The Healthy Holiday Guide

HEADWAY BOOKS

First published 1988

This 5th Edition published in 1993 by Catherine Mooney and Headway Books
Saddlers Cottage, York Rd, Elvington, York, YO4 5AR

© Catherine Mooney, 1993

ISBN 0 9513045 7 7

Printed by The Redwood Press, Melksham, Wiltshire.

Designed and typeset on Rank Xerox Ventura by Lisa Pickering

This book is sold subject to the condition that it
shall not, by way of trade or otherwise, be lent, re-sold,
hired out or otherwise circulated without the publisher's prior
consent in any form of binding or cover other than that in which
it is published and without a similar condition including this
condition being imposed on the subsequent purchaser.

For Christopher
whose cooking is the quintessence of whole-heartedness

Introduction

I wrote this book because I kept looking for it in bookshops and was fed up with not finding it there: occasionally I'd phone up a store and ask if they had such a thing as a guide to hotels which serve healthy food. "Yes madam... just one minute..." was the usual reply. They'd return, "I'm sorry, we don't seem to have one..." They seemed surprised - and so was I: with the upsurge of interest in all matters healthy - it seemed an obvious kind of book to have around. However I'm *glad*, now that it has been my privilege to collate the information to make this book. I've had great fun doing it and the hoteliers I've come into contact with have been a great bunch of people.

Who is it for? Well it is for everyone who is concerned about healthy eating; it is for strict vegetarians who do not like to see people eating meat in their hotel restaurant and it is also for that growing number of people best described as part-time vegetarians who prefer sometimes to choose a non-meat option on the evening menu; it is for omnivores and for people who are on special diets for resons of health - low-calorie, low-fat, gluten-free, macro-biotic, etc. - and want to stay in a hotel which can cater for their needs; it is for strict health-fooders who want to continue to eat the wholefood or organic food on holiday that they prepare for themselves at home and it is for not-so-strict health-fooders who *prefer* to eat fresh vegetables, but are not too fussed if someone occasionally has to sling a tin of tomatoes in the Bolognese; it is for strict non-smokers who can detect and abhor fortnight-old cigarette smoke in their bedrooms, and it is for the tolerant non-smoker who is happy with non-smoking zones in the dining room; it is for the healthy walker, jogger, stroller, swimmer, slimmer, coeliac, diabetic.... I could go on. Basically it is for anybody who cares as much about their health on holiday as they do at home.

Obviously in a something-for-everyone book of this sort, not *everything* is going to be suitable for *everyone*. There are smoking vegetarians, omnivorous husbands with meat-free wives (*sic.*), and strict wholefood parents with beans-and-chips offspring. This is called normal life. However in a mixed bag selection of hotels and guest houses such as this book provides - there should be something for everyone. Read the small print - I've made it clear which hotels and guest houses have priorities in which areas.

And while we're on the subject I've also included a wide range of types of holiday provision: some are tiny small-holdings in the middle of nowhere offering basic accommodation, healthy food and a warm welcome, while some are fully-fledged don't-forget-your-dinner-jacket stately homes. Most are in-between. Again - something for everyone: it should be clear from the write-up, however, which hotel offers which standard of amenity.

A word about my research. I decided very early on that it would be impossible to visit every hotel in order to assess its provision: no less than 10,000 establishments now claim to cater for vegetarians and it would take me the best part of 30 years of very pleasurable (but ultimately fruitless) labour to visit them all! I'm also not too sure about the validity of personal hotel recommendations: one woman's 'pretty chintz curtains' can be another's 'over-fussy furnishings'. Also until someone invents a portable nitrate-ometer there is no way of knowing if the vegetables on your plate have been organically grown or are fresh from Fisons - neither will you be any wiser by visiting the hotel.

However information published by the hotel is, of course, subject to trade regulations and as such is as reliable an indicator as any of the provision to be had therein. The best plan seemed to collect as detailed information as possible from each hotel and publish it as soon as possible thereafter. But under any circumstances, no matter how hard you try, it's impossible for a guide book to *guarantee* that the hotel facilities they describe will be available when guests visit, so I do not make this claim. Instead I present the information in good faith as a *guide* not a *gospel* and, in common with virtually every other travel-book on the market, urge you to *check when booking that the facilities you require are still available*. It has been my experience that hoteliers are generally becoming far more conscientious about healthy food provision - however *check before booking*. And do let me know of any improvement (or otherwise) in service that you encounter (there is a tear-out slip for this purpose at the back of the book).

Oh - and one final thing (which may surprise you). When I collected the information for this edition from hoteliers, one consistent comment that came back to me from them was how *nice* (in the broadest sense of the word I'm sure!) were the guests who had come to stay with them from this guide! And, while I must admit that that was something I could not have stage-managed, it just goes to show - hoteliers have feelings too!

So thankyou for using this book and for patronising those hotels and guest houses I have recommended: I hope you all have some very happy holidays - apparently you are all very deserving of them indeed!

Catherine Mooney

HOW TO USE THIS BOOK

This guide is divided into five sections: **England, The Channel Islands, Northern Ireland, Scotland** *and* **Wales**. *The* **England** *section of the book is divided into 11 principal areas in which the English counties within these areas are listed alphabetically; hotels and guest houses are listed within each county section under an alphabetical list of cities, towns and, if they are especially significant, villages. Establishments themselves are listed alphabetically by name under their city, town or village heading.*
Scotland, Wales, Northern Ireland *and* **The Channel Islands** *are smaller sections so it was not thought necessary to divide them into area by area sections. Instead the regions within* **Scotland, Wales** *and* **N. Ireland** *(and the islands for* **The Channel Islands***) are listed alphabetically and within that format the listing is exactly the same as for the English entries.*

The information given about each establishment is largely self-explanatory but the following should be noted:

- *The prices for B. & B. are per person per night and represent the cheapest high season price offered by each establishment - this is usually based on the price of a couple sharing a room, and it should be noted therefore that single rooms may cost significantly more than the B. & B. price given. Prices are correct at the time of going to press but it is impossible to guarantee that prices will not have increased by the time you use this book. We therefore strongly advise you to check with any establishment before booking.*
- *The reference to access for the disabled is based on the information we have been supplied with by the establishments. It has not been possible to verify the extent of the provision for those with varying degrees of physical disability - whether a room has wheelchair access, for instance. So do check that the establishment meets your requirements before booking.*

Contents

ENGLAND

The South West — 1
Avon, Cornwall, Devon, Dorset, Somerset, Wiltshire

The South of England — 23
Hampshire, Isle of Wight, West Sussex

South East England — 30
East Sussex, Kent, Surrey

London & Middlesex — 37
London, Middlesex

Thames & Chilterns — 40
Berkshire & Bedfordshire, Buckinghamshire, Hertfordshire, Oxfordshire

Central England — 45
Gloucestershire, Herefordshire, Shropshire, Staffordshire, Warwickshire, West Midlands, Worcestershire

East Anglia — 62
Cambridgeshire, Essex, Norfolk, Suffolk

East Midlands — 74
Derbyshire, Leicestershire, Lincolnshire, Northamptonshire, Nottinghamshire

Cumbria & the North West — 81
Cumbria, Cheshire, Lancashire

Yorkshire & Humberside — 97
North Yorkshire, South Yorkshire, West Yorkshire, Humberside

The North East — 106
Co. Durham, Northumberland, Tyne and Wear

CHANNEL ISLANDS — 114
Alderney, Guernsey, Jersey, Sark

NORTHERN IRELAND — 115
Co Antrim, Belfast, Co Down, Co Fermanagh

SCOTLAND — 116
Borders, Central, Dumfries and Galloway, Edinburgh, Fife, Glasgow, Grampian, Highlands, Lothian, Orkneys and Shetlands, Strathclyde, Tayside, Western Isles

WALES — 145
Clwyd, Dyfed, Glamorgan, Gwent, Gwynedd, Powys, Pembrokeshire.

The South West

Avon

BATH

Avon Hotel, 9 Bathwick Street, Bath, BA2 6NX (0225) 446176 Fax: (0225) 447452
Elegant Georgian residence in Bath.
Open all year. No smoking in dining room & some bedrooms. Vegetarian & other diets by arrangement. Children welcome. En suite, tea/coffee-making & T.V. in all bedrooms. Credit cards. B. & B. from £19.50.

Haydon House, 9 Bloomfield Park, Bath, BA2 2BY (0225) 427351
From the outside Haydon House looks like many

another unassuming Edwardian detached house so typical of the residential streets of Bath. Inside, however, 'an oasis of tranquility and elegance' prevails; certainly the proprietor, Magdalene Ashman, has done everything possible to make your stay - so near and yet so far from the tourist throng of Bath - a truly happy and welcome one: rooms are tastefully decorated (lots of Laura Ashley and soft furnishings) and, although breakfast is the only available meal, this too has a little special something added (porridge is served with whisky and muscavado sugar, for instance, and a fresh fruit platter is available for less staunch appetites).
Open all year. No smoking in the house. Vegetarian b'fast available. Vegan & diabetic by arrangement. Children by arrangement. En suite, tea/coffee-making & T.V. in all rooms. Access, Visa. B. & B. from £25 (3 for the price of 2 mid-Nov. to mid-Mar. Sun. to Thurs.).

Holly Lodge, 8 Upper Oldfield Park, Bath, BA2 3JZ Tel: (0225) 424042 Fax: (0225 481138
Holly Lodge is a large Victorian house set in its own grounds and enjoying magnificent views over the city of Bath. The house has been extensively renovated and beautifully decorated in recent years but with an eye to retaining all the period features of the original building (marble fireplaces, ceiling cornices, etcetera) so that the original architectural elegance is maintained. Breakfast is the only meal available at Holly Lodge but guests dine in a charming room which has views of the city and gives diners a chance to contemplate which of Bath's 80 fine restaurants they will choose for their evening meal. Facilities are also available for small conference parties under the supervision of the proprietor, Carrolle Sellick.
Open all year. No smoking. Vegetarian and other special diets by arrangement. Children by arrangement. En suite, tea/coffee-making, T.V. and phone in all rooms. Credit cards. B. & B. from £34.

Kinlet Villa Guest House, 99 Wellsway, Bath, BA2 4RX (0225) 420268
Open all year. No smoking. Special diets available. Children welcome. Tea/coffee & T.V. in all bedrooms. B. & B. from £15. ETB 2 Crowns Commended.

Leighton House, 139 Wells Rd, Bath, BA2 3AL (0225) 314769
Leighton House is a fine Victorian residence

which stands in its own grounds enjoying magnificent views over the city and surrounding hills; it is family owned and run, and each of the elegant and spacious en suite bedrooms has been tastefully decorated and furnished (the house also enjoys the benefit of its own car park and is just 10 minutes' walk from the city centre). A hearty breakfast is served in a charming dining room, and the beautifully prepared 4-course dinner* is complemented by an excellent wine list; vegetarians and those on other special diets are sympathetically catered for. Bath is one of only three United Nations World Heritage Cities and its history dates back to the Bronze Age; modern Bath owes much of its character to the Georgians, and present day visitors are lured by its many museums, art galleries and parks, as well as its splendidly elegant shops and antique

markets. *Evening meals are from Tuesdays to Saturdays from Nov. to April inc.*
Open all year. No smoking in dining room. Vegetarian & other diets on request. Licensed. Children welcome. Pets by arrangement. En suite. Tea/coffee-making and T.V. in all bedrooms. Access, Visa. B. & B. from £52.

21 Newbridge Road, Bath, BA1 3HE (0225) 314694

Victorian family house on the A4 Bristol road. Traditional or vegetarian, vegan and gluten-free b'fasts on request; health-food shop muesli, soya milk, organic wholemeal bread and decaffeinated coffee.
Open Feb. to Nov. No smoking. Vegetarian, vegan, dairy free and gluten free diets available. Children welcome. T.V. in lounge. Tea/coffee-making facilities available. B. & B. from £15-£18.

Oldfields, 102 Wells Rd, Bath, BA2 3AL (0225) 317984

This beautiful Victorian building, constructed of

the warm, honey-coloured stone for which Bath is famous, has been lovingly restored by its owners, the O'Flahertys, who have complemented the spacious architecture, moulded ceilings, high windows and marble fireplaces with such 20th C. refinements as Laura Ashley wall coverings and delicate pastel paintwork. Although breakfast is the only meal available at Oldfields the O' Flahertys are a health-conscious couple and offer, in addition to the traditional breakfast fare, a healthy alternative with wheatmeal bread, muesli (the heavy-duty variety) and herbal teas. Incidentally you are invited to *linger* over breakfast, with unlimited coffee, tea, toast & newspapers for those who like to dawdle at this hour.
Vegetarian, vegan, diabetic & other diets by arrangement. Open all year ex. Xmas. Disabled access: 2 ground floor rooms but showers and WC do not allow wheelchair access. Children welcome. En suite in 8 rooms. Tea/coffee & T.V. in all bedrooms. Visa, Mastercard.

The Old Red House, 37 Newbridge Rd, Bath, Avon (0225) 330464

Romantic Victorian guest house with stained glass windows and canopied beds. B'fast is served in a sunny conservatory - hearty or healthy, the choice is yours. Private parking.
Open all year. No smoking in the house. Vegetarian standard. Other diets by arrangement. 1 ground floor room. Children welcome. Pets by arrangement. En suite, TV & tea/coffee-making in all bedrooms. Access, Visa. B. & B. £17.

The Old School House, Church Street, Bathford, Bath, BA1 7RR (0225) 859593

Converted village school; rooms with views & 2 ground floor rooms for the less mobile. Home-made food.
Open all year. No smoking. Most special diets on request. Licensed. Disabled access: 2 ground floor, level-entry bedrooms available. En suite, tea/coffee & T.V. in rooms. Credit cards. B. & B. from £29.50.

Parkside Guest House, 11 Marlborough Lane, Bath, BA1 2NQ (0225) 429444

Parkside is an Edwardian family house, with a serene atmosphere, situated on the fringe of Bath's famous Royal Victoria Park and the famous Royal Crescent; it has a delightful town

garden, and it is just a short, beautiful walk from thence to the city centre. Parkside has a total of five bedrooms - three of which have en suite facilities, with colour TV and welcome tray - and the breakfast menu includes a choice of traditional and health food; evening meals, with vegetarian specailities, are also available.
Vegan and other special diets by arrangement. Organic when available. Wholefoods always. Open all year. No smoking in the house. Children: over 5s only. Pets by arrangement. B. & B. from £18.50.

Smiths, 47 Crescent Gardens, Upper Bristol Road, Bath, BA1 2NB (0225) 318175

Recently renovated Victorian house 5 mins from city centre; friendly welcome. Breakfast only.

Open all year. No smoking. Any diet by arrangement. Children welcome. Tea/coffee-making & T.V. in all bedrooms. 1 room en suite. B. & B. from £14.

Somerset House, 35 Bathwick Hill, Bath, BA2 6LD (0225) 466451

Somerset House is a listed Regency building perched atop of Bathwick Hill with splendid views across to the city. Jean and Malcolm Seymour spent some years as restaurateurs in the Lake Distict specialising in imaginative, home-cooked food using fresh, local ingredients. They have brought their high culinary standards to Bath and guests in the south west can now dine on excellent meals prepared from organically home-grown, wholefood and/or local ingredients; all bread, cakes, pâtés and soups are home-made and, as the Seymours like to add a bit of intellectual spice to their already savoury fare, you are likely to find food for the mind, as well as the palate, on the menu and wine list (their Shrove Tuesday menu featured, for instance, a Pease Soup for Lent which the Seymours found in the 18th C. recipe book of the otherwise anonymous Mr Farley).

Vegetarian & vegan by arrangement. Diabetic & other special diets by arrangement. Organic when avail. (much home-grown). Wholefood always. Open all year. No smoking. Licensed. Children: over 10s only. Pets: 'small ones, by arrangement.' En suite & tea/coffee in all bedrooms. T.V. in lounge. Visa, Amex, Mastercard. B. & B. around £31, Breaks available.

Sydney Gardens Hotel, Sydney Road, Bath, BA2 6NT (0225) 464818/445362

Fine Victorian mansion with lovely garden, in parkland setting 5 minutes' from the city centre.

Open all year ex. Xmas & Jan. No smoking. Some special diets by arrangement. Children: over 4s only. Pets by arrangement. En suite, tea/coffee, T.V. & telephone in all bedrooms. B. & B. only from £32.50.

Wellsgate, 131 Wells Road, Bath, BA2 3AN (0225) 310688

Victorian residence. B'fast has vegn. options & generous jugs of orange juice on the table.

Vegetarian, vegan and other special diets by arrangement. No smoking. Open all year. Children welcome. En suite, TV & tea/coffee in all bedrooms.

BRISTOL

Arches Hotel, 132 Cotham Brow, Cotham, Bristol, BS6 6AE (0272) 247398

Victorian house offering B. & B. Healthy b'fasts.

Open all year, ex. Xmas. No smoking. Vegetarian, vegan & other diets by arrangement. Children welcome. Pets by arrangement. Tea/Coffee & T.V. in all bedrooms.

Courtlands Hotel, 1 Redland Court Rd, Redland, BS6 7EE (0272) 424432

Open all year. Separate area of dining room for smokers. Vegetarian & other diets by arrangement. Licensed. B. & B. from £27.

Vicarage Lawns, Bristol Rd, West Harptree, Bristol, BS18 6HF (0761) 221668

Vicarage Lawns is is a comfortable country home which stands amidst an acre of lovely walled gardens in the pretty village of West Harptree at the foot of the Mendip Hills. Accommodation is in exceptionally well-appointed and tastefully decorated bedrooms (all with garden views), one of which has a spa bath and most of which have en suite facilities; a wholesome breakfast is offered to guests (evening meals can be provided by prior arrangement). The tranquil rural setting of Vicarage Lawns, with its proximity to Chew Valley Lake with its fishing, wildlife and lovely walks, makes it a perfect choice for a relaxing away-from-it-all break; additionally you will find yourself within easy reach of Bath, Bristol, Wells, Cheddar and Weston-Super-Mare.

Open all year. No smoking. Vegetarian & other diets by arrangement. Children welcome. En suite in some rooms. Tea/coffee making & T.V. in rooms. T.V. in lounge. B. & B. from £13.50.

WESTON-SUPER-MARE

Moorlands Country Guest House, Hutton, Nr. Weston-super-Mare, BS24 9QH (0934) 812283

Moorlands is an attractive Georgian house which has been the family home of Margaret and David Holt for over 25 years; it stands in 2 acres of mature landscaped gardens and enjoys peaceful views of nearby wooded hills. The food is delicious and wholesome; everything has been prepared on the premises from fresh produce - some of it home-grown - and vegetarian diets can be accommodated by arrangement. Hutton is a pretty little village which stands just 3 or 4 miles from the sea at Weston super Mare; it is within easy reach of a wide range of attractions in both Avon and North Devon, and as such is a good centre for day trips. Children are very welcome at Moorlands and pony rides from the paddock can be arranged on request.

Open Feb. to Oct. No smoking in dining room. Vegetarian & other diets by arrangement. Licensed. Wheelchair access (& 1 ground floor room suitable for physically less able). Children welcome. Pets by arrangement. Some rooms en suite. Tea/coffee in rooms. T.V. in lounge & some bedrooms. Visa, Access, Amex 2%. B. & B. from £16, D. from £8. ETB 3 Crown approved.

Cornwall & Isles of Scilly

BOSCASTLE

Lower Meadows House Licensed Hotel & Restaurant, Penally Hill, Boscastle, PL35 0HF (08405) 570

Exceptional cuisine of French influence; all dishes are home-prepared from the finest of fresh, local ingredients including the bread
Open all year. No smoking in part of the dining room. Vegetarian and diabetic standard. Other diets by arrangement. Licensed. Disabled access. Children welcome. Pets by arrangement. En suite in all rooms. Tea/coffee-making: room service. T.V. in lounge.

CALSTOCK

Danescombe Valley Hotel, Calstock, Cornwall, PL18 9RY (0822) 832414

Splendid southfacing villa set in tranquil wooded valley on a bend of the River Tamar; highly acclaimed cuisine using fresh, local produce.
Open Easter to end Oct. No smoking in dining room. Vegetarian & other diets by arrangement. Licensed. Children: over 12s welcome. En suite in all rooms. Tea/coffee on request. D.,B.& B. from £77.50.

CRACKINGTON HAVEN

Crackington Manor, Crackington Haven, EX23 0JG (08403) 397/536

Meals prepared from local produce where possible. Gym, sauna, solarium & pool.
Open all year. No smoking. Vegetarian standard. Other diets by arrangement. Licensed. Disabled access. Children welcome. T.V. in lounge.

FALMOUTH

Melvill House Hotel, 52 Melvill Road, Falmouth, TR11 4DQ (0326) 316645

Lovely centrally heated hotel, refurbished, yet retaining its Victorian atmosphere, close to town & beaches. Large car park.
Open all year ex. Xmas. No smoking in bedrooms & dining room. Licensed. Children: over 7s welcome. En suite, tea/coffee-making & T.V. in all bedrooms. B. & B. from £15.50. D., B. & B. from £21.

Tresillian House Hotel, 3 Stracey Road, Falmouth, TR11 4DW (0326) 312425/311139

Tresillian House is a small, friendly, family run hotel which is situated in a quiet road near the main sea front and close to the beach and coastal walks at Falmouth. The 12 comfortable, en suite bedrooms have each been tastefully decorated and furnished with a good range of amenities including colour TV, hair dryer, radio intercom and baby listening service. The cooking is excellent: traditional food is served in generous portions, in an attractive dining room with lovely garden views, and after-dinner coffee is served in the comfortable lounge. Falmouth is a perfect fishing town with one of the world's deepest natural harbours and, for those wanting to spend a day lazing on its lovely beaches, the proprietors will prepare picnic lunches on request.
Open Mar. to Oct. Smoking banned in dining room and in one lounge. Vegetarian, diabetic, gluten-free and low-fat diets by arrangement. Licensed. Children welcome. En suite, tea/coffee-making & T.V. in all bedrooms. Access, Visa. D., B. & B. from £24. ETB 3 Crowns Commended.

ISLES OF SCILLY

Covean Cottage Guest House, St Agnes, Isles of Scilly (0720) 22620

Charming little house overlooking the sea on the peaceful island of St Agnes. Meals are home-cooked from fresh, local produce.
Vegetarian & other diets by arrangement. Open Jan. to Nov. No smoking in dining room & separate cottage for non-smokers. Disabled access: 1 ground floor bedroom. Children: over 12s only. En suite & TV. Tea/coffee in rooms. L., B. & B. from £21.

Four Seasons Guest House, Little Porth, Hugh Town, St Mary's, Isles of Scilly, TR21 0JG (0720) 22793

Small comfortable guest house 2 mins from Porthcressa Beach. Food prepared from fresh produce where possible. Fish a speciality.
Open Easter to end Oct. No smoking in dining room & 1 bedroom. Vegetarian by arrangement. Licensed. Children: over 7s only. En suite some rooms. Tea/coffee in rooms. T.V. lounge. D., B. & B. from £27.

Hell Bay Hotel, Bryher, Isles of Scilly, TR23 0PR (0720) 22947

An old Scillonian farmhouse forms on Bryher. Most food prepared from fresh produce.
Vegetarian by arrangement. No smoking in dining room. Open Mar. 22nd to Oct. 6th. Licensed. Children welcome. All rooms private sitting room & bathroom. Tea/coffee & T.V. in rooms. B. & B. from £37.50.

LAUNCESTON

Highfield Country House, St. Giles on the Heath, DL15 9SD (0566) 772937

Elegant Edwardian house set in its own grounds surrounded by beautiful countryside. Food prepared from natural produce.

Open all year. No smoking in dining room and drawing room. Diabetic standard. Vegetarian, vegan and other special diets by arrangement. Older children welcome. Pets by arrangement. Tea/Coffee-making in all bedrooms. T.V. B. & B. from £13.50.

MARAZION
Old Eastcliffe House, Eastcliffe Lane, Marazion, TR17 0AZ (0736) 710298

Originally built for the wealthy mine owning Michell family, this fine old Georgian residence stands in a charming walled garden which slopes gently to the sea, and enjoys a most dramatic and uninterrupted view of St Michael's Mount. Beautifully decorated and with lots of character (brass beds, log fires, interesting antiques...) it is the place to come if you're in search of peace; it is also the place to come if you are looking for a good breakfast: your generous hosts, the Haverys, offer a splendid morning meal with lots of choices, including home-baked ham with Oxford Sauce (a house speciality) and smoked haddock with poached egg, as well as the usual traditional Great British Breakfast options.

Open Easter to end Sept. No smoking in dining room & bedrooms. Vegetarian & other diets by arrangement. Children welcome. En suite some rooms. Tea/coffee all rooms. T.V. lounge. B. & B. from £17.

MAWGAN PORTH
Bedruthan Steps Hotel, Mawgan Porth, Cornwall, TR8 4BU (0637) 860555

The Bedruthan Steps is a splendid modern hotel which stands amidst 5 acres of grounds overlooking the spectacular Cornish coast at Mawgan Porth. There are spacious hotel bedroom suites which have been very comfortably furnished and overlook the sea, and a number of villa suites which open out onto spacious lawns and are ideal for families (there is a children's play area in the grounds, a wonderful indoor play complex and a childrens' dining room). The food at Bedruthan Steps is outstanding: everything is home-made (including the bread, croissants and desserts), and fresh, local produce plus vegetables, fruit and herbs from the hotel's market garden, are always used in cooking. The leisure facilities are excellent: there is an indoor pool complex, tennis and squash courts, snooker and pool - and there is even an on site beauty therapist and masseuse.

Open Mar. to Nov. No smoking in dining room, lounges & part of bar. Vegetarian and most other special diets by arrangement. Licensed. Children welcome. En suite, tea/coffee-making & T.V. in all rooms. Access, Visa. D., B. & B. from £28.

MEGAVISSEY
Steep House, Portmellon Cove, Megavissey, PL26 2PH (0726) 843732

House in 1 acre of grounds in a natural cove with safe sandy beach; covered pool.

Open all year. No smoking in part of dining room and in bedrooms. Vegetarian and other special diets by arrangement. Licensed. Children: over 10s only.

MOUSEHOLE
Carn du Hotel, Raginnis Hill, Mousehole, TR19 6SS (0736) 731233

Detached hotel in terraced gardens overlooking the sea & St Michael's Mount; excellent cuisine.

Open Mar. to Feb. No smoking in dining room. Vegetarian by arrangement. Licensed. Disabled access. En suite, tea/coffee-making & T.V. in rooms.

Marconi Private Hotel, Cove Road, Mullion, Nr Helston (0326) 240483

Victorian house overlooking cricket field. Food prepared from fresh, local produce.

Open all year. Smoking banned in bedrooms and sun lounge. Vegetarian standard. Most other special diets by arrangement. Licensed. One room disabled access. Children welcome. En suite in some rooms. Tea/coffee-making in bedrooms. T.V. in all bedrooms. B. & B. from £13.50.

NEWQUAY

Sheldon, The Haven for Non-Smokers, 198 Henver Road, Newquay, TR7 3EH (0637) 874552

Fresh ingredients & bread, rolls & pastries baked fresh each day; home-made marmalade.

Open June to Aug. inc. No smoking. Children: over 10s only. Tea/Coffee-making on request. T.V. in lounge. B. & B. from £11.50 (based on weekly rate).

PADSTOW

The Dower House Hotel, Fentonluna Lane, Padstow, PL28 8BA (0841) 532317

Fabulous food prepared from fresh ingredients.

Vegetarian, diabetic, low-fat or low-cal. diets standard. Vegan by arrangement. Open all year ex. Xmas. Licensed. Children welcome. Pets by arrangement. En suite in most bedrooms. Tea/coffee making & TV in all bedrooms. B. & B. from £16.

PENRYN

Prospect House, 1 Church Rd, Penryn, TR10 8DA (0326) 373198

Prospect House was built as a 'gentleman's residence' around 1830, probably for a local ship owner, and it stands within its pretty walled rose garden, on the edge of Penryn just 2 miles from Falmouth. It is a listed building which has recently undergone some (sympathetic) refurbishment and has been redecorated and furnished in a style which complements the original features of the building, such as the stained glass windows, mahogany doors, and elaborately painted plaster cornices; Your hosts, Cliff Paul and Barry Sheppard, have endeavoured to create an atmosphere in which comfort combines happily with elegance: accordingly each of the bedrooms have been individually styled and named after sailing ships which were known to have worked from Penryn, and log fires blaze in the public rooms in cooler weather. The food is first-rate: everything has been prepared on the premises from fresh ingredients, and a typical evening menu might feature Cucumber Soup with Mint followed by Salmon en Papillote (served with boiled potatoes and green vegetables), and a tempting dessert such as Truffle Torte with local Raspberries. With its proximity to both Falmouth and Truro, Prospect House is a perfect base from which to explore a wide range of Cornwall's many lovely beaches, public gardens, National Trust properties and English Heritage monuments; there are also facilities nearby for sailing, windsurfing, deep-sea fishing and golf.

Open Jan. to Dec. No smoking in dining room. Vegetarian and other special diets by arrangement. Children: over 12s only. Pets by arrangement. En suite in all rooms. Tea/coffee making in guests' pantry. T.V. in bedrooms on request. B. & B. from £23.

The Higher Faugan Country House Hotel, Newlyn, Penzance, TR18 5NS (0736) 62076

Higher Faugan is a gracious country house built by Stanhope Forbes at the turn of the century. It stands at the end of a 1/3 mile drive, surrounded by 10 acres of lawns and woodlands, some 300 feet above sea level, overlooking Penzance and St Mounts Bay. All 12 bedrooms have been comfortably and tastefully furnished (each has private facilities), and your hosts are on hand throughout the day to ensure that your stay is, in keeping with your gracious surroundings, as relaxing and enjoyable as possible. The food is excellent: from the optional bar-lunches, served by the swimming pool in the garden to the dinner menu, with options which change daily, everything has been prepared from fresh local produce (including organic when possible), and a typical evening menu would feature Home-made soup, followed by Duck Breast with Apricot and Honey Sauce, followed by Chocolate and Brandy Flan (with fresh cream), coffee and mints. There is a wealth of intersting places to visit locally and the beaches, moors and cliffs are a short drive away.

Open all year. No smoking in dining room. Vegetarian & other diets by arrangement. Licensed. Children welcome. Pets by arrangement. En suite, tea/coffee, T.V., & phone in all bedrooms. B. & B. from £30.

Penalva Guest House, Alexandra Road, Penzance (0736) 69060

Small, private hotel in tree-lined avenue.

Open all year; no evening meals Jul. & Aug. No smoking in the house. Vegetarian and most other special diets by arrangement. Children welcome. En suite in 2 rooms. Tea/coffee-making in bedrooms. T.V. in lounge. B. & B. from £12. D. £9.

PORTSCATHO

Roseland House Hotel, Rosevine, Nr Portscatho, TR2 5EW   Tel: (0872580) 644 Fax: (0872580) 801
18 bedroom hotel set in 6 acres of National Trust and Heritage coastline; wonderful views.
Open all year. No smoking in dining room. Vegetarian and most other special diets by arrangement. Licensed. Some rooms disabled access. Children welcome. En suite, TV & tea/coffee-making in bedrooms. Credit cards. D., B. & B. from £36.50.

ST BLAZEY

Nanscawen House, Prideaux Road, St Blazey, Nr Par (0726) 814488
16th C. house in 5 acres of grounds & gardens with outdoor heated pool and whirlpool spa. All meals home-prepared from fresh ingredients (many culled from the extensive garden).
Open all year ex. Xmas. No smoking. Vegetarian by arrangement. Residential licence. Children: over 12s only. En suite, TV & tea/coffee in bedrooms.B. & B. from £27.50 (prices include afternoon tea).

ST COLUMB

Brentons Farm, Goss Moor, St Columb, TR9 6WR   (0726) 860632
Small farm close to the A30; free-range eggs, home-baked rolls.
Open Feb. to end Nov. No smoking throughout. Vegetarian and most other special diets by arrangement. Children welcome. Tea/coffee on request. T.V. facilities. B. & B. from £10.

ST IVES

Boswednack Manor, Zennor, St Ives, TR26 3DD   (0736) 794183
Spacious granite-built in stone-walled fields with magnificent views of moorland and sea. The food is 'plentiful and good' (vegetarian meals are a speciality) and the 3 acre smallholding provides much of the fresh vegetables used in cooking.
Open all year. No smoking. Vegetarian evening meals ex. on course weeks. Vegan by arrangement. Children welcome. Tea/coffee in bedrooms. En suite rooms. B. & B. from £13.50, D. £6.

Woodcote Vegetarian Hotel, The Saltings, Lelant   (0736) 753147
Long-established vegetarian hotel overlooking the estuary and bird sanctuary of Hayle.
Open Mar. to Oct. No smoking in dining room, bedrooms & lounge. Vegetarian exclusively. Diabetic, gluten-free, and some other special diets by arrangement. Bring your own wine. No babies or toddlers. En suite & TV in some rooms. Tea/coffee-making in all rooms. D., B. & B. from £22.

TINTAGEL

Bossiney House Hotel, Tintagel, PL34 0AX   (0840) 770240
Bossiney House stands in 2½ acres of grounds overlooking the coast. Heated pool, sauna and solarium.
Vegetarian, vegan and other special diets by arrangement. Open Mar. to Oct. Licensed. Disabled access. Children welcome. Pets by arrangement. En suite & tea/coffee in all rooms. B. & B. from £25.

Trevervan Hotel, Trewarmett, Tintagel, PL34 0ES   (0840) 770486
White-washed building looking out over Trebarwith Strand; healthy home-cooked fare.
Vegetarian, vegan & diabetic standard. Low-cal., low-fat, allergen-free or macrobiotic diets by arrangement. Wholefood & additive-free meat and fish used. Open all year. No smoking in dining room and some bedrooms. Licensed. Children welcome. Tea coffee. T.V. in lounge. B. & B. from £13.50.

TORPOINT

The Copse, St Winnolls, Polbathic, Torpoint, PL11 3DX   (0503) 30205
The Copse is part of a mixed farm in the hamlet of St Winnolls in a lovely rural setting yet A374 just 1m away; home-produced milk, beef, lamb and vegetables.
Open Mar. to Sept. No smoking. Children: over 10s only. En suite in some rooms. Tea/coffee-making & T.V. in all bedrooms. B. & B. from £11.

TRURO

Marcorrie Hotel, 20 Falmouth Rd, Truro (0872) 77374
Privately owned, family-run Victorian hotel pleasantly situated in a conservation area just a few minutes' walk from Truro town centre. Ideal base for touring Cornwall. Car parking.
Open all year. No smoking in dining room & some bedrooms. Vegetarian & other diets by arrangement. Children & pets welcome. Licensed. En suite, tea/coffee-making & TV in all bedrooms. Credit cards. B. & B. from £19.

Polsue Cottage, Ruan High Lanes, Truro, TR2 5LU   (0872) 501596
Six acre organic smallholding 1 mile from the sea; own vegetables, herbs and soft fruit.
Open all year. No smoking. Vegetarian standard (fish may be served on request). Low-fat, vegan and diabetic by arrangement. Children welcome. Tea/coffee-making. B. & B. from £11. E.M. £7.

Devon

ASHBURTON

Cuddyford, Rew Rd, Ashburton, TQ13 7EN (0364) 53325

Country house in rural setting within Dartmoor National Park, wholesome food including home-baked bread, free-range eggs & honey.
Open all year ex. Xmas. No smoking. Vegetarian, vegan, gluten-free & macrobiotic diets standard. Children welcome. Pets by arrangement. Tea/coffee in own kitchen. T.V. by arrangement. Evening meals by arrangement (3-course, £7). B. & B. from £12.

Holne Chase Hotel, Nr Ashburton (03643) 471

Described by a 19th C directory as "being in a particularly secluded and romantic situation", Holne Chase Hotel has been offering hospitality since 1934 and, for the last 20 of those years, the Bromage family has been providing a sanctuary from "the pressures of modern life" with an efficacy that won them commendation by the BTA since 1974. Although, as the hotel brochure points out, there are telephones and televisions in bedrooms "for those who need to keep up with the news", there is every incentive not to do so, and to spend your time instead fly fishing on the hotel's mile length of the River Dart or wiling away an hour or two on the croquet lawn, cricket pitch or putting green. Those seeking a day's energetic walking on Dartmoor may do so safe in the knowledge that they return to the good food and a sound night's sleep that the Holne Chase Hotel has to offer. ETB 4 Crown Highly Commended.
Open all year. No smoking in dining room. Vegetarian on request. Wheelchair access to all public rooms and ground floor bedroom. En suite, tea and coffee making and T.V. in all bedrooms. B. & B. from £41.

The Old Coffee House, 27-29 West Street, Ashburton, Devon, TQ13 7DT (0364) 52539

Beautifully situated next to the 15th C. church of St Andrews in the ancient stannary town of Ashburton, this charming 16th century Grade II listed building offers most comfortable accommodation to guests, including a guests' lounge. Ashburton, on the southern edge of Dartmoor National Park, is a perfect place from which to explore both the coastal resorts of Torbay and Torquay as well as the charms of Exeter and the unspoilt beauty of Dartmoor. Guests will be likewise pleased to discover that the Old Coffee House is open throughout the day as a restaurant serving delicious teas and snacks, in the cooking of which fresh local produce (including vegetables) have been used wherever possible.
Open all year. No smoking throughout. Vegetarian by arrangement. Tea/coffee-making & T.V. in all bedrooms. B. & B. from £12.50

AXMINSTER

Goodmans House, Furley, Membury, Nr Axminster, EX13 7TU Tel: (040488) 690

When the Spencer family removed in 1987 to Goodmans House with a solid reputation behind them at Lea Hill Farm Hotel, they wondered if they would ever complete the daunting task of restoring this potentially charming 16th C. cum Georgian residence with its stone barn. Miles of hand-stripped pine later, they have converted the barn to four fabulously equipped self-catering cottages - complete with oak beams and natural stone features - which are furnished throughout with Laura Ashley fabrics and antiques; there are two further en suite rooms in the house. Guests dine by candlelight in a superb arched room on succulent home-produced fare - all prepared from fresh ingredients (home-produced free-range eggs, lamb and pork) - and a typical evening menu would feature Seafood Platter, followed by Pork with Apricot and Orange Stuffing (served with fresh vegetables), and some delicious desserts, such as Hazelnut Meringues or home-grown raspberries with cream. Goodmans House stands amidst 12 acres of grounds and as such is a haven of peace and tranquillity; additionally guests will find themselves within easy reach of Dartmoor, Exmoor and the East Devon coast.

Open Feb. 1st - Jan. 3rd. No smoking throughout house ex. in conservatory. Vegetarian & other diets by arrangement. Children & pets at owners' discretion. En suite, tea/coffee-making & colour TV in bedrooms. 7 days from £125 per week.

BARNSTAPLE

Huxtable Farm, West Buckland, Barnstaple, EX32 0SR (05986) 254

Beautiful secluded 16th C. listed building lovingly restored to reveal oak beams, screen panelling & open fireplaces (with bread ovens).

Open all year ex. Xmas & New Year. No smoking in dining room. Vegetarian by arrangement. Good disabled access (3 ground floor rooms). Children welcome. 3 en suite rooms. Tea/coffee in bedrooms. T.V. in 2 bedrooms. Amex. B. & B. from £18.

BIDEFORD

Mount Hotel, Northdown Road, Bideford, EX39 3LP (0237) 473748

Charming Georgian building in semi-walled garden a short walk from town. Home-cooked fare cooked from fresh produce where possible.

Open all year. No smoking in bedrooms & dining room. Vegetarian, vegan and other special diets by arrangement. Licensed. Children by arrangement. En suite in most rooms. Tea/coffee-making in bedrooms. T.V. in lounge, or in a bedroom for a small charge. Access, Visa, Mastercard. B. & B. from £16.

Yeoldon Country House Hotel, Durrant Lane, Northam, Bideford, EX39 2RL (0237) 474400

Vegetarian, vegan and diabetic standard. Licensed. Wheelchair access. Children welcome. Pets by arrangement. En suite, tea/coffee-making and T.V. in all rooms. Access, Visa, Amex, Diners.

BOVEY TRACEY

Blenheim Country House Hotel, Brimley Road, Bovey Tracey, TQ13 9DH (0626) 832422

The Blenheim is a country house hotel which stands amidst delightful grounds on the edge of Dartmoor National Park; in fact Bovey Tracey is in the unique position of being the perfect centre for touring Dartmoor as well as for visiting the South Devon coastal resorts. Run under the personal supervision of Mr and Mrs John Turpin, the Blenheim has six bedrooms which have magnificent views of either the moors or the grounds.

Open all year. No smoking in dining room & T.V. lounge. Vegetarian & other diets by arrangement. Licensed. Children welcome. Pets by arrangement. Some en suite, private showers & colour T.V. in rooms. Tea/coffee-making on request. B. & B. from £22.

BRAUNTON

The Whiteleaf at Croyde, Croyde, Braunton, EX33 1PN (0271) 890266

"Small and intimate", this highly acclaimed and beautiful guest house offers first-class cuisine.

Vegetarian, vegan and other special diets by arrangement. Open all year. Licensed. Children welcome. Pets by arrangement. En suite, tea/coffee-making & T.V. in all bedrooms. Access, Visa. B. & B. from £27. D. £17.

BRIXHAM

Mimosa Cottage, 75 New Rd, Brixham, Devon, TQ5 8NL Tel: (0803) 855719

Spacious 19th C. guest house just a short, level walk from the town, seafront and harbour. Large, well-furnished centrally-heated rooms. Mid-week bookings welcome. Senior citizens discount off-season.

Open all year. No smoking in dining room. Vegetarian & other special diets on request. Children: over 2s welcome. En suite in some rooms. Tea/coffee-making, T.V. & Sky in all bedrooms. B. & B. from £13.

CULLOMPTON

Tredown Farm, Clayhidon, Cullompton, EX15 3TW (0823) 662421

Comfortable modern bungalow on a working dairy farm high on the Blackdown Hills in an area of Outstanding Natural Beauty. Most ingredients locally produced including home-grown produce. Wheelchair ramp. Junction 26 off M5 to Wellington, then following signs to Ford Street; at the top of the hill turn left, then after 300 yards, turn right.

Open all year ex. Xmas. No smoking in dining room and lounge. Vegetarian & other diets by arrangement. Disabled access. Children welcome. Tea/coffee-making & TV in bedrooms.

DARTMOOR

Two Bridges Hotel, Two Bridges, Dartmoor, PL20 6SW (0822) 89581

This 18th century posting inn, set in the heart of Dartmoor some 1,000 feet above sea-level, is situated near to the junction of the two main roads over the moor and has boundless views on each side of the unspoilt beauty of this lovely National Park. In the heart of a beautiful wilderness it is therefore reassuring to discover that the atmosphere at Two Bridges is cosy: log fires warm footsore travellers in the beautifully furnished lounge and bar, and good home-cooked food accompanied by sensibly priced wines is the order of the day at the carvery or in the dining room (cream teas are also served daily). With some 60 acres of hotel grounds alone, holiday-makers could walk for days within the vicinity of Two Bridges and not retrace a single path - but the proprietors organise guided National Park walks and there is riding and fishing to be enjoyed nearby (the West Dart River flows through the grounds).

Open all year. No smoking dining room, lounge & most bedrooms. Vegetarian standard. Other diets by arrangement. Licensed. Disabled access. Children welcome. Pets by arrangement. En suite most rooms. Tea/coffee & T.V. (+ satellite) in bedrooms. B. & B. from £24.50 (2-day breaks from £62.50 D., B. & B.).

DARTMOUTH

Ford House, 44 Victoria Rd, Dartmouth, TQ6 9DX (0803) 834047

Comfortable rooms & good food, wholefood & organic where possible, much of it home-grown.

Vegetarian by arrangement. Other diets by arrangement. Open Mar. to Dec. No smoking in part of dining room. Well-behaved children & pets by arrangement. En suite some rooms. Tea/coffee & T.V. all rooms. B. & B. from £22.50. D., B. & B. from £40.

EXETER

Claremont, 36 Wonford Rd, Exeter, EX2 4LD (0392) 74699

Regency style town house in quiet part of Georgian Exeter, offering accommodation of a very high standard. Special diets catered for with advance notice.

Open all year. No smoking in the house. Vegetarian & other diets by arrangement. Children: over 5s welcome. En suite, TV & tea/coffee-making in bedrooms. B. & B. £16-22 per person per night.

Copplestone Farm, Dunsford, Exeter, EX6 7HQ (0647) 52784

Comfortable farmhouse in the beautiful Teign Valley just within Dartmoor National Park; deer, badgers and buzzards are all regularly seen in the locality; home-baked bread, free-range eggs and poultry; small adjoining cottage to let.

Open Easter to Oct. inc. No smoking. Vegetarian, vegan and most other special diets by arrangement. Tea/coffee-making in bedrooms. T.V. in sitting room. B. & B. from £113

Down House, Whimple, Exeter, EX5 2QR (0404) 822860

Eelegant Edwardian gentleman's country house in 5 acres of gardens and paddocks. Country-house-party style hospitality. Home-baked bread and organically home-produced fruit and vegetables in season. Temporary membership of a local swimming club with sauna and solarium can be arranged.

Open Apr. to Sept. No smoking in public areas. Vegetarian & other diets by arrangement. Children welcome. 2 rooms en suite. TV & Tea/coffee-making in bedrooms. B. & B. from £16.

KINGSBRIDGE

Burton Farm, Galmpton, Kingsbridge, TQ7 3EY (0548) 561210

Working farm in the South Huish Valley. Home-produce used wherever possible.

Open all year ex. Xmas & New Year. No smoking. Vegetarian & other diets by arrangement. Licensed. Children welcome. Some rooms en suite Tea/coffee. T.V. lounge. B. & B. from £16, D., B. & B., £24.

Start House, Start, Slapton, Nr Kingsbridge, TQ7 2QD (0548) 580254

South facing home with log fire. B'fast features locally made sausages & bread, & free-range eggs. Home-cooked prepared from local meat or fish and home-grown vegetables.

Open all year ex. Xmas. No smoking. Vegetarian, diabetic & low-fat diets by arrangement. Bring your own wine. Children welcome. Some en suite. Tea/coffee. T.V. in lounge. B. & B. from £16. D. £9.

The White House, Chillington, Kingsbridge, TQ7 2JX (0548) 580580

Open all year. Vegetarian and other diets by arrangement. Children welcome. En suite in 1 room. Tea/coffee-making & T.V. in lounge. D., B. & B. £27.50.

The White House is a lovely Georgian house with an acre of lawned and terraced gardens midway between Salcombe and Dartmouth and just 2 miles from the sea. Recently refurbished to a very high standard, the hotel has nonetheless retained both its original architectural features and serene ambience of relaxed, unhurried calm. Each of the several en suite bedrooms has been furnished with care - the south-facing Master Suite is a particularly spacious room with a comfortable sitting area - and there is a cosy bar lounge with exposed stone work and an open log fire; guests may also enjoy the log fire which blazes in the drawing room - perhaps browsing through one of the wide selection of books. The food is first-rate: everything is home-made from fresh local produce wherever possible, and menus are an imaginative blend of familiar and not-so-familiar dishes, a typical evening meal featuring Savoury Roulade followed by Rack of Lamb with Garlic and Rosemary and Peach and Hazelnut Galette. One guest recently remarked that "whatever direction you take from the White House you discover somewhere nice". Hardly surprising given that the nearby coast is some of the most spectacular and beautiful in the country, and the historic towns of Kingsbridge, Totnes and Dartmouth are such a short distance away.
Open Easter - Xmas. No smoking in dining room & drawing room. Vegetarian & other diets by arrangement. Licensed. Children: over 5s only. Pets welcome. En suite, TV & tea/coffee in rooms. Credit cards. B. & B. from £31, D., B. & B. from £42.50.

LEWDOWN

Hayne Mill, Lewdown, Nr Oakhampton, EX20 4DD (056683) 342

Friendly holiday accommodation for dogs and their owners in lovely old mill house surrounded by 3 acres of naturally landscaped garden; good food prepared from organically produced fruit and vegetables; nearby walks.

LYDFORD

Lydford House Hotel, Lydford, EX20 4AU Tel: (082282) 347 Fax: (082282) 442

Granite-built Victorian house in 8 acres of garden and pastureland just outside village of Lydford; food home-made from fresh produce.
Open all year ex. Xmas. No smoking in dining room. Vegetarian & diabetic by arrangement. Licensed. Disabled access. Over 5s only. TV, En suite, tea-making & D.D. phone in rooms. B. & B. £28.50.

LYNTON

Longmead House Hotel, 9 Long Mead, Lynton, EX35 6DQ (0598) 52523

Lovely hotel quietly situated in beautiful gardens. Imaginative, home-cooked food prepared from fresh produce when possible, served in an oak-panelled dining room.
Open all year. No smoking in the house. Vegetarian, & other diets by arrangement. Licensed. Children welcome. En suite in 4 rooms. Tea/coffee-making in bedrooms. T.V. B. & B. from £14.

Neubia House Hotel, Lydiate Lane (0598) 52309

Highly commended Victorian farmhouse in old Lynton. Excellent healthy food. & veg. options.
Open Mar. to Nov. No smoking in dining room. Vegetarian & vegan standard. Other diets by arrangement. Licensed. Children welcome. En suite, TV & tea/coffee-making in rooms. B. & B. from £27.

Sylvia House Hotel, Lydiate Lane, Lynton, EX35 6HE (0598) 52391

Set in England's romantic little Switzerland, Sylvia House offers elegance at moderate terms. Delightful en suite bedrooms. Exquisitely scrumptious fare and old-fashioned hospitality.
Open all year. No smoking in public rooms & some bedrooms. Vegetarian & other diets by arrangement. Licensed. Children welcome. En suite. TV & Tea/coffee-making in rooms. B. & B. from £14.

Waterloo House, Lydiate Lane (0598) 53391

The Waterloo House Hotel is a delightful Georgian building, one of the oldest lodging houses in Lynton, in which are combined the spirit of the 19th century with all the comforts of modern day life; there are two comfortable lounges, one of which is reserved for non-smokers. Accommodation is in spacious bedrooms which have been furnished to a high standard (most have en suite facilities). Imaginative 4-course meals are served by

WATERLOO HOUSE HOTEL

candlelight in an elegant dining room, a typical evening meal featuring Fish Paté followed by Poultry cooked in Cider with Dried Fruits (accompanied by fresh vegetables), and a tempting dessert such as Rhubarb and Ginger Crumble; everything has been prepared from fresh produce. Vegetarians are most welcome and can be accommodated by arrangement. Quietly set in the heart of 'old' Lynton, Waterloo House is a perfect base from which to enjoy the variety of pursuits which the area offers.

Open all year. No smoking in dining room, some bedrooms & 1 lounge. Vegetarian by arrangement. Children welcome. En suite most bedrooms. TV & tea/coffee in rooms. B. & B. from £16.50. ETB 3 Crown Commended. AA Selected Award for High Standard of Cooking, Comfort & Hospitality 1990-92.

MORETONHAMPSTEAD

White Hart Hotel, The Square, Moretonhampstead, TQ13 8NF (0647) 40406

Beautiful listed building. Fresh local produce used in cooking where possible; everything home-prepared, including pastries & sweets.

Open all year ex. Xmas. No smoking in dining room. Vegetarian & vegan by arrangement. Licensed. Children: over 10s only. Dogs welcome. En suite, tea/coffee-making, T.V. & phone in all bedrooms. Credit cards. B. & B. from £29.

NEWTON ABBOT

Cleave Hotel, Lustleigh, Newton Abbott, TQ13 9TJ (06477) 223

15th C. thatched inn, inglenook fireplace. home-cooked food prepared from fresh produce.

Vegetarian standard. Other diets by arrangement. Open Feb. to Nov. No smoking in dining room. Licensed. Wheelchair access. Tea/coffee making & T.V. in rooms. Visa, Masterpcharge. B. & B. from £20.

Rutherford House, Widecombe in the Moor, Nr Newton Abbot, TQ13 7TB (03642) 264

Large detached house amidst pretty gardens in beautiful valley. Vegetarian b'fast option & a choice of fresh fruit salad.

Open Easter to end of year. No smoking. Vegetarian, vegan and diabetic on request. Children: over 9s only. T.V. in lounge. B. & B. from £13.50.

NEWTON POPPLEFORD

Jolly's, The Bank, Newton Poppleford, EX10 0XD (0395) 68100

Friendly smoke-free establishment offering accommodation and food to both residential and non-residential guests. Predominantly vegetarian, but a good range of meat and fish dishes also available. Imaginative & delicious.

Open all year. No smoking Vegetarian standard. Most other diets by arrangement. Licensed. Children welcome. Tea/coffee-making facilities. Colour T.V's. Credit cards. B. & B. from £12.50.

NORTH BOVEY (DARTMOOR)

Slate Cottage, The Green, North Bovey, Nr Moretonhampstead, TQ13 8RB (0647) 40060

18th C. cottage offering peace and comfort, overlooking thatched houses, 13th C. church, oak-tree'd green and undulating moorland, all in a picturesque Dartmoor village.

Open all year. No smoking in the house. Vegetarian & other diets by arrangement. Children: over 12s only. TV & tea/coffee-making in bedrooms. B. & B. from £19.50, single £24.50.

OKEHAMPTON

Howard's Gorhuish, Northlew, Okehampton, EX20 3BT (0837) 53301

Charming 16th C. Devon longhouse in 7 acres of beautiful gardens. Meals are prepared from organically home-grown fruit & vegetables.

Open all year. No smoking in the house. Vegetarian and vegan by arrangement. Children: over 10s only. Some rooms en suite. TV lounge. Tea/coffee-making in bedrooms. B. & B. from £15.

Pumpy Cottage, East Week, Okehampton, Devon, EX20 2QB (0647) 23580

Mediaeval Dartmoor cottage, formerly a yeoman farmer's long house, in beautiful countryside, with its own herb garden & paddock. Comfortable & charming. Healthy b'fast using home-grown & local produce.

Open May to Oct. No smoking throughout. Vegetarian on request. Children: over 5s only. B.& B. from £10.

Stowford House, Stowford, Lewdown, Okehampton, EX20 4BZ (056 683) 415

Stowford House is a charming former rectory which stands amidst peaceful gardens just a few minutes from the old A30 and a short drive from Okehampton, Tavistock and Launceston. Your hostess, Jenny Irwin, offers a warm welcome to guests, and comfortable acommodation in beautifully appointed guest rooms (single, double and twin rooms are available). The food is outstandingly good: everything is prepared on the premises from fresh ingredients (vegetarian meals are available with notice), and there are three or four starters and main courses to choose from, a typical selection featuring Fried Camembert with Gooseberry Preserve or Creamy Parsnip and Apple Soup followed by Grilled Whole Plaice with Orange Butter or Rack of Lamb with Wine, Mint & Caper Sauce; a selection of home-made desserts, ranging from light and fruity to rich and creamy, are also served, and there is the option of a generous wedge of Stilton; there is a well-stocked bar and an interesting wine list to accompany your meal. Stowford is an excellent touring base: beautiful Dartmoor & Lydford Gorge are easily reached, & the coasts of North & South Devon are only 40 mins drive away.
Open Mar. to Nov. No smoking in dining room. Vegetarian & other diets by arrangement. Licensed. Children by arrangement. En suite, TV & tea/coffee in rooms. Credit cards. B. & B. £17.50, D., B. & B. £29.50.

OTTERY ST MARY

Fluxton Farm Hotel, Ottery St Mary, EX11 1RJ (040481) 2818

Once a 16th C. long house, this charming white-washed hotel is pleasantly situated in beautiful open country and stands in pretty sheltered gardens complete with stream and trout pond; almost all the bedrooms enjoy splendid views over the Otter Valley. There is a healthy emphasis in the preparation of the excellent cuisine on the use of fresh, locally purchased or home-produced ingredients: free-range eggs come from the house hens. Meals are served in a bright airy dining room (log fires in cooler weather) with candlelight in spring and autumn. You are 4m. from the sea & a stone's throw from the pretty town of Ottery St Mary.
Open all year. No smoking in dining room & 1 lounge. Vegetarian & other diets by arrangement. Licensed. Children & pets welcome. En suite, TV & tea/coffee in rooms. B. & B. from £22.50 D., B. & B. from £28.50.

SEATON

The Bulstone, Higher Bulstone, Branscombe, Nr Seaton, EX12 3BL (0297) 80446

Lovely 16th C. hotel offering very high standard of cuisine & accommodation; especially welcoming to families with young children.
Open Feb. to Nov. Smoking only allowed in 1 lounge. Vegetarian standard. Other diets by arrangement. Licensed. Children welcome. Pets by arrangement. En suite most rooms. Tea/coffee in bedrooms. T.V. lounge. B. & B. from £19.75.

SIDMOUTH

Applegarth Hotel & Restaurant, Church St, Sidford, EX10 9QP (0395) 513174

16th C. building with oak beams & log fires; ornamental gardens; fresh produce in cooking.
Open all year. No smoking in dining room, bedrooms & lounge. Vegetarian & other diets by arrangement. Licensed. Disabled access. Children: over 10s. En suite. Tea/coffee & TV in rooms. B. & B. from £17.50

SOUTH BRENT

Brookdale House, North Huish, South Brent, TQ10 9NL (0548 82) 402/415

Grade II listed mansion; excellent cuisine from fresh, additive-free, local ingredients.
No smoking in dining room. Vegetarian by arrangement. Licensed. Most rooms en suite Tea/coffee-making & TV in rooms. B. & B. £37.50.

The Rock, TQ10 9JL (0364) 72185

Lovely old house overlooking Lydia Bridge and the falls; largely built in 1843, the house electricity is partly generated by water wheel!
Open Feb. - Nov. inc. No smoking. Vegetarian & other diets by arrangement. Babies/ over 8s only. En suite most rooms. Tea/coffee. T.V. avail. B. & B. from £20.

SOUTH MOLTON

Whitechapel Manor, South Molton, EX36 3EG (07695) 3797

Beautifully restored Elizabethan manor house with wonderful views; excellent cuisine.

Open all year. No smoking in dining room. Vegetarian & other diets by arrangement. Licensed. Children welcome. En suite & T.V. in rooms. B. & B. from £40.

TAVISTOCK

The Stannary, Mary Tavy, Tavistock, PL19 9QB (0822) 810897

Elegant house functioning as both a restaurant & guest house; all food is vegetarian and cooked from fresh produce. Second position in the 'Vegetarian Restaurant of the Year' Awards.

Open all year (restaurant closed some evenings). No smoking in bedrooms & dining room. Vegetarian exclusively. Other meat-free diets by arrangement. Licensed. Over 12s only. 1 en suite room. Tea/coffee-making & TV in rooms. B. & B. from £20.

TEIGNMOUTH

Fonthill, Torquay Rd, Shaldon, Teignmouth, TQ14 0AX (0626) 872344

Beautiful Georgian house in 25 acres of private grounds. Very tranquil and peaceful.

Open Mar. to Dec. No smoking in the house. Vegetarian & other diets by arrangement. Children welcome. 1 private bathroom. Tea/coffee-making in bedrooms. B. & B. from £17.50.

TIVERTON

Harton Farm, Oakford, Tiverton, EX16 9HH (03985) 209

Beautiful south-facing 17th C. farm built of local stone; all produce used in cooking has been organically grown on the farm; all bread home-baked. Herbs and flowers are grown & Harton Farm Jam is made!

Vegetarian & other diets by arrangement. Organic always. Mostly wholefood. No smoking in dining room Open all year ex. Xmas. Bring your own wine. Over 4s only. Tea/coffee in rooms. T.V. B. & B. from £11.

TORQUAY

Brookesby Hall Vegetarian Hotel, Hesketh Road, Meadfoot Beach, Torquay, TQ1 2LN (0803) 292194

Exclusively vegetarian hotel; imaginative cuisine cooked from natural ingredients including free-range eggs & organic vegetables.

Open Easter to Oct. inc. Vegetarian. No smoking. Children welcome. Some en suite rooms. Tea/coffee. T.V. in 1 of 2 lounges. D., B. & B. from £25.

Hotel Protea, Seaway Lane, Chelston, Torquay, TQ2 6PW Tel: (0803) 605778 Fax: (0803) 690171

Hotel Protea is a spacious, elegant Victorian villa which stands in secluded south-facing grounds overlooking Torbay. Family-owned and run, the Hotel Protea offers the ultimate in efficient, personal service thus creating an atmosphere of friendly informality in which you are able to relax and feel at home: each of the 11 spacious en suite bedrooms has been luxuriously appointed with direct dial phones, remote-control TVs, hairdryers and mini bars - and most overlook Torbay; the sunny sitting room is particularly inviting - the perfect place in which to let an hour or two pass playing chess or listening to music. The food is fabulous - everything is prepared with care from fresh local produce - and a typical evening menu would feature Fanned Melon with Raspberry Sauce, followed by home-made soup or sorbet, Roast Leg of Pork (with fresh vegetables - there are also vegetarian options), and a selection of home-made desserts; cheese, biscuits, coffee and mints would complete the meal.

Open Feb. - Dec. No smoking in the house. Vegetarian & other diets by arrangement. En suite, TV & tea/coffee-making in bedrooms. Licensed. Credit cards. D., B. & B. from £40.

Trees Hotel, Bronshill Rd, Babbacombe, Torquay, TQ 1 3HA (0803) 326073

The Trees Hotel is a small, elegant licensed hotel which is peacefully situated amidst spacious lawned gardens just a short distance from the centre of Babbacombe and the beach. A

family-run hotel, The Trees has a happy, friendly atmosphere and your hosts, Gwen and Stewart Ferguson, will do everything they can to make your stay a happy and memorable one. The rooms are pleasantly furnished - everything is scrupulously clean - and there is a cosy bar for pre-dinner drinks. The food is 'good, plain, Devonshire cooking', and is served in a light, airy dining room. Torquay offers a wealth of entertainments and attractions to visiting tourists and additionally there are numerous safe, sandy beaches and coves within easy striking distance.
Open all year. No smoking thoughout. Licensed. Wheelchair access.Over 7s only. En suite, tea/coffee making & T.V. in rooms. Visa. D., B. & B. from £20.

Hotel Sydore, Meadfoot Road, Torquay, TQ1 2JP (0803) 294489

Very comfortable villa-style hotel situated near Meadfoot Beach; the evening menu includes some tasty and imaginative vegetarian options.
Vegetarian standard. Other diets by arrangement. Open all year. Licensed. Disabled access. Children welcome. Pets by arrangement. En suite, tea/coffee-making, T.V, trouser press and hairdryer in all bedrooms. Credit cards. B. & B. from £20.

TOTNES

Hatchlands, Bluepost, Avonwick, Nr Totnes, TQ9 7LR (0364) 72224

Luxury farmhouse in panoramic countryside; 4 course English b'fast; beaches nearby. Fresh, organic ingredients used when possible.
Open all year ex. Xmas. No smoking in dining room. Vegetarian by arrangement. TV lounge. Children & pets welcome. Tea/coffee-making. B. & B. £10.

The Old Forge at Totnes, Seymour Place, Totnes, TQ9 5AY (0803) 862174

This charming stone-built hotel was converted recently from a 600 year-old smithy; it has a lovely walled garden which makes it a rural

retreat in the heart of Totnes; the property has had an interesting history and has partly reverted back to its primary use - Peter Allnutt now runs a busy wrought iron business while his wife, Jeannie, runs the hotel. The highest standard of accommodation is offered to guests: the cottage-style bedrooms are prettily and tastefully furnished, and the food (served in very plentiful quantities) is prepared from the best of healthy ingredients. A typical breakfast menu features a variety of fish & vegetarian options and, in addition to four different types of bread, *two* different sorts of decaffeinated coffee are also offered. Healthily conscientious indeed. Traditional breakfasts are also available - the Smithy Special - as well as fruit, yoghurts, waffles & pancakes. **Holder of AA Merit Award & ETB Highly Commended.**
Open all year. No smoking in the house. Vegetarian & other diets by arrangement. Licensed. Some ground floor rooms. Children welcome. En suite in most rooms. Tea/coffee-making & TV in bedrooms. Credit cards. B. & B. from £20.

Dorset

BLANDFORD FORUM

La Belle Alliance, White Cliff Mill Street, Blandford Forum, DS11 7BP (0258) 452842

La Belle Alliance is an elegant country house style restaurant and hotel offering first-rate accommodation and food just a short walk from the centre of the attractive town of Blandford Forum. Each of the six guest bedrooms has been individually decorated and styled and has a wide range of helpful little extras (bottled Dorset water, toiletries, magazines and books) in addition to other useful amenities (trouser press, direct dial phone). You are invited to take an aperitif in the comfortable lounge, with its attractive draped curtains, before dining in the pretty dining room (flowers and linen on the table); all dishes have been prepared from fresh ingredients (local wherever possible), and the imaginative menu, which changes seasonally, would typically feature Lettuce in Walnut Oil with grilled Goat's Cheese, followed by Fillet of Sea Bream with a Herb Crust (accompanied by Ratatouille and Red Wine Sauce) and an extraordinary selection of desserts (Creamy Lemon Tart with Fresh Garden Mint and Yoghurt Sauce). As well as being an excellent centre for visiting Dorset, Blandford Forum is architecturally interesting in that it was totally rebuilt in the 30 years succeeding 1731 when it was almost completely destroyed by fire; it is, therefore, unique in England in being a whole town conceived in the high Georgian period.

Open Feb. to Dec. Smoking banned in dining room. Vegetarian and most other special diets by arrangement. Licensed. No disabled access. Children welcome, babies by arrangement. Pets by arrangement. En suite, tea/coffee-making & T.V. in all bedrooms. Access, Visa, Amex. B. & B. from £29.

BOURNEMOUTH

Durley Grange Hotel, 6 Durley Road, West Cliff, Bournemouth, BH2 5JL (0202) 554473/290743

Large, white-washed & pantiled hotel 5 mins walk from the sea; traditional British menu; new smoke-free conference room plus ozone treated indoor pool, sauna, solarium & whirlpool.

Open all year. No smoking in dining room, part of bar area, pool area & solarium. Vegetarian and diabetic diets by arrangement. Licensed. Wheelchair access. Children: over 5s only. Pets by arrangement. En suite, tea/coffee-making, T.V. & phone in all rooms. Access, Visa. Car parking. B. & B. from £26.50-£29.50.

Edgewood Guest House, 26 Foxholes Road, Southbourne, Bournemouth, BH6 3AT (0202) 429798

Large, detached Edwardian house 6 mins from beach; all food prepared from fresh ingredients.

Open all year. No smoking. Vegetarian and most other special diets, but not Khosher, by arrangement. Licensed. Children welcome. Tea/coffee-making in bedrooms. T.V. in lounge. B. & B. from £14.50.

Kingsley Hotel, 20 Glen Rd, Boscombe, Bournemouth, BH5 1HR (0202) 398683

Small, 11-bedroomed hotel offering personal service and a warm, friendly atmosphere.

Open Mar. - Oct. No smoking throughout. Licensed. Children welcome. En suite in most rooms. TV & tea/coffee-making in all bedrooms. Access, Visa. D. B. & B. from £174 p.w.

Langtry Manor Hotel, Derby Rd, East Cliff, Bournemouth, BH1 3QB (0202) 553887

Open all year. No smoking in dining room & some bedrooms. Vegetarian standard. Licensed. Disabled access. Children by arrangement. Pets by arrangement. En suite, tea/coffee-making & T.V. in all rooms. Credit cards. B. & B. from £39.50.

CHARMOUTH

Newlands House, Stonebarrow Lane, Charmouth, West Dorset, DT6 6RA (0297) 60212

Former 16th C. farmhouse set in 2 acres of gardens and orchard on the fringe of the pretty village of Charmouth near Lyme Regis.

Open Mar. to Oct. Smoking permitted in bar lounge only. Vegetarian by arrangement. Licensed. Children: over 6s only. En suite, tea/coffee-making & T.V. in all bedrooms. D., B. & B. from £34.60.

DORCHESTER

"Badgers Sett", Cross Lanes, Melcombe Bingham, Nr Dorchester, DT2 7NY (0258) 880697

Mellow 17th C. flint and brick cottage carefully modernised to retain original features; all bedrooms are sunny and light.

Open all year. No smoking in dining room & sitting room. Vegetarian by arrangement. Children welcome. Pets by arrangement (garden facilities). En suite, tea/coffee, T.V. & radio in rooms. B. & B. from £16.50.

The Creek, Ringstead, Dorchester, DT2 8NG (0305) 852291

Lovely white-washed house with garden overlooking the Heritage Coast of Dorset. All ingredients "as fresh as possible!".

Open all year. No smoking. Vegetarian, vegan and other special diets by arrangement. Children welcome. Tea/coffee-making in bedrooms. T.V. in lounge. B. & B. from £13.50.

The Manor Hotel, Beach Road, West Bexington, Nr Dorchester, DT2 9DF Tel: (0308) 897785 Fax: (0308) 897035

The Manor Hotel is the ancient Manor House of Bexington and snuggles in a pocket of tree-and-garden on a gentle slope just a saunter from the great sea-washed sweep of Chesil Bank.

Mentioned in the Domesday Book, this beautiful oak-panelled stone building has been mellowed by nine centuries of sun and sea, and the several years of care and love lavished on it by its present owners; bedrooms are beautifully appointed - many have panoramic views of the Dorset Coast - and the residents' lounge looks over a flowered garden which is, in turn, surrounded by miles of peaceful countryside. The food is of an exceptionally high standard: meals are prepared by a master chef who works with imagination and flair to create a range of tempting dishes, a typical evening menu selection featuring Crab and Ginger Filo Parcels and Tarragon Sauce, followed by Poached Salmon (in a delicate Lime Hollandaise Sauce) and an enticing choice of desserts. Within easy reach of the Manor Hotel are the sandy stretches of Weymouth, Charmouth and Lyme Regis.

Open all year. Vegetarian standard. Vegan and other special diets by arrangement. Licensed. Children welcome. En suite, tea/coffee-making, T.V. & phone in all bedrooms. Credit cards. B. & B. from £37.50

LYME REGIS

Kersbrook Hotel, Pound Road, Lyme Regis (02974) 42596

Thatched, 18th C. listed building in 1 acre of gardens & grounds on a hillside overlooking Lyme Bay. Delicious à la carte meals.

Open Feb. to Dec. No smoking in dining room & bedrooms. Vegetarian and most other special diets by arrangement. Licensed. Children not allowed in dining room. Pets by arrangement. En suite, tea/coffee-making & T.V. in bedrooms. Credit cards.

POOLE

Gull Cottage, 50 Twemlow Avenue, Lower Parkstone, Poole, BH14 8AN (0202) 721277

Large family house overlooking Poole Park and close to harbour.

Smoking banned throughout the house. Vegetarian by arrangement. Children welcome. En suite in all rooms. B. & B. from £16.

Sunridge Hotel, Bleke St, Shaftesbury, Dorset (0747) 53130

The Sunridge Hotel is a listed 19th C. building in the centre of Shaftesbury, a thriving market town with an extensive history. The hotel has been comfortably furnished and tastefully decorated throughout, and has many leisure amenities for guests, including a sauna and a heated indoor swimming pool in addition to an elegant Victorian bar and restaurant. The food is imaginative and delicious: main dishes are served with a selection of fresh, locally grown vegetables, and a typical evening meal would feature deep-fried Camembert followed by lemon chicken, and a tempting dessert. Shaftesbury is town of great character and charm: standing on a hilltop overlooking the Blackmore Vale, it dates its origins from Saxon times and its many notable features include its abbey ruins and Gold Hill (the steep cobbled street featured in the Hovis ads!). A little further afield, visitors will find themselves within easy reach of Stonehenge, Avebury and the beautiful cathedrals of Salisbury and Wells.

Open all year. No smoking in dining room & 50% of bedrooms. Vegetarian & other diets by arrangement. Children welcome. Licensed. En suite, TV & tea/coffee-making in bedrooms. Credit cards. B. & B. from £26.

SHERBORNE

Middle Piccadilly Natural Healing Centre, Holwell, Sherborne (096323) 468

In spite of its urbane title, Middle Piccadilly is a 17th C. thatched cottage set in the heart of the Dorset countryside. Its proprietors describe themselves as "natural healers" and a wide range of treatments is offered at Middle Piccadilly including Acupressure, Bach Flower Remedies, Reflexology and Remedial Yoga. Guests have an initial consultation during which treatments are prescribed and during the course of their stay these are carried out while the additional recuperative benefits of living in a beautifully furnished cottage and being fed exceptionally good vegetarian cuisine also work their therapeutic magic. The food is 100% wholefood, the produce is organic (mostly home-grown), and the menu imaginative (a typical meal might feature Vegetable Wellington followed by pears in red grape juice).

Vegetarian standard. Vegan & other special diets by arrangement. Wholefoods when available. Open all year ex. Xmas. No smoking throughout the house. Tea/Coffee-making facilities. Full board from £46. 2,3 & 4 day packages available including treatments.

WEYMOUTH

The Beehive, Osmington, Nr Weymouth, DT3 6EL (0305) 834095

Mary Kempe is keen to point out that the Beehive is not so much a guest house as her home and visitors to this lovely little thatched Georgian cottage in the picturesque village of Osmington will be welcomed as friends. Healthy food is of prime importance at The Beehive ("by wholefoods I mean real foods") and breakfast is a feast of free-range eggs, bacon and wholemeal bread. Mary is something of a county patriot when it comes to the evening meal and guests might be treated to Wessex Chicken in Local Cider Sauce followed by a scrumptious dessert. Those who enjoy walking are excellently placed at The Beehive: many footpaths begin from the village and the Dorset Coast Path, on an inland loop, goes past the cottage.

Open Feb. to Dec. No smoking in the house. Vegetarian and some other special diets, but not vegan, by arrangement. Children: over 5s only. Pets by arrangement. En suite in one room. Tea/coffee-making in bedrooms. T.V. in sitting room. B. & B. from £14.

Fairlight, 50 Littlemoor Rd, Preston, Weymouth, Dorset, DT3 6AA

Family-run establishment with good home-cooking. All food fresh.

Open all year. No smoking. Vegetarian by arrangement. Children: over 4s. B. B. & D. from £18.

Somerset

BRENDON

Bridge Cottage, Brendon, Nr Lynmouth (05987) 247

Beautiful old stone house in woodland overlooking river. Home-cooked food with garden produce.

Vegetarian by arrangement. B. & B. from £11.

BRIDGWATER

Pear Tree House, 16 Manor Rd, Catcott, Bridgwater, TA7 9HF (0278) 722390

Comfortable family home situated in peaceful village on Polden Hills overlooking Somerset levels. Ideal as a base for touring Somerset.

Open all year. No smoking dining room & bedrooms. Vegetarian & other diets by arrangement. Licensed.

Children welcome. H. & C., shaver points, tea/coffee-making. T.V. B. & B. from £13.50.

Poplar Herb Farm, Mark Rd, Burtle, Nr Bridgwater, TA7 8NB (0278) 723170

Organic smallholding, herb & nursery gardens.

Open all year. No smoking. Vegetarian and vegan standard. Tea/coffee. T.V. B. & B. from £11. D. £6.

CREWKERNE

Adams Field House, West Chinnock, Crewkerne, TA18 7QA (0935 881249

300-year-old former shop and bakery.

Open April to Oct. No smoking in dining room, T.V. room & bedrooms. Vegetarian & diabetic diets by arrangement. Children welcome. Dogs by arrangement. Tea-making & T.V. in rooms.

Somerset

Merefield House, East St, Crewkerne, TA18 7AB (0460) 73112

Listed 16th C. building in quiet gardens with unrivalled views of the town; plentiful food.

Open Mar. to Dec. No smoking in dining room & all public areas. Exclusively vegetarian and vegan. Well-behaved children welcome. En suite & TV in 1 room. Tea/coffee-making all rooms.

Yew Trees Cottage, Silver Street, Misterton, Crewkerne (0460) 77192

A warm welcome and comfortable rooms await guests in this beautiful 17th century timber-beamed cottage with attractive gardens, in a quiet Somerset village. The food is excellent. A typical menu might offer Baked Avocado with Herb and Cheese stuffing followed by Silver Chicken, mange-touts and Dauphinoise potatoes, with Apple and Almond Dessert Cake to finish. A vegetarian main course option might be Harvesters' Crumble with Aubergine and Tomato Casserole. You are in lovely country near the Dorset border, with interesting old churches and National Trust properties, an excellent place for walkers with good coastal walking.- and Spring and Autumn walking breaks are offered at the cottage with the loan of maps and guides.

Open all year. No-smoking house-hold. Vegetarian and most other special diets by arrangement. Children: over 8s only. Tea/coffee-making in all bedrooms. T.V. in lounge. B. & B. from £15. D. £10.

HENSTRIDGE (Nr Shaftesbury)

Quiet Corner Farm, Henstridge, Templecombe, BA8 0RA (0963) 63045

Farm with stunning views across the Blackmore Vale. B'fast features yoghurt & fresh fruit from the garden, or bacon & eggs, & fresh filter coffee.

Open all year. No smoking in dining room, bedrooms & sitting room. Vegetarian standard. Other special diets by arrangement. Children welcome. En suite. Tea/coffee in all rooms. T.V. B. & B. £16-£18.50.

MINEHEAD

Meadow House, Sea Lane, Kilve, Nr Minehead, TA5 1EG Tel: (0278 74) 546 Fax: (0278 74) 663

Georgian rectory, full of character, surrounded by landscaped gardens and situated amidst rolling countryside just minutes from Kilve beach. Award-winning wine list

Open all year. No smoking in dining room & 1 lounge. Vegetarian and most other special diets by arrangement. Licensed. 4 ground floor bedrooms. Children welcome. Pets by arrangement. En suite, tea/coffee-making & T.V. in bedrooms. Credit cards. B. & B. from £39. D. £19.

Periton Park Hotel, Middlecombe, Minehead, TA24 8SW (0643) 706885

Handsome 19th C. country residence in an elevated position amidst 4 acres of woodland. Excellent food prepared from fresh ingredients with good vegetarian options.

Open all year. No smoking in dining room & 1 bedroom. Vegetarian standard. Other special diets by arrangement. Licensed. Disabled access. Children: over 12s only. En suite, tea/coffee-making & T.V. in all rooms. Credit cards. B. & B. fron £17.50.

MONTACUTE

Milk House Restaurant (with accommodation), The Borough, Montacute, TA15 6XB (0935) 823823

Open all year ex. Xmas Day. No smoking in dining room, lounge & bedrooms; separate smoking room. Vegetarian & vegan standard. Licensed. Children: over 12s only. En suite in both rooms. D. from £15.50.

King's Arms Inn, Montacute, TA15 GUU (0935) 822513

Pub specialising in home-cooking & baking.

Open all year. Smoking discouraged in dining room. Special diets by arrangement. Licensed. Disabled access difficult. Children welcome. En suite, TV & tea/coffee-making in all rooms. Credit cards.

PORLOCK

Lorna Doone Hotel, High St, Porlock, TA24 8PS (0643) 862404

Small, family-run hotel in Porlock village. Menu has a Somerset flavour & dishes are prepared from local, seasonal ingredients.

Open all year. No smoking in dining room. Vegetarian standard. Most other special diets by arrangement. Dogs welcome. En suite in most rooms. Tea/coffee-making & TV in all rooms. Visa, B. & B. from £17.50. ETB 3 Crown & RAC Acclaimed.

SHEPTON MALLET

The Long House Hotel, Pilton, Shepton Mallet, BA4 4BP (0749) 890701

An 18th C. house with character and a relaxed atmosphere in a picturesque village setting.

Open all year. No smoking in dining room & discouraged in lounge; smoke-free bedrooms usually available. Vegetarian & wholefood standard. Licensed. Children welcome. En suite in all rooms. Tea/coffee & T.V. on request. Access, Visa, Mastercard, Amex. B. & B. from £17. D. from £10.

TAUNTON

Watercombe House, Huish Champflower, Wiveliscombe, Taunton TA4 2EE (0984) 23725

Modernised old school house in a beautiful unspoilt valley in a secluded riverside setting. Imaginative dinners are freshly prepared.

Open Mar. to end Oct. No smoking. Vegetarian and most other diets by arrangement. Bring your own wine. En suite in 1 room. Tea/coffee-making in rooms. T.V. in lounge. B. & B. from £15. D. from £11.50.

WELLINGTON

Greenham Hall, Greenham, Wellington, TA21 0JJ (0823) 672603

A large, friendly home set in a beautiful garden which is lovingly cared for by the family. The garden itself is a plant lovers' paradise with a large collection of perennials - and plenty of room for children. Only bed and breakfast is available, but excellent meals are available at many of the surrounding pubs and hotels. Walking is the favoured occupation at this peaceful location but the more energetic may choose fishing, golf, riding, coastal trips, visits to historic houses or use of the excellent sports facilities in nearby Wellington. Special study weekends are also available at Greenham Hall; planned subjects include painting, homeopathy and the Alexander Technique (further details are available on request). The worst complaint from visitors is that it is so quiet at night, that it makes the birds' dawn chorus almost deafening!

Open all year. Vegetarian and most other special diets by arrangement. Children welcome. En suite in 2 rooms. Tea/coffee-making in lounge. T.V. lounge. B & B from £17.50.

Worth House Hotel, Worth, Wells, BA5 1LW (0749) 672041

15th C. farmhouse & restaurant with exposed beams and open fireplaces.

Open all year. No smoking in dining room & T.V. residents' lounge. Special diets by arrangement. Licensed. Children welcome. En suite, tea/coffee in all rooms. T.V. in lounge. Visa, Mastercard. B. & B. from £28. D. £15. ETB 3 Crowns. Les Routiers.

YEOVIL

Self-Realization Healing Centre, Laurel Lane, Queen Camel, Nr Yeovil, Somerset, BA22 7NU

Run by a spiritual family under the direction of

Mata Yogananda, this centre welcomes everyone seeking peace and unconditional love whatever their beliefs or station in life. Accommodation is available all year round, with use of a heated therapy pool, meditation room, Library and, in winter, a log fire. The gardens open out onto open coutnryside with well-marked footpaths and walks to suit all abilities. The centre offers vegetarian meals which have been cooked by the family with organic produce wherever possible. The centre offers individual training in meditative peace, yoga, relaxation, spiritual knowledge and philosophy and self-development; additionally healing, counselling and individual guidance are available at Queen Camel, Bristol and Wells.

Open all year. No smoking throughout. Vegetarian standard. Other diets by arrangement. Tea/coffee-making. 1 en suite room. 1 downstairs room. B. & B. from £14.50. Half/full board also avail.

Wiltshire

AVEBURY

Windmill House, Winterbourne Monkton, Nr Avebury, SN4 9NN (06723) 446

Beautifully renovated miller's house (some old chalk blocks are still visible in the walls) set amidst stunning scenery; comfortably furnished; excellent cuisine with home-baked bread and home-grown vegetables, and natural spring water from own well.

Open all year. No smoking in dining room and discouraged throughout. Vegetarian, diabetic and other special diets by arrangement. Children welcome. B. & B. from £14.50.

BRADFORD ON AVON

Bradford Old Windmill, 4 Masons Lane, Bradford on Avon, BA15 1QN (0225) 866842

Beautifully restored mill with timber sail gallery with lots of stripped pine and 'the flotsam and jetsam of beachcombing trips around the world'. The food is as imaginative and eclectic.

Open all year. Smoking banned throughout the house. Vegetarian standard. Vegan and other special diets by arrangement. Children: over 6s only. En suite in some rooms. Tea/coffee-making in all bedrooms. T.V. free on request. B. & B. from £24.50.

Woolley Grange, Woolley Green, Bradford on Avon, BA15 1TX (02216) 4705

Jacobean Manor House built from mellow Bath stone in the early part of the 17th C. All dishes have been home-prepared from the finest of fresh, local, and often home-grown, ingredients.

Vegetarian, vegan, diabetic & some other special diets by arrangement. Organic when avail. Wholefood when avail. Open all year. Licensed. Children welcome. Pets by arrangement. En suite in most rooms. Room service. T.V. B. & B. from £45.

CORSHAM

Rudloe Park Hotel and Restaurant, Leafy Lane, Corsham, SN13 0PA (0225) 810555

Splendidly appointed gothic country house hotel with sweeping wooded drive; exceptional cuisine prepared from fresh, local produce.

Open all year. No smoking in dining room. Vegetarian standard. Vegan, diabetic, candida, coeliac or any other diet by arrangement. Licensed. Some disabled access. Children: over 10s (hotel), over 5s (restaurant). Pets by arrangement. En suite, tea/coffee-making & T.V. in all rooms. Credit cards

DEVIZES

Pinecroft Guest House, Potterne Rd (A360), Devizes, SN10 5DA (0380) 721433

Comfortable Georgian family house; five minutes' walk from the centre of the ancient market town of Devizes; free-range eggs and bacon; vegetarians catered for by arrangement.

Open all year. No smoking in dining room & bedrooms. Vegetarian always available. Children welcome. En suite most rooms. Tea/coffee making. T.V. in all rooms. Credit cards. B. & B. from £17.

Longwater, Erlestoke, Nr Devizes, Wilts. Tel & Fax: (0380) 830095

Set a quarter of a mile from the 160 acre organic farm buildings, Longwater overlooks its own parkland and lakes (one for coarse fishing, one a waterfowl conservation area) and is a perfect base from which to explore the Wiltshire countryside. Accommodation is in comfortable en suite rooms, and guests have the use of a conservatory and spacious lounge with log fire (which overlooks the waterfowl area). Your hosts hold the Soil Association's symbol of approval and accordingly much of the organic produce used in cooking is home-grown; other items have been locally produced - such as the wine which comes from a nearby vineyard - and the traditional farmhouse fare can be adapted to meet the particular likes or dislikes of guests. In addition to Longwater there is an attractive farmhouse which is available for self-catering let.

Vegetarian, vegan, diabetic and some other special diets by arrangement. Organic when avail. Wholefood when avail. Open Jan 1 - Dec. 22. No smoking in dining room, conservatory & bedrooms. Licensed. Disabled access: ground floor rooms available. Children welcome. Pets welcome. En suite, tea/coffee making & T.V. in all bedrooms. B. & B. from £19.

EAST KNOYLE

Milton House, East Knoyle, Salisbury, SP3 6BG (0747) 830397

Charming old house. B'fast features farm-fresh eggs, fresh fruit juice, wholemeal bread.
Open all year. No smoking. Vegetarian & other special diets by arrangement. Children welcome. Pets by arrangement. Private bathroom leading to twin-bedded room with T.V. and tea/coffee making facilities. Hard tennis court. B. & B. from £19-£22.

MARLBOROUGH

Laurel Cottage, Southend, Ogbourne St George, Marlborough (0672) 84288

Exquisite 16th C. thatched cottage standing in an acre of lawned gardens; oak beams, inglenook fireplaces, etc; excellent breakfast menu includes smoked haddock and kippers.
Open March to Oct. No smoking. Vegetarian by arrangement. Children welcome. En suite some rooms. Tea/coffee & T.V. in rooms. B. & B. from £15.

SALISBURY

The Coach and Horses, Winchester St, Salisbury, SP1 1HG (0722) 336254

Salisbury's oldest Inn; well-deserved reputation for food and wine.
Open all year. No smoking in restaurant and bedrooms. Vegetarian standard. Other special diets by arrangement. Licensed. Some disabled access. Children welcome. Pets by arrangement. En suite, TV & tea/coffee in all rooms. B. & B. from £38.

The New Inn at Salisbury, 41-43 New St, Salisbury, SP1 2PH (0722) 327679

Charming 15th C. timbered building offering a very high standard of food and accommodation.
Open all year. No smoking throughout. Vegetarian standard. Licensed. Disabled access. Children welcome. En suite, tea/coffee-making & T.V. in all rooms. Credit cards. B. & B. from £39-£55.

Stratford Lodge, 4 Park Lane Castle Rd, Salisbury, SP1 3NP Tel: (0722) 325177 Fax: (0722) 412699

Stratford Lodge is an elegant Victorian house which stands in a quiet lane overlooking Victoria Park. Your host, Jill Bayly, offers a special brand of gracious hospitality: the complementary sherry before dinner speaks volumes - and is a welcome herald to a first-rate meal prepared by Jill from fresh ingredients, some home-grown. It is always advisable to book for dinner lest you miss such delights as Baked Roquefort Pears followed by Salmon Steak with Herb Butter and a selection of home-made desserts, all served by candlelight on beautiful china. Each of the bedrooms has en suite facilities and has been decorated and furnished with flair - one room has a brass Victorian bed; the house has been

furnished throughout with antiques and there is a lovely garden with flowering shrubs. Salisbury is a beautiful city - not the less appealing because of its proximity to so much unspoilt countryside and historically interesting towns and villages.
Open 22 Jan - 23 Dec. No smoking in the house. Vegetarian & other diets by arrangement. Children: over 8s welcome. Licensed. En suite, TV & tea/coffee-making in bedrooms. Credit cards.

Templeman Old Farmhouse, Redlynch, Salisbury, SP5 2JS (0725) 20331

Large, gracious 17th C. farmhouse in beautiful rural situation near to the New Forest.
Open April to Oct. No smoking in dining room & bedrooms. Vegetarian by arrangement. Children welcome. H. & C. in all rooms, but no en suite. T.V. in lounge. B. & B. from £16.

Yew Tree Cottage, Grove Lane, Redlynch, Salisbury, SP5 2NR (0725) 21730

Attractive, comfortable 'Guest Home' standing in a lovely, large garden & smallholding in the pretty village of Redlynch 1m. from the New Forest. Breakfast features traditional, wholefood, vegetarian or vegan options.
Open all year. No smoking throughout the house. Vegetarian and vegan standard. Other special diets by arrangement. Children welcome. Tea/coffee on request. T.V. in lounge. B. & B. from £14.

ZEALS

Cornerways Cottage, Longcross, Zeals, BA12 6LL (0747) 840477

18th C. house of great character comfortably furnished throughout; breakfast is a generous feast of, amongst other things, fresh croissants and muffins (mint, herb or decaffeinated tea or coffee are also avail.; alternative breakfast menus may be selected for those on special diets).
Open all year. No smoking in the house. Vegetarian and other special diets by arrangement. Children welcome. Pets (small dogs) by arrangement. En suite in 2 rooms. Tea/coffee making. T.V. in lounge. B. & B. from £14.

The South of England

Hampshire

ANDOVER
Abbotts Law, Abbotts Ann, Andover, SP11 7DW (0264) 710350
Charming country house in 3 acres of attractive gardens overlooking water meadows. Cordon Bleu cook & the garden provides much of the fresh fruit and vegetables used in cooking.
Open April to Oct. No smoking. Vegetarian and other special diets by arrangement. Children welcome. En suite, tea/coffee & T.V. in rooms. B. & B. from £20.

BASINGSTOKE
Fernbank Hotel, 4 Fairfields Road, Basingstoke, RG21 3DR (0256) 21191
Victorian building forming 18-bedroom hotel. Healthy b'fast options.
Open all year. No smoking in dining room & some bedrooms. Children welcome. En suite rooms avail. Tea/coffee & T.V. in all rooms. B. & B. from £17.50.

Oaklea Guest House, London Rd, Hook, Nr Basingstoke, RG27 9LA (0256) 762673

Oaklea is a fine Victorian house standing in an acre of walled gardens just a mile from junction 5 of the M3. It has been quite beautifully furnished throughout and offers first-class accommodation and food to guests. The food is basically of the good-old-fashioned-home-cooking variety - but everything is beautifully presented and has been prepared from fresh ingredients wherever possible. Breakfast is a hearty feast - smoked haddock or manx kippers feature in the otherwise traditional meal - and the 4-course dinner menu would typically feature Chicken and Sweetcorn Soup followed by Roast Lamb with all the trimmings and a delicious home-made dessert, such as Gooseberry Upside-down Cake; a good cheese board, and coffee, would complete the meal. Oaklea is ideally situated for Heathrow (35 mins.) and those wishing to visit Basingstoke, Farnborough, Camberley and Reading, and additionally there is a half-hourly train service to Waterloo.
Open all year. No smoking in dining room & some bedrooms. Vegetarian and other special diets by arrangement. Licensed. Some disabled access. Children welcome. Pets by arrangement. En suite in some rooms. Tea/coffee making in some rooms. T.V. in some rooms, and in lounge. B. & B. from £17.

CHANDLERS FORD
St Lucia, 68 Shaftesbury Avenue, Chandlers Ford, Eastleigh SO5 3BP (0703) 262995

St Lucia is a 1920's detached home standing in a third of an acre of mature and well-maintained gardens in a quiet residential area of Chandlers Ford. The bedrooms are all comfortable and centrally heated and each has a range of helpful amenities, including T.V. and tea and coffee-making facilities. A traditional or Continental breakfast option is served to guests (in your room, if you wish!), and the evening meal consists of either a choice of snacks or lighter meals, which can be prepared at short notice, or a full 4-course menu which can be offered if a few hours' notice is given. A typical 4-course evening meal would feature home-made Spring Soup (lettuce and Spring Onion), followed by home-made Steak and Kidney Pie (with home-grown vegetables), and a traditional dessert, such as Lemon Meringue Pie; tea or coffee would complete the meal. There is a sports centre and 18-hole golf course nearby, and you are within easy reach of the M3 and M27.
Open all year. No smoking. Vegetarian and most other special diets by arrangement. Children: over 10s only. H & C, tea/coffee-making & T.V. in all bedrooms. Parking for 5. B. & B. from £14.

Hampshire

FAREHAM

Mrs M. Mitchell, Avenue House Hotel, 22 The Avenue, Fareham (0329) 232175

Highly acclaimed guest house offering very comfortable accommodation and healthy breakfasts prepared by qualified dietician.
Vegetarian & diabetic standard. Vegan, low-fat, low-cal. and some other special diets by arrangement. Children & pets welcome. En suite, tea/coffee-making & T.V. in all rooms. Access, Visa. B. & B. from £21.

FORDINGBRIDGE

Ashburn Hotel and Restaurant, Station Rd, Fordingbridge (0425) 652060

Comfortable, warm family-run country house hotel close to historic village amidst miles of scenic beauty. Renowned for food and friendly atmosphere. Outdoor heated swimming pool.
Open all year. No smoking in dining room & garden room (adjacent to bar). Vegetarian & other diets by arrangement. Licensed. Children & pets welcome. En suite, tea/coffee-making & T.V. B. & B. from £31.

HOOK

Oakley Barn Guest House, Oakley Barn, Searles Lane, Hook (0256) 766104

Restored 17th C. thatched barn with panoramic views of the Whitewater Valley.
Open all year. No smoking in the house. Vegetarian by arrangement. Disabled access. Children welcome. Tea/coffee-making & T.V.

KILMESTON

Dean Farm, Kilmeston, Nr Alresford, SO24 0NL (0962) 771 286

This welcoming 18th C. farmhouse in the picturesque village of Kilmeston forms part of a working mixed farm on the edge of the Hampshire Downs. The comfortable accommodation consists of two double bedrooms and one family room (all with lovely views), and the large sitting room and separate dining room each have log fires and a relaxing atmosphere. Situated on the Wayfarers Walk and approximately one and a half miles from the South Downs Way, the farm is an ideal stopping-off point for walkers and horse-riders alike (there is stabling and grazing for horses and superb riding over 170 acres of farmland). Several nearby pubs serve good food and real ale, and you are within easy reach of Winchester (8 miles) and the New Forest (35 mins drive).
Open Jan. to Dec. No smoking. Vegetarians standard. Diabetic and low-fat by arrangement. Children: over 5s welcome. Tea/coffee on request at any time. T.V. in sitting room. B. & B. from £15. ETB listed.

LYMINGTON

Albany House, 3 Highfield, Lymington, SO41 9GB (0590) 671900

Elegant Regency house built around 1840 on the higher ground to the western edge of Lymington. Views of the Solent and the Isle of Wight from most of the bedrooms. Log fires in winter. Afternoon tea served in spacious sitting room overlooking walled garden. Excellent food prepared from fresh, local ingredients.
Open seasonally. No smoking in dining room & actively discouraged elsewhere. Vegetarian by arrangement. Children 'accepted'. Pets by arrangement. 3 en suites. Tea/coffee-making in all rooms. T.V. available. B. & B. from £18.50.

Redwing Farm, Pitmore Lane, Sway, Lymington, SO41 6BW (0590) 683319

Farmhouse forming part of a working farm; bedrooms are cosy and beamed.
Open all year. No smoking. Vegetarian and most other special diets by arrangement. 2 bedrooms on ground floor. T.V. in lounge. B. & B. from £15.

Stanwell House Hotel, High St, Lymington, SO41 9AA (0590) 677756

Charming small hotel, beautifully equipped; ground floor rooms available.
Vegetarian standard. Vegan, diabetic and some other special diets by arrangement. Open all year. Licensed. Disabled access: ground floor rooms available, one with wheelchair access. Children welcome. En suite, TV & tea/coffee all rooms. B. & B. from £44.

LYNDHURST

Forest Cottage, High Street, Lyndhurst, SO43 7BH (0703) 283461

Charming 300-year-old cottage with an extensive library of natural history books.
Open all year ex. Xmas. No smoking in dining room & bedrooms. Vegetarian, vegan and diabetic standard. Children: over 12s only. Tea/coffee provided from kitchen on request. B. & B. from £13.

PETERSFIELD

Mizzards Farm, Rogate, Petersfield, GU31 5HS (0730) 821656

Lovely 17th C. farmhouse in a peaceful setting with 13 acres of gardens and fields. Sympathetically restored and furnished. Covered swimming pool.
Open all year ex. Xmas. No smoking. Vegetarian by arrangement. Licensed. Children: over 6s only. En suite, TV & tea/coffee-making in all bedrooms. B. & B. from £20.

Trotton Farm, Rogate, Petersfield, GU31 5EN (0730) 813618

Lovely farmhouse situated in an area of outstanding natural beauty with many attractions within 1 hour's drive; many walks and fishing may be enjoyed within the environs of the farm.
Open all year. No smoking. Vegetarian standard. Children welcome. En suite & tea/coffee-making in all bedrooms. T.V. in sitting/games room.

RINGWOOD

Moortown Lodge, 244 Christchurch Road, Ringwood (0425) 471404

Charming country house hotel; excellent food prepared from fresh local produce.
Open all year. No smoking in dining room. Vegetarian & other diets by arrangement. Licensed. Children welcome. En suite in most rooms. Tea/coffee & T.V. in all bedrooms. Credit cards. B. & B. from £26.

ROTHERWICK

Tylney Hall, Rotherwick, Nr Hook, RG27 9AJ (0256) 764881

Tylney Hall is a magnificent, Grade II listed mansion which was 'respectfully restored' in 1985 and now offers hospitality of an

exceptionally high standard to guests. The original features of the building have been largely retained, from the wood panelling in the library where pre-dinner drinks may be enjoyed, to the delicate plaster work in the Grey Lounge. Cordon Bleu meals are served in the elegant glass-domed restaurant and accommodation is in spacious bedrooms or suites, each of which have been individually designed and exquisitely furnished. A wide range of leisure pursuits may be enjoyed at Tylney Hall: there is a sauna, gym and an indoor and outdoor heated pool, and tennis, snooker and croquet may also be enjoyed; archery, clay-shooting and hot-air ballooning may be arranged in the grounds with prior notice.
Open all year. No pipes & cigars in dining room. Vegetarian standard. Vegan, diabetic & other diets by arrangement. Organic & wholef'd when avail. Licensed. Children welcome. En suite & T.V. in all rooms. Credit cards.

SOUTH WARNBOROUGH

Street Farmhouse, Alton Rd, South Warnborough, Hants, RG25 1RS (0256) 862225

Listed Jacobean farmhouse with many original features, including inglenook and beamed ceilings; heated outdoor pool in season.
Open all year. No smoking in dining room & bedrooms. Vegetarian by arrangement. Children welcome. Pets by arrangement. En suite in 2 rooms. TV & tea/coffee-making in bedrooms. Amex. B. & B. £30 (per twin room).

SUTTON SCOTNEY

'Dever View', 17 Upper Bullington, Sutton Scotney, Nr Winchester, SO21 3RB (0962) 760566

Dever View is an attractive guest house set in the peaceful rural village of Bullington: a tiny place

with a population of just 23 people who live in the handful of houses which are surrounded by miles and miles of open countryside. Accommodation is in very comfortable rooms which have a helpful range of amenities and there is a pretty garden and comfortable lounge for guests' use. The breakfast is first-rate: your hostess, Mrs Somerton, offers a variety of delicious options including some healthy alternatives (low-fat, etc.) as well as more traditional fare. Bullington is just ½ mile from where the A34 crosses A303 and 9 miles from Winchester; there are numerous walks to be enjoyed in the locality and additionally you are within easy reach of Stonehenge, Romsey and the New Forest. ETB 2 Crown Commended.
Open all year. No smoking in the house. Vegetarian and diabetic diets by arrangement. Children welcome. Pets by arrangement. Tea/coffee-making in all bedrooms. T.V. in guests' lounge. B. & B. from £15-18.

WINCHESTER

Camellia's, 24 Ranelagh Rd (0962) 864129

Beautiful Grade II listed house with a warm, friendly atmosphere on a quiet road near the city centre; lovely garden & trad. English b'fast.
Open all year. Vegetarian & other diets by arrangement. No smoking in the house. Children welcome. En suite, tea/coffee-making & TV in bedrooms. B. & B. from £15.

Sandy Lodge, 47 Christchurch Road, St Cross, Winchester, SO23 9TE (0962) 53385

Charming detached house built of flint and red brick set in beautiful gardens just 10 mins walk from the city centre; good food, including lunch on request, served in dining room or in guests' own room; newspapers & magazines may be ordered.
Open all year. Smoking banned in one of the two dining rooms and in bedrooms. Vegetarian by arrangement. Disabled access. Children welcome. Tea/coffee-making in all rooms. T.V. available.

Sycamores, 4 Bereweeke Close, Winchester, SO22 6AR (0962) 867242

Detached family house with an open garden in a quiet area just 10 mins walk from the station.
Open all year. No smoking. Vegetarian breakfast on request. Children: over 8s only. Tea/coffee-making & T.V. in all bedrooms. B. & B. from £16.

The Wykeham Arms, 75 Kingsgate Street, Winchester, SO23 9PE (0962) 853834

17th C. public house - one of the oldest in Winchester - offering very comfortable accommodation and excellent food prepared exclusively from fresh, local produce.
Open all year. No smoking in 2 of 4 eating areas and in breakfast room. Vegetarian standard. Licensed. Disabled access. Children: over 14s only. Pets welcome. En suite in all rooms. Tea/coffee-making in all bedrooms. T.V. in all bedrooms.

64 Middlebrook St (0962) 862222

Bright, sunny private house offering B. & B.
Open Feb - Nov. No smoking in the house. Vegetarian standard. Any other diet on request. Tea/coffee-making. TV in lounge. B. & B. £15.

Parkhill Country House Hotel, Beaulieu Road, Lyndhurst, New Forest, SO43 7FZ (0703) 282944

Beautiful country house. Excellent food cooked from fresh, seasonal produce. Swimming pool.
Open all year. No smoking in dining room. Vegetarian and other special diets catered for. Licensed. Children welcome. Pets welcome. En suite, TV & tea/coffee-making in all bedrooms. Credit cards. B. & B. from £27.50.

Isle of Wight

CHALE

Clarendon Hotel and Wight Mouse Inn, Chale, PO38 2HA (0983) 730431

17th C. stone-built coaching inn; excellent food, home-made from fresh, local ingredients.
Vegetarian standard. Vegan, diabetic and other special diets by arrangement. Open all year. Licensed. Children welcome. Pets by arrangement. En suite. Tea/coffee-making & T.V. in all rooms.

FRESHWATER

Brookside Forge Hotel, Brookside Rd, Freshwater, PO40 9ER (0983) 754644

Substantial detached property with attractive terraced gardens, standing in a pleasant tree-lined road close to the centre of Freshwater. All food is home-made from fresh ingredients, including the soups and sweets.
Vegetarian, vegan and diabetic standard. Open all year. No smoking in dining room & bedrooms. Licensed. Children welcome. Pets by arrangement. En suite in most rooms. Tea/coffee-making. T.V. in lounge. Access, Visa. B. & B. from £18.50. Proprietors will book your ferry at substantial savings.

RYDE

Hotel Ryde Castle, The Esplanade, Ryde, PO33 1JA Tel: (0983) 63755 Fax (0983) 68925

Ryde Castle is an imposing 16th C. ivy-clad building which was commissioned by Henry VIII in 1540 in order to defend the island and its surrounding waters from invasion. With such perils happily past, Ryde Castle's more peaceably-motivated guests may now enjoy magnificent views of the Solent from this beautiful hotel which, under the direction of its

proprietors, has recently undergone careful restoration and retains many beautiful period features (open fires, moulded ceilings) while offering every modern facility to guests. Food is first-rate: freshly caught fish features highly on the menu and all dishes have been home-cooked from fresh island ingredients; a typical evening meal would feature Avocado Vinaigrette followed by Golden Apricot Chicken (breast of chicken poached in Rose Wine with Apricot and Cointreau), and a truly delectable dessert such as Chocolate Roulade.

Open all year. Smoking banned in part of dining room, some bedrooms, and in bar areas. Vegetarian, always avail. on à la carte menu. Vegan, diabetic, low-fat and other special diets on request. Licensed. No disabled access. Children welcome. Pets by arrangement. En suite, T. V. & tea/coffee-making in all rooms. Access, Visa, Amex, Diners. B. & B. from £39.50.

SEAVIEW

Seaview Hotel and Restaurant, High St, Seaview, PO34 5EX (0983) 612711

Exquisite hotel in the small Victorian seaside resort of Seaview; beautifully furnished with antiques and designer fabrics; excellent cuisine prepared from fresh local produce.

Vegetarian standard. Vegan, diabetic & other diets by arrangement. Open all year. 'Licensed. Children welcome. Pets by arrangement. En suite & T.V. in all rooms. Access, Visa, Amex. B. & B. from £33.

SHANKLIN

Culham Lodge Hotel, Landguard Manor Rd, Shanklin, PO37 7HZ (0983) 862880

Attractive hotel in a beautiful tree-lined road; excellent food prepared from fresh produce.

Vegetarian standard. Open March to Oct. Smoking banned in dining room and lounge. Children: over 12s only. En suite in most rooms. Tea/coffee making in all rooms. T.V. in lounge. B.B. & D. from £17.

Edgecliffe Hotel, Clarence Gardens, Shanklin, PO37 6HA (0983) 866199

Charming, family-run hotel in peaceful tree-lined road. Food prepared from fresh, local produce; imaginative vegetarian meals by arrangement.

Vegetarian, diabetic and some other special diets, but not vegan, by arrangement. Open Feb. to Nov. No smoking. Licensed. Children: over 3s only. En suite in most rooms. Tea/coffee making & T.V. in all rooms. Access, Visa, Amex. B. & B. from £15.

VENTNOR

Hotel Picardie, Esplanade, Ventnor, PO38 1JX (0983) 852647

Attractive villa-type hotel on the Esplanade; imaginative vegetarian options..

Open March to Oct. No smoking, ex. bar area. Vegetarian & other diets on request. Licensed. Children welcome. Pets by arrangement. Private facilities, tea/coffee & T.V. in all rooms. Credit cards. B. & B. from £16.50.

WOOTTON BRIGE

Bridge House, Kite Hill, Wootton Bridge, PO33 4LA (0983) 884163

Bridge House is a listed Georgian residence of tremendous character standing in a beautiful garden on the water's edge at Wootton Bridge. It was not always so appealing: when its present owners first took it under their wing it was in a very sorry state of repair and it took a whole year of very careful and sympathetic restoration to transform it into the elegant and comfortable house you see today. Breakfast is the only meal to be served at Bridge House - but what a treat it is! All preserves are home-made from fruit culled from garden bushes or trees (grape and apple jam is a house speciality), and the toast, butter and coffee are served 'as long as guests want them'! There is much to see and do in the area immediately around Bridge House: Wootton Creek feeds into the Solent (there is a slipway adjacent to the property) and there is an abundance of forest walks in nearby Firestone Copse. There are lots of good local eating places for those seeking an evening meal, and 3 very good pubs are just a short walk away.

Vegetarian, diabetic and some other special diets, but not vegan, by arrangement. Organic when avail. Wholefood on request. Open all year. Smoking banned throughout. Children by arrangement. Pets by arrangement. En suite in some rooms. Tea/coffee making in all rooms. T.V. on request. B. & B. from £15.

West Sussex

ARUNDEL
Burpham Country Hotel and Restaurant, Burpham, Arundel, BN18 9RJ (0903) 882160
Charming country house with mature garden in Burpham village, with superb views over the South Downs.
Open all year. No smoking in dining room. Vegetarian and most other diets by arrangement. Licensed. En suite, TV & tea/coffee-making in all bedrooms. Access, Visa. B. & B. from £29.

BOGNOR REGIS
Crouchers Bottom Country Hotel, Birdham Rd, Apuldram, Chichester, PO20 7EH (0243) 784 995
Rurally set amidst fields with fine view of Chichester Cathedral. Good imaginative food prepared from fresh produce.
Open all year. No smoking in dining room, bedrooms & toilets. Vegetarian and most other special diets by arrangement. Licensed. Good disabled access: 4 ground floor bedrooms, one specifically designed for the disabled. Children welcome. En suite, tea/coffee-making & T.V. in all bedrooms.

COPTHORNE
Broad Oak, West Park, Rd, Copthorne, W. Sussex, RH10 3EX (0342) 714882
Country house in 3 acre garden opposite 9-hole golf course just 10 mins drive from Gatwick airport. Ideal for early flights! Courtesy service to airport. Good pubs nearby with smoke-free areas.
Open all year. No smoking in the house. Vegetarian & other diets by arrangement. Children welcome. Pets by arrangement. Tea/coffee-making available. TV in lounge. B. & B. from £19.50, single £23.

EAST GRINSTEAD
Gravetye Manor, Nr East Grinstead, RH19 4LJ (0342) 810567
An Elizabethan mansion set in wonderful gardens. Hotel, restaurant and country club.
Open all year. No smoking in dining room. Vegetarian and most other special diets by arrangement. Licensed. Disabled access for the restaurant. Children: over 7s only. En suite in all rooms. T.V. all bedrooms. B. & B. from £45.

'Toads Croak House', 30 Copthorne Road, Felbridge, Nr East Grinstead, RH1 2NS (0342) 328524
Charming 1920's Sussex-style house in beautiful gardens, easy access to Gatwick airport.
Open all year. No smoking. Vegetarian and most other special diets by arrangement. Children welcome. En suite & T.V. in all bedrooms. B. & B. from £15.

EAST ASHLING
Englewood, East Ashling, PO18 9AS (Bosham) 575407
Modern bungalow in the conservation village of East Ashling; Cordon Bleu trained hostess offers superb home cooked food using organic home grown vegetables, fruit & herbs when possible.
Open all year but full menu from March - end Oct. Vegetarian standard and most other special diets by arrangement. No children or pets. No en suite. Tea/coffee-making in bedrooms. T.V. in bedrooms. No credit cards.

HENFIELD
Little Oreham Farm, Nr Woodsmill, Henfield, BS5 9SB (0273) 492931
Lttle Oreham Farm is *gorgeous*. Tucked away

down a quiet country lane and next door to footpaths that will lead you (if energetic!) to the South Downs, this 300-year old listed building is a picture-book cottage; prettily pantiled and set in a beautiful garden complete with (inhabited) dovecot. Inside the house are the oak beams and inglenook fireplace that one would expect from such a cottage, and outside the barn has been comfortably converted to accommodate further guests. Evening meals are available by arrangement; your hostess, Josie Forbes, is not able these days to do all the home-baking for which she was hitherto famed, but everything she *does* prepare is done so carefully and with the use of organic and wholefood ingredients - some home-grown (she has her own herbary).

PETWORTH

**Eastwood Farm, Graffham, Petworth,
GU28 0QF (07986) 317**
Large country house set in 15 acres of grounds with tennis court and swimming pool.
Open all year. No smoking in dining room & public areas. Vegetarian by arrangement. Licensed. Disabled access. Children welcome. En suite in 1 room. T.V. on request. B. & B. from £16.

**River Park Farm, Lodworth, Petworth,
GU28 9DS (079 85) 362**
17th C. farmhouse. All food home-prepared from fresh ingredients.
Open Easter to 2nd week Oct. No smoking in dining rooms & bedrooms. Vegetarian standard. Other diets by arrangement. Children welcome. TV lounge. Tea/coffee-making in all bedrooms. B. & B. from £15.

PULBOROUGH

**The Barn Owls Restaurant and Guestel,
London Rd, Coldwaltham, Pulborough,
RH20 1LR (07982) 2498**
Home-cooked cuisine prepared from fresh, seasonal ingredients; tasty vegetarian options.
Open all year. No smoking in dining room. Vegetarian & vegan standard. Most other special diets by arrangement. Licensed. Pets by arrangement. En suite & tea/coffee-making facilities in bedrooms. T.V. lounge. Access, Visa. B. & B. from £22. D. £15. Recommended in Vegetarian Good Food Guide.

**Chequers Hotel, Church Place,
Pulborough, RH20 1AD (0798) 872486**
17th C. hotel on sandstone ridge overlooking the beautiful Arun Valley and South Downs.
Open all year. Vegetarian & most other special diets by arrangement. Licensed. Children welcome. Pets by arrangement. En suite, tea/coffee-making & T.V. in all bedrooms. B. & B. from £32.50. D. £15.50.

STEYNING

**Nash Hotel, Horsham Rd, Steyning
(0903) 814988**
A beautiful 16th C. country house with lawns, paddocks and pond near to the coast and South Downs; a productive vineyard adjoins the property.
Open all year. No smoking in the house. Vegetarian, vegan and most other special diets by arrangement. Licensed. Children welcome. Pets by arrangement. En suite in 2 rooms. Tea/coffee-making & T.V. in all bedrooms. B. & B. from £21.

South East England

East Sussex

BEXHILL-ON-SEA
'Helensholme', Heatherdune Rd, Bexhill-on-Sea (0424) 223545
Lovingly furnished chalet home; vegetarian cuisine prepared from fresh produce a speciality.
Open all year. No smoking. Exclusively vegetarian. All special diets with good advanced notice. Children: over 10s welcome. Vanity units in 2 rooms. Tea/coffee making. T.V. lounge. B. & B. from £15.

BRIGHTON
'Brighton' Marina House Hotel, 8 Charlotte St, Marine Parade, Brighton, BN2 1AG Tel & Fax: (0273) 605349 Tel: (0273) 679484

Cosy, well-maintained and family-run, the Brighton Marina House Hotel is a pleasantly furnished and well-equipped hotel, highly recommended for its cleanliness, comfort and hospitality; it stands in the heart of Kemp town, the Regency side of Brighton. Traditional English fare is served in the dining room but, perhaps uniquely amongst privately owned Brighton hotels, you may also dine on Indian, Chinese, vegetarian, Halal or Kosher dishes on request; if you have other special dietary requirements your host, Mr Jung, will do his very best to accommodate them. The Brighton Marina House Hotel is in a quiet street leading to the beach which is a minute's walk away.
Open all year. Vegetarian, kosher & other diets by arrangement. Licensed. Children welcome. En suite, TV & tea/coffee-making in bedrooms. Credit cards. B. & B. £15-29.

Rozanne Mendick, 14 Chatsworth Rd, Brighton, BN1 5DB (0273) 556584
Large, comfortable family home.
Open all year. No smoking. Vegetarian and vegan standard. Most other diets by arrangement. Children welcome. Tea/coffee making. T.V. B. & B. from £14.

HASTINGS
Norton Villa, Hill St, Old Town, Hastings (0424) 428168
Delightful house built in 1847 set on cliffs overlooking the Channel, Old town and harbour. 4-poster room available in B. & B.; self-catering cottage available for summer let.
Open all year. No smoking in dining room and most bedrooms. Children: Over 8s. En suite in 3 rooms. Tea/coffee making facilities. T.V. Overnight car parking. B. & B. from £16.

LEWES
Berkeley House Hotel, 2 Albion St, Lewes, BN7 2ND (0273) 476057
Elegant Georgian town house in quiet conservation area in historic county town. South-facing roof terrace. Candle-lit restaurant.
Open all year. No smoking in the restaurant. Vegetarian & other diets by arrangement. En suite, TV & tea/coffee-making in bedrooms. Children welcome. Licensed. Credit cards. B. & B. £25 - 48.

PEVENSEY
Montana B. & B., The Promenade, Pevensey Bay, Pevensey, BN24 6HD (0323) 764651
Quiet house in a convenient situation close to village shops, pubs and the beach.
Open all year ex. Xmas & part of Oct. No smoking. Special diest on request. Children welcome. Tea/coffee in all rooms. T.V. lounge and in 1 bedroom. B. & B. from £13.

RYE
Green Hedges, Hillyfields, Rye Hill, Rye, TN31 7NH (0797) 222185

Green Hedges is a large Edwardian country house superbly situated on rising ground, with wonderful views of the ancient town of Rye and the sea beyond. It is a comfortable family home and stands in a beautiful landscaped garden, just a short walk from the town; during the summer months the heated outdoor swimming pool is available for guests' use. Breakfast is prepared from seasonal garden produce, home-made preserves and free range eggs. You can explore the cobbled streets of mediaeval Rye and are within easy reach of Royal Tunbridge Wells, the beautiful Cathedral city of Canterbury and many National Trust properties. There is ample parking in the private road beside the house.

Open all year ex. Xmas. No smoking throughout. Vegetarian standard. Any other special diet by arrangement. Children: over 12s only. En suite, tv & Tea/coffee making in all rooms. B. & B. from £22.50.

Jeake's House, Mermaid St, Rye, TN31 7ET Tel: (0797) 222828 Fax (0797) 222623

This beautiful listed building derives its name from the remarkable Jeake family of Rye who built the oldest part of the house (oak-beamed and wood-panelled) in 1689. It stands on a picturesque cobbled street in the heart of mediaeval Rye and has, in its time, seen service as a wool store, a Baptist School and, for 23 years home to the American Poet and author Conrad Aitken. The house is comfortably and interestingly furnished: antiques abound and there are 'brass and mahogany bedsteads, linen sheets and lace'; there is also a honeymoon suite. Wide choice of delicious breakfast fare.

Open all year. No smoking in dining room. Vegetarian and vegan menu; other diets by arrangement. Licensed. Children welcome. Pets by arrangement. En suite most rooms. Tea/coffee & T.V. all rooms. B. & B. from £19.50. RAC Highly Acclaimed & AA Selected. Winner of Good Hotel Guide César Award 1992.

The Old Vicarage Hotel & Restaurant, East St, Rye, TN31 7HF (0797) 222119

The Old Vicarage is a listed 16th C. building in the heart of the ancient town of Rye. Originally the home of the Taverner family, it became a vicarage at the end of the 19th C. until 1976 when it again became a private house. Now converted to a small, comfortable hotel, it has been beautifully converted: each of the en suite bedrooms are furnished in a period style and

several have Tester beds with full closing curtains. The restaurant has extensive views out over Romney Marsh; candle-lit and warmed by log fires in winter it is a splendid setting in which to enjoy the delicious meals which have been prepared from fresh, local produce wherever possible.

Open Feb. - Dec. Vegetarian standard. Other diets by arrangement. Children & pets welcome. Licensed. En suite, tea/coffee & T.V. all rooms. B. & B. £28 - 39.

ST LEONARDS-ON-SEA
Merryfield House, 3 St Matthews Gdns, St Leonards on Sea (0424) 424953

Large Victorian house. Exclusively vegetarian.

Open all year except Christmas. No smoking. Exclusively vegetarian. Children and well behaved dogs welcome. Tea/coffee-making & T.V. in all bedrooms. B. & B. from £14.50. D. £8.50.

WADHURST
New Barn, Wards Lane, Wadhurst, E. Sussex, TN5 6HP (0892) 782042

New Barn is a beautiful 18th C. farmhouse overlooking Bewl Water and Trout fishery and standing amidst magnificent and peaceful countryside near Wadhurst. The house is beamed throughout and is warm and comfortable: log fires blaze in the sitting room inglenook and bedrooms are light and spacious with lovely views. Breakfast is the only meal to be served at New Barn, but it is a hearty feast of home-made jams, marmalades and preserves with local home-baked bread and free range eggs; there are plenty of pubs and restaurants nearby for an evening meal. You are just 55 minutes by train from Charing Cross and 30 mins' drive from the South Coast; other nearby attractions include Vita Sackville-West's garden at Sissinghurst, Hever Castle & Canterbury (1½ hours away).

Open all year. No smoking ex in 1 lounge. Vegetarian & other diets by arrangement. Children welcome. Pets by arrangement. En suite & TV in bedrooms. Tea/coffee. B. & B. £19-24, Single £21.

Kent

ASHFORD
Woodman's Arms Auberge, Hassell St, Hastingleigh, Ashford (0233) 75250
17th C. inn in quiet cul-de-sac hamlet of Hassell Street. Exceptionally good food prepared from finest local ingredients & fresh herbs and spices.
Open all year ex. Sept. No smoking. Vegetarian and most other special diets by arrangement. Licensed. En suite & T.V. in all bedrooms. B. & B. from £30.

BECKENHAM
Crockshard Farmhouse, Wingham, Canterbury, CT3 1NY (0227) 720464
Regency farmhouse set in pleasant gardens amid orchards. Families welcome, babysitting avail; home-produced bread, jam, eggs & vegetables.
Open all year. No smoking Vegetarian and most other special diets by arrangement. Children welcome. Pets by arrangement. En suite in some rooms. Tea/coffee-making in kitchen. T.V. in lounge. Amex. B. & B. from £17. D. from £10.

CANTERBURY
Magnolia House, 36 St. Dunstan's Terr., Canterbury, CT2 8AX. (0227) 765121.

Magnolia House is a charming detached late Georgian house situated in a quiet residential street near to the city centre and just 2 minutes' drive or 20 minutes' walk from the university. The house itself has much of architectural interest to commend it and has been decorated sympathetically with each bedroom being individually designed and coordinated in a light, bright decor (lots of Laura Ashley fabrics and wallcoverings); there is a walled garden with fishpond, terraces and shrubberies (the perfect place to relax in after a day's sightseeing). Ann Davies, the proprietor, tells me, "because we only take 10 guests, each one is special," and guests are aware of this care from the moment they arrive, when a welcome tray is offered and information on the city given, to their first morning at breakfast where a wide range of options are available including special diets.
Vegetarian, vegan and diabetic diets as standard; other diets by arrangement. Open all year. No smoking ex. lounge. Children welcome. En suite, tea/coffee-making & T.V in all rooms. Access, Visa, Amex, Mastercard, Eurocard. B. & B. from £22.50.

The Tanner of Wingham, 44 High St, Wingham, Canterbury (0227) 720532
Charming 17th C. building in quiet village; freshly-prepared food; separate vegetarian menu with wide range of healthy, meat-free options.
Vegetarian & vegan standard. Diabetic & other diets by arrangement. Open all year. Licensed. Children welcome. Tea/coffee-making & TV in rooms. Access, Visa. B. & B. from £12.50.

Thruxted Oast, Mystole, Chartham, Canterbury, CT4 7BX (0227) 730080
Converted 18th C. oast houses offering luxurious accommodation in pretty rooms with stripped pine, patchwork quilts, etc. Eggs from own hens.
Open all year ex. Xmas. No smoking. Vegetarian by arrangement (b'fast only). Children: over 10s only. En suite, TV & tea/coffee in rooms. B. & B. from £37.50.

Upper Ansdore, Duckpit Lane, Petham, Canterbury, CT4 5QB (022770) 672
14th C. house, with later additions; beautiful views. Home-grown produce, free-range eggs, home-grown bacon.
Vegetarian by arrangement. Open Feb. to Nov. No smoking dining room & bedrooms. Children welcome. En suite & tea/coffee in rooms. B. & B. from £16.

Walnut Tree Farm, Lynsore Bottom, Upper Hardres, Canterbury, CT4 6EG (022787) 375.
14th C. thatched farmhouse situated in 6 acres. Perfect location for walking & birdwatching in peaceful valley yet close to Canterbury. Many beautiful villages. Close to channel ports.
Vegetarian, vegan & diabetic by arrangement. Wholefoods always. Open Jan. - Dec. No smoking. Children welcome. En suite, radio & tea/coffee in rooms. B. & B. from £18. Red. for children under 13.

Yorke Lodge, 50 London Rd, Canterbury, CT2 8LF (0227) 451243
Lovely Victorian town house.; all food prepared to suit. Lots of home-made items, including the marmalade, stewed apple and fruit salad.
Open 10 Jan. to 20 Dec. No smoking ex. in library. Vegetarian & other diets by arrangement. Children welcome. Pets by arrangement. En suite, TV & tea/coffee in all rooms. Visa, Amex. B. & B. from £20

CHARING
Barnfield, Charing (023) 371 2421
15th C. farmhouse log fires in inglenooks, huge oak beams, carved doors; bedrooms with views of River Stour; fresh produce used in cooking.
Vegetarian & vegan by arrangement. Open all year. No smoking. Children welcome. Tea/coffee & T.V in all bedrooms. B. & B. from £17.50.

CRANBROOK
Hancocks Farmhouse, Tilsden Lane, Cranbrook, TN17 3PH (0580) 714645

The earliest mention of Hancocks is in a will of 1520 in which the house was left by a clothier, Thomas Sheaffe, to his son Gervase. Today this fine well-preserved timber-framed building is a family home which also takes guests. Hancocks has been decorated and furnished with antiques, in keeping with its period origins and there is a large inglenook fireplace with log fires for cooler evenings. Set in a lovely garden and surrounded by farmland and beautiful views, Hancocks is the perfect place to come for those in search of peace and tranquillity. The food is first-rate: dinner is by prior arrangement and there is a complimentary afternoon tea served daily in addition to a very generous breakfast; organic and wholefood ingredients are used in cooking whenever availability permits. A typical evening menu would feature garlic stuffed mushrooms with home-made brown rolls, followed by fresh white fish cooked with leeks and ginger, and a tempting dessert such as creme brulée or fresh lime tart.
Open all year. No smoking. Vegetarian and most other special diets by arrangement. Some disabled access. Children: over 9s welcome. Pets by arrangement. En suite & TV in some rooms. Tea/coffee-making in all rooms. B. & B. from £18.

Hartley Mount Country House Hotel, Hartley Rd, Cranbrook, TN17 3QX (0580) 712230
Hartley Mount Hotel is a fine old Edwardian country manor house set in 2 acres of gardens overlooking the glorious views of Cranbrook and the Weald of Kent. It has been sympathetically

refurbished - all the grace and elegance of the Edwardian era have been retained in the decor and furnishings - yet it has all the modern conveniences of a luxury hotel: breakfast is served, in an Edwardian conservatory and the bedrooms are decorated in keeping with the period (there is a 'granny' brass double bed, a heavily draped 4-poster & fringed lampshades). Meals are served in an elegant dining room and the menus reflect an age in which the priveleged classes had little to do but sleep and feed: a typical appetiser might be Scotch Woodcock followed by Blanquette of Lamb and a home-made dessert. There is a good vegetarian menu & food is prepared from fresh produce.
Vegetarian as standard and most other special diets by arrangement. Organic & wholefoods when avail. Open all year. No smoking ex. in conservatory. Licensed. Children welcome. En suite, TV & tea/coffee in rooms. Access, Visa. B. & B. from £35.

DARTFORD
Rosedene Guest House, 284-286 Lowfield St, Dartford, DA1 1LH (0322) 277042
Comfortable B. & B. Vegetarian & other diets catered for. Wholefoods on request. Payphone.
Vegetarian & low-fat standard;other diets by arrangement (b'fast only). Wholefoods on request. Open all year. No smoking in dining room & bedrooms. Children welcome. Tea/coffee & colour T.V in all bedrooms. Visa. B. & B. from £18.

DEAL
Beaconhill (E. Kent Field Centre), Beaconhill Cottage, Great Mongeham, Deal, CT14 0HW (0304) 372809
A beautiful restored period country house set in quiet, peaceful garden with its own nature reserve. Excellent home-cooked meals. Convenient Canterbury, Dover & Sandwich.
Open all year. No smoking ex. smoking room. Vegetarian & other diets by arrangement. Children welcome. Tea/coffee & TV avail. B. & B. from £14.50.

DOVER

Sunshine Cottage, The Green, Shepherdswell, Nr Dover, CT15 7LQ. (0304) 831359.
17th C. cottage on village green; oak beams, inglenook fireplace; evening meal available using fresh produce; all home-cooking & baking.
Vegetarian & other diets by arrangement. Organic & wholefoods when avail. Open all year. No smoking in dining room & bedrooms. Children welcome. Tea/coffee in all rooms. T.V in lounge. B. & B. from £16.

EDENBRIDGE

Harman's Orchard, Froghole, Crockham Hill, Edenbridge, TN8 6TD (0732) 866417
Extended 16th C. house with lovely views and gardens. Home-baking and cooking.
Open by request. No smoking. Vegetarian & other diets by arrangement. Children: over 6s. Tea/coffee &. T.V. in rooms. B. & B. from £16.

RAMSGATE

Goodwin View Hotel, 19 Wellington Crescent, Ramsgate, CT11 8JD (0843) 591419
Goodwin View Hotel occupies a fine sea-front position in Ramsgate, overlooking the sea, sands, and harbour and is conveniently situated just a short walk from the ferry terminal, town centre and all holiday amenities. The hotel, run by the resident proprietors Joe and Patsy Denne, has a homely and friendly atmosphere; bedrooms are comfortable and centrally heated, and all have tea and coffee making facilities and colour T.V. Breakfast is served in the spacious dining room; all food is home-cooked and is prepared from fresh ingredients whenever possible. Goodwin View is an ideal base for touring the South East.
Vegetarian & other special diets by arrangement. Open all year. Licensed. Children welcome. En suite in some rooms. Tea/coffee-making & T.V in all bedrooms. Visa, Mastercard, Eurocheques. B. & B. from £16.50-£25. D. from £8.25.

SEVENOAKS

The Gables, 36 Dartford Rd, Sevenoaks, TN13 3TQ (0732) 456708
Spacious Victorian house on the A225 near Sevenoaks. Cooked English breakfast. Non-smokers only.
Vegetarian, diabetic & other diets by arrangement (b'fast only). Open all year ex. Christmas. Non-smokers only. Private bathroom & shower room. Tea/coffee & T.V in all bedrooms. B. & B. from £16.50.

Pond Cottage, Eggpie Lane, Weald, Sevenoaks, TN14 6NP (0732) 463773
16th C. listed house with inglenook, oak beams & quarry floors, in 3 acres of land, including fish pond. Home-made bread and cakes.
Open all year ex. Xmas. No smoking. Children welcome. Pets by arrangement. En suite in some rooms. Tea/coffee-making & T.V in all bedrooms. B. & B. from £20.

SITTINGBOURNE

Hempstead House, London Rd, Bapchild, Sittingbourne, ME9 9PP (0795) 428020
Exclusive private country house offering luxury accommodation and friendly hospitality; Home grown produce, home-baked bread, fresh herbs.
Vegetarian, diabetic & other diets by arrangement. Wholefoods always. Low-fat, high-fibre cooking. Open all year. No smoking ex. smoker's lounge. Children welcome. Pets by arrangement. En suite, tea/coffee & T.V. in all bedrooms. B. & B. from £50.

TENTERDEN

Brattle House, Cranbrook Rd, Tenterden, TN30 6UL (05806) 3565
Handsome Grade II listed Georgian farmhouse, timber-framed and hung with Kent-peg tiles and weatherboard in an acre of gardens amidst the Wealden countryside minutes away from Tenterden. Beautiful bedrooms with views. Imaginative cooking using fresh, organic and wholefood ingredients where possible.
Open all year. No smoking. Vegetarian by arrangement. Diabetic & other diets by arrangement. Children: over 12s only. En suite & tea/coffee-making in all rooms. T.V. in some bedrooms. B. & B. from £26.

TONBRIDGE

Poplar Farm Oast, Three Elm Lane, Golden Green, Nr Tonbridge, TN11 OLE (0732) 850723
Traditional Kentish Oast house; b'fast prepared from fresh ingredients whre possible; special diets plus a range of diabetic foods
Open all year ex. Xmas. No smoking. Vegetarian and diabetic on request. Children welcome. Tea/coffee making in all rooms. T.V. in lounge. B. & B. from £17.

TUNBRIDGE WELLS

Danehurst House Hotel, 41 Lower Green Rd, Rusthall, Tunbridge Wells, TN4 8TW (0892) 527739
Danehurst is a charming gabled guest house standing in a lovely rural setting in the heart of Kent; accommodation is in tastefully decorated rooms - all of which have private bathrooms and

beverage-making facilities. The food is excellent: everything has been home-prepared from fresh, seasonal ingredients, and a typical evening menu would feature Carrot and Orange Soup followed by Chicken in Cream and Tarragon (with a selection of five seasonal vegetables and baby new potatoes), and a tempting dessert, such as Strawberry and Kiwi Fruit Shortcake with Cream; an English Cheeseboard, coffee and mints would complete the meal. You are just a short distance from the lovely town of Royal Tunbridge Wells and all the gracious country houses of Kent are easily reached from Rusthall.

Open all year. No smoking ex. lounge. Vegetarian and most other special diets by arrangement. Licensed. Children welcome. En suite in some rooms. Tea/coffee-making & T.V. in all bedrooms. Credit cards. B. & B. from £21.50.

Scott House, High St, West Malling, ME19 6QH (0732) 841380 /870025

Scott House is a Grade II listed Georgian town house situated opposite the library in the lower part of West Malling High Street. It is a family home from which the owners, the Smiths, also run an antique business and is therefore, unsurprisingly enough, quite beautifully decorated in keeping with its period origins; all bedrooms are furnished with taste and style. Only breakfast is offered at Scott House but there

are lots of healthy options on the menu including muesli, yoghurt and porridge as well as the usual 'Full English' fare. The Smiths assure me that there are several good restaurants in West Malling which has, in addition to this, several other features to commend it to the touring visitor including an 11th C. abbey, a craft centre and a lakeside country park with numerous delightful walks.

Open all year ex. Xmas. No smokin.g Vegetarian and most other special diets by arrangement. En suite, TV & tea/coffee-making in all rooms. Access, Visa, JCB, Mastercard. B. & B. from £25.

Surrey

CAMBERLEY

Tekels Park Guest House, Camberley, GU15 2LF (0276) 23159
Comfortable accommodation in a large house owned by the Theosophical Society set in a beautiful and secluded estate of 50 acres, forming a wildlife sanctuary; 35 miles from London.
Open all year. No smoking. Vegetarian and vegan standard. Other meat-free special diets on request. B. & B. from £25.85 D. £5.55. Non-residents welcome but booking essential.

CROYDON

Selsdon Park Hotel, Sanderstead, Croydon, Surrey (081) 657 8811
170-bedroom hotel with comprehensive sport and leisure facilities; fresh vegetables, meat, fish.
Open all year. Vegetarian standard. Other diets by arrangement. Children & pets welcome. Licensed. En suite, TV & tea coffee-making in bedrooms. Credit cards. Room only from £57.

DORKING

Crossways Farm, Raikes Lane, Abinger, Hammer, Nr Dorking, RH5 6PZ (036) 730173
Listed Jacobean farmhouse, with oak beams and log fires, set amidst the lovely Surrey hills just 30 mins from Gatwick and 40-45 mins from Heathrow, London and the coast.
Open all year. No smoking in dining room and bedrooms. Vegetarian & other special diets by arrangement. Children welcome. En suite in 1 room. Tea/coffee-making in all bedrooms. T.V. lounge. B. & B. from £14.

GUILDFORD

Weybrook House, 113 Stoke Road, Guildford, GU1 1ET (0483) 302394/36625
Large Edwardian town house offering comfortable accommodation and with warm, friendly family atmosphere; half hour from Heathrow and convenient for Gatwick and London.
Open all year. No smoking in dining room and all public areas. Vegetarian and most other special diets by arrangement. Disabled access. Children welcome. Pets by arrangement. Tea/coffee-making T.V. in all bedrooms. B. & B. from £14.

KINGSTON-UPON-THAMES

Chase Lodge, 10 Park Rd, Hampton Wick, Kingston-Upon-Thames, KT1 4AS (081) 943 1862
Pretty Victorian villa, recently been refurbished to a very high standard. Excellent food prepared from fresh ingredients.
Open all year. No smoking in dining room, sitting room & 1 bedroom. Vegetarian and most other special diets by arrangement. Children welcome. Pets by arrangement. Most rooms en suite. Tea/coffee, T.V. & phones in all bedrooms. Credit cards. B. & B. from £18. ETB 4 Crowns Highly Acclaimed, AA Selected & RAC Highly Acclaimed.

LEATHERHEAD

Hazelgrove, Epsom Rd, West Horsley, Near Leatherhead, KT24 6AP (04865) 4467
Friendly family home set off the road amidst pleasant gardens. Everything at breakfast prepared from fresh produce where possible.
Open Mar. to Oct. No smoking. Children: over 6s only. Tea/coffee-making in all bedrooms. T.V. lounge. B. & B. from £15.

WEST MOLESEY

Alderton Guest House, 30 Cannon Way, West Molesey, KT8 2NB (081) 9791055
Small, friendly guest house within easy reach of the Thames and Hampton Court Palace. Breakfast is a hearty feast of yoghurt, grapefruit, brown bread and honey; the traditional English breakfast features black pudding and fried bread in addition to the usual bacon, egg and sausage, and Scottish kippers are also available; coffee is fresh and filtered - and herbal teas are available on request.
Open all year. No smoking. Vegetarian and most other special diets by arrangement. Children: over 10s only. Tea/coffee making & T.V. in all bedrooms. B. & B. from £16.50. ETB Commended.

London and Middlesex

London

N1

Regent Palace Hotel, Piccadilly Circus, N1A 4BZ (071) 734 7000
Elegant well-appointed hotel in Piccadilly Circus.
Open all year. Smoking banned in part of restaurant and some bedrooms. Vegetarian standard. Licensed. Some disabled access. Children welcome. Pets by arrangement. No en suite. Tea/coffee making in all rooms. T.V. in all rooms. Credit cards accepted.

N19

Parkland Walk Guest House, 12 Hornsey Rise Gardens, London, N19 3PR (071) 263 3228
Parkland Walk Guest House is a small, friendly B. & B. in a pretty, comfortable Victorian family house. Listed and commended by the English Tourist Board, the Parkland Walk Guest House has easy access to the M1 and A1, central London, King's Cross and Euston; visitors will also find themselves within easy reach of Hampstead, Alexandra Palace, Muswell Hill and Islington. The breakfast menu features a wide range of home-cooked dishes plus home-made jams, fresh fruit, yoghurt and wholemeal bread. Both single and double rooms are available (the bathrooms are gorgeous!), and the house is centrally heated throughout. You are conveniently near to many good restaurants - including those serving Vegetarian, Caribbean, French and Italian food - as well as possibly the best tea rooms in London. A brochure - including a map - is available on request.
Open all year. No smoking. Vegetarian & other diets on request. Children welcome. Tea/coffee making & T.V. in all rooms. B. & B. from £18.

NW3

Hampstead Village Guest House, 2 Kemplay Rd, Hampstead, NW3 1SY Tel: (071) 435 8679 Fax (071) 7940254
Typical Victorian house with many original features.
Open all year. No smoking throughout. Vegetarian by arrangement. Some disabled access. Children welcome. Tea/coffee making & T.V. in all rooms. B. & B. from £19.

NW8

London Regents Park Hilton, 18 Lodge Rd, St John's Wood, NW8 7JT (071) 722 7722
Large, modern hotel adjacent to Regents Park and overlooking Lord's Cricket Ground; good business facilities and restaurants.
Open all year. No smoking in part of dining room. Vegetarian and other special diets by arrangement. Licensed. Some disabled access. Children welcome. Pets by arrangement. En suite, TV & tea/coffee in all rooms. Credit cards accepted.

W1

Berner Plaza Hotel London, 10 Berners St, W1 (071) 636 1629
Splendid Edwardian hotel with classical ceilings and marble columns.
Open all year. No smoking in 50% of dining room and some bedrooms. Vegetarian standard. Some other special diets by arrangement. Licensed. Disabled access: '10 rooms equipped for disabled guests'. Children welcome. En suite & T.V. in all rooms. Credit cards.

The Hilton on Park Lane, 22 Park Lane, W1A 2HH (071) 493 8000
Luxurious business-class hotel in prestigious position overlooking Hyde Park.
Open all year. No smoking in part of dining room & some bedrooms. Vegetarian and some other special diets by arrangment. Licensed. Disabled access. Children welcome. Pets by arrangement. En suite, TV & tea/coffee-making in all rooms. Credit cards. B. & B. from £90.

Hospitality Inn, Piccadilly, 39 Coventry St, London, W1V 8EL (071) 930 4033
Vegetarian and other special diets on request. Open all year. Smoking discouraged in dining room and banned in some bedrooms. Licensed. Children welcome. En suite, TV & tea/coffee making in rooms.

The Mayfair Hotel, Stratton St, W1A 2AN (071) 629 1459
Stylish and elegant luxury-class hotel with excellent business and leisure facilities.
Open all year. No smoking in part of dining room. Vegetarian standard, other special diets by arrangement. Licensed. Disabled access. Children welcome. Pets by arrangement. En suite & T.V. in all rooms. B. & B. from £100.

WC1

Bloomsbury Crest Hotel, Coram St, WC1N 1HT (071) 837 1200

Large, modern business-class hotel with two fine restaurants.
Open all year. Smoking banned in 66% of dining room and some bedrooms. Vegetarian and diabetic on request. Licensed. Disabled access. Children welcome. No pets. En suite in all rooms. Tea/coffee making in all rooms. T.V. in all rooms. Credit cards accepted. B. & B. from £120.

Bonnington Hotel, Southampton Row, WC1B 4BH (071) 242 2828

Well-established family-run hotel conveniently situated on Southampton Row within two miles of most of the attractions of London. Meals are served in either the elegant Waterfalls restaurant or in the Waterfalls Brasserie which has a marble tiled floor and atrium with hanging baskets of plants.
Vegetarian and vegan standard. Diabetic and some other special diets by arrangment. Open all year. Licensed. Disabled access. Children welcome. Pets by arrangement. En suite, TV & tea/coffee in all rooms. Access, Visa, Amex. B. & B. from £47.

W8

Kensington Close Hotel, Wrights Lane, W8 5SP (071) 937 8170

Business-class hotel in central London with good conference and leisure facilities and extensive health and fitness club with pool.
Open all year. No smoking in part of restaurant and some bedrooms. Vegetarian standard. Other special diets on request. Licensed. Children welcome. Pets by arrangement. En suite, TV & tea/coffee making in all rooms. Credit cards.

W9

Colonnade Hotel, 2 Warrington Crescent, W9 1ER (071) 286 1052

Charming Grade II listed Victorian building in a quiet residential area of Little Venice. Family-owned and run. 50 well-equipped bedrooms. Recent winners of 'Best Business' prize and award for its garden and window-box displays.
Vegetarian standard. Open all year. Smoking banned in part of dining room and some bedrooms. Licensed. Disabled access. Children welcome. Pets by arrangement. En suite, TV & tea/coffee making in all rooms. Access, Visa, Amex, Diners.

SW1

The Cavendish Hotel, Jermyn St, St James's, SW1Y 6JE (071) 930 2111

One of London's most elegant hotels, furnished in a contemporary style and with a very fine restaurant.
Vegetarian on request. Open all year. No smoking in some bedrooms. Licensed. Disabled access. Children welcome. Pets by arrangement. En suite & T.V. in all rooms. Credit cards. B. & B. from £150.

The Chelsea Hotel, 17 Sloane St, Knightsbridge, SW1X 9NU (071) 235 4377

Elegant hotel furnished throughout in bold contemporary style; very comfortably appointed.
Vegetarian and other special diets on request. Open all year. No smoking in part of bar & some bedrooms. Licensed. Disabled access. Children welcome. En suite & T.V. in all rooms. Credit cards. B. & B. from £168.

Stakis London St Ermin's Hotel, Caxton St, SW1H 0QN (071) 222 7888

Elegant, traditional, Edwardian-style hotel which is quietly situated in a peaceful corner of stately Westminster just a few minutes' walk from Buckingham Palace. There are two excellent restaurants which together offer a contrasting choice of dishes: the air-conditioned Carving Table offers traditional and international cuisine while guests might choose to dine in the more intimate surroundings of the Caxton Grill.
Vegetarian standard. Diabetic on request. Open all year. Smoking banned in some bedrooms. Licensed. Children welcome. En suite, TV & tea/coffee making in all rooms. Credit cards.

SW5

Swallow International Hotel, Cromwell Rd, SW5 0TH (071) 973 1000

Modern business-class hotel with excellent business, conference and leisure amenities.
Open all year. No smoking in some bedrooms. Vegetarian and other special diets on request. Licensed. Disabled access. Children welcome. Pets by arrangement. En suite, TV & tea/coffee making in most rooms. Access, Visa, Amex, Diners, Air Plus.

SW7

Aster House Hotel, 3 Sumner Place, SW7 (071) 581 5888

Aster House is at the end of an early Victorian terrace situated right in the heart of London on the borders of South Kensington and Knightsbridge, within walking distance of the museums and Harrods department store. Its proximity to the hustle and bustle of central London notwithstanding, Aster House has a charming situation in a peaceful residential area and its country house atmosphere is enhanced by its pretty walled garden; the elegant facade of the building has not been marred by any hotel signs, so just ring the bell at No 3 to be welcomed by your hosts. The house has been beautifully decorated: bedrooms have been furnished with thought and care (each room is individually styled and has fresh flowers and lots of lovely little extras) and meals are served in the charming L'Orangerie in an atmosphere of relaxed elegance; you are cordially invited to garb yourself in suitably elegant attire!

Open all year. No smoking in restaurant and bedrooms. En suite & T.V. in all rooms. Access, Visa. B. & B. from £30.

The Regency Hotel, One Hundred Queen's Gate, SW7 5AG (071) 370 4595

Open all year. Vegetarian standard. Vegan, diabetic and other special diets by arrangement. Organic and wholefood always. Licensed. Children welcome. En suite & T.V. in all rooms. Credit cards. B. &. B. from £99.

SE10

Traditional Bed and Breakfast, 34 Devonshire Drive, Greenwich, SE10 8JZ (081) 691 1918

Pleasant Victorian house near Cutty Sark, the Thames, and local antique markets; 25 mins to central London.

Open all year. Smoking banned in dining room. Vegetarian standard. Vegan, diabetic and other special diets by arrangement. Organic when avail. Wholefood on request. Children welcome. T.V. & tea/coffee-making in all bedrooms. B. & B. from £16.

Middlesex

HEATHROW AIRPORT/WEST DRAYTON

Holiday Inn London Heathrow, Stockley Rd, West Drayton, UB7 9NA (0895) 445555

Large business-class hotel with excellent conference and leisure facilities, including pool.

Open all year. Smoking banned in 50% of restaurant. Vegetarian and other special diets on request. Licensed. Disabled access. Children welcome. Pets by arrangement. En suite in all rooms. Tea/coffee making in all rooms. T.V. in all rooms. Credit cards accepted. B. & B. from £92-£122.

Excelsior Hotel, Heathrow, Bath Rd, West Drayton, UB7 ODU (081) 759 6611

858-bedroom hotel opposite the airport; excellent conference and leisure facilities; regular courtesy service to all terminals.

Open all year. Smoking banned in part of restaurant and in some bedrooms. Vegetarian standard. Some other special diets by arrangement. Licensed. Disabled access. Children welcome. Pets by arrangement. En suite in all rooms. Tea/coffee making in all rooms. T.V. in all rooms. Access, Amex, Diners, JCB, Carte Blanche, THF Gold Card. B. & B. from £110.

Thames and Chilterns
Berkshire & Buckinghamshire

AYLESBURY
Foxhill Farmhouse, Kingsley, Aylesbury, HP17 8LZ (0844) 291650
Peaceful 17th C. Grade II listed oak-beamed house with views. Breakfast only.
Open Feb. to Nov. No smoking. Vegetarian breakfast on request. Children: over 5s only. En suite in some rooms. Tea/coffee-making & T.V. in all bedrooms. B. & B. from £15.

LITTLE MARLOW
Monkton Farm, Little Marlow, SL7 3RF (0494) 21082
Charming 14th C. 'cruck' farmhouse with 150 acre working dairy farm. English breakfast served in the large farm kitchen.
Open all year. No smoking. Vegetarian and most other special diets by arrangement. Children: over 5s welcome. Tea/coffee-making & T.V. in all bedrooms. Credit cards. B. & B. from £16.

MILTON KEYNES
Chantry Farm, Pindon End, Hanslope, Milton Keynes (0908) 510269
Old farmhouse built of Northamptonshire Stone. Swimming pool and trout lake.
Open all year. No smoking. Vegetarian standard. Most other special diets by arrangement. Disabled access. Children welcome. Pets by arrangement. Tea/coffee-making & T.V. in all bedrooms. B. & B. from £12.50.

NEWBURY
The Bell at Boxford, Lambourn Road, Newbury, RG16 8DD (048838) 721
Traditional inn; log fires, real ale, good food.
Open all year. Separate dining room for smokers Vegetarian and most other special diets by arrangement. Licensed. Children welcome. Pets by arrangement. En suite & T.V. in bedrooms.

Fishers Farm, Shefford Woodlands, Newbury, RG16 7AB (048838) 466
Lovely, spacious farmhouse with 600 acre farm in rural setting; indoor swimming pool.
Open all year. No smoking ex. sitting room. Vegetarian and most other special diets by arrangement. Wine included in price of meal. Children welcome. En suite. Tea/coffee-available at all times. B. & B. from £20.

Foley Lodge Hotel, Stockcross, Newbury, RG17 0NE (0635) 528770
Open all year. No smoking in 50% of dining room & some bedrooms. Vegetarian and most other special diets by arrangement. Licensed. Children welcome.

READING
Neals Farm, Wyfold, Reading, RG4 9JB (0491680) 258
Neals Farm is a spacious Georgian farmhouse which stands high in the Chilterns in a totally rural and peaceful setting. The house has a very warm and friendly atmosphere - cosy and snug

in winter, light and airy in summer - and a holiday spent there is very relaxed and informal; guests are treated as part of the family. The bedrooms are attractively furnished (the exceptionally comfortable beds have soft, downy pillows) and the delicious home-cooked food is all prepared from fresh, often home-produced ingredients. There is much to enjoy on the farm itself: guests are welcome to make friends with the animals and, in addition to an outdoor heated pool, there are numerous walks in the woods.
Vegetarian & other diets by arrangement. No smoking in the house. Open all year ex. Xmas. Children welcome. Pets by arrangement. Tea/coffee-making in all bedrooms. T.V. in lounge. B. & B. from £15.

St Hilda's Guest House, 24 Castle Crescent, Reading, RG16 6AG Tel: (0734) 568296/595699
St Hilda's is a large family-run guest house which stands very close to the town centre in Reading. It is very cosy and welcoming - there is central; heating throughout - and although breakfast is the only meal available at St Hilda's, there are a number of good eating places in the town to which your host, Mrs Hales, will gladly direct you. Vegetarians by arrangement.
Open all year. No smoking in the house. Vegetarian and other special diets by arrangement. Tea/coffee & colour TV in all bedrooms. B. & B. from £15-20.

Hertfordshire

BISHOP'S STORTFORD

The Cottage Guest House, 71 Birchanger Lane, Birchanger, Bishop's Stortford, CM23 5QA (0279) 812349
17th C. Grade II listed building. Panelled reception rooms with log-burning stove. Large attractive garden in quiet rural village yet with good access Stanstead airport.
Open all year. No smoking. Vegetarian by arrangement. Licensed. Disabled access. Children welcome. Some en suite. Tea/coffee & T.V. in all rooms. Credit cards. B. &. B. from £32.

HERTFORD

The Hall House, Broad Oak End, Off Bramfield Rd, Hertford, SG14 2JA (0992) 582807
Charming country home built around a 15th C. Hall House timber frame in 1985, standing in attractive wooded gardens on the edge of town; exceptionally good service, excellent cuisine prepared from fresh produce. Heated pool.
Open all year. No smoking. Vegetarian & other diets for b'fast, but not dinner, by arrangement. En suite in some rooms. Tea/coffee & T.V. in all rooms. Access, Visa, Mastercard. B. &. B. from £27.50.

RICKMANSWORTH

27 Mount View, Rickmansworth, WD3 2BB (0923) 774408/776529
Detached house with an attractive garden situated in a quiet road close to the M25.
Open all year. Smoking banned in bedrooms. Vegetarian by arrangement. Children: over 8s only. T.V. in lounge. B. & B. from £15.

6 Swallow Close, Nightingale Road, Rickmansworth, WD3 2DZ (0923) 720069
Bed and breakfast for the discerning traveller! A charming guest house, furnished throughout with antiques, and situated in a quiet cul-de-sac just half an hour's tube ride from central London (the underground station is nearby). All food is home-cooked - including the bread and preserves - and there are home-grown vegetables and home-laid eggs!
Open all year. No smoking. Vegetarian by arrangement. Children: over 5s only. B. &. B. from £17.

ST ALBANS

The Squirrels, 74 Sandridge Rd, St Albans, AL1 4AR (0727) 40497
Edwardian terrace house within 10 mins walk of historic St Albans town centre & 20 mins to mainline station with frequent & all night trains to London. Imaginative breakfast options.
Open mid Jan. - mid Dec. No smoking. Vegetarian & other diets by arrangement. En suite, TV & tea/coffee in rooms. B. & B. £12.50, single £15.

25 Ridgmont Rd, St Albans, AL1 3AG (0727) 862755
Friendly, comfortable family home; lots of books; wide choice of breakfasts. Convenient for London (trains to Kings Cross 20 mins). Easy access M1, M25.
Open all year. No smoking. Vegetarian by arrangement. Children welcome. TV & tea/coffee in all rooms. B. & B. from £14.

TRING

Rose & Crown Hotel, High St, Tring, HP23 4BN (044282) 4071
28-bedroom hotel built in Tudor style at the turn of the century; high standard of food and accommodation; good business facilities.
Open all year. 30% no smoking dining room and bedrooms. Vegetarian and most other special diets by arrangement. Licensed. Disabled access. Children welcome. En suite, TV & tea/coffee-making in all rooms. Credit cards. B. & B. from £40.

Oxfordshire

ABINGDON

Fallowfields, Southmoor with Kingston Bagpuize, Abingdon (0865) 820416

Beautiful 17th C. house in 12 acres of private gardens; luxuriously appointed with excellent food prepared from home-grown ingredients.
Open Apr. to Sept. No smoking in dining room. Vegetarian & other diets by arrangement. Licensed. Children: over 10s only. Pets by arrangement. En suite in most rooms. Tea/coffee-making & T.V. in all bedrooms. Access, Visa. B. & B. from £27 - 44, D. £18.

BANBURY

Studleigh Farm, Wales St, Kings Sutton, Banbury, OX17 3RR (0295) 811979

17th C. renovated and modernised farmhouse on 8 acres of pastureland in picturesque village; several good village pubs nearby and fishing rights on the Cherwell are available.
Open all year. No smoking in the house. Vegetarian & other diets by arrangement. En suite & tea/coffee in all rooms. T.V. in lounge. B. & B. from £19.

Sugarswell Farm, Shenington, Banbury, OX15 6HW (0295) 680512

This lovely large stone-built farmhouse looks as though it has been part of the lush Oxfordshire countryside in which it stands, for centuries. In fact it has been built relatively recently and as such boasts all the modern conveniences you could wish for, but also has a standard of cosiness and character that you would only expect with much older buildings: there are log fires in the lounge and the prettily decorated bedrooms are furnished in a cottagey style. Food is of great importance at Sugarswell combining the best of British farmhouse fare with continental dishes. Your hostess is a Cordon Bleu cook, so you can be sure of an excellent meal (a speciality is home-produced fillet of beef in port & cream). There is much to see and do in the area: Warwick, Woodstock, Oxford and Stratford are all nearby while Banbury has much of historic interest (including its cross) to commend it.
Open all year. No smoking in the house. En suite & tea-making in rooms. Amex. B. & B. from £20.

Wroxton House Hotel, Wroxton St Mary, Nr Banbury, OX15 6QB (0295) 730777

Wroxton House Hotel is the product of the sensitive restoration of three 17th C. village houses and a clocktower! All food home-prepared from fresh, local produce (some home-grown); bread is home-baked).
Open all year. No smoking in dining room & part of bar. Vegetarian & other diets by arrangement. Licensed. Children welcome. Pets by arrangement. En suite, TV & tea/coffee in all rooms. Credit cards. B. & B. from £45.

BURFORD

The Bay Tree Hotel, Sheep St, Burford, OX18 4LW (099382) 2791

Beautiful country house. The food is of an exceptionally high standard.
Open all year. No smoking in dining room & some bedrooms. Vegetarian standard; other diets by arrangement. Licensed. Disabled access. Children welcome. En suite, TV & tea/coffee-making in all rooms. Access, Visa, Amex, Diners.

OXFORD

Combermere House, 11 Polstead Rd, Oxford, OX2 6TW (0865) 56971

Family-run guest house in a quiet tree-lined road off Woodstock Road in residential North Oxford.
Open all year. No smoking in dining room. Vegetarian & other diets by arrangement. Disabled access: 'to ground floor & dining room'. Children welcome. Pets by arrangement. En suite, tea/coffee & T.V in all bedrooms. Visa, Mastercard. B. & B. from £22.

Cotswold House, 363 Banbury Rd, Oxford, OX2 7PL (0865) 310558

Charming, comfortable and highly acclaimed guest house in North Oxford.
Open all year. No smoking. Vegetarian standard. Most other special diets by arrangement (breakfast only). Children: over 6s only. En suite, tea/coffee & T.V. in all bedrooms. B. & B. from £23.

The Dial House, 25 London Rd, Headington, Oxford, OX3 7RE (0865) 69944

Elegant half-timbered house in beautiful gardens just a mile from Oxford city centre.
Open all year ex. Xmas. No smoking in dining room and bedrooms. Vegetarian breakfast standard. Children: over 6s only. Pets by arrangement. En suite, tea/coffee-making & T.V. in all bedrooms. B. & B. from £21.

Earlmont Guest House, 322-32 Cowley Rd, Oxford, OX4 2AF (0865) 240236

12 bedroom guest house; vegetarian and healthy options at breakfast.

Open Jan. 1st to Dec 15th. No smoking in dining room & some bedrooms. Vegetarian & other diets by arrangement. Ground floor rooms and shower/toilet. Children: over 5s only. Tea/coffee-making & T.V. in all rooms. Access, Visa, Amex. B. & B. from £17.50.

The Farmhouse Hotel & Restaurant, University Farm, Lew, Oxford, OX8 2AU (0993) 850297/851480

This beautiful 17th C. Cotswold stone farmhouse forms part of a working farm and has a herd of black and white Friesian milking cows; it stands amidst rolling countryside just 12 miles west of Oxford in the tiny village of Lew. The farmhouse has been carefully and comfortably furnished - each of the pretty bedrooms has beamed ceilings and rural views (one ground floor room is specially designed to have wheelchair access) - and there is a comfortable, airy lounge with a massive inglenook fireplace (filled with flowers in summer and blazing logs in winter!). The cuisine has earned a very high reputation amongst the locals: the daily changing menu features a range of tasty options which have all been prepared from the finest of fresh ingredients; meals are served in either the cosy dining room with its beamed ceilings and stone walls, or in the lovely Garden Room - which also forms the perfect venue for private functions.

Open all year ex. Xmas. No smoking in 75% dining room & corridors. Vegetarian & other diets by arrangement. Licensed. Disabled access. Children: over 5s only. En suite, TV & tea/coffee-making in all rooms. Access, Visa. B. & B. from £23.50.

Morar Farm, Weald St, Bampton, West of Oxford, OX18 2HL Tel: (0993) 850162 Fax: 0993 851738

Morar Farm is a spacious stone-built farm house which is pleasantly situated in the little village of Bampton which is famous for its beautiful 11th C. church and annual Spring festival of Morris dancing and wild flower garlands. Morar is the home of Janet and Terry Rouse - a lively couple who enjoy bell-ringing, barn dancing, Morris dancing and spinning! They also enjoy welcoming guests to their home, and offer a special brand of helpful hospitality which has earned them a Highly Commended status from the English Tourist Board. The food is plentiful and excellent and features lots of wholesome items such as home-made preserves and home-baked bread. There are a wealth of things to enjoy and places to visit within the area: Cheltenham, Bath, Cirencester and Oxford are all easily visited (to add to the many attractions of the latter there is now the Oxford Story: an animated recreation of Oxford's history); garden lovers would enjoy visiting nearby Waterperry Gardens, and there is a wildlife park and rare breed farm within a short drive of Morar. Blenheim Palace, Avebury Stone Circle and Didcot Steam Railway Centre are nearby. For those seeking to relax *in situ* there are lovely walks to the Thames from the farmhouse.

Open Jan. to early Dec. No smoking throughout. Vegetarian & other diets by arrangement. Licensed. Over 6s only. En suite in 2 double rooms; 1 twin room has private bathroom. Tea/coffee-making in all rooms. T.V. in lounge. Credit cards. B. & B. from £16.

Mount Pleasant Hotel, 76 London Rd, Headington, Oxford, OX3 9AJ Tel & Fax: (0865) 62749

The Mount Pleasant Hotel is a small family-run hotel which stands in the shopping area of Headington but is within easy reach of the main shops and colleges of Oxford. Mr and Mrs Papamichael are especially welcoming hosts and will do all they can to make you feel at home: the food is excellent - Greek, English and Continental dishes are all home-cooked from fresh ingredients - and special diets can be catered for by arrangement. Accommodation is in comfortable bedrooms - each of which has en suite facilities - and there is a safe car park for guests' use.

Open all year. No smoking ex. in the bar. Vegetarian & other diets by arrangement. Licensed. Wheelchair access. Children welcome. En suite, TV & tea/coffee-making in rooms. Credit cards. B. & B. from £35.

Oxfordshire

Randolph Hotel, Beaumont St, Oxford, OX1 2LN (0865) 247481

The Randolph Hotel is a well-known Oxford landmark; first-rate meals are served in the excellent restaurant (open to non-residents).

Open all year. No smoking in 60% of dining room and some bedrooms. Vegetarian standard. Other diets by arrangement. Licensed. Disabled access. Children welcome. Pets by arrangement. En suite, TV & tea/coffee-making in all rooms. B. & B. from £67.

Westwood Country Hotel, Hinksey Hill Top, Oxford, OX1 5BG. (0865) 736408

The brochure of the Westwood Country Hotel

shows, instead of the pleasing facade of this attractive small hotel, a badger standing near an oak tree; this is a significant emphasis - as the hotel, which is just 3 miles from Oxford, boasts an exceptional abundance of wildlife in its 4 acres of grounds: woodpeckers, nightingales, badgers, foxes and, if you are lucky, deer have all been spotted in and around the 400 acres of woodland which surround the hotel grounds - which is a testament to the peace and tranquillity to be found at this charming hotel. The bedrooms are exceptionally comfortable and well-appointed and the food (served on lace tablecloths in the oak beamed dining room) is exceedingly good; the comfortable bar welcomes walkers returning from exploring the many footpaths that radiate from the hotel's front door.

Open all year ex. Xmas. Smoking banned in dining room and T.V. lounge. Vegetarian and most other special diets by arrangement. Licensed. Disabled access. Children welcome. En suite, tea/coffee-making & T.V. in all bedrooms. All major credit cards accepted. Two day country breaks £46 p.p. per night, 7-days £242. Winner of Daily Mail Award 1991 for Tourism for All.

Windrush Guest House, 11 Iffley Rd, Oxford (0865) 247933

Family-run guest house near Magdalen Bridge. Easy walk to shops, restaurants & all the places of interest. Healthy Eating Award. Non-smokers preferred. Coaches to and from London airport.

Open all year. No smoking in the dining room. Vegetarian by arrangement. Children welcome. TV & tea/coffee-making facilities. Credit cards. B. & B. from £11-21.

TOWERSEY

Upper Green Farm, Manor Rd, Towersey, OX9 3QR (0884) 212496

Very comfortable farmhouse accommodation. Peacefully quiet.

Open all year. No smoking. Vegetarian and most other special diets by arrangement. Disabled access: 'wide doorways, level entrance, 2 ground floor bedrooms, no room for wheelchairs in bedrooms'. En suite in most rooms. Tea/coffee-making & T.V. in all bedrooms.

WOODSTOCK

Bear Hotel & Restaurant, Park St, Woodstock, OX7 1SZ (0993) 811511

Famous 16th C. coaching inn offering accommodation of an exceptionally high standard.

Open all year. Smoking banned in 30% dining room and bedrooms. Vegetarian standard. Licensed. Disabled access. Children welcome. No pets. En suite in all rooms. Tea/coffee-making in all rooms. T.V. in all bedrooms. All major credit cards accepted. B. & B. from £50.

Gorselands, Boddington Lane, Nr Long Hanborough, Nr Woodstock, OX8 6PU (0993) 881202

Cotswold stone house with oakbeams and flagged floors set in 1 acre of grounds in idyllic rural setting between Oxford and Woodstock. Breakfast and home-cooked evening meal, using fresh local produce, on request.

Open Apr. to Nov. No smoking. Vegetarian and other special diets by arrangement. Children welcome. En suite in one room. Tea/coffee-making in lounge. Satellite T.V. in lounge. B. & B. from £12.50, D £8.50.

Central England

Gloucestershire

BERKELEY

The Old Schoolhouse Hotel and Restaurant, Canonbury St, Berkeley, GL13 9BG (0453) 811711
Comfortable hotel offering various health and beauty treatments under the supervision of Ann Leighton. High proportion of home-made food. Vegetarian and most other special diets by arrangement. Open all year ex. Xmas. No smoking in part of dining room. Licensed. Disabled access: 2 ground floor bedrooms. Children welcome. En suite, tea/coffee & T.V in all rooms. W/E course from £130.

BOURTON ON THE WATER

Coombe House, Rissington Rd, Bourton on the Water, GL54 2DT (0451) 821966
Coombe House is a family-run concern quietly situated in pretty lawned gardens in Bourton on the Water. This delightful village is often dubbed The Venice of the Cotswolds on account of the River Windrush which gracefully wends its way through willow-draped banks on which delightful stone houses and cottages nestle. Coombe House interior is bright, fresh and airy with an overall feeling of relaxation (it has been awarded a Highly Commended status by the English Tourist Board and your hosts, Graham and Diana Ellis, will make you very welcome). Breakfast is the only meal available at Coombe House and it can be 'as healthy or as non-healthy as each guest wishes.' Accordingly yoghurt is available as an alternative to cereal and Flora as an alternative to butter; decaffeinated coffee is available on request and a pleasant light continental alternative is a warm croissant with apricot jam.
Open all year. No smoking in the house. Vegetarian standard; other diets by arrangement. Licensed. Some disabled access: '2 ground floor rooms'. Children welcome. En suite, TV & tea/coffee in all rooms. B. & B. from £24.50.

Dial House Hotel, Bourton on the Water, GL54 2AN (0451) 22244
Centrally situated in Bourton on the Water this 17th C. house with an acre of lovely garden has been charmingly converted into a hotel complete with open inglenook fireplaces and oakbeams; excellent cuisine.
Open all year. No smoking in dining room & some bedrooms. Vegetarian and some other special diets by arrangement. Licensed. Disabled access. En suite, tea/coffee-making & T.V. in all bedrooms. Access, Visa. B. & B. from £32.

Farncombe, Clapton, Bourton on the Water, GL54 2LG (0451) 820120
Beautifully appointed Cotswold family house standing in 2 acres of gardens some 700 ft above sea-level in the tiny hamlet of Clapton on the Hill; prettily decorated and furnished bedrooms.
Open all year. No smoking. Vegetarian & other diets by arrangement (breakfast only). Children welcome. 1 double room with shower. Tea/coffee-making in dining room. T.V. in lounge. B. & B. from £14.50.

The Strathspey, Lansdown, Bourton on the Water, GL54 2AR (0451) 20694
Small, friendly, family home run by Sue and Andrew Firth; quietly situated 5 mins walk from the centre of Bourton on the Water.
Open all year. No smoking. Vegetarian and most other special diets by arrangement. Children: over 5s welcome. En suite in some rooms. Tea/coffee, TV & radio alarm clock in all rooms. B. & B. from £14.

CHELTENHAM

Charlton Kings Hotel, London Rd, Charlton Kings, Cheltenham, GL52 6UU (0242) 231061
Visitors to Cheltenham Spa or the Cotswolds

could not do better than spend their stay at the recently refurbished Charlton Kings Hotel just 2 miles from the centre of Cheltenham. Situated in an area of Outstanding Natural Beauty, this elegant building stands in an acre of lawned gardens and feature trees, the whole surrounded by the rolling Cotswold hills. Guests are accommodated in the 14 beautiful en suite bedrooms - each of which have views of the hills (one has a private balcony); in fact a gentle stroll from the hotel will take you to the hills (a footpath runs alongside the building) or you can see them by one of the Hot Air Balloon flights (lazy but romantic) which depart from the hotel lawn. There are plenty of good eating houses in the area, but a varied and interesting menu is served in the Bistro style restaurant; the charming reception lounge and welcoming conservatory (with its snug leather sofa by the fire) is open to both residential and non-residential guests for tea and coffee.

Open all year. No smoking in dining room & some bedrooms. Vegetarian standard. Licensed. Disabled access. Children & pets by arrangement. En suite, TV & tea/coffee-making in rooms. Access, Visa, Mastercard. B. & B. from £29.

Hallery House Hotel, 48 Shurdington Rd, Cheltenham Spa, GL53 0JE (0242) 578450

Hallery House is a lovingly-restored listed Victorian building which functions as a small, family-run hotel with a welcoming, relaxed and informal atmosphere. There are sixteen light, airy bedrooms - each with individual furnishings and lots of character - and there is an elegant dining room and comfortable lounge; guests may chose to while away an hour or two on the patio in sunny weather, and the grounds include lots of space for parking. Hallery House food is fresh, healthy and simple, prepared from the best local produce to imaginative and tasty recipes; traditional or continental breakfasts are provided and the evening meal would typically feature a choice of dishes such as Galantine of Chicken followed by Rack of Lamb Vin Herb and a tempting choice of desserts, such as Fresh Apricot and Passion Fruit Brulee. Hallery House is within walking distance of Cheltenham town centre, and within a short drive are all the charms of the Cotswolds.

Open all year. No smoking in dining room & non-smoking bedrooms available. Vegetarian & other diets by arrangement. Licensed. Children & pets very welcome. En suite in most rooms. Tea/coffee-making, T.V. & satellite T.V. in all rooms. Visa, Amex, Mastercard. B. & B. from £20.

Northfield B. & B., Cirencester Rd, Northleach, Cheltenham, GL54 3JL (0451) 60427

Northfield is a lovely detached family home set in large gardens overlooking open countryside. Although functioning principally as a bed and breakfast, packed lunches and evening meals can be taken at Northfield by arrangement and fresh, home-grown produce - including free-range eggs - are used wherever possible in cooking; in sunny weather meals may be enjoyed in the garden either on the lawn or relaxing by the pond. Northfield is conveniently situated just off the A429 a mile from the market town of Northleach, with its beautiful church and musical museum; its proximity to so many other lovely towns and villages in the Cotswolds makes it a perfect base from which to explore all the charms and delights of this lovely part of the world.

Open all year. No smoking Vegetarian and most other special diets by arrangement. Licensed. Children welcome. En suite & tea/coffee-making in all rooms. T.V. in lounge. B. & B. from £15.

Prestbury House Hotel, The Burgage, Prestbury, Cheltenham, GL52 3DN (0242) 529533

Georgian manor house built in 1700 standing in secluded grounds in pretty village of Prestbury. Elegantly appointed with chandeliered dining room and four-posters in some of the bedrooms.

Open all year. No smoking in part dining room and bedrooms. Vegetarian, vegan and diabetic standard. Other diets by arrangement. Licensed. Disabled access: 3 specially equipped rooms'. Children welcome. En suite, TV & tea/coffee-making in all rooms. Access, Visa. B. & B. from £36.

Stretton Lodge, Western Rd, Cheltenham, GL50 3RN (0242) 528724 or 570771

Beautiful late Victorian house, quietly situated in central Cheltenham. Healthy b'fast options (yoghurt, fruit) and evening meal (by arrangement) cooked from fresh produce.

Vegetarian by arrangement. Open all year. Smoking banned throughout the house. Licensed. Children welcome. En suite, TV & tea/coffee-making in all rooms. Access, Visa. B. & B. from £27.50.

Turret House, Aldsworth, (between Burford & Bibury), Cheltenham, GL54 3QZ (04514) 547

Converted chapel now a private country house offering B. & B. only but local pub serves excellent and acclaimed meals.

Open all year. No smoking. Vegetarian and most other special diets by arrangement, (breakfasts only). Children: over 14s only. Tea/coffee-making & T.V. in all bedrooms. B. & B. from £12.50.

Gloucestershire

Wyck Hill Lodge B. & B., Wyck Hill, Cheltenham, GL54 1HT (0451) 830141

Wyck Hill Lodge is an early Victorian building which stands in country surroundings enjoying extensive views over the Vale of Bourton. Comfortably furnished throughout, Wyck Hill Lodge has several guest bedrooms (2 of which are on the ground floor) and each is equipped with a range of helpful amenities including TV & tea and coffee-making facilities; there is a comfortable guest lounge, an attractive garden and ample space for parking. Breakfast is a generous meal with choices to suit all tastes, including kippers, smoked haddock and mushrooms on toast in additional to the usual fare; evening meals may be ordered by arrangement and there are several good restaurants nearby. Wyck Hill is just 1 mile from Stow-on-the-Wold (on the A424 Burford Road); several other interesting places are close at hand including Cirencester, Stratford and Oxford.
Open most of the year. Vegetarian standard. Other diets by arrangement. En suite, TV & tea/coffee in bedrooms. B. & B. £19 - 22. D. £12 - 13.

CHIPPING CAMPDEN

The Cotswold House Hotel, Chipping Campden, GL55 6AN (0386) 840330

Beautifully restored 17th C. country house elegantly furnished with antiques & paintings to complement its period features. Lovely garden, open fires, excellent cuisine.
Open all year ex. Xmas. No smoking in dining room. Vegetarian & other diets by arrangement. Licensed. Children: over 8s welcome. En suite, TV & room service in bedrooms. Credit cards. B. & B. from £40.

CIRENCESTER

Raydon House Hotel, 3 The Avenue, GL7 1EH (0285) 653485

Small family hotel close to town centre. Warm welcome. Light airy bedrooms. Good food prepared from fresh, local produce
Open all year. Vegetarian standard. Other diets by arrangement. Licensed. Children welcome. Ground floor rooms. Dogs by arrangement. En suite, TV & tea/coffee in rooms. B. & B. from £17.50, D. from £10.

Wimborne House, 91 Victoria Rd, Cirencester, GL7 1ES (0285) 653890

Lovely old house situated just 5 mins from the centre of the historic city of Cirencester.
Open all year ex. Xmas. No smoking in the house. Vegetarian & other special diets by arrangement. Children: over 5s only. En suite, tea/coffee-making & T.V. in all bedrooms. B. & B. from £14.

KILCOT

Orchard House, Aston Ingham Rd, Kilcot, Nr Newent, GL18 1NP (0989) 82417

Orchard House is a beautiful Tudor-style country

home which stands amidst 5 acres of peaceful grounds (including well-tended lawns, paddocks and country walks) in a tranquil country setting close to the unspoilt Wye Valley and the Forest of Dean; the oldest parts of the house date from the 18th C. and many original beams are still to be seen - in, for example, the TV lounge with its log fires. Your hosts, Anne and Basil Thompson, have done everything they can to make their home as warmly welcoming as possible: the elegant and finely furnished rooms provide a very high standard of accommodation (Orchard House has been awarded a Highly Commended status by the ETB) but there is, nonetheless, a friendly relaxed feel about the place. Anne is an excellent cook and provides a wide selection of delicious and imaginative fare: only fresh produce - with local specialities - are ever used in cooking, and a typical evening menu would feature Green Pea and Mint Soup followed by Poached Salmon or Spinach Roulade with Cottage Cheese, and fresh fruit salad; coffee and mints would complete the meal. You are within easy reach of a number of interesting places including the Brecon Beacons, the Malverns, the Cotswolds and Ross-on-Wye.
Open all year. No smoking. Vegetarian & other diets by arrangement. Licensed. Children: over 12s only. En suite & tea/coffee-making in bedrooms. Credit cards. B. & B. from £17.50, D. from £12.50.

MINSTERWORTH
Severn Bank Guest House, Minsterworth, GL2 8JH (0452) 75357
Fine country house in 6 acres of grounds on the banks of the Severn 4 miles West of Gloucester.
Open all year. No smoking in dining room, hall & bedrooms. Vegetarian & other diets by arrangement. Children welcome. En suite, TV & tea/coffee-making in all bedrooms. B. & B. from £17.50.

MORETON IN MARSH
Blue Cedar House, Stow Rd, Moreton in Marsh, GL56 0DW (0608) 50299
Beautiful detached residence set in attractive gardens within easy reach of the centre of the picturesque town of Moreton in Marsh.
Open all year ex. Xmas. No smoking ex. T.V. lounge. Vegetarian & other diets by arrangement. Disabled access: 'one ground floor suite'. Children welcome. En suite some rooms. Tea/coffee & colour TV all rooms. T.V. in lounge. B. & B. from £13, D. from £6.

Mr & Mrs Malin, 21 Station Rd, Blockley, Moreton-in-Marsh (0386) 700402
Modern, Cotswold stone house.
Open all year. No smoking. Vegetarian & other diets by arrangement. Children: 'depends on age'. Tea/coffee & T.V. in rooms. B. & B. from £12.50.

PAINSWICK
Upper Dorey's Mill, Edge, Nr Painswick, GL6 6NF (0452) 812459
18th C. Cotswold stone mill house in tranquil valley; beams & woodburning stoves.
Open all year. No smoking. Vegetarian and most other special diets by arrangement (breakfast only). Children welcome. En suite & tea/coffee-making in all rooms. T.V. in lounge. B. & B. from £17.50.

RUARDEAN
The Lawn, Ruardean, GL17 9US (0594) 543259
18th C. Grade II listed building, formerly the village gaol. Good provision for vegetarians.
Open all year ex. Xmas. No smoking. Vegetarian & other diets by arrangement. Children: over 8s only. En suite. Tea/coffee. T.V. in lounge. B. & B. from £14.

ST BRIAVELS
Cinderhill House, St. Briavels, GL15 6RH (0594) 530393
14th C. building with oakbeams, inglenook fireplaces and bread oven, nestling in hillside. Home-prepared food from fresh, local produce. Two self-catering cottages are also available.
Open all year. No smoking ex. in sitting room. Vegetarian and most other special diets by arrangement. Licensed. Children welcome. En suite & tea/coffee-making in all rooms. B. & B. from £21.

STROUD
Burleigh Cottage, Burleigh, Minchinhampton, Stroud, GL5 2PW (0453) 884703
Charming cottage with splendid views. Healthy b'fast options (fruit, yoghurt, etc.).
Open all year. No smoking. Vegetarian and most other special diets by arrangement. En suite in two rooms. Tea/coffee-making & T.V. in all bedrooms.

Reddings, Burleigh, Stroud, GL5 2PH (0453) 882342
Comfortable, spacious house standing in 5 acres of gardens and paddocks splendidly set with mature trees. Healthy food a speciality.
All special diets by arrangement. Open all year ex. Xmas. Licensed. Children welcome.

TETBURY
Calcot Manor, Nr Tetbury, GL8 8YJ (0666) 890391
Beautiful manor converted from a farmhouse; lovely gardens with outdoor heated pool. Individually styled bedrooms and excellent meals prepared from fresh, local produce.
Open all year. No smoking in dining room. Vegetarian & diabetic standard. Other diets by arrangement. Licensed. Children: over 12s. En suite & TV in rooms. Room service. B. & B. from £73, D. from £29.

TEWKSBURY
Puckrup Hall Hotel, Puckrup, Tewksbury, GL20 6EL (0684) 296200
Grand Regency house providing superb accommodation and excellent cuisine.
Open all year. No smoking in dining room. Vegetarian standard. Other diets by arrangement. Licensed. Children welcome. En suite & T.V. in all bedrooms. Credit cards. B. & B. from £49.50.

WOTTON UNDER EDGE
Coombe Lodge Vegetarian B. & B., Wotton under Edge, GL12 7NB (0453) 845057
Grade II listed Georgian house 1 acre of gardens Free-range eggs, local mushrooms and wholemeal bread. Good vegetarian food.
Open all year ex. Xmas and New Year. No smoking. Vegetarian standard. Children: over 3s only. Tea/coffee-making & T.V. in all bedrooms. B. & B. from £15. ETB 2 Crowns Commended.

Herefordshire

HAY-ON-WYE

The Haven, Hardwicke, Hay-on-Wye, HR3 5TA (04973) 254

Early Victorian vicarage in 2 acres of mature gardens and paddocks 2m from Hay on Wye. All food prepared from fresh, often home-grown, ingredients. Open air pool.
Open Mar. to Nov. No smoking ex. in library. Vegetarian & other diets by arrangement. Licensed. Disabled access: '1 ground floor en suite room.' Children welcome. Pets by arrangement. En suite in most rooms. Tea/coffee-making & T.V. in all bedrooms. Amex. B. & B. from £19.50

Kilvert Court Hotel, Bullring, Hay-on-Wye, HR3 5AG (0497) 821042

Acclaimed hotel in the centre of Hay on Wye serving a wide range of excellent cuisine.
Open all year. No smoking. Vegetarian & other diets by arrangement. Licensed. Disabled access: 'to restaurant and rear gardens'. Children welcome. Pets by arrangement. En suite, tea/coffee-making & T.V. in all bedrooms. B. & B. from £30.

HEREFORD

Grafton Villa, Grafton, Nr Hereford, HR2 8ED (0432) 268689

Farmhouse of character in 1 acre of lawns & garden; panoramic views; superb home-cooking with fresh, organic vegetables & local produce.
Open all year. No smoking. Vegetarian and most other special diets by arrangement. Children welcome. Pets by arrangement. En suite twin & double rooms. Tea/coffee & T.V. in all bedrooms. B. & B. from £15.

KINGTON

Church House, Lyonshall, Kington, HR5 3HR (05448) 350

Small, Georgian country house with lovely views in 4 acres of gardens and paddocks; meals are 'generous and simple yet imaginative' and are prepared from fresh local produce.
Open all year ex. Xmas. No smoking in dining room and bedrooms. Vegetarian and most other special diets by arrangement. Children welcome. En suite in some rooms. Tea/coffee-making in all rooms. T.V. in lounge. B. & B. from £14.

LEDBURY

Wall Hills Guest House, Hereford Rd, Ledbury, HR8 2PR (0531) 2833

Elegant Georgian mansion standing in lovely garden on hill overlooking Ledbury. Imaginative meals prepared from fresh, local produce.
Open all year ex. Xmas. No smoking in dining room. Vegetarian & other diets by arrangement. Licensed. Children welcome. En suite or priv. fac.& tea/coffee in all rooms. TV lounge. B. & B. from £17.50.

LEOMINSTER

Copper Hall, 134 South St, Leominster, HR6 8JN (0568) 611622

Charming 17th C. house on the outskirts of town; good home-cooking using fresh, local produce.
Open all year ex. Xmas. No smoking in dining room & bedrooms. Vegetarian by arrangement. Children: if well behaved. Tea/coffee & T.V. B. & B. from £17.

Highfield, Ivington Rd, Newtown, Leominster, HR6 8QD (0568) 613216

Set amidst the rolling Herefordshire countryside in an acre of garden just 1½ miles from attractive market town of Leominster, this elegant

Edwardian house is home to twins, Marguerite and Catherine Fothergill, who offer quite exceptional hospitality to guests. The 3 bedrooms are large and tastefully decorated - all have lovely country views - and the sun-filled morning room and cosy lounge with its crackling fire in the evening all enhance the home-from-home atmosphere (house parties are especially welcome!). Meals are served in an elegant dining room and the food, which is outstandingly good, has been "lovingly prepared from fresh, seasonal produce" - certainly the home-made brioches served for breakfast suggest quite serious culinary commitment. Guests will be loathe to tear themselves away from the peace and tranquillity of Highfield but you are within easy reach of Hereford and Hay-on-Wye and it would be a shame to miss the charms of these lovely towns.
Open all year. No smoking in dining room & bedrooms. Licensed. Children by arrangement. Private bath/en suite all rooms. Tea/coffee. TV lounge. B. & B. from £18, D. £10. ETB 2 Crowns Commended.

Herefordshire

Kimbolton Court, Kimbolton, Leominster, HR6 0HH (0568) 87259
Charming stone-built farmhouse in nearly an acre of partially wild garden 3m. from town; home-made produce includes bread, preserves, marmalade & organically grown vegetables.
Open all year ex. Xmas and New Year. No smoking in bedrooms & dining room. Vegetarian & other diets by arrangement. Children welcome. En suite. Tea/coffee all rooms. T.V. lounge. B. & B. from £13.

Lower Bache Farm, Kimbolton, Nr Leominster (0568) 87304
Lovely 17th C. stone farmhouse and a small farm which is currently being restored to an organic system of husbandry; home produce including home-smoked Finnan Haddock, home-made sausages and bacon, and free-range eggs, organic meat and vegetables.
Open all year ex. Xmas. No smoking in dining room. Vegetarian & other diets by arrangement. Licensed. Children: over 8s only. En suite. Tea/coffee-making in all suites. T.V. B. & B. from £17.

Ratefield Farm, Kimbolton, Leominster, HR6 0JB (0568) 2507
Lovely 18th C. house forming part of a 110 acre livestock farm in a secluded position less than a mile from Kimbolton. Home-produce used in cooking and home-baked bread and rolls.
Open Mar. to mid Feb. No smoking in dining room & bedroom. Vegetarian, diabetic, coeliac by arrangement and low-fat as standard. Children welcome. Pets by arrangement. Tea/coffee-making available. T.V. in lounge. Amex. B. & B. from £13.50.

MORDIFORD

Orchard Farm, Mordiford, Nr Hereford, HR1 4EJ (0432) 870253
17th C. stone-built farmhouse with large, natural garden and 57 acres of traditional farmland.
Open all year ex. Xmas. No smoking ex. sitting room. Vegetarian and most other special diets, but not vegan, by arrangement. Licensed. Children: over 10s only. Tea/coffee-making available. T.V. available. Amex. B. & B. from £14.

MUCH BIRCH

The Old School, Much Birch, Nr Hereford, HR2 8HJ Tel: Rita Ayers (0981) 540006
Comfortable, attractive, converted Victorian school with a lovely large garden and fantastic views. Really good home-made food. Marvellous walking country. Guest lounge with colour TV and extensive library. Central heating.

Open all year. No smoking in dining room and bedrooms. Vegetarian, vegan, diabetic and most other special diets by arrangement. Children welcome. Trained pets welcome. En suite in 2 rooms. Tea/coffee-making in all rooms. T.V. in lounge, radio in all bedrooms. B. & B. from £15. ETB 2 Crown Commended.

ROSS ON WYE

The Arches Country House, Walford Rd, Ross-on-Wye (0989) 63348
Small family-run guest house in ½ acre of lawns & 10 mins walk from town centre. All bedrooms overlook the garden. Very high standard of decor. *RAC Acclaimed. AA listed. Routier Award.*
Open all year. No smoking in the dining room & bedrooms. Vegetarian & other diets by arrangement. En suite, TV & tea/coffee-making in bedrooms. Children & pets welcome. B. & B. £15 - 20.

Brook House, Lea, Nr Ross on Wye, HR9 7JZ (098981) 710
Brook House is a fine Grade II listed Queen Anne building standing on the site of a medieval hospice for weary travellers! Now extensively - and sympathetically - renovated, Brook House offers quite exceptionally comfortable accommodation to guests: all bedrooms have been furnished in keeping with the period details of the house's architecture, and there are many fine, family antiques in the public rooms. The emphasis at Brook House is on comfort and good food; accordingly there is a very friendly and relaxed atmosphere and your hosts will always find time to chat to help you plan your stay. Breakfast is stupendous: the bread and muffins are all home-made and the bacon, sausages and eggs (free-range of course!) represent the best of local produce. Evening meals are imaginative and tasty, and snacks can be provided for late arrivals. Lea is a pleasant Herefordshire village just 4 miles from Ross on Wye on the Gloucester road; you are perfectly placed therein for visiting both the Wye Valley and the Forest of Dean.
Open all year. No smoking ex. in lounge, where smoking is discouraged. Vegetarian standard. Most other special diets by arrangement. Children: over 7s only. Pets by arrangement. En suite shower in 2 rooms & bathroom in one room. Tea/coffee-making in all rooms. T.V in lounge. B. & B. from £15.

Edde Cross House, Edde Cross St, Ross on Wye, HR9 7BZ (0989) 65088
This delightful Georgian Grade II listed town house with its charming walled garden stands in a convenient position in Ross on Wye overlooking the river. It has a very friendly and warm atmosphere - a bit like staying in a house

with friends - and all bedrooms have been comfortably furnished to a very high standard with extensive use of mellow old pine and have excellent facilities, including a welcome tray and a hairdryer. Breakfast is the only meal available at Edde Cross but it is a meal with lots of options including three different fish dishes, an extensive choice for vegetarians, and a continental alternative for lighter appetites.

Open Feb. to Nov. No smoking in the house. Other diets by arrangement. Children: over 10s. Some en suite. Tea/coffee & TV in all rooms. B. & B. from £17.

Lavender Cottage, Bridstow, Ross on Wye, HR9 6QB (0989) 62836

Lavender Cottage is a delightful character property with parts dating back to the 17th century; it enjoys a tranquil location just one mile from Ross on Wye and has fine views of Bridstow church and May Hill; Ross church spire can be seen clearly amidst the backdrop of the trees of Chase Woods and Goodrich Castle with the Forest of Dean beyond. The cottage has been comfortably furnished and decorated and a generous breakfast is offered to guests.

Open all year. No smoking. Vegetarian & other diets by arrangement. En suite in some rooms. Tea/coffee in all rooms. T.V. lounge. B. & B. from £12.50.

Linden House, 14 Church St, Ross on Wye, HR9 5HN (0989) 65373

Linden House is a William and Mary/Georgian town house built around 1680 and now comfortably decorated and furnished. It is situated in a quiet street opposite St Marys church just off the market square. The proprietors, Claire and Patrick take great pride in the fine food that they offer: for breakfast you help yourself from the sideboard to a selection of cereals, fruit, yoghurt and juice, followed by warm croissants and toast (served with home-made jam and marmalade) or a piping hot traditional or vegetarian cooked meal. The proprietors take care of the environment as well as you! All cleaning products are bio-degradable - and even the loo rolls are made from recycled paper.

Open all year. No smoking throughout. Vegetarian & other diets by arrangement. Licensed. Children: over 8s only. En suite in some rooms. Tea/coffee-making & T.V. in all rooms. B. & B. from £16.50.

Pengethley Manor Hotel, Nr. Ross on Wye, HR9 6LL (0989) 87211

Although much of the this original Tudor Manor was destroyed by fire in the 19th C. some parts have survived, such as the oak panelling in the entrance hall; now superbly rebuilt and sumptuously appointed, this splendid country house stands in 15 acres of stunning English countryside. The cuisine is exceptional and is prepared from the freshest and finest of local ingredients - much of the herbs, fruit and vegetables used in cooking have been culled from the Pengethley estate; a typical 6-course evening menu would feature Avocado with Orange and Grapefruit followed by Beef Consomme, Cod Meuniere, Chocolate Profiteroles and a selection of cheeses; freshly ground coffee and petit fours would complete the meal. The amenities at Pengethley include a croquet lawn, a 9-hole golf improvement course, a trout lake and an outdoor swimming pool which is heated in summer. The area is a walkers' paradise, and there are 3 'customised' walks of different lengths available.

Vegetarian and vegan standard. Diabetic and most other special diets by arrangement. Organic and wholefoods when available. Open all year. Licensed. Disabled access. Children welcome. Pets by arrangement. En suite facilities, tea/coffee-making, T.V., direct dial phones and hairdryers in all rooms. Credit cards accepted. D., B. & B. from £65.

ULLINGSWICK

The Steppes Country House Hotel, Ullingswick, HR1 3JG (0432) 820424

Listed 17th C. building beamed ceilings, inglenook fireplaces & tiled floors. The 5-course evening meal, served by candlelight, is a gourmet treat; all meals have been prepared from the finest fresh ingredients.

Open all year. No smoking in most public rooms. Vegetarian & other diets by arrangement. Licensed. Disabled: 'not for wheelchair bound'. Children: over 12s. Pets by arrangement. En suite, tea/coffee, T.V. & mini-bar in rooms. B. & B. from £32.50.

Shropshire

BRIDGNORTH

The Croft Hotel, St Marys St, Bridgnorth, WV16 4DW (0746) 767155/6

The Croft Hotel is a small, licensed family hotel situated in a Grade II listed building in St Marys Street in the historically interesting town of Bridgnorth; the hotel's architecture is interesting and includes some half-timbered 16th C. sections as well as some 18th and 19th century additions. The bedrooms have each been very comfortably furnished (there is central heating in cooler weather), and the meals which are served in the intimate dining room with inglenook fireplace and beamed ceilings, have all been prepared from fresh, seasonal vegetables. Bridgnorth dates from the 10th C. and is divided by the River Severn, its High Town being approached by steep streets; it is an interesting, picturesque location, and additionally you will find you are within easy reach of the Stretton Hills and the Long Mynd.
Open all year. No smoking in part of dining room & bedrooms. Vegetarian & other diets by arrangement. Licensed. Children welcome. Pets by arrangement. En suite in most rooms. Tea/coffee-making on request. T.V. in all rooms. Credit cards. B. & B. from £23.50.

The Old Vicarage Hotel, Worfield, Bridgnorth, WV15 5JZ (07464) 497

The Old Vicarage is a magnificent Edwardian house which stands in two acres of beautifully tended grounds, overlooking fields and farmland, in the quiet Shropshire hamlet of Worfield. The proprietors, Christine and Peter Iles, have been in residence since 1979 and since that time have lovingly restored this handsome Edwardian parsonage into a country house hotel of quite exceptional quality: decorated and furnished in keeping with the period, the en suite guest rooms are nonetheless individually styled (each is named after a local village), and offer a wide range of facilities. The candlelit dinner is based around the availability of fresh, regional produce, changes daily and virtually everything is home-made, including the bread, ice-cream, sorbets and preserves (plus vegetarian options).
Open all year. No smoking in dining room & some bedrooms. Vegetarian & other diets by arrangement. Licensed. Ramps & special suite for disabled. Children welcome. En suite, tea/coffee-making & T.V. in all bedrooms. Credit cards. B. & B. from £78.50 for 2 persons. D. from £19.50.

CHURCH STRETTON

Cwm Head House, Cwm Head, Marshbrook, SY6 6PX (069 46) 279

19th century farmhouse in large gardens.
Open all year. No smoking ex. lounge. Vegetarian, vegan, diabetic and other diets by arrangement. Over 8s only. Tea/coffee-making in all bedrooms. T.V. in lounge. B.& B. from £11.50.

Hope Bowdler Hall, Church Stretton, SY6 7DD (0694) 722041

Peaceful manor house on the edge of village.
Open Apr - Oct. No smoking in the house. B. & B. £15.

Mynd House Hotel, Little Stretton, Church Stretton, SY6 6RB (0694) 722212

Standing high above the road with extensive views across the Stretton Gap to Ragleth Hill, this small Edwardian house hotel and restaurant offers a perfect window on the Shropshire Hills. The rather severe Edwardian brick exterior belies the intimate interior of the house which Janet and

Robert Hill have enhanced with period furniture and decor (a log fire blazes in the lounge in cooler weather); no reception or room numbers here: you are received as a guest in a country house. The candlelit restaurant - open to non-residents - features an excellent fixed price 4-course Table d'hote or an à la carte menu (both offer imaginative dishes and good meat-free options), and there is an outstanding wine list (the Mynd House Hotel was the 1991 winner of the Mercier Prix d'Elite award) which features over 300 selections - including English country and French organic wines - and an incredible 50 item half bottle list. For the walker the area is a delight in all seasons - the hotel produces a booklet of six walks from the door - and your proximity to the ancient towns of Shrewsbury and Ludlow make the Mynd House Hotel a perfect destination for a break in the Shropshire Hills.

Open March to Dec. No smoking in dining room & bedrooms. Vegetarian by arrangement. Organic French wines available. Licensed. Children welcome. Pets. En suite, TV & Tea/coffee-making in rooms. Credit cards. B. & B. from £57.

CLEOBURY MORTIMER

The Redfern Hotel, Cleobury Mortimer, Shrops., DY14 8AA (0229) 270395

The Redfern Hotel is situated in the tree shaded main street of this ancient market town, alongside half timbered and 18th century houses. The conservatory, used as a breakfast room and a day lounge, is on the roof of the building and has lovely views across the town to the hills beyond. The English Kitchen Restaurant specialises in home-cooked traditional English food using organic and wholefood ingredients when available; steaks and fish dishes feature prominently on the menu. A log fire is lit in the bar in cooler seasons. Of particular interest locally is the Ironbridge Museum, Acton Scott Working Farm Museum and the Severn Valley Railway, and the Severn Gorge is easily reached.

Open all year. Vegetarian standard. Most other special diets by arrangement. Licensed. Limited disabled access. Children welcome. Pets by arrangement. En suite, TV & tea/coffee-making facilities. Credit cards. B. & B. from £30.

The Old Rectory, Hopesay, Craven Arms, SY7 8HD (05887) 245

17th century rectory; home-grown/local produce

Open all year. No smoking. Vegetarian & other diets by arrangement. En suite, tea/coffee-making & TV in all bedrooms. B & B from £26, D. £16.

LUDLOW

Corndene, Coreley, Ludlow, SY8 3AW (0584) 890324

Corndene is a house of great charm, the original part of which dates from the 18th C.; it stands amidst 2 acres of lovely gardens, some distance from any main road, and has lovely views over woods and farms. Accommodation is in very comfortable twin-bedded rooms, three of which are on the ground floor and have full wheelchair access; additionally there is a pleasant sitting room with an open fire, colour T.V., games, books and level access to the terrace. The food is tasty, wholesome and home-cooked: special diets - such as vegetarian - are catered for very competently if prior notice is given, and packed lunches can be provided on request. Corndene is situated 7 miles East of Ludlow and 4 miles North of Tenbury Wells on the South side of Titterstone Clee Hill; as such it is a perfect base from which to explore the attractions of the lush, countryside immortalised in A.E. Housman's poem, *The Shropshire Lad*.

Open all year ex. Xmas and New Year. No smoking Vegetarian & other diets by arrangement. Excellent disabled access. Children welcome. En suite & tea/coffee-making in rooms. T.V. in lounge. B. & B. from £18. ETB 3 Crowns.

Dinham Weir Hotel, Dinham Bridge, Ludlow, SY8 1EH (0584) 874431

Dinham Weir Hotel and Restaurant was recorded as being worked as an iron foundry until the late 19th century; it occupies the site of the original 17th century Castell Myll in the historic town of Ludlow and is surrounded by the beautiful rolling Shropshire countryside. These days the hotel has been carefully restored and tastefully decorated, and each of the comfortably appointed bedrooms overlooks the landscaped garden and the River Teme. A full à la carte or table d'hote menu is served in the intimate candlelit restaurant and there is a vegetarian option on the evening menu.

Open all year. Vegetarian standard. Most other special diets by arrangement. Licensed. Children: over 5s only. No pets. En suite, tea/coffee-making & T.V. in all bedrooms. B. & B. from £30.

Shropshire

The Feathers at Ludlow, Bull Ring, Ludlow, SY8 1AA (0584) 875261
One of the world's most famous and historic inns with a magnificent half-timbered front elevation and a richly decorated interior.
Open all year. No smoking in part of dining room. Vegetarian standard. Most other special diets by arrangement. Licensed. Disabled access. Children welcome. En suite, tea/coffee & T.V. in all bedrooms. Credit cards. B. & B. from £43. D £18.

Haynall Villa, Little Hereford, Ludlow, SY8 4BG (058472) 589
Comfortable Victorian farmhouse kitchen garden - and with an adjoining working farm.
Open all year ex. Xmas. Vegetarian & other diets by arrangement. Licensed. Children welcome. En suite in 1 room. Tea/coffee-making in all bedrooms. T.V. in lounge. B. & B. from £13.

MINSTERLEY

Cricklewood Cottage, Plox Green, Minsterley, SY5 0HT (0743) 791229
A delightful 18th century character cottage in an old fashioned garden.
Open all year. No smoking. Vegetarian and most other special diets by arrangement. Children welcome. Pets by arrangement. En suite 1 room. Tea/coffee-making in all bedrooms. T.V. in lounge. B. & B from £12.

OSWESTRY

April Spring Cottage, Nantmawr, Oswestry, SY10 9HL (0691) 828802
In spite of its lyrical name, April Spring Cottage

was a derelict cottage housing cattle for a number of years - although the sympathetic renovations by its previous owners 8 years ago give no indication of its former use. Situated down a peaceful country lane with no passing traffic, the cottage stands amidst an acre of garden which, although just 5 years old, is already a mass of flowers and herbs in summer. Both guest bedrooms overlook the garden (through which a stream runs), and are cosy and prettily furnished. The food is wholesome and delicious: home-grown vegetables (rabbits permitting) and home-produced eggs are used in cooking and a typical evening meal would feature home-made soup followed by Welsh Lamb with Rosemary and home-made ice-cream. Vegetarians are more than welcome - please let your host know when booking.
Open all year. No smoking in dining room & bedrooms. Vegetarian & diabetic by arrangement. Children: over 8s only. Tea/coffee-making in bedrooms. T.V. in lounge. B. & B. from £15, D. £7.50.

SHREWSBURY

Frankbrook, Yeaton Lane, Baschurch, Shrewsbury SY4 2HZ (0939) 260778
Peaceful country house with interesting garden, set in lovely countryside. Home-grown produce.
Open all year. No smoking. Vegetarian & other diets by arrangement. Children welcome. Tea/coffee-making in all bedrooms. T.V. in lounge and some bedrooms. B. & B. from £12.50. D. £6.50.

The Lion, Wyle Cop, Shrewsbury, SY1 1UY (0743) 353107
Now a Forte Heritage hotel, The Lion dates from the 14th century.
Open all year. No smoking in dining room some bedrooms and lift. Vegetarian and vegan standard. Most other special diets by arrangement. Licensed. Children welcome. Pets by arrangement. En suite, TV & tea/coffee in rooms. Credit cards . B.& B. from £40.

The Old House, Ryton, Dorrington, SY5 7LY (0743) 73585
The Old House is a 17th C. manor house which stands in 2 acres of superb gardens (complete with orchard and lily pond) which are the pride and joy of Susan Paget-Brown. Most of the original timber frame and panelling remains: the oak-panelled dining room, in which breakfast is served, has remained largely unchanged over the centuries and is crammed with antiques, pewter and fine paintings. 6m South of Shropshire.
Open all year. No smoking. Vegetarian and vegan standard. Most other special diets by arrangement. Children welcome. En suite & tea/coffee-making in all bedrooms. T.V. lounge. B. & B. from £17.50, with 10% reduction for 5 nights or more.

TELFORD

The Cottage, Lydbury North, SY7 8AU (05888) 224
Cottage guest house in village. Home-grown vegetables and herbs used in cooking.
Open all year. Vegetarian and most other special diets by arrangement. Children welcome. Pets by arrangement. En suite in 1 room. T.V. in lounge. B. & B. from £13.

Staffordshire

BURTON-ON-TRENT

The Edgecote Hotel, 179 Ashby Rd, Burton on Trent, DE15 0LB (0283) 68966

The Edgecote is an attractive family-run hotel situated on the A50 Leicester road less than 5 minutes from the centre of Burton. All 12 centrally heated bedrooms are clean and comfortable - several have en suite facilities - and each is equipped with a range of helpful amenities such as a radio intercom and colour T.V.; there is a licensed bar and a comfortable lounge. Breakfast at the Edgecote is a real treat (the proprietors believe it to be the best in Burton!): a selection of cereals, yoghurt, fresh fruit and fruit juice is arranged on a self-service buffet, and to follow there is a choice of a traditional cooked breakfast or a lighter Continental option with home-baked rolls and croissants; dinner is served in the oak-panelled dining room and the delicious 3-course meal features imaginative vegetarian options and excellent home-cooked puds - and, at £9 it has got to be one of the best bargains to be found in Burton!

Open all year. No smoking in dining room, bedrooms and corridors. Vegetarian and most other special diets by arrangement. Licensed. Children welcome. Pets by arrangement. En suite in some rooms. Tea/coffee-making & T.V. in all rooms. Access, Visa, Amex. B. & B. from £16.50, D. £9.

ECCLESHALL

Glenwood, Croxton, Eccleshall, ST21 6PF (063082) 238

Originally a 16th C. coaching inn, this timber-framed cottage offers peaceful accommodation in a beautiful rural setting.

Open all year. No smoking in dining room & bedrooms. Vegetarian & other diets by arrangement. Disabled access. Children welcome. Pets by arrangement. Tea/coffee-making in all rooms. T.V. in lounge. B. & B. from £13

LEEK

Choir Cottage & Choir House, Ostlers Lane, Cheddleton, Nr Leek, ST13 7HS (0538) 360561

Choir Cottage is a small 17th C. stone-built cottage and Choir House is just 20 years old and was built on what was originally the cottage herb garden. Some rooms have four-posters.

Open all year ex. Xmas. No smoking. Vegetarian & other diets by arrangement. Children welcome. En suite, tea/coffee & T.V. in rooms. B. & B. from £18.

Pethills Bank Cottage, Bottomhouse, Nr Leek, ST13 7PF (0538) 304277/304555

18th century Derbyshire stone farmhouse. B'fast includes fresh fruits & home-made jam.

Open Mar. to Dec. No smoking in most of house Vegetarian & other diets diets by arrangement. Children: over 5s welcome. En suite, tea/coffee & T.V in all bedrooms. B. & B. from £17.50.

The White House, Grindon, Nr Leek, ST13 7TP (0538) 304250

South-facing 17th C. house with uninterrupted views; stone mullions and oak beams. Breakfast features home-baked bread and preserves and free-range eggs from the village.

Open all year ex. Xmas and New Year. No smoking ex. lounge. Vegetarian & other diets by arrangement. Children: over 10s only. En suite, tea/coffee & T.V. in all bedrooms. B. & B. from £17.

STOKE-ON-TRENT

Hayden House Hotel, Hayden St, Basford, Stoke-on-Trent, ST4 6JD (0782) 711311

Large Victorian house retaining the period charm and features of the original building.

Vegetarian & vegan standard. Diabetic and most other special diets by arrangement. Licensed. Disabled access. Children welcome. En suite, tea/coffee & T. V. in all rooms. B. & B. from £32.

The Hollies, Clay Lake, Endon, Stoke-on-Trent, ST9 9DD (0782) 503252

The Hollies is a lovely Victorian house with a large garden, quietly situated in the village of Endon off the B5051/A53

Open all year. No smoking. Vegetarian and most other special diets by arrangement. Children welcome. Pets by arrangement. En suite some rooms. Tea/coffee in all rooms. T.V. lounge. B. & B. from £14.

WOLVERHAMPTON

Moors Farm and Country Restaurant, Chillington Ln., Codsall, Nr Wolverhampton (09074) 2330

Working livestock farm (traditional methods only!). All food cooked from organically home-grown and wholefood ingredients.

Vegetarian, diabetic & other diets by arrangement. No smoking in part of restaurant. Licensed. Some disabled access. Children welcome. Pets by arrangement. En suite, tea/coffee & T.V. in all rooms.

Warwickshire

HENLEY IN ARDEN

Irelands Farm Bed & Breakfast, Irelands Farm, Irelands Lane, Henley in Arden, B95 5SA (0564) 792476

Irelands Farm is a spacious Georgian farmhouse which stands amidst 220 acres of unspoilt countryside just north of Henley-in-Arden off the A3400 Stratford to Birmingham Road. Your hosts, Pamela and Colin Shaw, offer both bed and breakfast and self-catering holiday accommodation to guests: the delightful self-catering cottages are oak-beamed and stand in a sheltered courtyard setting; they are well-appointed with a range of amenities including microwave cookers, electric blankets, washing machines and gas-fired central heating. Guests staying at the farmhouse enjoy a similarly high standard of accommodation in spacious guest bedrooms with splendid country views - and they are treated to a wholesome and delicious farmhouse breakfast each morning.

Open all year, ex. Xmas & New Year. No smoking in dining room & bedrooms. Vegetarian and other special diets by arrangement. Dogs by arrangement. En suite in some rooms. Tea/coffee making & T.V. in all rooms. B. & B. from £15.

OXHILL

Nolands Farm & Country Restaurant, Oxhill, Warwickshire, CV35 0RJ Tel: (0926) 640309 Fax: (0926) 641662

Nolans Farm is a working arable farm situated in a tranquil valley just off the main A422. Your hosts, Sue and Robin Hutsby, have converted a block of 19th C. stables to provide exceptionally comfortable accommodation for guests: the old timbers and beam of the original building have been preserved, but the interior of each bedroom has been decorated and furnished with care and style - there are four-poster bedrooms, a family room (sleeps 4), double rooms, twins and a single room. Something for everyone - and a self-catering cottage too for those who are able to resist the fabulous farm cuisine: everything is prepared from fresh ingredients and a typical

evening menu would feature warm Spinach and Cheese Tart with Garlic Mayonnaise, followed by Poached Salmon in White Wine and Lemon Juice, and a selection of home-made desserts. There are numerous places to visit within the vicinity of Nolands Farm, such as Stratford-upon-Avon, Warwick and the Cotswolds.

Open 15 Jan. - 15 Dec. No smoking in dining room, sitting room & lounge. Vegetarian by arrangement. Wheelchair access. Children: over 7s welcome. En suite, TV & tea/coffee-making in bedrooms. Credit cards (with surcharge). B. & B. from £15, self-catering £145 p.w., D. from £14.50.

ROYAL LEAMINGTON SPA

Agape, 26 St Mary Rd, Royal Leamington Spa (0926) 882896

Pleasant guest house situated on the southern edge of town & within easy walking distance of its many attractions. Warm, friendly atmosphere. BTA member. Home-made jams for b'fast.

Open all year. No smoking in the house. Vegetarian & other diets by arrangement. Children: over 5s welcome. En suite, TV & tea/coffee-making in bedrooms. B. & B. from £18.50.

The Willis, 11 Eastnor Grove, Royal Leamington Spa, CV31 1LD (0926) 425820

Lovely, spacious Victorian town house with a pretty garden set in a quiet cul-de-sac just a short walk from the centre of Leamington Spa; English or continental breakfast.

Open all year. No smoking. Vegetarian and most other special diets by arrangement. Children welcome. Pets by arrangement. En suite in one room. Tea/coffee-making in all rooms. T.V in some bedrooms. B. & B. from £15.

York House Hotel, 9 York Rd, Royal Leamington Spa, CV31 3PR (0926) 424671
Exquisitely furnished Victorian house retaining many period features; views of the River Leam and the Royal Pump Gardens from the hotel.
Open all year ex. Xmas. No smoking in dining room and bedrooms. Vegetarian & other diets by arrangement. Licensed. Children welcome. Pets by arrangement. En suite most rooms. Tea/coffee & T.V. in all bedrooms. Credit cards. B. & B. from £15.

RUGBY

The School House Guest House, Bourton on Dunsmore, Nr Rugby, CV23 9QY (0926) 632959
Beautifully converted village school. All meals have been home-cooked from fresh ingredients (including free-range eggs), and vegetarians and diabetics can be accommodated by arrangement.
Open Jan. to Dec. No smoking in dining room. Vegetarian & diabetic diets by arrangement. Children by arrangement. En suite in 1 room. Tea/coffee making and T.V. in all rooms. B. & B. from £16-£23. ETB 3 Crown Commended.

SHIPSTON-ON-STOUR

Longdon Manor, Shipston-on-Stour, CV36 4PW (0608) 82235
14th C. manor house with history and records dating from 10th C. Home-grown & organic produce used when possible.
Open Mar. to Nov. No smoking. Vegetarian diets by arrangement. Children welcome. En suite & TV in all rooms. Tea/coffee on request. B. & B. from £30.

STRATFORD UPON AVON

Ashburton Guest House, 27 Evesham Place, Stratford upon Avon. CV37 6HT. Tel: (0789) 292444 Fax: (0789) 415658

Ashburton is a small, friendly guest house in a Victorian terrace which is conveniently situated just 10 minutes' walk from the town centre and Royal Shakespeare Theatre. The new owners of Ashburton, Jeremy Rose and Junko Yamamoto offer traditional Japanese breakfast as an alternative to the traditional English fare. The 6-dish Japanese breakfast is virtually cholesterol-free and would typically consist of Japanese rice, miso soup with vegetables, home-made tofu, spinach and sesame-seed roll, stir-fried Japanese radish and Japanese pickles. Pre-theatre dinners are also available by prior arrangement. Here again the menu is Japanese and, although Japanese cuisine caters for omnivores, many Japanese dishes are naturally vegetarian. Junko has a range of vegetarian dishes on offer and a typical dinner would consist of chawan mushi (steamed savoury custard with chestnuts), tempura (lightly deep-fried vegetables in batter), steamed vegetable rice, and Japanese clear soup followed by fruit and Japanese tea.
Vegetarian and vegan standard. Organic and wholefood ingredients used when available. Open all year ex. Xmas. No smoking in public rooms. Children welcome. En suite showers (but no W.C. en suite). Tea/coffee & T.V in all bedrooms. B. & B. from £16.

Parkfield, 3 Broad Walk, Stratford-upon-Avon, CV37 6HS (0789) 293313

Parkfield is an elegant Victorian house which is quietly situated in the peaceful 'old town' part of Stratford. Bedrooms are all warm, comfortable and centrally heated, and have been equipped with a range of helpful amenities including TV, hot-drink facilities and an easy chair. Your hosts offer a delicious breakfast which includes pancakes and vegetarian sausages in addition to the more traditional English breakfast fare: everything is free-range, home-made and organic wherever possible and unrefined sugar, wholemeal bread and low-fat milk are all available. Travellers by car will be glad to know that they can leave their car safely at Parkfield without having to worry about parking in town: it is just a few minutes' pleasant walk along the river from Parkfield to the Royal Shakespeare Theatre or to the centre of Stratford-upon-Avon.
Open all year. No smoking in the dining room & some bedrooms. Vegetarian & other diets by arrangement. Children welcome. En suite, TV & tea/coffee-making in bedrooms. Credit cards. B. & B. £16-22.

WARWICK

The Croft, Haseley Knob, Warwick, CV35 7NL (0926) 484 447

The Croft is a large family house and smallholding set in the picturesque village of Haseley Knob. It has a large flower and vegetable garden in which guests can relax. A friendly family atmosphere is a very important part of life at the Croft - for business or tourist traveller alike - and there are ample quantities of food, often featuring home-made produce like fresh farm eggs, vegetables and home-made jam and marmalade. There is lots to see and do in the area including visiting Warwick, Kenilworth, Stratford, Coventry and the Birmingham areas (there are many leaflets at The Croft to give you information). The croft is convenient for both Birmingham airport and the NEC.

Open all year. No smoking. Vegetarian and most other special diets by arrangement. Disabled access: 'ground floor bedroom but not suitable for wheelchairs'. Children welcome. Pets by arangement. En suite in some rooms. Tea/coffee & T.V. in all bedrooms. Touring caravan site also available. B. & B. from £16. ETB 3 Crowns Commended, AA Listed and RAC Acclaimed.

The Garden Suite, 44 High St, Warwick, CV34 4AX (0926) 401512

Its owners tell me that while the origins of their lovely old home have been lost in the mists of time, it nevertheless has the dubious distinction of having been one of the first houses to have been burned in the fire of 1694; an event unlikely to be repeated as No. 44 is now a completely smoke-free establishment! It has much else to commend it: overlooking (as its name suggests) a tranquil private garden, it provides a haven of peace for visitors to this historically interesting, active old town. Accommodation is in one of two superbly appointed suites, equipped to the very highest standards, with hairdryer, fridge, a large hot drinks selection, and books and magazines - a home from home! Supper trays and evening meals are available only by prior arrangement.

Open all year. No smoking. Disabled access: '1 ground floor suite of rooms'. Children welcome. En suite, TV & tea/coffee-making in all rooms. B. & B. from £17.50.

Northleigh House, Five Ways Rd, Hatton, Nr Warwick, CV35 7HZ (0926) 484203

This small, country house, set in the quiet of rural Warwickshire, is really rather a special

place: from its beautiful furnishings (all rooms have been individually designed with colour coordinating linen and upholstery) to its glorious setting amidst private gardens and open fields (several rooms have views), Northleigh House is, as its proprietor endeavours to make it, an exceptionally nice small hotel. Service is an important feature of a stay at Northleigh, where nothing seems to be too much trouble to your hostess (a laundry service, a hot water bottle, some shoe-cleaning equipment...just ask and it's there). The food is first-rate - breakfasts are freshly prepared to suit individual requirements and evening meals or supper trays are available on request (although guests might want to sample the many fine restaurants in the area). ETB 3 Crowns Highly Commended.

Open all year ex. Xmas & Jan. No smoking in the house. Vegetarian & some other diets by arrangement. Children welcome. Pets by arrangement. En suite, tea/coffee-making, T.V. & fridge in all rooms. Visa, Mastercard, Eurocard. Single from £28, double from £40.

Willowbrook House B. & B., Lighthorne Rd, Kineton, Nr Warwick, CV35 0JL Tel: (0926) 640475 Fax: (0926) 641747

Very comfortable house & smallholding with sheep, chickens, gardens & paddocks in lovely rolling countryside. Near Warwick, Stratford, Cotswolds, NEC & NAC. Furnished with antiques. *3 miles J12 M40.*

Open all year ex. Xmas. No smoking in the house. Vegetarian & other diets by arrangement. Pets by arrangement. En suite, TV & tea/coffee-making in bedrooms. B. & B. from £14.

West Midlands

COVENTRY
Westwood Cottage, Westwood Heath Road, Westwood Heath, Coventry, CV4 8GN (0203) 471084
One of 4 sandstone cottages built in 1834 and set in rural surroundings; pleasingly renovated and retaining many period features.
Open all year ex. Xmas. No smoking in dining room, bedrooms and lounge. Vegetarian and most other special diets by arrangement. Disabled access. Children welcome. En suite in some rooms. Tea/coffee making in reception. T.V. in lounge. B. & B. from £17.

FILLONGLEY (Nr COVENTRY)
Mill Farmhouse, Mill Lane, Fillongley, Nr Coventry, CV7 8EE (0676) 41898
Peace and tranquillity in country residence in idyllic countryside. Good home-cooking. Private gardens and car park. Exceptionally comfortable bedrooms. Nr NEC Birmingham.
Open all year. No smoking in the house. Vegetarian & other diets by arrangement. En suite, TV & tea/coffee-making in bedrooms. B. & B. £45 apartment (double) or £35 single; £17 single room.

SUTTON COLDFIELD
New Hall, Walmley Road, Sutton Coldfield, B76 8QX (021) 378 2442

New Hall is reputed to be the oldest moated manor house in England and stands in 26 acres of private gardens surrounded by a lily-filled moat. It has been beautifully renovated and is now a most comfortable hotel - but almost all of the original features of the building have been retained (including latticed windows and oak-panelled dining room); furnishings have been chosen to complement the style and imposing presence of the manor, and bedrooms look out over beautiful gardens to wooded arbours and sunlit glades. The food is first-rate: everything has been prepared from the finest fresh ingredients and a typical evening menu would feature a Casserole of Baby Leeks followed by Honey Roast Goose Breast and a selection of extraordinary puddings, such as Iced Blueberry and Mint Parfait.
Open all year. No smoking in dining room. Vegetarian and most other special diets by arrangement. Licensed. Disabled access. Children: over 7s only. En suite, TV & tea/coffee making in bedrooms.

Standbridge Hotel, 138 Birmingham Road, Sutton Coldfield, B72 1LY (021) 354 3007
The Standbridge Hotel is a converted family

house of great character which stands in substantial mature gardens just a short distance from the 2,400 acre Sutton Park yet just one mile from the town centre. The food is excellent: the proprietors received the 1991 Heartbeat Award for their comprehensive selection of healthy food choices, and special diets are catered for competently and sympathetically: the breakfast menu offers a hearty choice of 6 different main courses (English, Texan, Greek, Swedish, Danish or Dutch) and each is prepared from fresh, wholesome ingredients such as free-range eggs, Greek yoghurt, Edam cheese, bananas and honey; wholemeal toast, home-made marmalade and freshly brewed coffee (or tea) complete the meal.
Open all year. No smoking in dining room. Vegetarian & other diets by arrangement. Licensed. Children: over 5s. En suite in most rooms. Tea/coffee making & T.V. in all bedrooms. Access, Visa. B. & B. from £20.

WEST BROMWICH
West Bromwich Moat House Hotel, Birmingham Road, West Bromwich, B70 6RS (021) 5536111
Very comfortable business-class hotel.
Open all year. No smoking in some bedrooms. Vegetarian & other diets by arrangement. Licensed. Disabled access. Children welcome. Pets by arrangement. En suite, tea/coffee making & TV in bedrooms. B. & B. from £43 (w/es).

Worcestershire

BROADWAY

Orchard Grove, Station Rd, Broadway, WR12 7DE (0386) 853834
Modern detached house built of Cotswold stone and traditionally furnished and decorated to a high standard; warm and friendly welcome.
Open all year. No smoking. Vegetarian & other diets by arrangement (b'fast). Children welcome. En suite some rooms. Tea & T.V. in rooms. B. & B. from £17.

Pye Corner Farm, Broadway, WR12 7JP (0386) 853740
Working farm situated on a quiet lane within walking distance of Broadway.
Open May. to Oct. No smoking. Vegetarian & other diets by arrangement. Children welcome. Tea/coffee-making in all rooms. B. & B. from £12.

The Old Rectory, Church St, Willersey, Nr Broadway, WR12 7PN (0386) 853729

Standing in a beautiful, flower-filled walled garden, this splendid 17th C. rectory, built of mellow Cotswold stone, has been lovingly restored by its owners who have been careful to retain all the original period features of the building such as the oak beams and quaint stone-built fireplaces. It has been charmingly decorated and furnished: the bedrooms, with charming four-poster beds, have an individual style and are very romantic (honeymooners are very welcome!); some rooms have views of Bredon and the Welsh hills. Breakfast is the only meal to be served at the Old Rectory, but it is a generous feast and vegetarian or continental options are available for meat-free or lighter appetites. The Old Rectory stands opposite the ancient church (first built in the 11th C.). Willersey, with its picturesque duck pond and quaint cottages, is typical of all that is best in the Cotswolds, and is an ideal centre for touring this lovely area. RAC Guest House of the Year 1992.
Open all year. No smoking in the house ex. smoking lounge. Vegetarian b'fasts by arrangement. Children: over 8s only. En suite, tea/coffee-making & Satellite T.V. in rooms. Access, Visa. B. & B. from £34.50 p.p.

EVESHAM

Evesham Hotel, Cooper's Lane, Off Waterside, Evesham, WR11 6DA (0386) 765566
Standing in 2 acres of lovely gardens, this charming hotel was built in 1540 as a Tudor farmhouse. Indoor-heated pool.
Vegetarian standard and most other special diets by arrangement. Open all year. Licensed. Well behaved children welcome. Pets welcome but not in public rooms. En suite, tea/coffee-making & TV in all rooms. Credit cards. B. & B. from £37.

GREAT MALVERN

Holdfast Cottage Hotel, Welland, Nr Malvern, WR13 6NA (0684) 310288

Holdfast Cottage was originally built in the 17th C., although Victorian extensions have since added to its already considerable charm: guests enter through the plant-filled conservatory into the oak-beamed hall, and the lounge, with its log fire and cosy Victorian-style bar, opens out onto a wisteria covered terrace. Food is of prime importance and the à la carte menu features imaginative dishes prepared from fresh, local produce such as Hot Asparagus and Blue Wensleydale Flan in a wholemeal pastry case or Lambs Kidneys in Cumberland Sauce.
Open all year. No smoking in dining room & bedrooms. Vegetarian standard. Other diets by arrangement. Licensed. Disabled: 'two steps into building'. Children welcome. En suite, TV & tea/coffee all rooms. B. & B. from £34, D. from £14.

The Nupend, Cradley, Nr Malvern, WR13 5NP (0886) 880881
A former farmhouse in 2 acres of grounds just 10 minutes drive from the Malvern Hills; tastefully furnished south-facing bedrooms with views of the Malvern Hills. Good breakfast choices.
Open all year. No smoking in the house. Vegetarian by arrangement. Children: 'discretionary'. Pets: 'discretionary'. En suite, TV & tea/coffee-making in all rooms. B. & B. from £16, D. from £12.50.

Worcestershire   Central England

*Oakwood, Blackheath Way, Malvern,
WR14 4DR (0684) 575508*

Oakwood is one of Malvern's most notable houses: a beautiful, detached Victorian residence standing in 4 acres of grounds on the south-west slopes of the Malvern Hills looking towards Wales (on warm summer evenings guests can enjoy these views while relaxing on the terrace). There are lots of lovely little touches at Oakwood; the house is furnished throughout with antiques - the bedrooms are all prettily decorated and there is a sitting room where letters may be written on house notepaper. The cuisine is of Cordon Bleu standard (although simpler meals can be prepared for those who prefer them) and a typical evening menu would feature Avocado and Citrus Salad, followed by Chicken Breasts stuffed with Stilton and wrapped in bacon, and a dessert such as Apricot Pavlova.
Open all year. No smoking. Vegetarian & other diets by arrangement. Licensed. Children welcome. En suite most rooms. Tea/coffee & T.V in all bedrooms. B. & B. from £16. ETB 3 Crown Highly Commended.

One Eight Four, 184 West Malvern Rd, Malvern, WR14 4AZ (0684) 566544

Beautiful 5-storey Victorian house high on the western side of the Malvern hills; beautifully decorated (lots of stripped pine) and west-facing rooms each have views to the Welsh mountains.
Open all year. No smoking ex. one lounge. Vegetarian b'fasts by arrangement. Licensed. En suite, T.V. & Tea/coffee-making in all rooms. Access, Visa. B. & B. from £18.

The Red Gate, 32 Avenue Rd, Great Malvern, WR14 3BJ (0684) 565013

Family-run hotel with atmosphere of a country home. Home-made food & vegetarian options.
Open all year. No smoking in dining room & bedroom. Vegetarian & other diets by arrangement. Licensed. Children: over 6s only. B. & B. from £22.

Rock House, 144 West Malvern Rd, Malvern, WR14 4NJ (0684) 574536

Charming Victorian guest house quietly situated with wonderful views. Home-cooked food. Suitable for groups or active elderly.11 pretty bedrooms. Stamp for brochure please.
Open Feb. to Nov. No smoking in dining room and bedrooms. Vegetarian diets by arrangement. Licensed. Children welcome. Pets by arrangement. En suite 1 room. Tea/coffee all rooms. T.V. in lounge. B. & B. from £16, D. £10. ETB 1 Crown Commended.

MALVERN WELLS

The Cottage in the Wood Hotel, Holywell Rd, Malvern Wells (0684) 573487

Twice voted the hotel with the best view in England, this charming country hotel is in fact three separate white-painted buildings perched in the Malvern Hills in 7 acres of woods.
Open all year. No smoking in dining room. Vegetarian standard. Licensed. Children welcome. Pets welcome. En suite, tea/coffee-making & T.V in all bedrooms. Credit cards. B. & B. from £44.50.

PERSHORE

Samares Guest House, 11 Cherry Orchard, Charlton, Nr Pershore, WR10 3LD (0386) 860461

Comfortably furnished dormer bungalow.
Open all year. No smoking. Vegetarian and most other special diets by arrangement. Disabled: '2 ground floor bedrooms'. Children: over 10s. Tea/coffee on request. T.V. lounge. B. & B. from £13.50, D. from £8.

TENBURY WELLS

Court Farm, Hanley Childe, Tenbury Wells, WR15 8QY (0885) 410265

15th C. farmhouse. Good home-cooking.
Open Apr. to Oct. No smoking in the house. Vegetarian and most other special diets by arrangement. Children welcome. Tea/coffee-making in all rooms. T.V. in lounge. Moderately priced.

WORCESTER

Ye Olde Talbot Hotel, Friar St, Worcester, WR1 2NA (0905) 23573

A 13th C. coaching inn near to the cathedral with oak-panels, low, beamed ceilings & a high standard of food, accommodation & service.
Open all year. 50% no-smoking dining room & bedrooms. Vegetarian standard. Other diets by arrangement. Licensed. Disabled access. Children welcome. En suite, tea/coffee & T.V. in rooms. B. & B. from £25.

East Anglia

Cambridgeshire

CAMBRIDGE

Arundel House Hotel, 53 Chesterton Road, Cambridge CB4 3AN (0223) 67701

Bon Accord House, 20 St. Margaret's Square, Off Cherry Hinton Road, Cambridge, CB1 4AP (0223) 411188/246568

The Arundel House Hotel is privately owned and has been converted from a fine terrace of Victorian houses - modernisation has, thankfully, impaired neither the interiors nor the facade. Health is taken very seriously at the Arundel where, every year since the start of the scheme, they have won the city's Clean Kitchen Award and for 5 successive years have added the Heartbeat award to their list of accolades. The hotel's reputation for providing some of the finest food in the area at a reasonable cost is matched by a something-for-everyone policy in which guests can choose from an à la carte, table-d' hote, exclusively vegetarian or (for parents) an extensive children's menu. Bar meals are also available. Additionally, it is just a short walk across the river bridge to the city centre with its wide range of quality restaurants.

Vegetarian as standard. Vegan and other special diets by arrangement. Wholefood when available. Open all year ex. Xmas. Smoking only permitted in small part of restaurant. Licensed. Children welcome. En suite in most rooms. Tea/coffee-making, T.V., video, radio, telephone and hairdryer in all bedrooms. Credit cards. B. & B. from £28.50.

Established as a guest house some 12 years ago, the Bon Accord is situated down a quiet cul-de-sac on a good bus route to Cambridge city centre. The Northrops are non-smokers themselves and decided to make the Bon Accord completely smoke-free four years ago - since which time they have found (surprise, surprise!) that their business has not collapsed and they are inundated with visitors in search of a comfortable guest house, good food - and clean air! Only breakfast is served at the Bon Accord - but there is a wide variety of options to choose from and skimmed milk and low-fat margarine are available on request. You are within easy access of Cambridge city centre from the Bon Accord (which has, incidentally, received numerous other acclaims and commendations) and the Northrops can arrange cycle hire for you if you wish.

Open all year ex. Xmas. No smoking in the house. Vegetarian and most other special diets by arrangement. Children welcome. One room en suite. Tea/coffee-making & T.V. in all bedrooms. Visa, Mastercard. B. & B. from £17.50.

Belsar Lodge, 155 Rampton Road, Willingham, Cambridge, CB4 5JF (0954) 60359

Pleasant guest house serving quite excellent cuisine; everything home-made including bread and soups.

Vegetarian, vegan and most other special diets by arrangement. Organic always. Wholefoods when avail. Open all year. Disabled access. Children welcome. Pets by arrangement. Tea/coffee-making & TV in bedrooms. B. & B. from £14.

The Coach House, Scotland Road, Dry Drayton, Cambridge, CB3 8BX (0954) 782439

19th C. converted coach house standing in 2 acres of delightful grounds with a lily pond; 5 miles North of Cambridge.

Open mid March to Christmas. No smoking Vegetarian and most other special diets by arrangement. Disabled access. En suite & tea/coffee-making in bedrooms. T.V. in lounge. B. & B. from £19.

Purlins, 12 High Street, Little Shelford, Cambridge, CB2 5ES (0223) 842643

Purlins is a relatively new house set in two acres of maturing woodland and lawned gardens in the quiet and picturesque village of Little Shelford. Although of recent origin its architecture is, as its brochure suggests, redolent of an English Country Manor and there are many fascinating original features. Accommodation is in exceptionally well-furnished and appointed rooms and, although breakfast is the only meal available at Purlins, it is a generous feast, satisfying most tastes, from English to Continental, from kippers to croissants, and is served in the galleried dining hall. The proprietors have other interests apart from running their small family business, including conservation and the protection of wildlife. (You may have seen them and their house featured on a BBC *QED* programme in March 1990, *A Man who Writes Birdsong*.) Little Shelford is a charming village with a flint church which was mentioned in the Domesday Book; it is just 4 miles south of Cambridge and as such is a perfect base from which to explore the infinite charms of this timeless city, and the many other places of interest near at hand.

Open Feb. to Dec. 18th. No smoking. Vegetarian and most other special diets by arrangement. Disabled access. Children: over 8s only. En suite & colour T.V. in all rooms. Tea/coffee on request. B. & B. from £20.

St. Mark's Vicarage, Barton Road, Cambridge, CB3 9JZ

Victorian vicarage with garden; breakfast only - but wide choices, including 'Victorian breakfast'; short walk into central Cambridge.

Open all year ex. Xmas. No smoking. Vegetarian and most other special diets by arrangement. Children welcome. Tea/coffee-making & T.V. in all bedrooms. B. & B. from £14.

The Willows, 102 High Street, Landbeach, Cambridge CB4 4DT (0223) 860332

The Willows is a beautiful Georgian farmhouse which is pleasantly situated in the small village of Landbeach just off the A10 and just three miles north of the historic city of Cambridge. There are two comfortable guest rooms in which up to six people can be easily accommodated and as your hostess, Mrs Wyatt, welcomes children and can also accommodate some pets by arrangement, The Willows is the ideal family holiday destination. For everyone's added comfort and enjoyment smoking is banned throughout the house.

Open all year ex. Xmas. No smoking throughout the house. Vegetarian by arrangement. Not licensed. Disabled access: 1 ground floor room. Children welcome. Pets by arrangement. Tea/coffee-making. T.V. in all bedrooms. B. & B. from £15.

ELY

Fenlands Lodge Hotel and Restaurant, Soham Road, Stuntney, Ely (0353) 66704

Small luxury hotel converted from a former farm and set in 2 acres of grounds just 2m from Ely.

Vegetarian standard. Other special diets by arrangement. Open all year. No smoking in part of dining room. Licensed. Disabled access. Children welcome. En suite, tea/coffee-making & TV in bedrooms. B. & B. from £27.

Springfields, Ely Road, Little Thetford, Ely, CB6 3HJ (0353) 663637

Springfields is a lovely large home set in an acre of beautiful landscaped gardens and orchard in which guests are invited to wander and sit awhile to enjoy the tranquillity of the setting and (in summer) to smell the roses! The guest accommodation is housed in a separate wing and consists of three pretty double rooms which have each been tastefully furnished and appointed with many delightful touches and everything you could wish to make your stay a happy and memorable one; all rooms have wash hand basins. Breakfast is served in a pleasant dining room in which guests sit around a large table to

enjoy together the delicious, freshly prepared food. Springfields is set in a very quiet location yet is only two miles from historic Ely with its famous cathedral, Oliver Cromwell's house (he lived here from 1637 to 1644) and many other buildings of architectural and historic interest; and of course it is a perfect base from which to explore the changeless beauty of the Fens!
Open all year, ex. Dec. No smoking. Vegetarian by arrangement. En suite available. Tea/coffee-making & T.V. in all rooms. B. & B. from £20.

Warden's House, Lode Lane, Wicken, Ely CB7 5XP (0353) 624165

Home of headwarden of Wicken Fen Nature reserve - so ideal for amateur naturalists. B. & B.
Open all year ex. Xmas. Smoking banned throughout. Vegetarian b'fast standard. Dogs by arrangement. Tea/coffee-making in bedrooms. B. & B. from £10.50.

HUNTINGDON

Mrs Sue Rook, 38 High St, Hemingford Grey, Huntingdon (0480) 301203

38 High Street is a quiet, modern detached house which stands in is own large garden in the peaceful surroundings of the picturesque village of Hemingford Grey, the centre of the Ouse Valley Walk. It is an entirely smoke-free establishment and the proprietors, Gerry and Sue Rook, offer comfortable accommodation to guests. Good home-cooking is prepared from fresh produce (including free range eggs) by Sue, and the fruit and vegetables have all been organically grown at home or locally; vegetarians, vegans and diabetics can be accommodated by arrangement. You are within easy reach of a number of interesting places at Hemingford Grey including Cambridge (20 minutes' drive), St Ives, the Fens, Huntingdon and National Trust properties such as Wimpole Hall, Anglesey Abbey and Wicken Fen.
Open Jan - Nov. No smoking in the house. Vegetarian & other diets by arrangement. Bring your own wine. Children: over 10s only. Tea/coffee-making in bedroom. TV lounge. B. & B. £16. D. £10. **ETB 1 Crown Approved.**

PETERBOROUGH

Chesterton Priory, Priory Gardens, Chesterton, Peterborough, PE7 3UB (0733) 230085

Victorian gothic former rectory in 2 acres.
Open 2 Jan. to 24 Dec. No smoking in dining room and 3 bedrooms. Any special diets by arrangement. Licensed. Children: over 10s only. En suite, tea/coffee & T.V. in all bedrooms. B. & B. from £25.

Stoneacre, Elton Rd, Wansford, Peterborough (0780) 783283

Charming modern house in a secluded spot with views across the Nene Valley. Half a mile A1.
Open all year. No smoking in dining room and bedrooms. Vegetarian and most other special diets by arrangement. Good disabled access: 4 ground floor rooms. B. & B. from £13.

Swallow Hotel, Peterborough Business Park, Lynch Wood, Peterborough, PE2 6GB Tel: (0733) 371111 Fax: (0733) 236725

The Swallow Hotel is a luxuriously appointed 163-bedroom business class hotel conveniently situated just 2 minutes from the A1 and within easy reach of Peterborough city centre.

Accommodation is in luxuriously appointed en suite bedrooms, with a range of excellent amenities including remote control Colour TV, two direct dial phones and a refrigerator and mini-bar. Fully air-conditioned, the hotel's two restaurants are designed around a Romanesque theme and offer guests a comprehensive choice including a Carvery, cold buffet and charcoal grill. The Swallow Leisure Club is free to resident guests and features an indoor heated pool, sauna, steam room, gym and sunbed; massage and beauty treatments are available by trained therapists. There are excellent conference facilities for up to 300 delegates and a courtesy mini-bus is available from Peterborough station.
Open all year. 50% no-smoking dining room/pub/bar area, and 55% of bedrooms. Vegetarian, vegan and diabetic diets catered for, most other special diets by arrangement. Licensed. Disabled access. Children welcome. Dogs allowed in bedrooms. En suite, tea/coffee-making & T.V. in all bedrooms. Credit cards. B. & B. from £42 p.p. sharing twin room.

Essex

CASTLE HEDINGHAM
The Pottery, St James Street, Castle Hedingham, CO9 3EW (0787) 60036
Comfortable Georgian house 5 mins from castle in mediaeval village of Castle Hedingham.
Open all year ex. Xmas. No smoking. Vegetarian and most other special diets by arrangement. Children: over 12s only. Tea/coffee-making in all bedrooms. B & B from £16.50.

CHELMSFORD
Boswell House Hotel, 118 Springfield Road, Chelmsford, CM2 6LF (0245) 287587
Beautifully converted 19th C. town house now a charming small hotel; fresh food.
Open all year ex. Xmas. No smoking in dining room, sitting room & 9 bedrooms. Vegetarian & other special diets by arrangement. Licensed. Disabled access: ground floor bedrooms and just one step at the hotel entrance. Children welcome. En suite, tea/coffee-making & T.V. in all bedrooms. Credit cards. B & B from £28, £38 single.

COLCHESTER
Gill Nicholson, 14 Roman Road, Colchester, CO1 1UR (0206) 577905
14 Roman Road is a spacious Victorian town house situated in a quiet square near the centre of Colchester with easy access to both the bus and railway station. In fact those who choose to bring cars can park them and forget about driving during their visit, as all the places of interest - the castle, the museums, shops and sports facilities - are within easy walking distance of the house. A full, home-cooked English breakfast is served by Gill which features a number of home-made items - including the bread, jam and lemon curd - and some healthy, vegetarian and low-cholesterol options, such as muesli, prunes and low-fat yoghurt; the nearby Foresters Arms serves excellent home-cooked lunches and evening meals. Whether visiting Colchester on business - or just taking a holiday break in this beautiful part of Eastern England - the comfortable family atmosphere at 14 Roman Road will make your stay a special and memorable one.
Open all year ex. Xmas week. No smoking. Vegetarian and other special diets by arrangement. Children by arrangment. One room en suite. Tea/coffee-making & TV in bedrooms. B & B from £30 (double).

FORDHAM
Kings Vineyard, Fossetts Lane, Fordham, Nr Colchester, CO6 3NY (0206) 240377
Lovely large detached house, situated on a southfacing slope amongst gentle rolling countryside close to the Essex/Suffolk border.
Open all year. No smoking. Vegetarian standard. Children welcome. Private bathroom available. Tea/coffee-making & T.V. Amex. B. & B. from £16.

SOUTHEND-ON-SEA
Strand Guest House, 165 Eastern Esplanade, Southend-on-Sea, SS1 2YB (0702) 586611
Small, family-run guest house on the Thorpe Bay sea front. Healthy breakfast options.
Open April to Nov. Smoking banned in dining room and in one bedroom. Vegetarian by arrangement. Children welcome. Most rooms en suite. Free coffee in lounge. T.V. in all bedrooms. B. & B. from £16.

THAXTED
Piggot's Mill, Watling Lane, Thaxted, CM6 2QY (0371) 830379
A range of traditional Essex barns, retaining many original features, now a farmhouse standing in a secluded yet central position in mediaeval village of Thaxted; lovely garden; very good breakfast.
Open all year. No smoking in dining room & bedrooms. Vegetarian and most other special diets by arrangement. Children: over 12s only. En suite, tea/coffee-making & TV in all bedrooms. B. & B. from £19.50.

Norfolk

BLAKENEY

Flintstones Guest House, Wiveton, Blakeney, NR25 7TL (0263) 740337

Flintstones Guest House is a charming single storey residence set in picturesque surroundings near to the village green in the quiet village of Wiveton one mile from the sea at Cley and Blakeney. It has been beautifully furnished throughout - the bedrooms have each been very comfortably appointed - and a friendly and relaxed atmosphere prevails. Food is of the good old-fashioned British variety and is served in good old-fashioned quantities, too: a typical evening meal would feature fresh grapefruit followed by Roast Chicken with all the trimmings and a home-made dessert such as Sherry Trifle; tea and coffee would complete the meal. The area is perfect for walkers and birdwatchers: the heathland at Salthouse and Kelling offers stunning scenery, while the North Norfolk Coastal Path passes nearby.

Open all year. No smoking. Vegetarian and some special diets by arrangement. Licensed. Children welcome. Pets by arrangement. En suite, TV & tea/coffee-making in all rooms. B. & B. from £15.

CASTLE ACRE

The Old Red Lion, Bailey Street, Castle Acre, PE32 2AG (0760) 755557

Unusual brick & flintstone building with private rooms or dormitories. Wholefood & vegetarian meals or self-catering. Courses offered; a retreat for artists, writers or 'seekers after solace.'

Open all year. No smoking. Vegetarian, diabetic, gluten-free, yeast-free, dairy-free & other diets by arrangement. Licensed (restaurant) and bring your own wine. Children welcome. Pets by arrangement.

CROMER

Birch House, 34 Cabbell Rd, Cromer, NR27 9HX (0263) 512521

Birch House is a warm, friendly guest house, close to all the amenities of Cromer. It has been tastefully furnished throughout - everything is scrupulously clean - and there is a residents' lounge with a Satellite T.V. There is a traditional British breakfast menu including oak-smoked kippers and haddock. Cromer is,. as its residents point out, 'bright but breezy', but its fine sandy beaches are still very beautiful and Birch House is situated just a short walk from the pier.

Open all year. No smoking. Children welcome. Pets by arrangement. Some en suite. Tea/coffee. B. & B. from £15.

Morden House, 20 Cliff Ave., Cromer, NR27 0AN (0263) 513396

Morden House is a beautiful detached late Victorian residence, full of character and peacefully situated in a quiet avenue in Cromer just a few minutes walk from the beach and the town centre. Furnished and decorated sympathetically throughout, the house retains the style and charm of its original period - the hall has a polished oak floor and open fireplace and the bedrooms are all airy, spacious and comfortable - yet the house has the feel of a real home, and service is friendly and efficient. The food is excellent: everything has been prepared on the premises from fresh, local produce and a typical evening meal would feature (after a complimentary sherry served in the lounge) Tomato and Avocado Salad with Vinaigrette, followed by Chicken cooked in Red Wine with Mushrooms (and a selection of fresh vegetables), and a dessert, such as Apple Brown Betty.

Most special diets catered for. Open all year. No smoking in dining room & lounge. Licensed. Children welcome. En suite in some rooms. Tea/coffee making & radio alarms in all bedrooms. T.V. in lounge. B. & B. from £18.50. D. £11.50.

DEREHAM

Travellers Cottage, Horningtoft, Dereham, (0328) 700205

Travellers Cottage is situated in the quiet hamlet of Horningtoft and was built in 1848 as two farmworkers cottages. Delicious vegetarian meals are served in the cottage style kitchen with its wood-burning stove; everything is home-made including the bread, rolls & yoghurt; home-grown fruit & vegetables are served in season (including fresh strawberries at breakfast); evening meals are available a few evenings a week and on other occasions there are good meat-free meals to be had at nearby restaurants; tea, coffee and home-made cakes and biscuits are available throughout the day.

Vegetarian standard, other special diets by arrangement. Wholefood always. Organic when available. Open April to Oct. Children welcome. B. & B. from £11. D. £7.

DISS

The Old Rectory, Gissing, Diss, IP22 3XB (037 977) 575

The Old Rectory is a large, spacious Victorian house standing amidst 3 acres of garden and woodland in the peaceful hamlet of Gissing; the village has an abundance of mature trees from the time when it formed part of a private estate and the church has an unusual round tower and double hammer beam roof. The guest bedrooms at the Old Rectory are large and beautifully appointed: each has en suite or private facilities and fresh flowers, hairdryers and notepaper in addition to the usual amenities; the elegant drawing and dining room each have welcoming open fires. A delicious 4-course evening meal, or lighter option, is available by prior arrangement, and packed lunches can be prepared on request; breakfast, which is often served in the conservatory, offers an extensive menu choice. There is much to enjoy - guests may play croquet on the lawns, swim in the indoor heated pool, or relax on the terrace - while those venturing a little further afield will find much to enjoy nearby including the part-Tudor town of Diss, Bressingham Gardens, Thetford Forest and the quiet unspoilt coast-line at Southwold and Walberswick.

Open all year. No smoking in dining room, bedrooms and most public areas. Vegetarian & low-fat diets by arrangement. En suite, tea/coffee-making & T.V. in all rooms. B. & B. from £23.

Swan House Country Crafts and Tea Room, Swan House, Hopton Rd, Garboldisham, Nr Diss, Norfolk, IP22 2PQ Tel: (095381) 8221

Attractive 17th C. former coaching inn with original character including beams & inglenooks. Comfortable bedrooms. The tea room has quality crafts, paintings & antiques. All the bread, rolls & cakes are home-baked; a log fire blazes in the grate in cooler weather

Open all year ex. Xmas & Jan. No smoking. Vegetarian by arrangement. Wheelchair access to teashop. Children welcome in tea shop only. T.V. in bedrooms. Diners card. B. & B. from £15.

Strenneth Farmhouse, Old Airfield Rd, Fersfield, Diss (0379) 888182

This beautiful red brick 16th/17th C. former farmhouse stands in a lovely lawned garden close to the market town of Diss; it has been renovated to a very high standard indeed while retaining the period features of the building - oak beams, casement windows, open fires, window seats - and the bedrooms are decorated and furnished with taste and style (one has a four-poster and the rooms in the newer East wing are all on the ground floor); there is an especially attractive residents' lounge which has been furnished with period and reproduction furniture to harmonise with the beamed ceilings and walls. The food is very good; special diets are treated sympathetically and there is a high proportion of home-baking. Diss is a charming town & central to East Anglia's attractions.

Open all year. No smoking in part of dining room & 1 lounge. Vegetarian & other diets by arrangement. Licensed. Children welcome. Pets by arrangement. En suite most rooms. Tea/coffee in all rooms. T.V. lounge. Credit cards. B. & B. from £20. D. £12.50.

DOWNHAM MARKET

The Dial House, Railway Rd, Downham Market, PE38 9EB (0366) 388358

Large, local 'Carr Stone' Georgian House; lots of health foods at breakfast.

Open all year. No smoking in bedrooms & most public areas. Vegetarian, coeliac, vegan, low-fat, low-sugar, diabetic or any other special diet by arrangement. Children welcome. En suite. Tea/coffee & T.V.

FAKENHAM

Manor Farmhouse, Stibbard Rd, Fulmodestone, Nr Fakenham, NR21 0LX (032 878) 353

Lovely white-painted Georgian farmhouse with beautiful lawned gardens; lots of home-prepared food (including icecream) from fresh or home-produce, including lamb, free-range eggs

and poultry. ETB 1 Crown Commended.
Open all year. No smoking. Vegetarian & other diets by arrangement. Access, Visa. B. & B. from £17.

FELMINGHAM
Felmingham Hall Country House Hotel, Felmingham, NR28 OLP (0692) 69631
16th C. mansion which has been sumptuously furnished and appointed; 17th C. candlelit dining room; French & British cuisine prepared from fresh, often home-grown, produce.
Open all year. No smoking in dining room & bedrooms. Vegetarian & other diets by arrangement. Licensed. Children: over 12s only. En suite, tea/coffee-making & T.V. in rooms. B. & B. from £35.

HOLT
The Blakeney Hotel, Blakeney, Nr Holt, NR25 7NE (0263) 740797
Hotel overlooking the beautiful National Trust Harbour of Blakeney. All food is home-cooked from fresh ingredients. There is a heated indoor pool, snooker, a games room, also a spa bath, sauna, mini gym and a hair salon.
Vegetarian standard. Vegan, diabetic and some other special diets by arrangement. Open all year. Licensed. Disabled access. Children welcome. En suite, TV & tea/coffee making in all rooms.

HUNSTANTON
Salacia Lodge, 56 Greevegate, Hunstanton, PE36 6AE (0485) 533702
Salacia Lodge is a warm, friendly well-established guest house which offers superb, well-appointed accommodation and an excellent breakfast. You are conveniently situated close to several sports and recreational facilities, and additionally you are just a few minutes' walk from the town centre, theatre and sea front; there are a number of good eating places in the town. Hunstanton is a perfect centre for walkers and birdwatchers.
No smoking. Vegetarian and other special diets by arrangement. En suite in all rooms. B. & B. from £15.

KINGS LYNN
Congham Hall Country House Hotel and Restaurant, Grimston, Kings Lynn, PE32 1AH (0485) 600250
Elegant Georgian manor in 40 acres of parkland; swimming pool, tennis court and stabling.
Open all year. No smoking in dining room. Special diets by arrangement. Licensed. Some disabled access. Children: over 12s only. En suite & T.V. in all rooms. Credit cards. B. & B. from £70.

Corfield House, Sporle, Nr Swaffham, Kings Lynn, PE32 2EA (0760) 23636
Lovely period detached house which has been beautifully furnished and maintained.
Open Easter-Dec. No smoking. Vegetarian & diabetic by arrangement. Licensed. Some disabled access. Children welcome. Pets by arrangement. En suite & T.V. in rooms. Credit cards. B. & B. from £18.50.

The Tudor Rose, St Nicholas St, Kings Lynn, PE30 1LR (0553) 762824
15th C. beamed and timbered inn - the only owner-run and fully licensed inn in Kings Lynn; excellent food prepared from fresh local ingredients; very good vegetarian options.
Open all year. No smoking in dining room. Vegetarian standard. Other special diets by arrangement. Licensed. Children welcome. Pets by arrangement. En suite, tea/coffee, T.V. & D.D. phones in all rooms. Credit cards. B. & B. from £36.

MORSTON HOLT
Morston Hall, Morston Holt, NR25 7AA (0263) 741041
Acclaimed hotel offering first-rate food and accommodation.
Open all year. No smoking in dining room & some bedrooms. Vegetarian & other diets by arrangement. Licensed. Some disabled access. Children: over 8s. En suite most rooms. Credit cards. B. & B. from £40.

NEATISHEAD
Regency Guest House, Neatishead, Nr Norwich, NR12 8AD (0692) 630233
Lovely 18th C. house in the unspoilt village of Neatishead on the Norfolk Broads; beautifully furnished rooms (all decorated with Laura Ashley fabrics & wallcoverings). Exceptionally generous breakfasts; good vegetarian options.
Open all year. No smoking in dining room & all public areas. Vegetarian and other special diets by arrangement. Children welcome. Pets by arrangement. Some rooms en suite. Tea/coffee & T.V. in all rooms. B. & B. from £16.50.

NORTH WALSHAM
Toll Barn, Norwich Rd, North Walsham, NR28 0JB (0692) 403063
Toll Barn lies one mile South of North Walsham amidst beautiful wooded countryside. The house was created within the shell of an 18th C. barn - the cosy en suite lodges form a courtyard around a delightful garden - and although it has retained all the charm and atmosphere of a 200 year-old building, it has also been equipped with every modern amenity and luxury you could wish for,

and provides a peaceful refuge away from the stresses and strains of 20th C. life. A traditional farmhouse breakfast is served in the exposed brick and beamed dining room (a lighter continental meal may be served in your room if you so wish), and there are several good eating places nearby for your evening meal. North Walsham was built on an original Danish settlement - and was also the site of the Peasants' Uprising in 1381; in spite of its troubled history it is a place of great tranquillity and is also the most central location for visiting all of Norfolk's attractions. Light suppers from £5.
Open all year. No smoking. Vegetarian by arrangement. Wheelchair access 'possible'. Children: over 5s welcome. Pets welcome. En suite. Tea/coffee & T.V. in all bedrooms. B. & B. from £18.

NORWICH

The Almond Tree Hotel and Restaurant, 441 Dereham Rd, Costessey, Norwich, NR5 OSG (0603) 748798/749114
Very comfortably appointed small hotel on the main A47 Dereham Road; excellent meals prepared from fresh, local produce.
Open all year. No smoking in dining room. Vegetarian, diabetic & other diets by arrangement. Licensed (restaurant). Some disabled access. En suite, TV & tea/coffee in all rooms. B. & B. from £41.75.

The Beeches Hotel, 4-6 Earlham Rd, Norwich, NR2 3DB (0603) 621167
The Beeches Hotel began life as private

mansions in the 19th C. for successful Norwich businessmen; Henry Trevor, one such resident, devoted some 15 years to creating an idyllic Italianate garden in his grounds. Sadly the houses and gardens were neglected until 1980 when they were rediscovered, beautifully renovated and revived, and now they stand surrounded by 3 acres of tranquil wooded gardens just 10 minutes stroll from the centre of Norwich. The houses - known collectively as the Beeches Hotel - provide a luxurious and unique holiday or business destination: accommodation is in prettily furnished bedrooms and the bistro-style dining room which overlooks the garden is a pleasant airy room in which excellent home-cooked meals are served to guests.
Open all year. No smoking in dining room & 50% of bedrooms. Vegetarian by arrangement. Licensed. Disabled access. Children welcome. En suite, tea/coffee making & T.V., radio & telephones in all bedrooms. Access, Visa. B. & B. from £37.

Grey Gables Country House Hotel and Restaurant, Norwich Rd, Cawston, Norwich, NR10 4EY (0603) 871259
Formerly Brandiston Rectory, this beautiful house offers very comfortable accommodation and fine food prepared from fresh ingredients and served by candlelight. Wine list includes some 200 items.
Open all year. No smoking in dining room. Vegetarian choice available. Most other special diets by arrangement. Licensed. Some disabled access. Children: over 5s only. En suite in most rooms. Tea/coffee-making, T.V. & telephone in all rooms. Access, Visa. B. & B. from £23. 2 day breaks: D., B. & B. from £64 pp.

Pine Trees, Holly Lane, Blofield, Norwich, NR13 4BV (0603) 713778
Large, modern country house peacefully situated in a quiet rural area one mile from Blofield Village and the by-pass. Accommodation for 2 to 6 in ground-floor suite with private bathroom and entrance. Healthy breakfast options.
Open all year. No smoking. Vegetarian & vegan standard. Other special diets by arrangement. Some disabled access. Children welcome. T.V. in lounge. B. & B. from £12-£16.

SLOLEY

Cubitt Cottage, Low St, Sloley, Nr Norwich, NR12 8HD (069) 269295

Cubitt Cottage is a delightful little 18th C. building set in an acre of pretty gardens in which (Mrs. Foulkes tells me) there are nearly 100 varieties of old-fashioned rose; the summer scent is intoxicating and a terrace leads out from the oak-beamed dining room where, weather permitting, breakfast is served to guests. As well as being a rose-grower, Mrs Foulkes also

cultivates (organically) a wide variety of vegetables and this produce is used in the preparation of her excellent evening meals in which a typical menu would feature Courgette and Spinach Soup (served with wholemeal rolls) followed by Vegetable Lasagne (with fresh, seasonal vegetables) and Wild Blackberry and Apple Crumble (with home-made yoghurt). The countryside is beautiful around Cubitt Cottage and *flat* - which is good news for cyclists and puffless runners and ramblers; there are two bikes for hire.
Open all year. No smoking throughout. Vegetarian, vegan, diabetic, gluten-free and other special diets on request. Children welcome. Tea/coffee-making in all rooms. T.V. in lounge. B. & B. from £18.50. D. £10.

THETFORD

Ivy Cottages, Blackmoor Row, Shipdham, Thetford, IP25 7PU (0362) 820665
Ivy Cottages are two beautiful 16th C. Norfolk cottages which have been sympathetically restored in order to retain their original features such as oak beams, pamment tiles and pantiled roofs; they stand in an acre of pretty gardens in a peaceful little road near the thriving village of Shipdham. One cottage is available to let for self-caterers and has been equipped with every modern convenience including a dishwasher, washing machine, tumbledryer and fridge-freezer! The second cottage is for the lazier amongst us who would like to be served - rather than to have to cook - a full English Breakfast; it does not have the self-catering amenities of the other cottage but has been very prettily furnished and a generous breakfast of free-range eggs and locally produced bacon is served daily. Just to make the choice even more difficult, guests staying in the self-catering cottage may elect to have an evening meal and a delivery of fresh organic vegetables!
Vegetarian and other special diets by arrangement. Open all year. Children welcome. Pets by arrangement. Tea/coffee-making in all rooms. T.V. in some rooms and lounge. B. & B. from £13.50.

WALSINGHAM

The Old Rectory, Waterden, Walsingham, NR22 6AT (0328) 823298
Beautiful Victorian rectory on the Holkham Estate in peaceful rural surroundings; beautifully furnished with antiques.
Open all year. No smoking ex. 1 bedroom. Vegetarian and other special diets by arrangement. Disabled access. Children welcome. Pets by arrangement. En suite & tea/coffee-making in all rooms. T.V. in one room. B. & B. from £16.

WALTON HIGHWAY

Stratton Farm, West Drove North, Walton Highway, West Norfolk, PE14 7DP (0945) 880162
Ranch-style bungalow set amidst 22 acres of grassland which supports a prize-winning herd of Short-horn cattle. Breakfast features home produced sausages, home-cured bacon, free-range eggs, home-made marmalade, and goat's milk if required. There is free fishing in the farm's carp lake and use of the heated swimming pool; additionally there is a fitness gym and facilities for horse-riding & golf nearby.
Open all year. No smoking. Vegetarian and diabetic by arrangement. Disabled access. Children: over 5s only. En suite, TV & tea/coffee making in all rooms. B. & B. from £18.

WORSTEAD

Geoffrey the Dyer House, Church Plain, Worstead, North Walsham, NR28 9AL (0692) 536562
Geoffrey the Dyer House stands across the

village square from Worstead's famous church which was built in the 13th C. by Flemish weavers. The beams and stays that hold up the house's lofty ceilings once supported the looms that made the famous Worstead cloth; careful restoration of this 17th C. listed building has preserved its unique character while creating a comfortable (and centrally heated) home of great charm: all the guest bedrooms have en suite facilities but the oak beams are intact and it is still possible to warm yourself in front of the inglenook fireplace on cooler evenings. Worstead is a conservation village in which the most dominant feature is its famous church; the village and the surrounding area have a beautiful, unspoilt quality despite the fact that Norfolk's most popular amenities and attractions are so near at hand (Norwich 12 miles, the coast 8 miles and the Broads 2 miles). Worstead station 1 mile.
Open all year. No smoking. Vegetarian and other special diets on request. Children welcome. Pets by arrangement. En suite, tea/coffee-making & T.V. in all rooms. B. & B. from £16. D. from £8.50.

Suffolk

ALDEBURGH

Uplands Hotel, Victoria Rd, Aldeburgh, Suffolk, IP15 5DX (0728) 452420

The Uplands Hotel is a family-run hotel and was formerly the home of Elizabeth Garrett Anderson, the first woman doctor and lady mayor of Aldeburgh. The hotel consists of 20 bedrooms, 12 in the main building and 8 in ground-floor rooms overlooking the gardens. The gardens recently won an Ashley Courtenay award and are filled with trees, shrubs, a herb garden, a rockery and pond area, and a 300 year old mulberry tree - all lovingly tended by the proprietors themselves. Breakfast and dinner are served in the restaurant overlooking the garden; the menu changes daily and all food is freshly prepared and cooked using many local specialities. Vegetarian and specail diets are catered for and special requests satisfied wherever possibe; the hotel is licensed and drinks may be enjoyed in the bar or by the log fire in one of the lounges.
Open all year ex. Xmas & New Year. No smoking in dining room & bedrooms. Vegetarian standard. Other diets by arrangement. Licensed. En suite, TV & tea/coffee i n rooms. Credit cards. B. & B. around £27.

BURY ST EDMUNDS

The Angel Hotel, Bury St Edmunds (0284) 753926

The Angel Hotel has 2 restaurants, one in the 12th C. undercroft, and one overlooking the square and Abbeygateway. Recommended by Mr Pickwick!
Open all year. No smoking in main dining room and some bedrooms. Vegetarian & other special diets by arrangement. Licensed. Children welcome. Pets by arrangement. En suite in all rooms. Credit cards B. & B. from £65.

Coney Weston Hall, Coney Weston, Nr Bury St Edmunds (035921) 441

Family owned & run country house.
Open Feb. to Dec. No smoking in dining room and bedrooms. Vegetarian standard. Other diets by arrangement. Licensed. Children welcome. En suite. Tea/coffee on request. T.V. lounge. B. & B. from £26.

Hamilton House, 4 Nelson Rd, Bury St Edmunds, IP33 3AG (0284) 702201

Elegant Edwardian villa situated in a quiet cul de sac offering accommodation of a very high standard. Home-made bread at breakfast. Italian, French and Spanish spoken.
Open all year. No smoking in the house. Vegetarian and most other special diets by arrangement. Children welcome. En suite in 2 rooms. Tea/coffee & TV in all bedrooms. Credit cards. B. & B. from £17.

CAVENDISH

Western House, High St, Cavendish, CO10 3AR (0787) 280550

Bed and breakfast establishment.
Open all year. Vegetarian standard. Most other special diets by arrangement. Children welcome. Tea/coffee in all bedrooms. B & B from £13.50.

FRAMLINGHAM

Shimmens Pightle, Dennington Rd, Framlingham, IP13 9JT (0728) 724036

B. & B. set in an acre of landscaped garden; convenient for countryside and coast.
Open all year ex. Xmas. No smoking. Vegetarian & other diets by arrangement. Disabled access. Children: over 8s only. Tea/coffee. T.V. lounge. B. & B. from £15.50. E.T.B Crown Commended.

HADLEIGH

Ash Street Farm, Ash Street, Semer, Nr Hadleigh, IP7 6QZ (0449) 741493

Approached down a single track country lane, this fine early 15th C. farmhouse stands in a Domesday-recorded hamlet in pretty countryside in the Brett Valley. All the rooms are tastefully decorated and have lovely views overlooking unspoilt water meadows. The food at Ash Street Farm is first-rate: everything has

been home-prepared from fresh produce including the home-made preserves and wholemeal bread; eggs are fresh from the farm hens and the proprietors say that "most eccentricities are catered for!". There is much to see and do in this part of the world: the gentle landscape is perfect for cycling and there are numerous mediaeval towns, houses and churches to visit nearby.
Open all year. No smoking in dining room & bedrooms. Vegetarian & other diets by arrangement. Children welcome. Pets by arrangement. En suite in one room. Tea/coffee-making in all bedrooms. T.V. lounge. B. & B. from £14. D. £8.50.

HALESWORTH
Broad Oak Farm, Bramfield, Nr Halesworth (098684) 232
Lovely farmhouse offering bed and breakfast, near the Heritage Coast. 6m. from Southwold.
Open all year. No smoking in dining room. Vegetarian and most other special diets by arrangement. Children welcome. Pets by arrangement. One room en suite. Tea/coffee-making. T.V. B. & B. from £13.

IPSWICH
Hill Farm House, Bury Rd, Hitcham, Ipswich. IP7 7PT (0449) 740657
18th C. farmhouse and adjoining 15th C. cottage set in large grounds overlooking the gently rolling countryside of South Suffolk.
Open March - end Oct. Vegetarian and most other special diets by arrangement. Children welcome. Pets by arrangement. En suite, TV & tea/coffee-making in all bedrooms. B. & B. from £12. D. £8.50.

Pipps Ford, Norwich Rd, Needham Market, Ipswich IP6 8LJ (044979) 208

Pipps Ford is a beautiful, half-timbered 16th C. farmhouse which was built on the site of a Stone-age battleground on a beautiful stretch of the River Gipping amidst several acres of rambling garden surrounded by farmland. Peace and rest are the key ingredients at Pipps Ford - together with the exceptionally nourishing food: only organic and wholefood ingredients are used in cooking - including the herbs - and the extensive breakfast menu includes waffles, cinnamon toast, crumpets and croissants as well as goose egg omelettes, additive-free bacon and sausages . . . the list is apparently endless; evening meals (which are available by arrangement) are similarly imaginative, and vegetarians can be accommodated by arrangement. Bedrooms have been decorated with style and flair (there is a 4-poster, a French Provincial and a Victorian brass bed), and there is also a cottage in the grounds which has been converted to accommodate four further guests.
Open mid-Jan. to mid-Dec. No smoking in dining room & bedrooms. Vegetarian and most other special diets by arrangement. Licensed. Disabled access. Children: over 5s only. En suite & tea/coffee-making in all bedrooms. T.V. in lounge. B. & B. from £26.

Redhouse, Levington, Ipswich, OP10 0LZ (0473) 659670
Early Victorian farmhouse standing in 3 acres of gardens, fields and trees with lovely views over the river estuaries.
Open Mar. to Nov. No smoking in part of dining room & bedrooms. Vegetarian by arrangement. Children welcome. Tea/coffee-making in bedrooms. B. & B. from £13.

LAVENHAM
The Swan, Forte Heritage, High St, Lavenham (0787) 247477
Splendid 14th C. inn still renowned for its hospitality. Excellent food..
Open all year. No smoking in dining room & some bedrooms. Vegetarian standard. Other diets by arrangement. Licensed. Disabled access. Children welcome. Pets by arrangement. En suite, tea/coffee-making & T.V. in all bedrooms.

SUDBURY
Bulmer Tye House, Nr Sudbury, CO10 7ED (0787) 269315
Historic and characterful house in beautiful gardens. Evening meals by arrangement.
Open all year. No smoking. D. by arrangement. Vegetarian and most other special diets catered for. Children welcome. B. & B. from £15.

Holly Cottage, 3 Borley Rd, Long Melford, Sudbury, CO10 9HH (0787) 79848
Lovely old beamed cottage and a large garden.
Open all year. Smoking only with agreement of all other guests; banned in bedrooms. Vegetarian & other diets by arrangement. Disabled: 4 steps into house, ground floor room. Children welcome. Tea/coffee on request. T.V. in rooms.

WOODBRIDGE

Church Cottage, Saxtead (0728) 724067

17th century family cottage with low ceilings, beams and winding staircase.

Open Easter - Nov. Non smoking house in practice though not banned. Exclusively vegetarian and vegan, most special diets by arrangement. Children welcome. Pets by arrangement. Tea/coffee-making facilities. T.V. in family sitting room. B. & B. from £12. D. £6-£8.

Old School, Saxtead, Woodbridge, IP13 9QP (0728) 723887

Pleasantly renovated - but not over-heated or over-fussy - school house offering excellent vegetarian and vegan cuisine prepared from home-grown produce and wholefood ingredients.

Open all year. No smoking in the house. Exclusively vegetarian. Vegan standard. Most other special diets by arrangement. Children welcome. Pets by arrangement. En suite in two rooms. Tea/coffee-making facilities. B. & B. from £10. D. £6.

Priory Cottage, Low Corner, Butley, Nr Woodbridge, IP12 3QD (0394450) 382

Surrounded by woods, fields and rivers, Priory Cottage is pleasantly situated near to the Suffolk Coast Path which follows the beautiful Heritage Coast.

Open all year ex. Xmas/Boxing Day. No smoking in the house. Vegetarian and most other special diets by arrangement. Children: over 5s only. Pets by arrangement. T.V. lounge. B. & B. from £14. D. £12.50.

East Midlands

Derbyshire

ALKMONTON
Dairy House Farm, Alkmonton, Longford, Derby, DE6 3DG (0335) 330359
Picturesque farmhouse on 82 acre working dairy farm in Peak District. Home-produced food.
Open all year. No smoking. Vegetarian & other diets by arrangement. Licensed. Children: over 5s welcome. En suite 3 rooms. Tea/coffee. T.V. lounge. B. & B. from £14.50. ETB 3 Crowns Commended.

ASHBOURNE
The Manse Vegetarian and Vegan Guest House, Wetton, Ashbourne, DE6 2AF (033527) 259
Small guest house with lovely views.
Open all year ex. Xmas and New Year. No smoking. Exclusively meat-free, mainly vegan. Children welcome. Pets by arrangement. En suite 1 room. Tea/Coffee. T.V. in sitting room. B. & B. from £12.50.

The Old Chapel, Wetton, Nr Ashbourne, DE6 2AE (033527) 378
Converted chapel now a luxurious country house offering a very high standard of accommodation. The proprietor is a 'dedicated Gourmet Cook'.
Open Feb. to Nov. No smoking in dining room & bedrooms. Vegetarian & other diets by arrangement. Children: over 7s only. Pets by arrangement. En suite & tea/coffee in bedrooms. T.V. B. & B. from £26.

BASLOW
Cavendish Hotel, Baslow, Derbyshire, DE4 1SP (0246) 582311
Splendid 18th C. building on Chatsworth Estate.
Open all year. No smoking in dining room. Vegetarian standard. Other diets by arrangement. Licensed. Children welcome. En suite, tea/coffee & T.V. in all bedrooms. Credit cards accepted. B. & B. from £37.

BELPER
Dannah Farm Country Guest House, Bowmans Lane, Shottle, Nr Belper, DE56 2DR Tel: (0773)550 273 or 630 Fax: (0773) 550590
Dannah Farm is an attractive Georgian building serving a 128 acre mixed farm on the beautiful Chatsworth Estate. The accommodation is very comfortable, and there is a superb 4-poster suite available. Joan Slack is very interested in (and knowledgeable about) healthy food and uses wholefood ingredients where possible in cooking. Muesli, yoghurt and fruit are always available at breakfast and the imaginative evening menu might feature Spinach and Cottage Cheese Filo, followed by Earl Grey

Sorbet, Seafood Pie and a delicious dessert such as Stuffed Apple Pancakes with Cream. Joan recently opened her highly acclaimed non-residential restaurant, The Mixing Place, on the Dannah Farm site, offering the same superlative food; the excellence of her achievements have been recognised by the English Tourist Board (Dannah Farm is 3 Crown Highly Commended) and she has won the National Award for Farm Catering. Lots to see and do in the area which is, incidentally, excellent for walking.
Open all year ex. Xmas. No smoking in bedrooms & dining room. Vegetarian & other diets by arrangement. Licensed. Children welcome. All rooms private facilities, tea/coffee & T.V. Credit cards. B. & B. from £24. ETB 3 Crown Highly Commended, AA 4Q Selected, RAC Highly Acclaimed. Finalists '92 Alternative Farmer of the Year.

BUXTON
Alpine Guest House, Hardwick Mount, Buxton, SK17 6PS (0298) 26155
Comfortable and friendly guest house near to the station and all amenities; good, wholesome food. Your landlady is a vegetarian but you can choose either traditional or vegetarian fare.
Open all year. No smoking. Vegetarian & other diets by arrangement. Children welcome. Tea/coffee-making in bedrooms & on landing. T.V. in all bedrooms. B. & B. from £14, D. £8 to order.

Biggin Hall, Biggin-by-Hartington, Buxton, SK17 0DH (0298) 84451
Beautiful 17th C. Grade III listed, stone-built house peacefully situated in 8 acres of spacious grounds in the Peak District National Park; spacious rooms are individually furnished with

antiques; several self-catering apartments also available; fresh, local produce used in cooking; b'fast features home-made brioches, croissants, jams and marmalades.
Open all year. No smoking in dining room & sitting room. Vegetarian & other diets by arrangement. Licensed. Children welcome for B. & B. but over 12s only for dinner. Pets by arrangement. En suite in most rooms. Tea/coffee in apartments. T.V. all apartments & sitting room. Mastercard. B. & B. from £18.

Coningsby Guest House, 6 Macclesfield Road, Buxton, SK17 9AH (0298) 26735

Conveniently situated within walking distance of the major attractions of this lovely spa town, this elegant Victorian house has been most tastefully decorated and furnished by its proud owners, John and Linda Harry. Meals are prepared by Linda and her mother who are careful to use *fresh* produce wherever possible in cooking, and in offering a varied - and imaginative - menu to guests. Accordingly a typical evening meal might feature Mushroom and Stilton Soup, followed by Pork Fillet in Sherry Sauce and a selection of tempting desserts, such as Home-made Apple, Rum and Raisin Pie or Iced Raspberry Souffle. Buxton is a charming town in its own right although visitors are equally well-placed for visiting other Peak District attractions such as Chatsworth, Haddon Hall and the Castleton Caverns.
Open all year ex. Xmas. No smoking in the house. Vegetarian & other diets by arrangement. En suite. tea/coffee & T.V. in all bedrooms. B. & B. from £20.

Ivy House, Newhaven, Biggin by Hartington, Buxton, Derbyshire, SK17 0DT (0298) 84709

19th C. former Grade II listed coaching inn recently renovated yet retaining many original features. including flag stone floors. Log fires. Ideal for walking, cycling, touring. Ground floor apartment.
Open all year. No smoking in the house. Vegetarian & other diets by arrangement. Ground floor apartment. Children & pets welcome. En suite, TV & tea/coffee-making in bedrooms. B. & B. from £19-25.

Poppies, Bank Square, Tideswell, Buxton, Derbyshire, SK17 8LA (0298) 871083

3 letting rooms & small, homely restaurant with excellent selection of home-cooked meat & vegetarian dishes. Continental b'fasts.
Open all year. No smoking in part of dining room. Vegetarian & vegan standard. Coeliac & other diets by arrangement. Wheelchair access to restaurant. Children welcome. Pets by arrangement. En suite in one room. TV & tea/coffee-making in all bedrooms. B. & B. from £12.75-17.25.

Westminster Hotel, 21 Broad Walk, Buxton, SK17 6JR (0298) 23929

The Westminster Hotel is a small, friendly family

hotel run by the resident proprietors, Derek and Norma Stephens. It enjoys an enviable position overlooking the Pavilion Gardens, yet is just a few minutes' stroll from the shops, market and Opera House. Bedrooms are spacious and have been comfortably furnished and appointed; each has a private shower or bath. There is also a large, welcoming lounge together with a cosy, well-stocked bar for guests' use. The food is good, traditional home-cooking using fresh, local ingredients wherever possible, and meals are served in a pleasant dining room overlooking the garden. Buxton, the highest market town in England, was first made popular by the Romans in 79 AD; attracting visitors for nearly 2 millenia (including Mary Queen of Scots), the town still charms present day tourists who will find several attractions within easy reach including Chatsworth house, Haddon Hall and the Blue John Caves.
Open Feb. to Nov. & Xmas. No smoking in the dining room. Vegetarian & other diets by arrangement. Licensed. Children welcome. En suite, TV & tea/coffee-making in bedrooms. B. & B. from £20, D. £8.

CHESTERFIELD

Sheeplea Cottage Farm, Baslow Road, Eastmoor, Chesterfield (0246) 566785
Lovely old stone cottage set in 22 acres of garden and farmland just 2 miles from Chatsworth and Baslow village; beautiful moorland views.
Open Mar. to Oct. inc. Smoking banned throughout the house. Vegetarian standard. Most other special diets by arrangement. Children: over 12s only. Pets by arrangement. Tea/Coffee-making in bedrooms. T.V. in lounge. B. & B. from £12.50.

DOVEDALE

The Izaak Walton Hotel, Dovedale, Nr Ashbourne (033 529) 555
Beautiful 17th C. stone-built ex-farmhouse where Izaak Walton stayed while collecting material for 'The Compleat Angler.' Very comfortably furnished. Very good food.
Open all year. No smoking in part of dining room & some bedrooms. Vegetarian standard. Other diets by arrangement. Children welcome. Pets by arrangement. En suite, TV & tea/coffee in bedrooms. Credit cards. B. & B. from £39.

MATLOCK

Cliffeside Bed & Breakfast, Brunswood Rd, Matlock Bath, DE4 3PA (0629) 56981
Cliffeside is a friendly, family-run bed and breakfast with a lovely garden, complete with patio and ponds, set in the heart of the beautiful Derbyshire Dales with spectacular country views. Accommodation is in very comfortable rooms - there is a new double en suite bedroom with an adjacent room with bunk beds which is ideal for families (a cot and highchair is available, and baby-sitting can be arranged); the other double room has the use of a bathroom with a corner bath. The breakfast is hearty and delicious - a real treat to set you up for the day - and there are plenty of restaurants and pubs nearby where you may enjoy an evening meal. Matlock Bath is a beautiful town, and you are within easy reach of such attractions as Chatsworth House, Haddon Hall, Gulliver's Kingdom and the Heights of Abraham.
Open all year. No smoking in the house. Vegetarian & other diets by arrangement. Children & pets welcome. 1 double/family en suite, 1 double. TV & tea/coffee-making in both rooms. B. & B. from £13.

Derwent House, Knowleston Place, Matlock, DE4 3BU (0629) 584681
Charming 17th C. Grade II listed house built of Derbyshire gritstone in a secluded setting near Hall Leys Park. 5 comfortable bedrooms are each named after Derbyshire rivers.
Open all year ex. Xmas and New Year. No smoking in the house. Vegetarians standard. Children welcome. Pets by arrangement. 1 room en suite. TV & Tea/coffee-making in all bedrooms. B. & B. from £16.

Lane End House, Green Lane, Tansley, DE4 5FJ (0629) 583981
Lane End is a small Georgian farmhouse set behind Tansley village green near to the church and with open fields and green hills to the rear. It is owned by a very welcoming couple, David and Marion Smith, who brought their 10 years of experience in running a very successful country house hotel in Leicestershire to bear on a smaller - and, they hope, therefore more personal - enterprise just two years ago. Much love and care has gone into the internal decoration and refurbishment of the house - there is a downstairs bedroom with shower room for those unable to cope with stairs - and the bedrooms are equipped, in addition to the usual facilities, with bathrobes, current magazines, tapes, fresh fruit and flowers. The food is prepared with a similar amount of attention to detail: everything is home-made - including the soups and patés - and vegetables are nearly always steamed; fromage frais - or yoghourt - is served as an accompaniment to the delicious desserts.
Open all year. No smoking. Vegetarian and most other special diets by arrangement. Licensed. Disabled access: 2 steps at front door. Children welcome. Pets by arrangement. En suite, tea/coffee-making & T.V. in all bedrooms. Credit cards. B. & B. from £21.

New Bath Hotel (THF Ltd), New Bath Road, Matlock (0629) 583275
Beautiful Regency building situated amidst 5 acres of landscaped gardens; swimming pool, sauna, solarium and tennis court.
Open all year. No smoking in dining room & some bedrooms. Vegetarian standard. Other diets by arrangement. Licensed. Disabled access. Children welcome. Pets by arrangement. En suite, TV & tea/coffee-making in bedrooms.

Sheriff Lodge Hotel, 51 Dimple Road, Matlock, DE4 3JX (0629) 582973
Hotel in a quiet and elevated position, overlooking the town and surrounding countryside. All home-cooking; free-range eggs.
Vegetarian standard. Vegan & other special diets by arrangement. Open all year. No smoking in bedrooms and dining room. Licensed. Children welcome. Pets by arrangement. En suite in most rooms. Tea/coffee-making & T.V. in all bedrooms. Access, Visa. B. & B. from £20.

Leicestershire

BROUGHTON ASTLEY

The Old Farmhouse, Old Mill Rd, Broughton Astley, LE9 6PQ (0455) 282254

18th C. farmhouse overlooking fields in a quiet position at the back of the village; public footpath adjoins house. Advance booking please.
Vegetarian, vegan, diabetic & other diets by arrangement. Wholefood always. Open all year. No smoking. Children welcome. Tea/coffee making in rooms. B. & B. from £16.

COTTESMORE

The House of Alice (incorporating The Looking Glass Natural Therapies & Madhatters Tearoom), 35 Main St, Cottesmore, LE15 7DH (0572) 813264

300-year-old thatched cottage 3 miles from Rutland Water functioning as a centre for natural healing and with a tea room serving home-made snacks and cakes; there is also a beauty parlour offering a range of natural beauty therapies.
Open all year. No smoking. Vegetarian & other diets by arrangement. Disabled access: 'reasonable'. Children welcome. Pets by arrangement. Tea/coffee-making & T.V. B. & B. from £18.

LEICESTER

Belmont House Hotel, De Montfort St, Leicester, LE1 7ER (0533) 544773

Elegant hotel forming part of the Victorian conservation area of New Walk in the centre of Leicester; very comfortable accommodation, excellent service and first-class cuisine.
Open all year. No smoking in 1 lounge & some bedrooms. Vegetarian standard. Licensed. Disabled access. Children welcome. Pets by arrangement. En suite, tea/coffee & T.V. in all rooms. B. & B. from £72.

Leicestershire Moat House, Wigston Rd, Oadby, Leicester, LE2 5QE (0533) 719441

Once a 19th C. gentleman's residence, this contemporarily refurbished hotel offers very comfortable accommodation and excellent food; flambéed dishes a speciality.
Open all year. No smoking in part of restaurant & some bedrooms. Vegetarian & other diets by arrangement. Licensed. Disabled access. Children welcome. Pets by arrangement. En suite, tea/coffee & TV in all rooms. Credit cards. B. & B. from £30.50.

Richard's Backpacker's Hostel, 157 Wanlip Ln., Birstall, Leicester, LE4 4GL (0533) 673107

Small, independent hostel catering for cyclists, backpackers and young tourists who are looking for cheap, comfortable accommodation near Leicester. Access from Stand B at the city bus station to the hostel's nearest stop at Windmill Avenue, Birstall. Fresh vegetarian food daily.
Open all year. No smoking. Vegetarian & vegan standard. Other diets by arrangement. Bring your own wine. Children: over 5s only. B. & B. from £8.

LUTTERWORTH

Highcross House, Highcross, Lutterworth, LE17 5AT (0455) 220840

Highcross House is a 16th C. Grade II listed building standing at the historic crossing of Fossways and Watling Street - the Roman Centre of England. Your hosts offer an exceptionally thoughtful and memorable welcome to guests: flowers and refreshments are ready to greet you on your arrival, and additional services, such as the provision of a picnic basket, are available on request. Rooms are tastefully decorated and beautifully furnished - there is a genuine antique four-poster in one - and the imaginative menu, prepared from fresh, local produce, is usually arranged by prior notice with guests and changes daily. Highcross caters for both the tourist and business traveller, but also offers excellent facilities for small conferences or special family occasions. There is much to see and do in the locality including diving at Stoney Cove, the country's foremost diving centre, or walking the Fosse.
Open all year. No smoking. Vegetarian & other diets by arrangement. Licensed. Disabled access. Children welcome. Pets by arrangement. En suite in some rooms. Tea/coffee & T.V. in all rooms. B. & B. from £20.

Wheathill Farm, Church Lane, Shearsby, Lutterworth, LE17 6PG (0533) 478663

Traditional Leicestershire-built Grade II listed farmhouse standing in a large garden with sloping lawns leading down to a small lake. Period features include low beams & inglenook fireplaces. The food is all prepared from fresh home-grown vegetables, meat and free-range eggs, and meals are served in a pleasant dining room with garden views.
Open all year. No smoking in dining room, lounge and bedrooms. Vegetarian by arrangement. Children welcome. Ground floor room has private facilities. Tea/coffee making in all rooms. T.V. in lounge. B. & B. from £14.

MELTON MOWBRAY

Stapleford Park Country House Hotel, Stapleford Park, Nr Melton Mowbray, LE14 2EF (057 284) 522

16th C. stately home of almost indescribable grandeur and eclecticism of style; 2 acres of walled gardens; designer bedrooms creating 'a museum of interior design'.
Open all year. No smoking in dining room. Vegetarian & other diets by arrangement. Licensed. Disabled access. Pets by arrangement. En suite in all rooms. T.V. Credit cards. B. & B. from £125.

OAKHAM

Rutland Cottages, 5 Cedar St, Braunston-in-Rutland, Oakham, LE15 8QS (0572) 722049

Rutland Cottages are charming stone-built houses which stand in the quiet conservation village of Braunston near Rutland Water. Your hosts, John and Connie Beadman offer B. & B. with a difference ... guests have the freedom of a cottage but have a substantial English Breakfast served in the elegant 17th C. dining room. All the rooms and cottages have been equipped with a range of helpful amenities, including TV and tea and coffee-making facilities - and totally self-catering cottages are also available.
Open all year. No smoking in dining room, lounge & most bedrooms. Vegetarian and other special diets by arrangement. No wheelchair access but ground floor rooms available. Children welcome. Some rooms with private facilities. Tea/coffee making & T.V. in all rooms. B. & B. from £16-£20.

The Whipper In Hotel, The Market Place, Oakham, Rutland, LE15 6DT (0572) 756971

Vegetarian standard & other diets by arrangement. Organic and wholefood on request. Open all year. Licensed. Disabled access. Children welcome. Pets by arrangement. En suite in all rooms. Tea/coffee-making & T.V. Credit cards. B. & B. from £68.

UPPINGHAM

Garden Hotel, High St West, Uppingham, LE15 9QD (0572) 822352

Charming small hotel with large, well-maintained walled garden in which meals, drinks and barbeques are served in summer; all food prepared from fresh ingredients; home-baked bread.
Open all year. No smoking in 66% of dining room, & first floor, including bedrooms. Vegetarian & diabetic on request, other special diets by arrangement. Licensed. Some disabled access. Children welcome. Pets by arrangement. En suite in all rooms. Tea/coffee-making. T.V. Access, Visa, Amex. B. & B. from £40.

The Lake Isle Hotel, 16 High East, Uppingham, LE15 9PZ (0572) 822951

Charming 18th C. house with lots of character, including log fires and pine tables and chairs in the restaurant; excellent and acclaimed cuisine prepared from fresh ingredients delivered twice weekly from Paris and England.
Open all year. Vegetarian standard. Vegan, diabetic and other special diets by arrangement. Organic and wholefood when avail. Licensed. Children welcome. Pets by arrangement. En suite in all rooms. Tea/coffee-making. T.V. Credit cards. B. & B. from £44.

Lincolnshire

CASTLE BYTHAM

Bank House, Castle Bytham, Nr Grantham, Lincs, NG33 4SQ (0780) 410523

Bank House is located just 3 miles east of the A1 between Stamford and Grantham. Owned by Richard and Marian Foers, this country home has

the rare and prestigious quality grading of De Luxe awarded by the English Tourist Board. It was voted Bed and Breakfast of the Year in the Middle England Best of Tourism Awards and was the East Midlands Tourist Board nominee for the national England for Excellence Awards. It is a superbly appointed and comfortable private home, set in well-maintained secluded grounds and overlooking rolling Lincolnshire countryside on the edge of the peaceful and historic conservation village of Castle Bytham. The spacious guests' lounges, dining room and the two twin bedrooms each have their own individually designed and created furnishings. Value for money, attention to detail and visitors' needs are of paramount importance to your hosts: menus feature healthy, home-made foods and there is an individually caring and personal service which enables guests to fully enjoy the many attractions of the area such as country houses and castles, walks, bird-watching, riding, water sports, golf and other country pursuits.

Open all year. No smoking in the house. Vegetarian & other diets by arrangement. En suite, TV & tea/coffee-making available. B. & B. from £20, 2-course dinner £6.

EAST BARKWITH

The Grange, Torrington Lne, East Barkwith, LN3 5RY (0673) 858249

Welcoming Georgian farmhouse quietly situated amidst extensive grounds with herb beds and lawn tennis courts; the spacious bedrooms have views of the farm and gardens.

Open all year. No smoking in bedrooms & most public areas. Vegetarian, diabetic & other diets by arrangement. Children welcome. En suite in all rooms. B. & B. from £18.50. 2 Crowns De Luxe.

NORTH ORMSBY

Abbey Farm, North Ormsby, Nr Louth, LN11 0TJ (0472) 840272

Vegetarian, diabetic & other diets by arrangement. Organic when avail. Open Mar. - Oct. Children welcome. Pets by arrangement. Tea/coffee in rooms. T.V. lounge. B. & B. from £14. D. £8.

NORTH THORSEBY

The Hen House, Hawerby Hall, North Thoresby, DN36 5QL (0472) 840278

Handsome Georgian manor house surrounded by gardens, fields and woods for women to come 'for reunions, celebrations, holidays, short breaks...or just to unwind'. Wonderful food & numerous good walks.

Open all year. No smoking ex. in small bar area. Vegetarian & other diets by arrangement. Licensed. Disabled access. Children welcome. Some en suite. T.V. D., B.& B. from £32.

SLEAFORD

The Mallards Hotel, Eastgate, Sleaford (0529) 303062

Grade II listed building; excellent food made from fresh, local produce. Many local walks.

Open all year. No smoking in part dining room. Vegetarian and diabetic standard. Licensed. Disabled access. Children welcome. TV, en suite & tea/coffee-making in all rooms. B. & B. from £24.50.

SPALDING

Guy Wells Farm, Whaplode, Spalding, PE12 6TZ (0406) 22239

Lovely Queen Anne family home on a flower farm. Fresh and wholesome food; home-produce includes vegetables and free-range eggs.

Open all year. No smoking. Vegetarian and other special diets on request. Tea/coffee making in all rooms. T.V. in lounge. B. & B. from £15.

WASHINGBOROUGH

Washingborough Hall Country House Hotel, Church Hill, Washingborough, LN4 1BE (0522) 790340

Beautiful stone-built residence in 3 acres. Fresh food including home-grown vegetables.

Vegetarian, vegan, diabetic & other diets by arrangement. Open all year. No smoking in dining room and some bedrooms. Licensed. Children welcome. Pets by arrangement. En suite, tea/coffee making & TV in all bedrooms. Credit cards. B. & B. from £42.

Northamptonshire

DAVENTRY

Barewell Fields, 1, Prestidge Row, Moreton Pinkney, Daventry, NN1 6NJ (0295) 76 754

Comfortable, centrally-heated modern home in rolling countryside. Wholesome food prepared with the use of some home-grown produce.
Open Jan. to Nov. No smoking in dining room & bedrooms. Vegetarian & other diets by arrangement. Children: over 5s only. Tea/coffee making in all rooms. B. & B. from £15. D. £10.

NORTHAMPTON

Hollington Guest House, 22 Abington Grove, Northampton, NN1 4QW (0604) 32584

Small, friendly B. & B. close to town centre. Easy access to M1, Kettering & Wellingborough.
Open all year ex. Xmas. No smoking in the dining room. Vegetarian & other diets if required. Children welcome. TV & tea/coffee-making in bedrooms. B. & B. from £12.50 (single £16, family of 3: £33; family of 4: £40.

Westone Moat House, Ashley Way, Weston Favell, Northampton, NN3 3EA (0604) 406262

Magnificent mansion; excellent cuisine.
Open all year. No smoking in part of dining room & some bedrooms. Vegetarian standard. Other diets by arrangement. Licensed. Disabled access. Children welcome. En suite, TV & tea/coffee. B. & B. from £65.

Wold Farm, Old, Northampton, NN6 9RJ (0604) 781258

Beautiful 18th C. oak-beamed stone farmhouse.
Open all year. No smoking in dining room & bedrooms. Vegetarian by arrangement. Children welcome. En suite. Tea/coffee. T.V.

YARDLEY GOBION

Old Wharf Farm, Yardley Gobion, Nr Towcester, NN12 7UE (0908) 542454

18th C. farmhouse by Grand Union Canal.
Open all year. No smoking in dining room. Vegetarian and most other special diets by arrangement. Children welcome. B. & B. from £17.

Nottinghamshire

NEWARK

The Appleton Hotel, 73 Appletongate, Newark, NG24 1LN (0636) 71616

Pleasant small hotel; à la carte menu with fresh produce used in cooking.
Vegetarian standard. Open all year. No smoking. Licensed. Children welcome. En suite, tea/coffee making, T.V. & phone in all rooms. B. & B. from £25.

NOTTINGHAM

Greenwood Lodge, 5 Third Ave., Sherwood Rise, Nottingham, NG7 6JH (0602) 621206

Beautiful Georgian house one mile from the centre of Nottingham; breakfast only.
Open all year. No smoking in dining room. Vegetarian standard. Other diets by arrangement. Children welcome. B. & B. from £25.

The Lucieville Hotel, 349 Derby Rd, Nottingham, NG7 2DZ Tel: (0602) 787389 Fax 0602 790346

Executive-class hotel exclusively for non-smokers. Vegetarian choices on menu.

Open all year. No smoking. Vegetarian standard. Licensed. Disabled access. En suite, T.V., tea/coffee & hairdryer in rooms. B. & B. from £49.50.

Waltons Hotel, 2 North Rd, The Park, Nottingham (0602) 475215

Vegetarian standard. Open all year. Licensed. Disabled access. Children welcome. Pets by arrangement. En suite, TV & tea/coffee making in all rooms. B. & B. from £55-£75.

RETFORD

The Barns, Morton Farm, Babworth, Retford, DN22 8HA (0777) 706336

Vegetarian by arrangement. Open all year. Disabled access: good, with one ground floor room. Children: babies and over 9s only. En suite, T.V. & tea/coffee making in all rooms. B. & B. from £17.

SOUTHWELL

Old National School Hotel, Nottingham Rd, Southwell, NG25 0LG (0636) 814360

Open all year. No smoking in dining room & lounge. Vegetarian by arrangement. Disabled access. Children welcome. Pets by arrangement.

Cumbria & the North West
Cumbria

ALSTON

The High Fell Hotel, Alston, CA9 3BP (0434) 381597
Reputed to be the highest farmhouse in England at 1200 ft, the High Fell Hotel enjoys wonderful views over unspoilt countryside; French provincial cooking with fresh produce.
Open all year. No smoking in dining room. Vegetarian & other diets by arrangement. Licensed. Children: over 14s welcome. En suite & tea/coffee in bedrooms. T.V. in lounge. Credit cards. B. & B. from £24.75.

Loaning Head Wholefood Vegetarian Guesthouse, Garrigill, Alston (0434) 381013
Converted 17th C. stone barn perched above the quiet village of Garrigill; woodburning stove in lounge & bar has a good selection of beverages (including organic and vegan wines).Everything home-made, including the bread, & and only fresh, seasonal vegetables are used.
Open all year. No smoking. Vegetarian standard. Most other meat-free diets by arrangement. Licensed. Ground floor bathroom & bedroom for the less mobile. Children: over 2s welcome. Tea/coffee in all bedrooms. B. & B. from £14. E.M. £9.

Lovelady Shield Country House Hotel, Nenthead Road, Nr Alston, CA9 3LF (0434) 381203
Pleasantly secluded Victorian house with 2 acres of garden; fresh, local produce.
Open Mar. to Jan. No smoking in dining room, lounge & some bedrooms. Vegetarian by arrangement. Licensed. Children welcome. Pets by arrangement. En suite & TV in all rooms. Tea/coffee.

AMBLESIDE

Borrans Park Hotel, Borrans Road, Ambleside, LA22 0EN (05394) 33454

Borrans Park Hotel is an exceptionally comfortable and well-appointed hotel standing in its own grounds so near and yet so far from the bustling centre of Ambleside. Bedrooms are superbly furnished and appointed: the De-luxe rooms have not only a double four-poster bed but also a private bathroom with a bubbling spa bath! Luxury indeed. A traditional English menu is served in the elegant Borrans Park dining room: all food is either home-baked or home-cooked and a typical evening menu would feature Mushroom and Coriander Paté served with fresh salad and melba toast, followed by roast ham with Cumberland Sauce and a tempting selection of home-made desserts; a selection of fine cheeses are served to round off your meal - and the menu has a helpful wine recommendation - chosen from among the 150 cases in the Borrans Park cellar.
Open all year. No smoking in bedrooms & dining room. Vegetarian and most other special diets by arrangement. Licensed. Disabled access. Children welcome. En suite, TV & tea/coffee-making in bedrooms. Credit cards. B. & B. from £27.50.

Chapel House Hotel, Kirkstone Road, Ambleside, LA22 9DZ (05394) 33143
Originally two 16th C. cottages, this small family hotel overlooks the village and fells; excellent food prepared by top hotel experienced chef.
Open Mar. to Oct.; limited opening Nov. and Dec.; closed Jan. and Feb. No smoking in dining room, and all bedrooms. Vegetarian and most other special diets by arrangement. Licensed. Children welcome. En suite in some rooms. D., B. & B. from £24.25.

Grey Friar Lodge Country House Hotel, Clappersgate, Ambleside, LA22 9NE (05394) 33158
19th C. lodge surrounded by woodland. Excellent food including home-baked bread & home-made chocolates.
Open weekends from Feb; fully open from Easter to end Oct. No smoking in dining room & bedrooms. Vegetarian, low-fat & wholefood diets catered for. Licensed. Children: over 12s only. En suite, TV & tea/coffee-making in bedrooms. D.,B. & B. from £30.

Grizedale Lodge Hotel and Restaurant in the Forest, Grizedale, Hawkshead, Ambleside, LA22 0QL (09666) 532
Comfortable shooting lodge. Excellent cuisine prepared using the best of local, fresh produce.
Open 15th Feb. to 2nd Jan. No smoking in dining room, bedrooms & sitting room. Vegetarian & other diets by arrangement. Licensed. Disabled access. Children welcome. En suite, tea/coffee-making & T.V. in all bedrooms. Access, Visa. B. & B. from £26.

Cumbria

Horseshoe Hotel, Rothay Rd, Ambleside, Cumbria (05394) 32000
Pleasant hotel near the centre of Ambleside yet with magnificent mountain views. Superbly appointed and with separate lounge for smokers. All food home-made from fresh ingredients.
Open all year. No smoking in dining room, bar, some bedrooms & other public areas. Vegetarian standard. Low-fat & some other diets by arrangement. Licensed. Disabled access to ground floor; rest. bars & lounge. Children welcome. Pets by arrangement. En suite in most rooms. Tea/coffee-making & T.V. in all bedrooms. Visa, Mastercard, Amex. B. & B. from £23. Mini-breaks.

Rothay Garth Hotel, Rothay Road, Ambleside, LA22 0EE (05394) 32217
Fine hotel constructed of traditional Lakeland stone and set in attractive gardens on the north shore of Lake Windermere. Excellent cuisine.
Open all year. No smoking ex. in bar. Vegetarian standard. Other special diets by arrangement. Licensed. Disabled access. Children welcome. Pets by arrangement. En suite, T.V. & Tea/coffee-making in bedrooms. Access, Visa. B. & B. from £32.

Rydal Holme, Rydal, Ambleside (05394) 33110
Lakeland stone house on a fell-side terrace overlooking Rydal water. Healthy b'fast cooked on a solid fuel Aga. Good old fashioned bacon and eggs with all of the flavour and no additional fat. Herb teas and decaffeinated coffee.
Open Mar. to Nov. No smoking. Vegetarian & other diets by arrangement. Children by arrangement. Pets by arrangement. En suite in 3 rooms. Tea/coffee in bedrooms. T.V. in lounge. B. & B. from £18.

APPLEBY-IN-WESTMORLAND

Appleby Manor Hotel, Roman Rd, Appleby-in-Westmorland, CA16 6JD (07683) 51571
Comfortable hotel set in private wooded grounds; swimming pool, sauna and solarium avail. All food prepared from fresh ingredients.
Vegetarian standard. Diabetic & other diets by arrangement. Open all year. Licensed. Disabled access good: some ground floor bedrooms avail. Children welcome. Pets in annexe only. En suite, tea/coffee-making & TV in bedrooms.

The Friary, Battlebarrow, Appleby in Westmorland, CA16 6XT (07683) 52702
Georgian House built on the site of a 12th C. Carmelite Friary and standing in its own wooded grounds; comfortable, centrally heated rooms and log fires in winter; hypnosis therapy offered for smokers, also aromatherapy and reflexology for relaxation.
Open all year. No smoking. Cordon Vert vegetarian, demi-veg., diabetic, vegan, arthritic, gluten-free and any other special diet by prior arrangement. Licensed. Children: over 6s only. En suite & tea /coffee making in all bedrooms. T.V. in lounge. B. & B. from £18.

ARNSIDE

Stonegate Guest House, The Promenade, Arnside (0524) 761171
Vegetarian owner. All food freshly cooked.
Vegetarian, vegan & other diets by arrangement (vegetarian owner). Open all year. No smoking. Children welcome. Pets by arrangement. Tea/coffee & T.V. in all bedrooms. B. & B. from £15.

BOWNESS ON WINDERMERE

Blenheim Lodge, Brantfell Road, Bowness-on-Windermere (05394) 43440
Lovely Lakeland stone house peacefully situated against National Trust lands yet just minutes from the lake & shops. Food is "an art form" and only fresh and local produce is used in cooking.
Open all year. No smoking in most areas. Special diets "any healthy diet can be prepared by arrangement." Licensed. Children: over 6s only. En suite, TV & tea/coffee in all bedrooms. Credit cards.

BUTTERMERE VALLEY

Pickett Howe, Brackenthwaite, Buttermere Valley, CA13 9UY (0900) 85444

After a successful first year at Pickett Howe, a '17th C. Lakeland statesman's long house' David and Dani Edwards, (ex of the highly acclaimed Low Hall) are looking forward to welcoming a second season of guests to their lovely home in the beautiful Buttermere Valley. With characteristic flair and meticulous attention to detail the Edwards have clearly taken great pleasure in decorating and furnishing their lovely home: bedrooms are individually styled and Laura Ashley fabrics, lace bedspreads, and elegant furniture (the bedsteads are restored Victorian) recreate the 17th & 18th centuries while power showers and whirlpool baths wash

away the cares of the 20th; the original features, such as mullioned windows, flagged floors and oak beams have been retained and add to Pickett Howe's already considerable charm. Dani's culinary skills are as exceptional as ever; and the 5-course evening menu includes such delights as Spiced Apple Soup, Fennel, Lemon and Walnut in a Gougère Pastry Ring and Juniper Pudding. Crystal, candlelight and chamber music all combine to provide the all important sense of occasion which is the hallmark of dining in the Edwards' home.
Open Mar. to Nov. No smoking. Vegetarian & meat dishes standard. Most other special diets by arrangement. Licensed. Children: over 10s welcome. En suite & tea/coffee in bedrooms. T.V. on request. D., B. & B. from £45. ETB Three Crowns De Luxe.

CALDBECK
High Greenrigg House, Nr Caldbeck (06998) 430
High Greenrigg House is a carefully restored stone-built 17th C. farmhouse situated at the foot of the Caldbeck Fells in the Lake District National Park. This little known Northern area of the National Park remains uncrowded even at the height of the season and, with its proximity to the Cumbria Way (just half a mile) and the Northern and Central Fells it forms an ideal centre for fell-walkers. The house itself has been comfortably furnished and appointed with an eye to enhancing and complementing the original features of the building: the lounge retains the original flagged floor and exposed beams, and guests can sit round the cosy open fire in cooler weather. The food is wholesome and imaginative: all meals have been home-prepared from fresh produce and are served in an attractive beamed dining room, and the evening meal consists of 3 courses plus a cheeseboard and coffee. Your hosts, Fran and Robin Jacobs, are used to accommodating intrepid fell-walkers, but for the days when the weather is inclement enough to deter the hardiest of them, there is a well-equipped games room complete with table tennis, darts and snooker.
No smoking in dining room, bedrooms & T.V. lounge. Special diets by arrangement. Licensed. Disabled access. Children welcome. Pets by arrangement. En suite in all rooms. Tea/coffee-making in T.V. lounge. B. & B. from £17.

CARLISLE
Bessiestown Farm, Catlowdy, Penton, Carlisle, CA6 5QP (0228) 77219
Situated virtually between two counties overlooking the Scottish border to the north of Charming farmhouse with beamed ceilings & log fires; food is prepared with imagination and flair from fresh, and where possible, local ingredients.
Open all year. Smoking allowed only in the bar. Vegetarian & other diets by arrangement. Licensed. Children welcome. En suite & tea/coffee in bedrooms. T.V. lounge. B. & B. from £18.50.

Cumbria Park Hotel 32 Scotland Rd, Carlisle, CA3 9DG Tel: (0228) 22887 Fax: (0228) 514796
On the road to Scotland and only minutes from the centre of Carlisle, the Cumbria Park Hotel stands amidst its magnificent award-winning gardens. Family-owned and run, the service is efficient but friendly, and the personal touch is in evidence everywhere: the bedrooms are comfortable and thoughtfully equipped, and the public rooms have been decorated and furnished with care. The food is wholesome and delicious: everything has been home-cooked from fresh ingredients, and there are always vegetarian options on the menu. Carlisle is an ideal starting point for visiting a wide range of interesting places - including Hadrian's Wall and the Lake District - while the town itself has a first-rate shopping centre as well as a museum and castle.
Open all year. No smoking in part of dining room, some bedrooms & some public areas. Licensed. Wheelchair access. Children welcome. En suite, TV & tea/coffee in rooms. Credit cards. B. & B. from £49.

Howard House, 27 Howard Place, Carlisle, CA11 1HR (0228) 29159
Quiet, friendly Victorian family house; 5 mins from city centre.
Vegetarian, vegan and other special diets by arrangement. No smoking in dining room. Open all year. Children welcome. Pets by arrangement. En suite in some rooms. Tea/coffee-making & T.V. in all bedrooms. B. & B. from £12.

New Pallyards, Hethersgill, Carlisle, Cumbria (0228) 577308
New Pallyards is a modern country farmhouse together with a converted barn, cottages and a new, purpose-built bungalow, which offers award-winning holiday accommodation to guests. Visitors can choose to stay in either the comfortably furnished farmhouse (and be treated to a first-rate breakfast each morning - the proprietors are the winners of a Salon Culinaire award for the Best Breakfast in Britain), or to self-cater in the other farm buildings (all units have been furnished and equipped to a very high standard). Whichever kind of holiday you prefer, you will find that you are excellently placed for enjoying both the unspoilt beauty of north-east Cumbria and the historically interes-

ting towns and countryside of the Scottish borders.
Vegetarian, vegan and other special diets by arrangement. Separate facilities for non-smokers. Some disabled access. Children welcome. Pets by arrangement only. En suite avail. Tea/Coffee in rooms. T.V. some rooms. Credit cards.

The Warren Guest House, 368 Warwick Road, Carlisle, CA1 2RU (0228) 33663/512916

The Warren Guest house is conveniently situated near to Hadrian's Wall (and thus just a short drive from the Lake District) but also just a short walk from Carlisle town centre with its Tullie House, museum, castle and cathedral. The proprietors specialise in the use of *fresh* produce in cooking, and meals are delicious and wholesome. Bedrooms have been very comfortably furnished and appointed and, as a further lure, I am reliably informed that the Warren Guest House boasts an outstanding collection of chamber pots!
Vegetarian, vegan and other special diets by arrangement. Low-fat cooking. Smoking banned in bedrooms and part of dining room. Open all year. Children welcome. En suite or private facilities in all rooms. Tea/coffee-making & TV in all bedrooms. Hairdryers & ironing facilities. B. & B. from £15.

CONISTON

Beech Tree, Yewdale Road, Coniston, LA21 8DB (05394) 41717

Exclusively vegetarian. A Victorian house full of character (used to be the parish vicarage) standing in its own grounds at the foot of the Old Man of Coniston. Beautiful walks from door.
Open all year. No smoking. Health food, vegetarian, vegan & other diets standard. Open all year. No smoking. Children: babies & over 6s only. Pets by arrangement. En suite some rooms. Tea/coffee in bedrooms. T.V. in lounge. B. & B. from £14.

Coniston Lodge, Sunny Brow, Coniston, LA21 8HH (05394) 41201

Managed by Anthony and Elizabeth Robinson who are the 3rd generation of hoteliers to have been looking after visitors since 1911! High standard of accommmodation and comfort. Fresh local ingredients used in cooking.
Vegetarian by arrangement. Diabetic by arrangement. Open all year ex. Xmas. No smoking. Licensed. Children: over 10s only. En suite, TV & tea/coffee-making in bedrooms. Access, Visa, Mastercard, Eurocard. B. & B. from £26.50.

GLENRIDDING

Moss Crag Guest House, Glenridding, CA11 0PA (07684) 82500

Moss Crag, a family-run guest house, is a charming stone-built house situated opposite Glenridding Beck in the heart of the Lake District hills and fells. Just 300 yards away is the hauntingly beautiful Lake Ullswater and, although you can fish, sail, canoe or windsurf thereon, it is best enjoyed (I feel) by just looking at it - perhaps the fishermen have got it right. Freshly prepared food is a feature of a stay at Moss Crag where a typical evening menu would feature Partan Bree (Crab Soup) followed byBeef and Noodle Bake or Spinach and Stilton Pancakes, and a delicious home-made dessert such as Citrus Conde or Coffee Fudge Pudding. Morning coffee, light lunch and afternoon tea are also served.
Open Feb. to Nov. inc. No smoking. Vegetarian, diabetic & other diets by arrangement. Licensed. Children welcome. En suite some rooms. Tea/coffee & TV in bedrooms. B. & B. from £15.50. D., B. & B. from £28. All inclusive D., B. & B. breaks available Nov. to March incl., ex Dec., Jan. 10% reduction for weekly stay summer.

GRANGE-OVER-SANDS

Graythwaite Manor Hotel, Fernhill Road, Grange-over-Sands, LA11 7JE (05395) 32001

Elegant and tranquil hotel, exceptionally well-appointed; fresh flowers and antiques; cuisine prepared from fresh, local ingredient.
Open all year. No smoking in dining room. Vegetarian and most other special diets by arrangement. Licensed. Disabled access. Children welcome. En suite, tea/coffee-making & TV in bedrooms. Visa, Mastercard. D., B. & B. from £40.

Prospect House Hotel, Kents Bank Rd, Grange-over-Sands, LA11 7DJ (05395) 32116

Prospect House Hotel has 7 spacious bedrooms which are centrally heated and have been comfortably equipped with brand new beds and duvets; the hotel also has a cosy, well-stocked residents' bar with 12 different table wines, (including some organic Scottish wines) together with real ale and malt whiskies. It is the food at Prospect House which has commended it to this guide, however: meals are imaginative and wholesome - only fresh food, no junk food, here! - and there is a vegetarian option at each meal for those who give advance notice. A typical evening meal would feature Stilton Pâté followed by Carrot and Courgette Bake, and a dessert such as Pears in Cider; fresh, seasonal vegetables would accompany the main course. Grange-over-Sands is a quiet and peaceful little town which hasn't been overtaken by 20th C. commercialism; it is a good centre for touring the Lake District, however, and Windermere and Coniston are each within easy reach.

Open all year. No smoking in dining room. Vegetarian standard. Diabetic by arrangement. Licensed. Children: over 6s only. Dogs by arrangement. 6 rooms en suite. TV & tea/coffee-making in bedrooms. B. & B. from £16, D., B. & B. from £23.80.

GRASMERE

Lancrigg Vegetarian Country House Hotel, Easedale, Grasmere, LA22 9QN (05394) 35317

It is now almost 7 years since a chance stay at Lancrigg inspired me to compile the first edition of *The Healthy Holiday Guide*. Happily (and unsurprisingly) Robert and Janet Whittington have continued to go from strength to strength in their provision of quite exceptional vegetarian hospitality. The house itself, set in 27 acres of gardens overlooking Easedale, has been converted from the Westmorland farm it originally was (a favourite haunt of the Wordsworths) and has been charmingly decorated - the sitting room with large, floral prints and ample armchairs, and the dining room with beautiful reproduction and period furniture, polished oak floor and prints by the lakeland artist W. Heaton Cooper. The 5-course evening menu is prepared from local organic produce (some home-grown) and would typically feature Greek Marinated Vegetables with Feta Cheese and wholemeal toast, followed by Spinach Soup, Savoury Stuffed Vine Leaves and a choice of desserts, such as Sticky Toffee and Date Pudding (digestion is enhanced by the gentle background music of Telemann and Vivaldi).

Open all year. No smoking in lounge & dining room. Vegetarian exclusively. Vegan & other special diets by arrangement. Licensed. Disabled access. Children welcome. Pets by arrangement. En suite in most rooms. Tea/coffee-making & TV in bedrooms. Credit cards. D., B. & B. from £35.

Michael's Nook Country House Hotel, Grasmere, Nr Ambleside, LA22 9RP (09665) 496

Exceptionally charming 19th C. house furbished with owner/antique dealer's collection of English rugs, prints, furniture and porcelain. Elegant, gracious - yet homely. Excellent cuisine.

Open all year. No smoking in dining room. Vegetarian & other diets by arrangement. Licensed. Children by arrangement. En suite & TV in all bedrooms. Room service. Credit cards. D., B. & B. from £74.

Oak Bank Hotel, Broadgate, Grasmere, LA22 9TA (05394) 35217

Small family run hotel in Grasmere: all meals are prepared from the finest of fresh ingredients by a Cordon Bleu trained chef. Special suite with spa bath available.

Open Feb. to Dec. No smoking in dining room. Vegetarian & other diets by arrangement. Licensed. Children welcome. Pets by arrangement. En suite, tea/coffee-making & TV in bedrooms. Access, Visa. B. & B. from £26.

Cumbria

White Moss House, Rydal Water, Grasmere, LA22 9SE (09665) 295
Splendid 18th C. house once owned by William Wordsworth and overlooking Rydal water. Award-winning cuisine.
Open Mar. to Nov. No smoking in the dining room. Vegetarian and other special diets by arrangement. Licensed. Disabled access. Children welcome. En suite & T.V. in all rooms. D. , B. & B. from £59.

KENDAL

Fairways, 102 Windermere Rd, Kendal, Cumbria, LA9 5EZ (0539) 725564
Victorian guest house with lovely views. 4-poster bedroom. Private parking. Golf nearby.
Open all year. No smoking in the house. Vegetarian & other diets by arrangement. Children welcome. En suite, tea/coffee-making & TV in all bedrooms. B. & B. from £15-17.

7 Thorny Hills, Kendal (0539) 720207
Grade II listed Georgian house.
Open Jan. to Nov. No smoking. Vegetarian by arrangement. Children welcome. En suite in one room. Tea/coffee & T.V. in all bedrooms. B. & B. from £12, D. £8. ETB 1 Crown Commended.

KESWICK

Anworth House, 27 Eskin Street, Keswick (07687) 72923
Anworth House is a small, friendly guest house which is conveniently situated just a few minutes walk from the attractive centre of Keswick with its interesting shops and pencil museum! Your hosts, Mandy and Dave Lanchester, offer an especially warm and friendly welcome to guests and do everything they can to make your stay enjoyable: the food is tasty and wholesome - everything having been prepared on the premises - and the comfortable bedrooms each have en suite facilities; packed lunches are available on request. You are within walking distance of local parks and Lake Derwentwater, and the Northern Lakes, fells and valleys are within easy reach.
Open all year. No smoking in the house. Special diets by arrangement. Children welcome. En suite, tea/coffee & T.V. in rooms. B. & B. from £16.50.

Brundholme Country House Hotel, Brundholme Rd, Keswick, CA12 4NL (07687) 74495
Georgian mansion frequented in the 18th C. by Wordsworth and Coleridge; exceptional cuisine.
Vegetarian standard. Other diets by arrangement. Open Feb. to Dec. No smoking in dining room. Licensed. Disabled access. Children: over 12s only. Pets by arrangement. En suite, tea/coffee & T.V. in all rooms. Visa, Mastercard. B. & B. from £37.

Chaucer House Hotel, Ambleside Road, Keswick (07687) 72318
A strong emphasis on home-cooking and baking (including bread, jams and chutneys).
Vegetarian standard. Other diets by arrangement. Wholefood almost always. Open Easter - Dec. inc. No smoking in dining room & lounge. Licensed. Lift to all floors. Children: over 4s. En suite most rooms. Tea/coffee & T.V. in rooms. B. & B. from £20.

Cottage in the Wood, Whinlatter Pass (07687) 78409
17th C. former coaching house in the heart of the pine forest with superb views of Skiddaw Range.
Vegetarian & other diets by arrangement. Organic & wholefoods on request. Open Mar. to Nov. No smoking. Licensed. Children welcome. Pets by arrangement. En suite & tea/coffee in bedrooms. B. & B. from £27, D. £8.50.

Dalegarth House Country Hotel, Portinscale, Keswick, CA12 5RQ (07687) 72817
Dalegarth House is a spacious, Edwardian

property standing in a sunny elevated position, amidst nearly an acre of gardens, in the village of Portinscale just one mile from Keswick. The resident proprietors, John and Carolyn Holloway, have worked hard to create a comfortable, relaxing atmosphere; indeed two guests phoned me just recently to enthuse about the service and hospitality they had enjoyed at Dalegarth House. The food is wholesome, delicious and home-cooked, a typical 6-course evening menu featuring Prawn Cocktail; home-made soup with hot, fresh rolls, followed by Poached Salmon with Dill Sauce and a choice of home-made sweets; cheese, biscuits and coffee would complete the meal and packed lunches are also available on request. Dalegarth House enjoys superb views of the beautiful northern fells which provide walks for the skilled climbers and ambling strollers; those seeking to explore the Lake District by car will find Dalegarth an ideal touring base.
Open all year. No smoking in the house. Vegetarian food by arrangement. Licensed. Children: over 5s only. En suite, TV & tea/coffee-making in bedrooms.

Access, Visa. B. & B. from £24. D., B.& B. £35.

Dale Head Hall Hotel, Lake Thirlmere, Keswick, CA12 4TN (07687) 72478

16th C. hall set in 3 acres of gardens on shores of Lake Thirlmere.
Open all year. No smoking in dining room, bedrooms & most public rooms. Vegetarian on request. Licensed. Children: over 12s only. En suite & tea/coffee in rooms. Credit cards. B. & B. from £34.

Derwentdale Guest House, 8 Blencathra Street, Keswick, CA12 4HP (07687) 74187

Traditional guest house in the centre of Keswick; friendly welcome and relaxed atmosphere.
Open all year. No smoking. Vegetarian as standard. Children welcome. Pets welcome (bedding provided). Tea/coffee-making in bedrooms. T.V. in lounge. B. & B. from £11.50.

Kendoon, Braithwaite, Keswick, CA12 5RY (07687) 78430

"A warm welcome for wet walkers!" Panoramic views from sitting room.
Open Feb. to Nov. No smoking. Vegetarian, vegan & other diets by arrangement. Pets by arrangement. Tea/coffee-making in lounge. B. & B. from £12.

The Keswick Hotel, Station Road, Keswick, CA12 4NQ (07687) 72020

Impressive Victorian hotel set in over 4 acres of gardens. Luxuriously appointed.
Open all year. No smoking in dining room. Vegetarian standard. Licensed. Disabled access. Children welcome. Pets by arrangement. En suite in most rooms. Tea/coffee-making & T.V. in all bedrooms. Credit cards. D., B. & B. from £40.

Orchard House, Borrowdale Road, Keswick, CA12 5DE (07687) 72830

This exclusively vegetarian guest house looks deceptively small from the outside but inside the three storeys of rooms are all attractively decorated and cosy - the loo boasting one of the best views of Grisedale Pike to be had in Keswick! More pertinently, perhaps, for visiting vegetarian guests, the exclusively meat-free cuisine is freshly prepared from wholefood and, in season, organic vegetables and fruit grown locally especially for Orchard House; a typical 4-course evening menu featuring Spanish Pepper Soup, Chicory with Cheese Sauce, and Mushroom Noisettes with accompanying vegetables, followed by a delicious dessert such as Banana Brulée (everyone's favourite!), with an accompanying selection from the short but well-chosen organic wine list. Keswick is an ideal base for exploring the Northern Lakelands and within a short drive are historic homes, stone circles and watermills.
Open mid Feb. to mid Nov. plus Xmas. No smoking in the house. Vegetarian exclusively, vegan and other special diets by arrangement. Licensed. Children by arrangement. Dogs by arrangement. En suite in some rooms. Tea/coffee-making in bedrooms. T.V. in separate lounge. D., B. & B. from £27. Open to non-residents for dinner.

Richmond House, 37/39 Eskin Street, Keswick (07687) 73965

Small, friendly personally run guest house a few minutes walk from the centre of Keswick. Fresh, local produce used wherever possible.
Open all year. No smoking. Vegetarian, vegan, additive-free & other diets by arrangement. Licensed. Children welcome. En suite most rooms. ETB 2 Crown

Squirrel Lodge, 43 Eskin Street, Keswick (07687) 73091

Attractive guest house in the centre of Keswick, with an emphasis on home-cooking.
Open all year. Smoking banned throughout the house. Vegetarian and all other special diets by arrangement. Licensed. Children welcome. Tea/coffee-making & T.V. in all bedrooms. Credit cards accepted. B. & B. from £13, D. £7.

Winchester Guest House, 58 Blencathra St, Keswick (07687) 73664

Spacious, end-of-terrace Victorian town house near the centre of the attractive market town of Keswick. Home-cooked breakfasts; traditional evening meals during winter months.
Open all year. No smoking in the house. Vegetarian by arrangement. Children: over 3s welcome. Tea/coffee-making & TV in all bedrooms. B. & B. from £13.50, D. £7.

KIRBY LONSDALE

Lupton Tower Vegetarian Country Guest House, Nr. Kirkby Lonsdale, LA6 2PR (04487) 400

Magnificent house offering exclusively vegetarian fare and standing in its own grounds amidst the beautiful open countryside. Everything home-cooked from fresh produce.

Open all year ex. Xmas. No smoking. Exclusively vegetarian. Licensed. Children welcome. Pets by arrangement. En suite most rooms. Tea/coffee in all bedrooms. B. & B. from £14.50

KIRKBY STEPHEN
Annedd Gwyn, 46 High St, Kirkby Stephen, Cumbria, CA17 4SH (07683) 72302
This late Victorian home is run along 'green' lines, with home-cooked wholefoods & a relaxing, healthy environment. Meditation room & guest lounge.
Open Jan. 7 - Dec. 22. No smoking in the house. Vegetarian standard. Tea/coffee-making. TV on request. Children & pets welcome. B. & B. £13.50.

KIRKOSWALD
Howscales Holiday Cottages for Non-Smokers, Howscales, Kirkoswald, Penrith, CA10 1JG (0768 83) 666
Converted sandstone barn and byres, exclusively let to non-smokers.
Open all year. No smoking. Children: over 12s only. Access, Visa, Diners.

THE LORTON VALE
New House Farm and The Barn, New House Farm, Lorton, Cockermouth, CA13 9UU (0900) 85404
Mid-17th C. house in the beautiful Lorton Vale between the villages of Lorton and Loweswater; exposed oak beams, stone fireplaces and flagged floors; excellent home-cooking.
Open all year. No smoking. Fully licensed. Vegetarian meals can be prepared with notice. Dogs welcome. D. B. & B. from £45.

MILLOM
Whicham Hall Farm, Silecroft, Millom, LA18 5LT (0229) 772637
Family farm in peaceful valley. Home cooking.
Open all year. No smoking. Vegetarian & other diets by arrangement. Disabled access. Children welcome. Pets by arrangement only. En suite in 1 room. Tea/coffee-making. T.V. B. & B. from £10.

MILNTHORPE
Eildan, 129 Church Street, Milnthorpe Cumbria, LA7 7DZ (05395) 63311
Home-baked bread and free-range eggs.
Vegetarian, vegan & other diets by arrangement. No smoking. Open Feb. to Nov. Children welcome. Tea/coffee-making. T.V. 1 bedroom.

MOSEDALE
Mosedale House, Mosedale (07687) 79371
An emphasis on home-made and home-grown provision: vegetables, fruit, produce (such as eggs and lamb), home-baked bread and rolls. Vegetarians welcome.
Open all year. No smoking in the house. Most special diets by arrangement. Disabled access. Children welcome. Pets by arrangement. En suite in 4 rooms. Tea/coffee-making in all bedrooms. T.V. B. & B. from £18, D. from £11.

PENRITH
'Fair Place' Wholefood and Vegetarian Guest House, Fair Place, Watermillock, Nr Penrith, CA11 0LR (07684) 86235

This handsome rag-stone building, set in secluded grounds 200 yards past Watermillock Church, used to be the village school. Its proprietors, whose family home it has been, converted it over 30 years ago, and it has been beautifully renovated and modernised. Now a charming small guest house (though retaining many of the original features), it is an exclusively vegetarian and vegan B. & B., serving only the best and freshest of free-range and 'whole' breakfasts. The bedrooms are all en suite (and have very comfortable beds), and, if you like music, there is an especially good room for listening (bring your own CDs). Drive if you must, but there is ample countryside within walking distance of 'Fair Place': Aira Force, a spectacular waterfall is 3 miles away, and Ullswater is an especially lovely Lakeland haunt.
Open Feb. to Nov. No smoking. Vegetarian & vegan b'fast standard, other diets by arrangement. Children welcome. Pets by arrangement. En suite. Tea/coffee & T.V. in all bedrooms. B. & B. from £17.50.

The Mill Hotel, Mungrisdale, Penrith, CA11 0XR (07687) 79659
Beautifully renovated 17th C. Mill Cottage at the foot of a mountain; excellent home-cooked food.
Open Feb. to Nov. No smoking in dining room & some bedrooms. Vegetarian standard. Other diets by arrangement. Licensed. Children welcome. En suite 5 rooms. Tea/coffee in rooms. T.V. B. & B. from £23.

Nunnery House Hotel, Staffield, Kirkoswald, Penrith, CA10 1EU (076 883) 537

Small, country house hotel in splendid grounds with beautiful walks. Bedrooms all have views and meals prepared from fresh, local produce are served in a panelled dining room.
Vegetarian & other diets by arrangement. Open Mar. to Jan. inc. No smoking. Licensed. Disabled access to dining room. Children welcome. Pets by arrangement. En suite in 7 rooms. Tea/coffee & T.V. in all bedrooms. B. & B. from £25.

Prospect Hill Hotel, Kirkoswald, Penrith, CA10 1ER (0768) 898 500

This cosy little huddle of farm buildings, nestling together on a green, unspoilt and ever so peaceful hillside overlooking the splendid Eden Vale, has been lovingly restored by its owners, John and Isa Henderson, to provide a most charming and comfortable hotel which retains the traditional features of the original buildings (low-beamed ceilings, sandstone walls). It offers a taste of "18th century England with 21st century amenities". The culinary emphasis is on freshly prepared traditional fare using the best of local ingredients (bread comes fresh from the Langwathby and Lazonby bakeries) and a typical evening menu would feature Wine and Nut Paté with Wholemeal Herb Bread followed by Courgette Roulade and a selection of desserts (including home-made ice-cream!) The vegetarian menu is being continually updated with new and interesting dishes. Prospect Hill Hotel is convenient for visiting Hadrians Wall by car and Tullie House by train; the Settle to Carlisle railway passes through Lazonby, 2 miles away. The surrounding area offers excellent opportunities for walking (there are many magnificent riverside walks) and energetic cycling, and local maps, wellingtons and wet-weather gear are all available from your hosts for a small charge. Incidentally there is a super new ground floor unit for families at just £73 for 4 people.

Vegetarian standard. Other diets by arrangement. Organic & wholefoods when avail. Open all year ex. Xmas. Licensed. Some disabled access, to restaurant. Children & pets by arrangement. En suite most rooms. Tea/coffee-making in all rooms. T.V. in lounge. Credit cards. B. & B. from £22.

Ullswater Trout, Sockbridge Mill Trout Farm, Tirril, Penrith, CA10 2JT (0768) 65338

Situated in a secluded spot on the banks of the River Eamont within 10 mins drive of Ullswater. Own trout smoking done on premises and own smoked trout pâte.
Vegetarian, vegan and some other special diets by arrangement. No smoking in bedrooms & dining room. Open Easter to end Oct. Children welcome. Pets by arrangement. En suite 1 room. Tea/coffee. T.V. in sitting room. B. & B. from £12.

The White House, Clifton, Nr Penrith (0768) 65115

Beautiful 18th C. farmhouse in the village of Clifton; home-grown produce in cooking.
Open Mar. to Nov., plus Xmas & New Year. No smoking. Vegetarian, diabetic and gluten-free diets by arrangement. Licensed. Children welcome. En suite in one room. Tea/coffee-making in all bedrooms. T.V. on request. B. & B. from £13, D. £8.50.

Woodland House Hotel, Wordsworth Street, Penrith, CA11 7QY Tel: (0768) 64177 Fax: (0768) 890152

An elegant and spacious licensed private hotel with a large car park, just five minutes walk from the centre of the town. All rooms are en suite and all have tea/coffee making facilities and a colour T.V. The meals are delicious and have been prepared from the best of fresh and local produce and, with notice, special dietary requirements can be catered for. There is a large library of maps and books for walkers, nature-lovers and sightseers and the proprietors will gladly help you plan your stay. Woodland House Hotel is an ideal centre for exploring the Lake District, Northern Pennines, Borders, Eden Valley, and is

a perfect spot for an overnight stop on journeys to and from Scotland.
Open all year. No smoking. Vegetarian & other diets by arrangement. Residential licence. Children welcome. En suite, tea/coffee-making & T.V. in all bedrooms. B. & B. from £19.

SEDBERGH
Cross Keys Hotel, Cautley, Sedbergh, Cumbria, LA10 5NE (05396) 20284
16th C. inn with beamed ceilings, flagged floors, mullion windows and log fires. All food prepared from fresh ingredients; home-baked bread.
Vegetarian, diabetic & other special diets by arrangement. No smoking. Open Easter to New Year. Children welcome. 1 en suite room. Tea/coffee in all bedrooms. B. & B. from £23.

ULVERSTON
Appletree Holme Farm, Blawith Via Ulverston, LA12 8EL (0229 85) 618
Exquisite farmhouse with beautiful gardens and views; welcoming log fires. Stupendous fare prepared from garden vegetables, home-laid free-range eggs and local dairy produce. Breakfast features oak-smoked kippers, porridge with Jersey cream & goat's milk yoghurt.
Open all year. No smoking ex. 1 lounge. Vegetarian & other diets by arrangement. Licensed. En suite, TV & tea/coffee in rooms. D., B. & B. from £49.

WASDALE
Low Wood Hall Hotel, Nether Wasdale, Wasdale, CA20 1ET (09467) 26289
Splendid Victorian country house hotel with retaining original features such as gas chandeliers, marble fireplaces and stained glass. Magnificent views over valley of Whinn Rigg.
Vegetarian food as standard. No smoking in dining room. Open all year. Licensed. Disabled access. Children welcome. En suite, TV & tea/coffee in all bedrooms. B. & B. from £19.

WINDERMERE
The Archway, 13 College Road, Windermere (05394) 45613
This guest house is the one about which I received the most readers' recommendations when I was compiling the second edition of the guide. A small, 'impeccable' Victorian guest house furnished tastefully throughout with antiques, paintings and fresh flowers allows its reputation, nevertheless, to rest (and rest soundly) on the high standard of its cuisine: the best of fresh local ingredients are brought

together in imaginative and nutritionally thoughtful menus (the breakfast fare offers everything from freshly squeezed fruit or vegetable juice to home-made spicy apple griddle cakes; bread, of course, is wholemeal and home-baked), while the 3-course evening menu includes a wine recommendation - and a refreshing tipple of home-made lemonade!
Open all year. No smoking. Vegetarian, vegan and diabetic diets standard. Licensed. Children: over 12s only. En suite in 5 rooms. Tea/coffee-making & T.V. in bedrooms. Credit cards. B. & B. from £20.

Ashleigh Guest House, 11 College Road, Windermere (05394) 42292
Delightful Victorian guest house in Windermere village; comfortably furnished and tastefully decorated throughout (there are fresh flowers in the bedrooms), many rooms have glorious mountain views.
Open all year. No smoking. Vegetarian by arrangement. Children: over 12s welcome. En suite available. Tea/coffee & T.V. in all bedrooms. B. & B. from £14.

Hazel Bank, Hazel Street, Windermere (09662) 5486
Handsome Victorian residence 2 mins walk from Windermere; home-made, healthy cuisine .
Open all Mar. to Nov. No smoking. Vegetarian by arrangement. Bring your own wine. Good disabled access, inc. ground-floor bedroom. Children: over 7s only. En suite & tea/coffee-making in bedrooms. T.V. in lounge. B. & B. from £16.

Hideaway Hotel, Phoenix Way, Windermere, LA23 1DB (09662) 3070
Highly acclaimed small hotel in quiet country lane just 5 minutes from Windermere Village centre. Imaginative home-cooked cuisine.
Open all year. No smoking in dining room & sitting room. Most special diets by arrangement. Licensed. Children welcome. Pets by arrangement. En suite, TV & tea/coffee in rooms. D., B. & B. from around £35.

Holbeck Ghyll Country House Hotel, Holbeck Lane, Windermere, LA23 1LU (05394) 32375

With a majestic location overlooking Windermere and surrounded by natural woodland and open fields this splendid country house hotel offers superlative food and accommodation.
Open Feb. to Dec. No smoking in dining room. Vegetarian standard. Most other special diets by arrangement. Licensed. Children welcome. Pets by arrangement. En suite, TV & tea/coffee-making in bedrooms. Access, Visa. D., B. & B. from £47.

Kirkwood Guest House, Prince's Road, Windermere, LA23 2DD (05394) 43907

Kirkwood is an attractive stone-built guest house peacefully situated in a quiet area of Windermere yet just a few minutes' walk from the town centre and shops; Lake Windermere is just 1 mile away. Your hosts, Carol and Neil Cox, do all they can to make your stay a happy and memorable one, and you will find that all the bedrooms have been individually furnished and have excellent amenities. The breakfast is first-rate: a range of options are offered - including a menu for vegetarians - and other special diets can be accommodated if a little notice is given. Open most of the year, Kirkwood Guest House is the perfect choice for those seeking to enjoy Lakeland in the uncrowded Autumn, Winter and Spring months, with their clear bright days and welcome absence of traffic!
Open all year. No smoking in dining room. Vegetarian and other diets by arrangement. Children welcome. Pets by arrangement. En suite in 5 rooms. Tea/coffee-making & T.V. in all bedrooms. Credit cards. B. & B. from £15.

Merewood Country House Hotel, Ecclerigg, LA23 1LH (09662) 6484

Vegetarian standard. Other special diets by arrangement. No smoking in dining room. Open all year. Licensed. Children welcome. En suite, TV & tea/coffee-making in rooms. D., B. & B. from £45.

Rockside, Ambleside Road, Windermere, LA23 1AQ (09662) 5343

Rockside Guest house is a traditional 19th C. stone and slate built Lakeland home which stands just 150 yards from Windermere centre and train station. It is a house of some charm: each of the 15 bedrooms is different in size and shape (passage ways and short flights of stairs go off in all directions), and each has en suite facilities and a range of other amenities including electric blankets and telephone; one bedroom is on the ground floor. Breakfast is excellent: there are six different options and a continental choice for those having to leave early. There is so much to se and do in the area that your hosts will gladly help you plan your stay by giving advice about car routes and how to plan walks.
Open all year. Car parking. No smoking in dining room and 2 bedrooms. Special diets by arrangement. Disabled access. Children welcome. En suite. Tea/coffee-making & T.V. in all bedrooms. Credit cards. B. & B. from £16.50. ETB 2 Crowns.

South View Hotel, Cross Street, Windermere, Cumbria, LA23 1AE (09662) 2951

Georgian house, formerly owned by local soft-drinks manufacturer, now converted to comfortable hotel. Excellent fitness facilities including indoor swimming pool, 'Trim-room' and whirlpool Spa.
Vegetarian, diabetic, low calorie but not vegan, diets by arrangement. Wholefoods on request. Smoking banned in bedrooms. Open all year. Children and pets by arrangement. En suite in most rooms. Tea/coffee-making & T.V. in all bedrooms. Amex, Access, Visa. B. & B. from £18.

WORKINGTON

Morven Guest House, Siddick Rd, Workington, CA14 1LE (0900) 602118

Morven Guest House is a large, detached late Victorian house with a car park and garden which stands to the north west of Workington. It has been very comfortably furnished and tastefully decorated and all four bedrooms have en suite facilities; there is a pleasant bar for guests' use. Easily accessible by car, Morven Guest House is the ideal choice for tourists and business travellers in west Cumbria. Large detached Victorian house with car park and garden.
Open all year. No smoking in dining room. Vegetarian and most other special diets by arrangement. Licensed. Children welcome. Pets by arrangement. En suite in 4 rooms. Tea/coffee-making & T.V. in all bedrooms. B. & B. from £19.

Cheshire

CHESTER

Frogg Manor, Fullers Moor, Nantwich Road, Broxton, Chester, CH3 9JH (0829) 782629

Superb Georgian manor house, recently refurbished to provide an exceptionally comfortable hotel with all the graceful elegance of the Georgian era. All food is freshly prepared using the best of local ingredients, and there is a separate vegetarian à la carte menu.

Open all year. Separate room for smokers. Vegetarian & other diets by arrangement. Licensed. Children welcome. Pets by arrangement. En suite, TV & tea/coffee in bedrooms. Credit cards. From £27.

Asquith House, 8 Waterloo Road, Chester, CH2 2AL (0244) 380620

Elegant Victorian home which was built in 1895 and was restored to its former glory nearly a century later in 1989 by its present owners.

Open all year ex. Xmas. No smoking. Special diets by arrangement only. En suite, TV & tea/coffee-making in bedrooms. B. & B. £25, single £29.

HOLMES CHAPEL

Holly Lodge Hotel, 70 London Road, CW4 7AS (0477) 37093

Built in the mid 19th C. by the local architect Massey, this large Victorian house in the centre of the charming village of Holmes Chapel retains all the character and charm of the first phase of its existence yet has been extensively modified and refurbished to provide an exceptionally comfortable and well-appointed hotel complete with function and conference facilities and a swimming pool, sauna, jacuzzi and mini-gym. Food is of an exceptionally high standard: only the finest ingredients are ever used in cooking and a typical evening menu would feature Sautéed Quail Breasts on a Julienne of Beetroot and Celeriac (with Raspberry Vinaigrette) followed by Medallions of Veal on home-made noodles, with yoghurt and basil sauce.

Vegetarian standard. Vegan & other diets by arrangement. Some no smoking bedrooms. Open all year. Licensed. Disabled access. Children welcome. Pets by arrangement. En suite, TV & tea/coffee-making. Credit cards. B. & B. from £34.

KNUTSFORD

Longview Hotel and Restaurant, 51-55 Manchester Road, Knutsford, Cheshire, WA16 0LX (0565) 632119

This charming small hotel overlooking the

common in the historic market town of Knutsford, offers a true haven for the holiday-maker or business man or woman visiting Cheshire. The present owners have refurbished the hotel - but have done so with care to ensure that the elegance and character that it enjoyed in former Victorian times has been retained. The culinary standard is very high indeed: all food is prepared from fresh ingredients wherever possible and cooked on the premises; and the vegetarian selection is excellent (the hotel is included in *The Vegetarian Good Food Guide*). A typical evening menu would feature perhaps Greek Salad, followed by Chicken Louchow (chicken in sauce with an Oriental influence) or, from the vegetarian menu, Vegetable Florina, tasty vegetables with a red wine sauce, topped with feta cheese sauce. A 'Vegetarian Medley' is also available, giving diners the chance to sample a little of each of the vegetarian dishes on the menu; you can complete your meal from a selection of tempting desserts.

Vegetarian as standard, other special diets by arrangement. Open all year. Licensed. Children welcome. Pets by arrangement. En suite in most rooms. Tea/coffee making & T.V. in all bedrooms. Credit cards. B. & B. from £25.

KNUTSFORD

Tatton Dale Farm, Ashley Road, Knutsford, WA16 6QJ (0565) 654692
Victorian farmhouse forming part of working farm in Tatton Park.
Open all year. No smoking. Vegetarian and most other special diets by arrangement. Disabled access. Children welcome. En suite. Tea/coffee-making in bedrooms. B. & B. £14.

Toft Hotel, Toft Road, Knutsford, WA16 9EH (0565) 3470
16th C. farmhouse set around courtyard; comfortably appointed rooms (old pine furniture, etc). Vegetarian emphasis, including separate restaurant.
Open all year. No smoking. Vegetarian standard. Licensed. Children: over 10s only. En suite & TV in 6 rooms. Tea/coffee-making in all bedrooms. Credit cards B. & B. from £15.

MACCLESFIELD

Shrigley Hall Hotel, Shrigley Park, Nr Macclesfield, SK10 5SB (0625) 575757
Regency style hotel in 262 acre estate; fine cuisine; golf course and swimming pool.
Open all year. No smoking in part of bar & leisure areas. Vegetarian & other diets by arrangement. Licensed. Disabled access. Children welcome. Pets by arrangement. En suite. TV & tea/coffee-making in bedrooms. B. & B. from £35.

MOBBERLEY

Laburnum Cottage, Knutsford Road, Mobberley, Nr Knutsford, WA16 7PU (0565) 872464
Laburnum Cottage is a small, luxurious country house set amidst the beautiful Cheshire countryside, with open views looking out towards Tatton Park. Standing in one acre of very pretty gardens (with ample room for parking) Laburnum Cottage is cosily furnished with antiques, and guests can enjoy the comfort of curling up in front of a log fire in colder weather (although the house is also centrally heated). Shirley Foxwell offers just breakfast to guests (vegetarians can be accommodated by arrangement) but she will gladly advise guests of good local pubs and restaurants. Knutsford is a lovely little town (just 15 mins from Manchester airport) and you are less than an hour's drive from both Chester and the Peak District.
Open all year. No smoking in the house. Vegetarian & other special diets by arrangement. Children: over 5s only. Some en suite. TV & Tea/coffee-making in bedrooms. B. & B. from £20.

NANTWICH

Rookery Hall, Worleston, Nr Nantwich, CW5 6DQ (0270) 610016
Splendid Georgian hall - converted to a hotel & conference centre - in 100 acres including 28 acres of gardens and wooded parkland. High standard of service, decor and cuisine.
Open all year. No smoking in dining room. Vegetarian & other diets by arrangement. Licensed. Disabled access. Children welcome. En suite & Satellite TV in all rooms. Room service.

NORTHWICH

Beechwood House, 206 Wallerscote Road, Weaverham, CW8 3LZ (0606) 852123
Comfortable farmhouse on 19 acre stock farm; peacefully situated 1m N.E. of Weaverham; home-cooking with a varied menu.
Open Jan. to Nov. No smoking. Vegetarian and other special diets by arrangement. Tea-making & T.V. B. & B. from £12. D. £6

Lancashire

BLACKPOOL

Mains Hall Country House Hotel, Mains Lane, Singleton, Nr Blackpool, FY6 7LE (0253) 894132
Grade II listed country houses standing in 4 acres of private grounds. Excellent food prepared from first-class seasonal ingredients. Good conference facilities. Private river frontage with sailing, fishing, etc.
Vegetarian, vegan & diabetic standard. Other diets by arrangement. Open all year. No smoking in bedrooms. Licensed. Disabled access. Children welcome. Pets by arrangement. En suite, TV & Tea/coffee in all rooms. Credit cards B. & B. from £25.

Ruskin Hotel, Albert Rd, Blackpool, FY1 4PW (0253) 24063
Well-appointed 80-bedroomed hotel close to Tower. First-rate food prepared from fresh, local ingredients and vegetarian option available.
Vegetarian & other diets by arrangement. Open all year. No smoking in part of dining room. Licensed. Disabled access. Children welcome. Pets by arrangement. En suite, TV & tea/coffee in all rooms.

CARNFORTH

Thie-ne-shee, Moor Close Lane, Over Kellet, Carnforth, LA6 1DF (0524) 735882
Attractive bungalow with superb views of Lake District, mountains and Morecambe Bay. Near to Steamtown Carnforth and Leighton Moss R.S.P.B. Nature Reserve. Healthy breakfasts!
Open all year ex. Xmas & New Year. No smoking. Vegetarian & other diets by arrangement. Children welcome. Room service. T.V. B. & B. from £12.

CHORLEY

Shawhill Hotel, Golf and Country Club, Preston Rd, Whittle-le-Woods, Chorley, PR6 7PP (02572) 69221
Vegetarian, vegan, diabetic standard. Most other special diets by arrangement. Open all year. Licensed. Children welcome. Pets by arrangement. En suite, TV & tea/coffee-making in all rooms. B. & B. from £40.

INGLETON

Bridge End Guest House, Mill Lane, Ingleton, Nr Carnforth, LA6 3EP (05242) 41413
Formerly a mill owner's Georgian home, this charming guest house, situated on the River Doe adjacent to the Ingleton Waterfalls Walk, is a listed building and has retained many period features including a fine, spacious staircase. The house is further interesting in that its patio cantilevers over the River Doe and the thus suspended terrace provides a spectacular dining location (weather permitting!); breakfast on sunny, summer mornings becomes a memorable occasion. The food at Bridge End is a further attraction: everything is home-cooked from fresh ingredients, and a typical evening menu would feature Courgette and Cumin Soup followed by Lentil Moussaka (or Steak and Kidney Pie), and a choice of desserts. You are just 3 minutes' walk from Ingleton village and surrounded by the wonderful, wild beauty of the Yorkshire Dales National Park.
Vegetarian standard and most other special diets by arrangement. Organic and wholefoods when available. Low-fat cooking. Open all year. Children welcome. Pets by arrangement. En suite, TV & tea/coffee-making in all rooms. B. & B. from £15.50.

LANCASTER

Elsinore House, 76 Scotforth Rd, Lancaster (0524) 65088
Large, detached house on the outskirts of the city; pretty terraced garden and fishpond.
Open all year. No smoking ex. lounge. Vegetarian and most other special diets by arrangement. En suite, TV & tea/coffee-making in all rooms. B. & B. £15.

Lancaster Post House (THF UK Ltd), Waterside Park, Caton Rd, LA1 3RA (0524) 65999
Open all year. No smoking in 30% dining room & bedrooms. Vegetarian standard. Diabetic on request. Licensed. Lifts to all floors; disabled bedroom and toilet. Children welcome. En suite, TV & Tea/coffee-making in all rooms.

LYTHAM ST ANNES

Dalmeny Hotel, 19-33 South Promenade, Lytham St Annes, FY8 1LX (0253) 712236
Large, modern family hotel overlooking the sea and gardens; indoor pool and squash court.
Open all year ex. Xmas. No smoking in dining room & lounge. Vegetarian & other diets by arrangement. Licensed. Disabled access. Children welcome. En suite, TV & tea/coffee in rooms. Room only from £18.

PRESTON

**Brickhouse Hotel & Restaurant,
Chipping, Nr Preston (0995) 61085**

Charming 18th C. house; everything home-made including the bread and icecreams.

Vegetarian standard. Vegan, diabetic and most other special diets standard. Open all year. No smoking in part of the dining room. Licensed. Disabled access. Children welcome. En suite, TV & tea/coffee-making in all rooms. B. & B. from £22.50.

ROSSENDALE

**Sykeside Country House Hotel,
Haslingden, Rossendale (0206) 831163**

A 19th C. country house superbly converted into award-winning hotel offering exceptionally good service. Wonderful food.

Open all year. No smoking in dining room & bedrooms. Vegetarian & other diets by arrangement. Licensed. Disabled access. Children welcome. En suite, TV & tea/coffee in all rooms. B. & B. from £40.

SILVERDALE

Lindeth House, Lindeth Rd, Silverdale, Carnforth, LA5 0TX (0524) 701238

Lindeth House is a pleasant country residence wonderfully situated in a area of outstanding

natural beauty, surrounded by woodland walks, yet just a few minutes' walk from the sea and a short distance from Leighton Moss RSPB Reserve. The house has been attractively decorated and appointed and each of the bedrooms have been individually furnished and have en suite facilities, a colour TV, a clock radio and tea and coffee-making facilities. The licensed restaurant provides the finest traditional English cuisine which has been prepared from fresh, local produce, and a typical evening meal would feature a range of options from which you might select Smoked Salmon Profiteroles with Lemon Mayonnaise, followed by soup or sorbet, Gressingham Duckling with Sage and Onion Cream, a delicious dessert and cheese, biscuits, a cafetiere of fresh coffee and Chocolate Kendal Mint Cake! The excellent food, combined with the warm and friendly atmosphere, makes

Lindeth House an excellent base for a quiet break or touring the Lake District.

Open Feb. to Dec. No smoking in dining room by request & bedrooms. Vegetarian by arrangement. Licensed. Disabled access. Children: over 12s. En suite, tea/coffee & T.V in rooms. B. & B. from £20.

SOUTHPORT

Ambassador Private Hotel, 13 Bath St, Southport, PR9 0DP (0704) 543998

The Ambassador Hotel occupies one of the most central positions in Southport adjacent to

beautiful Lord Street, with its covered boulevard and elegant shops, and just a short walk from the promenade. The bedrooms have all been very comfortably furnished and well-equipped with a range of helpful amenities including a hairdryer, a hospitality tray, (with drinks and snacks), a shoe cleaner and a mending kit. There is a comfortable bar (not open to non-residents) and in which the resident organist will entertain you during the evening! Your host, Margaret Bennett, is a qualified chef and prepares tasty meals from fresh, seasonal produce: the breakfast menu is tremendous and a wide variety of options are on offer including, in addition to the traditional English bacon, eggs and sausage, cheese on toast, kippers or smoked haddock. There are many interesting places to visit including a Wildfowl Sanctuary, Formby Red Squirrel Colony & Liverpool's Albert Dock and Maritime Museum. ETB 3 Crown Commended.

Open all year ex. Xmas. No smoking dining room & bedrooms. Vegetarian & other diets by arrangement. Licensed. Children: over 5s. En suite, TV & tea/coffee in rooms. Credit cards B. & B. from £23.

TODMORDEN

The Queen Hotel, Rise Lane, Todmorden, OL14 7AA (0706) 812961

Family-run hotel cum pub; 99% home-cooking.

Open all year. No smoking in one bar. Vegetarian & other diets by arrangement. Licensed. Children welcome. En suite, TV & tea/coffee. B. & B. from £18.

Yorkshire and Humberside

North Yorkshire

BEDALE

The Old Rectory, Patrick Brompton, Bedale, Dl8 1JN (0677) 50343
Georgian rectory, Grade II listed building, furnished in period style, surrounded by gardens.
Open Feb to Nov. No smoking. Vegetarian and most other special diets by arrangement. Licensed. Pets by arrangement. En suite, TV & tea/coffee-making in all rooms. B. & B. from £17. D. £11

'Southfield', 96 Southend, Bedale, DL8 2DS (0677) 423510
Well established 3 bedroomed bed and breakfast establishment.
Open all year ex. Xmas and New Year. No smoking in dining room & throughout upper floor. Vegetarian & other diets by arrangement. Children welcome. Tea/coffee facilities if requested. B. &. B. from £14.

Waterside, Crakehall, Bedale, DL8 1HS (0677) 22908
Modern house with an acre of mature gardens; home-cooked food prepared from organically grown vegetables, free range eggs and poultry.
Open all year. No smoking in dining room, sun lounge, sitting room & bedrooms. Vegetarian & other diets by arrangement. Children welcome. En suite 3 rooms. Tea/coffee & T.V. in rooms. B. & B. from £19. D. £12.

DANBY

Fox & Hounds Inn, Brook Lane, Ainthorpe, Nr Danby (0287) 660218
One of the oldest inns in the country and with an impressive guest list which has included Oliver Cromwell; all vegetarian, vegan and diabetic meals are home made from fresh ingredients wherever possible; excellent hand-pulled Theakstons ales.
Vegetarian & vegan standard. Other diets by arrangement. Open all year. No smoking in part of dining room. Licensed. Disabled access for dining only not to bedrooms. Children welcome. Tea/coffee & T.V. in all bedrooms. B. & B. from £14.

GRASSINGTON

Ashfield House Hotel, Grassington, Nr Skipton, BD23 5AE (0756) 752584
Ashfield House is a secluded 17th century hotel, superbly situated in a quiet backwater near the village square. Family-owned and run, the emphasis is on personal service and comfort: each of the bedrooms has been individually styled and furnished, and welcoming log fires blaze in the entrance and the lounge. All the food is home-cooked on the kitchen Aga and only fresh ingredients (some home-grown) are used; a typical evening meal might feature Cheese-topped Ratatouille, followed by Chicken with Grape and Cider Sauce, and a tempting dessert such as Nutcracker Tart or Burgundy Cream.
Open mid-Jan. to early Nov. No smoking ex. entrance lounge. Vegetarian & other diets by arrangement. Licensed. Children: over 5s. En suite 6 rooms. TV & Tea/coffee all rooms. B. & B. from £26.75, D. 12.25.

HARROGATE

Amadeus Vegetarian Hotel, 115 Franklin Rd, Harrogate, HG1 5EN (0423) 505151
Elegant private hotel on tree-lined road 5 mins from town centre, exhibition halls and conference centre. Healthy b'fast of natural cereals, fresh fruits, yoghurts, freshly cooked dishes, home made wholewheat toast, honey and preserves. Healthy dinners too!
Exclusively vegetarian/vegan. Open all year ex. Xmas. No smoking in the house, Licensed. Children welcome. En suite in 4 rooms. Tea/coffee-making in all bedrooms. T.V. in lounge and 1 bedroom. B. & B. from £22. D. £12.

Hookstone House Farm, Low Lane, Darley, Nr Harrogate, HG3 2QN (0423) 780572
Hookstone House farm is a 300 year old cottage farmhouse (with a variety of animals) which stands amidst wonderful countryside 10 miles from Harrogate, Knaresborough, Skipton, & Otley. It has a homely atmosphere (only 5 guests at any one time), & a log fire supplements the central heating in cooler weather. You are close to a number of golf courses & riding centres; additionally there are some lovely walks.
Open all year. No smoking in dining room & bedrooms. Gluten-free standard. Vegetarian & other diets by arrangement. Children welcome. Pets by arrangement. En suite in 1 room. Tea/coffee-making. T.V. B. & B. from £15. D. £7.

The Low Hall Hotel & Coachhouse Restaurant, Ripon Rd, Killinghall, Harrogate, HG3 2AY (0423) 508598
Luxurious 17th century hotel and restaurant with open fires and minstrels' gallery.
Open all year. No smoking in restaurants. Vegetarian by arrangement. Licensed. Disabled access. Children welcome. En suite, TV & tea/coffee in bedrooms.

Scotia House Hotel, 66 Kings Rd, Harrogate, HG1 5JR (0423) 504361

A small, comfortable hotel in the hub of Harrogate opposite the Conference Centre.

Open all year ex. Xmas & New Year. No smoking in dining room & bedrooms. Vegetarian & other diets by arrangement. Licensed. Children: over 7s only. Pets welcome. En suite in most rooms. Tea/coffee-making & T.V. in all rooms. B. & B. from £22.50. D. £9.75.

Wharfedale House Hotel, 28 Harlow Moor Drive, Harrogate, HG2 OJY (0423) 522233

Wharfedale House is a quiet, comfortable spacious house which is beautifully situated overlooking the lovely Valley Gardens yet just a leisurely walk from the centre of the elegant spa town of Harrogate with its exhibition and conference centre. The house has been beautifully furnished and appointed and each of the en suite bedrooms has tea and coffee-making facilities and a colour T.V. Food is first-rate: the proprietors are trained chefs and will often prepare meals only after consultation with guests about their individual requirements and, having eschewed the idea of incorporating a potentially noisy bar onto the premises, they offer a much more civilised Licensed Bar Service in the comfortable lounge; lots of other helpful services are also available including babysitting, dry cleaning and free collection from the station. Situated twixt the Moors and the Dales, Harrogate is a perfect base from which to explore both of these regions, and additionally you are just 45 minutes' drive from York.

Open all year. No smoking in dining room. Vegetarian & other diets by arrangement. Licensed. Children welcome. Pets welcome by arrangement. En suite, tea/coffee & T.V. in all rooms. B. & B. from £22.

The White House, 10 Park Parade, Harrogate, HG1 5AH (0423) 501388

Elegant 19th C. house; excellent food prepared from fresh produce.

Open all year. No smoking in part of dining room. Vegetarian & other diets by arrangement. Licensed. Children welcome. Pets by arrangement En suite & TV in all rooms. Tea/coffee. B. &. B. from £37.50.

HAWES

Rigg House West, Appersett, Hawes, DL8 3LR (0969) 667712

Historic house built by Edmund Hillary's forbears. All food home-cooked & freshly prepared - including the bread.

Open all year. No smoking in bedrooms. Vegetarian & low fat by arrangement. Licensed. Children welcome. Tea/coffee on request. T.V.

Simonstone Hall, Hawes, Wensleydale, DL8 3LY (0969) 667255

Simonstone Hall, dating from 1733, has been restored and converted into a most comfortable owner-run country house hotel. The menu offers freshly prepared English dishes using an abundance of local produce. The English Tourist Board recently adjudged owner John Jeffryes the hotelier offering the warmest welcome to visitors and one of a select few to receive the RAC top award - the Blue Ribbon - for the last 4 years. The large, south-facing panelled drawing rooms are beautifully furnished with antiques and command uninterrupted views of upper Wensleydale. You are in excellent walking country, and only five minutes from the Pennine Way.

Vegetarian & healthy choice standard. Most other special diets, including gluten-free & diabetic, by arrangement. Open all year. Smoking effectively discouraged in dining room. Licensed. Disabled access. Children & dogs always welcome. En suite, tea/coffee-making & TV in bedrooms. Access, Visa. B & B from £50. D. £22.50. Anytime Breaks: 2 nights D., B. & B. (high season) from £65. Reductions out of season & longer stay.

HELMSLEY

The Pheasant Hotel, Harome, Helmsley, YO6 5JG (0439) 71241/70416

Delightful hotel created from existing village dwellings with a large garden & paddock, overlooking pond. Indoor heated pool.

Open March to Nov. No smoking in dining room. Vegetarian & other diets by arrangement. Licensed. Disabled access. Children: over 12s only. Pets by arrangement. En suite, TV & tea/coffee-making in all rooms. T.V. in all rooms. D., B. & B. £48 - 58.

HUNMANBY

Wrangham House Hotel, Stonegate, Hunmanby, YO14 ONS (0723) 891333

Converted Georgian vicarage in half an acre of grounds, in a peaceful village 3m from coast.

North Yorkshire

Open all year. No smoking. Vegetarian & other diets by arrangement. Licensed. Disabled access. En suite, TV & tea/coffee in rooms. B. & B. £30.75. D. £11.75.

HUTTON-LE-HOLE

Burnley House Country Hotel, Hutton-le-Hole, YO6 6UA (07515) 548

Elegant Georgian farmhouse on the village green amidst the picturesque stone-built cottages with their red pantiled roofs. Stone-flagged floors, beamed ceilings & furnished with locally-made furniture; welcoming log fires. Most bedrooms have pleasant views. The home cooked traditional English food is often prepared from local produce.

Open March to Dec. No smoking. Vegetarian & other diets by arrangement. Licensed. Wheelchair access. No children - over 15s only. En suite, tea/coffee making & T.V. in all rooms. B. & B. from £23.

Hammer & Hand Country Guest House, Hutton-le-Hole, YO6 6UA (07515) 300

A charming, listed Georgian property in lovely village, facing the green and beck and within North York Moors National Park.

Open all year. No smoking in dining room & bedrooms. Vegetarian & other diets by arrangement. Licensed. Over 5s only. En suite, tea/coffee & T.V. in all bedrooms. B. & B. from £22. D. £9.50.

INGLETON

Storrs Dale, Hawes Rd, Ingleton, LA6 3AN (0468) 41843

Small guest house specialising in wholesome home cooking.

Open all year. No smoking. Vegetarian & other diets by arrangement. Licensed. Children welcome. Tea/coffee in rooms. T.V. B. & B. from £15.

KIRKBYMOORSIDE

Sinnington Common Farm, Kirkbymoorside, York, YO6 6NX (0751) 31719

Sinnington Common Farm is a 135-acre working, family-run farm, with sheep, cattle, poultry - and pet pigs! The ground floor accommodation adjacent to the farmhouse is comprised of one double and one twin room (each with its own separate outside entrance), and both rooms are spacious and have lovely views overlooking the paddock towards the open countryside beyond; the twin room has full disabled facilities (it has been given the seal of approval by various wheelchair users). Breakfast is served in the comfort of your own room, and the optional dinner has a choice of menus.

Open all year. No smoking in dining room & bedrooms. Vegetarian & other diets by arrangement. Good wheelchair access. Children welcome. Pets by arrangement. En suite, tea/coffee & T.V. in all rooms. B. & B. from £15. ETB 2 Crowns Commended.

LEYBURN

Countersett Hall, Countersett, Askrigg, Leyburn, DL8 3DD (0969) 50373

Ancient Hall with flagged floors, old panelling and open fires (but with all 20th C. comforts and plumbing). Lovely walks.

Open Feb - Oct. No smoking throughout. Vegetarian & other diets by arrangement. Licensed. Children: over 8s only. Pets by arrangement. Tea/coffee-making in all bedrooms. T.V. B. & B. from £17. D. £10.

The Holly Tree, East Witton, Leyburn (0969) 22383

16th C. listed house sympathetically restored and set in one of the prettiest villages in Wensleydale National Park.

Open Easter to end Oct. No smoking in dining room, bedrooms & lounges. Vegetarian & other diets by arrangement. Licensed. En suite. Tea/coffee on request. Separate T.V. lounge. D., B. & B. from £28.

MALTON

Newstead Grange Country House Hotel, Norton, Malton, YO17 9PJ (0653) 692502

Newstead is an elegant Georgian country house retaining authentic features such as working shutters and antique furniture; a log fire blazes in the lounge in cooler weather. Each bedroom is individually styled with period furniture, paintings & prints. The hotel is set in 2 acres of grounds with mature chestnut, copper beech and sycamore trees. All food has been prepared from organically produced fruit and vegetables from the extensive kitchen gardens wherever possible.

Open mid-Feb to Dec. No smoking. Vegetarian & other diets by arrangement. Licensed. Children: over 12s only. En suite, tea/coffee & T.V. in all rooms. B. & B. from £26. D. £11.50. Special breaks.

MIDDLEHAM

Miller's House Hotel, Market Place, Middleham, Wensleydale (0969) 22630

Peaceful Georgian country house commanding splendid views from its elevated position close to the cobbled village square of Middleham.

Open 1 Feb to 2 Jan. No smoking in dining room. Vegetarian standard. Other diets by arrangement. Licensed. Over 10s only. En suite, TV & tea/coffee-making in bedrooms. B. & B. from £30.

NORTHALLERTON

Solberge Hall Hotel, Newby Wiske, Northallerton, DL7 9ER (0609) 77919
Luxury hotel with an atmosphere of Victorian grandeur. Lots of interesting and imaginative special weekends on offer.
Vegetarian standard. Other diets by arrangement. Open all year. Licensed. Disabled access. Children welcome. En suite, tea/coffee & T.V. B. & B. £38.

The Sundial Hotel, Darlington Rd., Northallerton, DL6 2XF (0609) 780525
Modern hotel set in 3 acres of gardens and convenient for Teesside, the Moors and Dales.
Open all year. No smoking in part of dining room and in bedrooms. Vegetarian, vegan, and low-fat diets standard. Other diets by arrangement. Licensed. Disabled access. Children welcome. En suite, TV & tea/coffee-making in all bedrooms. Room from £33.

PATELEY BRIDGE

Moorhouse Cottage, Pateley Bridge, HG3 5JF (0423) 711123
Restored 18th century farmhouse in picturesque surroundings, overlooking Nidderdale.
Open Easter to end Oct. No smoking. Vegetarian & other diets by arrangement. Children welcome. Tea/coffee & TV in rooms. B. & B. from £12. D. £7.

PICKERING

The Blacksmith's Arms and Restaurant, Aislaby, YO18 8PE (0751) 72182
16th C. oak-beamed smithy with original forge in bar; log fires; imaginative food.
Open all year. No smoking in dining room. Vegetarian & vegan standard. Other diets by arrangement. Licensed. Disabled access. Children welcome. En suite in 3 rooms. Tea/coffee & TV in rooms.

Bramwood Guest House, 19 Hallgarth, Pickering, YO18 7AW (0751) 74066
Grade II listed building with comfortable lounge and open fire, set in a charming walled garden.
Open all year. No smoking. Vegetarian & other diets by arrangement. Children: over 3s only. Tea/coffee in all rooms. T.V. lounge. B. & B. from £13.50. D. £7.

RICHMOND

The Kings Head Hotel, Market Place, Richmond, DL10 4HS (0748) 850220
Elegant hotel overlooking cobbled market square. Meals cooked from fresh, local produce
Open all year. No smoking in dining room & some bedrooms. Vegetarian & vegan standard. Other diets by arrangement. Licensed. Disabled access. Children welcome. En suite, tea/coffee & T.V. in rooms.

Peat Gate Head, Low Row in Swaledale, Richmond, DL11 6PP (0748) 86388.
300 year old house on an elevated south facing site overlooking river and dale; excellent food home-prepared from fresh produce
Open all year. No smoking in dining room, 1 sitting room & bedrooms. Vegetarians standard. Other diets by arrangement. Licensed. Ground floor bedroom en suite. Over 5s only. En suite 3 rooms. Tea/coffee. T.V. lounge. D., B. & B. from £32.50.

Ridgeway Guest House, 47 Darlington Rd, Richmond, DL10 7BG (0748) 823801
Ridgeway is a 1920's detached house standing in an acre of lovely gardens, with ample unobstructed parking space. It has been built to a high standard from cut York stone, and stands under a steeply pitched, slated roof and is architecturally interesting both inside and out. A fascinating collection of furniture, clocks and china complement the house - and one bedroom contains a four-poster bed. Food and service are in the best English tradition and locally grown produce is used where possible in cooking. You are centrally situated for exploring the cobbled streets of Richmond, with its Norman castle and Georgian theatre.
Open all year. No smoking throughout. Vegetarian by arrangement. Licensed. Children & pets by arrangement. En suite & tea/coffee-making in rooms. T.V. in sitting room. B. & B. from £17. D. £9.50.

ROBIN HOODS BAY

Falconhurst Wholefood Guest House, Mount Pleasant South (0947) 880582
Double-fronted villa on the Bank Top of the village; all food home-cooked from fresh, sometimes organic, ingredients, including bread, yogurt, preserves and ice cream
Open Easter to Sept. No smoking. Vegetarian/wholefood standard. Children and pets by arrangement. Tea/coffee-making in all rooms. TV in lounge. B. & B. from £16. D. £10.

Meadowfield Bed & Breakfast, Mount Pleasant North, Robin Hood's Bay, Nr Whitby, YO22 4RE (0947) 880564
Delightful Victorian guest house, completely refurbished but retaining original character. Traditional, vegetarian and vegan options always available.
Open all year. No smoking in dining room & all public areas. Vegetarian and most other special diets by arrangement. Children welcome. Tea/coffee-making in all rooms. Portable T.V. available. B. & B. from £13.

SCARBOROUGH

Amber Lodge, 17 Trinity Rd, Scarborough, YO11 2TD (0723) 369088
Edwardian house of great charm and character, peacefully situated in a conservation area 10 mins walk from South Bay and the town centre. Centrally heated. Fresh ingredients used in cooking.
Open Mar. to Oct. No smoking in the house. Vegetarian standard. Other special diets by arrangement. Children welcome. En suite 5 rooms. Tea/coffee-making & T.V. in all rooms. Credit cards B. & B. from £14. D. £6.

Excelsior Private Hotel, 1 Marlborough St, Scarborough, YO12 7HG (0723) 360716

The Excelsior is a small private hotel beautifully situated on a corner of the North Bay; both the North and South bays can be seen from the hotel; there is a T.V. in the comfortable lounge. Much of the food is home made from fresh ingredients - including the bread, preserves, cakes, soups and sweets. You are well placed at the Excelsior for enjoying cliff and coastal walks, the beaches and parks and many attractions of Scarborough and your hosts, Raymond and Irene Brown, will do everything they can to make your stay a happy and memorable one. Weekly terms and short breaks available.
Open Easter to Oct. No smoking throughout. Special diets by arrangement. Children welcome. Tea/coffee-making in all bedrooms. T.V. in lounge. B. & B. from £15, D.B. & B. from £18.

Flower in Hand Hotel, Burr Bank, Scarborough, YO11 1PN (0723) 371471
The Flower in Hand, nestling beneath the castle walls and overlooking the harbour and South Bay, has for 150 years been a much-loved feature of Scarborough's Old Town. It is no longer a pub, but a warm and friendly hotel run by people who genuinely like people and is renowned for traditional sizzling Yorkshire breakfasts, as well as for the wide alternative choice offered to vegetarians and vegans.

Open all year ex. Xmas/New Year. No smoking in dining room. Vegetarians & other diets. Licensed. Children: over 2s only. En suite in 3 rooms. Tea/coffee-making & T.V. in all rooms. Credit cards. B. & B. from £16.50.

Foxcliffe Tearoom, Station Sq., Ravenscar, Scarborough (0723) 871028
19th C. building which is superbly situated overlooking the countryside. All items freshly prepared including light lunches & afternoon teas. The 4 spacious bedrooms have sea views.
Open Easter - Sept. No smoking in the house. Vegetarian by arrangement. TV & tea/coffee-making Children welcome. B. & B. £13, E.M. £7.

Glywin Guest House, 153 Columbus Ravine. Scarborough, YO12 7QZ (0723) 371311
Glywin Guest House is a clean, comfortable establishment close to the sea front and all the attractions of Scarborough. The proprietors specialise in vegetarian cuisine although omnivores are also catered for.
Open all year. No smoking in dining room. Vegetarian food a speciality. Other diets by arrangement. Children welcome. Tea/coffee-making & T.V. in all bedrooms. Credit cards. B. & B. from £10. D. £3.50.

'The Gypsy', Vegetarian Guesthouse, 'Ranworth', Church Rd, Ravenscar, Scarborough, YO13 OLZ (0723) 870366
A Victorian house in the small, peaceful village of Ravenscar overlooking Robin Hood's Bay. Aromatherapy massages also available.
Open all year. No smoking. Vegetarian/wholefood standard. Other diets by arrangement. Children welcome. Pets welcome, by arrangement. Tea/coffee-making in all bedrooms. T.V. lounge and portable T.V. for bedrooms. B. & B. from £14. D. £7.

Lea Grae Guest House, Seamer Crossgates, Scarborough, YO12 4ND (0723) 862465
Guest house in own grounds. Enjoy superb views of the Wolds from the comfort of the spacious sun lounge.
No smoking. Vegetarian and vegan standard. Other diets by arrangement. Disabled access. Children welcome. En suite, vanity units, TV & tea/coffee in all bedrooms. B. & B. from £15. D. £6.50.

Northcote Hotel, 114 Columbus Ravine, Scarborough, YO12 7QZ (0723) 367758
Modern semi-detached hotel pleasantly situated near the beach, Peasholm Park, Water Scene Theme Park and Kinderland.
Open May to Oct. No smoking. Vegetarian & other diets by arrangement. Children: over 3s welcome. En suite, T.V. & tea/coffee in all rooms. B. & B. from £16

Royal Hotel, St Nicholas St, Scarborough, YO11 2HE (0723) 364333

This recently restored Crown Hotel is an outstanding example of Regency architecture and has a restaurant, coffee shop, and Leisure Centre with swimming pool.
Open all year. No smoking in part of dining room & some bedrooms. Vegetarian standard. Other diets by arrangement. Licensed. Children welcome. Pets by arrangement. En suite, TV & tea/coffee in rooms. Credit cards. B. & B. from £47.50. D. from £19.

Wrea Head House, Wrea Head Farm, Barmoor Lane, Scalby (0723) 375844

Beautifully appointed house with panoramic views of the sea and surrounding countryside, set on the edge of the North York Moors Nat. Park.
Open all year. No smoking. Vegetarian & other diets by arrangement. Children: over 8s only. En suite, tea/coffee & T.V. in all rooms. Credit cards. B. & B. from £17.50-£22.

restaurant extends into the new, Georgian-style conservatory with its fine views over the lawned gardens to the hills and moors beyond. The food served therein is first-rate: a range of English and Continental dishes are prepared with imagination and flair, and a typical à la carte selection might feature Mille Feuille of Smoked Duck and Red Cabbage on a Raspberry Dressing followed by King Prawns Deep Fried in a Cinnamon Batter and Pan Fried Loin of Venison served with a Confit of Cabbage, Bacon and Thyme Spatzle; the desserts are irresistible. The extensive grounds include croquet lawns and a 9-hole putting green, and fly-fishing and clay-pigeon shooting may each be enjoyed locally.
Open all year. No smoking in dining room & bedrooms. Vegetarian & other diets by arrangement. Licensed. Disabled access. Children welcome. Pets by arrangement. En suite, tea/coffee-making & TV in all rooms. Access,Visa, Amex, Diners. B. & B. from £85.

SKIPTON

Ashfield House Hotel, Grassington, Nr Skipton, BD23 5AE (0756) 752584

Ashfield House is a secluded 17th century hotel, superbly situated near the village square.
Open mid-Feb to early Nov. No smoking in dining room & lounge. Vegetarian & other diets by arrangement. Licensed. Children: over 5s only. En suite in 5 rooms. Tea/coffee-making & TV in all rooms. B. & B. from £28.

Bridge End Farm, Grassington, Threshfield, Skipton, BD23 5NH (0756) 752463

A charming Dales cottage with beams, window seats & a spiral staircase; its large gardens run down to the river. Log fires.
Open all year. No smoking. Vegetarian and most other special diets by arrangement. Children welcome. T.V. in most bedrooms. B. & B. from £18.

Devonshire Arms Country House Hotel, Bolton Abbey, Skipton, BD23 6AJ (0756) 710 441

The Devonshire Arms is an historic hotel (hospitality has been offered on this site since the 17th C.) which stands in the heart of the Yorkshire Dales, midway between the east and west coasts. It has been carefully restored and extended, under the personal supervision of the Duchess of Devonshire, to create an hotel of great elegance, character and charm: a stone-flagged reception hall with an open log fire leads into handsome lounges furnished with antiques and family portraits from Chatsworth, and the recenty refurbished Burlington

WHITBY

Cote Bank Farm, Egton Rd, Aislaby, Whitby (0947) 85314

Cote Bank is a substantial, stone-built 18th C. farmhouse with mullioned windows, log fires and period furniture which stands in a sheltered position amidst a large garden enjoying wonderful country views. The food is wholesome and delicious: fresh produce is used wherever possible and, although this is primarily a bed and breakfast establishment, your hostess, Mrs Howard, will be happy to prepare an evening meal on request. You will find Cote Bank Farm an excellent base for exploring the varied scenery of the North York Moors; Goathland, Robin Hoods Bay and the North York Moors Railway are nearby, while visitors in search of safe, sandy beaches will find them just 5 miles away at historic Whitby with its famous abbey.
Open all year ex. Xmas. No smoking in the house. Vegetarian & other diets by arrangement. Children welcome. H & C, shaver points & tea/coffee-making in all rooms. T.V. in lounge. Amex. B. & B. from £16. D. £9.

'The Low House', Baysdale, Kildale, Nr Whitby, YO21 2SF (0642) 722880

A small 18th century guest house surrounded by moorland with a river nearby, commanding superb views on all sides.
Open Easter to Sept. No smoking. Vegetarian exclusively. Children: over 5s only. B. & B., picnic lunch and dinner from £25.

1 Well Close Terrace, Whitby, YO21 3AR (0947) 600173

Vegetarian B. & B. family guest house.
Vegetarian standard. Open most of year but subject to availability. No smoking. B. & B. from £8.50.

Wentworth House, 27 Hudson St, West Cliff, Whitby, YO21 3EP (0947) 602433

Beautiful 4-storey Victorian house 5 minutes' walk from the harbour, beach and town centre of Whitby. The food is wholesome and delicious: everything is freshly prepared (from organic ingredients wherever possible - including free-range eggs) and the proprietors specialise in wholefood vegetarian meals although non-vegetarian dishes are also available.
Open all year. No smoking. Vegetarian/wholefood a speciality. Other special diets by arrangement. Licensed. Disabled access: ground floor en suite room with suitable fittings in shower room. Children welcome. En suite in 3 rooms. Tea/coffee in all rooms. T.V. lounge. Credit cards accepted. B. & B. from £12.

YORK

Bowen House, 4 Gladstone St, Huntington Rd., York YO3 7RF (0904) 636881

Late Victorian town house, carefully decorated and furnished with antique and period furniture. Private car par. Close to city centre, restaurants and tourist attractions. Traditional English and vegetarian breakfasts. Reduced winter rates.
Open all year. Smoking banned throughout. Vegetarian standard. No disabled access. Children welcome. Pets by arrangement. En suite in 2 rooms. Tea/coffee-making & T.V. in all bedrooms. Credit cards. B. &. B. from £14. Reduced winter rates.

City Guest House, 68 Monkgate, York, YO3 7PF (0904) 622483

The City Guest House is a lovely Victorian terraced house which is conveniently situated in Monkgate, just a few minutes' walk from the ancient city walls. It is 'comfy, cosy, and a haven for non-smokers', with a choice of single, double or family rooms which have each been decorated and furnished to a very high standard and have en suite facilities; there is a comfortable lounge for guests' use. Breakfast is served in the elegant Victorian dining room (in addition to traditional English there are vegetarian, vegan and continental options available), and there is a wide choice of excellent restaurants within a few minutes' stroll. There is private parking at the City Guest House - an essential amenity in York - and you are within walking distance of all of the city's many attractions including the Jorvik Centre, York Minster and the Shambles. ETB 2 Crowns.
Open all year. No smoking. Vegetarian standard. Most other special diets by arrangement. Children welcome. En suite, tea/coffee & T.V. in all bedrooms. Credit cards. B. & B. from £14.

Dairy Wholefood Guesthouse, 3 Scarcroft Rd., York YO2 1ND (0904) 639367

A pleasant, tastefully renovated Victorian town house decorated and furnished throughout with plants and natural pine, with touches of Sanderson, Habitat and Laura Ashley. It enjoys full central heating and has a lovely enclosed courtyard. A full breakfast is served ranging from traditional British to wholefood/vegetarian. You are only 200 yards south of the mediaeval city walls, within easy walking distance of the many attractions of York city centre.
Open Feb. to Dec. No smoking in dining room & sitting room. Vegetarian/wholefood a speciality. Other diets by arrangement. Children welcome. En suite in 2 rooms. Tea/coffee-making & TV in all rooms. B. & B. from £15.

Kilima Hotel, 129 Holgate Rd, York YO2 4DE (0904) 625787

A restored Victorian rectory in a conservation area close to the centre of York. *AA **. RAC ***. ETB 4 Crown Commended.*
Open all year. No smoking in dining room. Vegetarian standard. Other diets by arrangement. Licensed. Disabled access: concrete ramp and 2 rooms speically adapted. Children welcome. Pets by arrangement. En suite, TV & tea/coffee-making in all rooms. Credit cards. B. & B. from £34. D. £17.25.

The Limes Hotel, 135 Fulford Rd, York (0904) 624548

The Limes is a family-run hotel in an Edwardian house situated on the main A19 road and particularly well placed for the university and the golf course. Home-cooked meals and home-baking from wholefood ingredients are a speciality. You are just a mile and a half from the many attractions of York city centre.
Open all year. No smoking ex. bar. Vegetarian by arrangement. Licensed. Children welcome. En suite, TV & tea/coffee in bedrooms. Credit cards. B. & B. from £26.

The Lodge, Earswick Grange, Earswick, York, YO3 9SW (0904) 761387

The Lodge is a modern family home which stands amidst large, well-kept gardens, complete with paddock, free-range hens and apiary (fresh eggs and plenty of honey for breakfast!) in a lovely rural setting near the historic city of York. The house has been very comfortably furnished throughout - there are two spacious bedrooms - and a welcoming open fire burns in the grate on cooler days. You are perfectly situated at The Lodge for visiting both the city of York and for touring the North York Moors and Dales; additionally you are within easy reach of both Ryedale Sports Stadium and York golf club.
Open all year. No smoking. Vegetarian b'fast option, & other diets by arrangement. Children welcome. Tea/coffee. T.V. lounge. B. &. B. from £13. ETB 1 Crown.

21 Park Grove, York, YO3 7LG (0904) 644790

Exclusively vegetarian B. & B. in spacious Victorian town house quietly situated in a residential area 10 mins. walk from the centre of York and the Minster. En suite accommodation. Organic food including home-made bread. 3 good vegetarian restaurants nearby.
Open all year. No smoking. Exclusively vegetarian. Vegan and other special diets standard. En suite & tea/coffee-making in all rooms. T.V. in lounge. B. & B. from £15.

Pauleda House Hotel, 123 Clifton, York YO3 6BL (0904) 634745

Small, comfortable hotel with four-posters in some rooms 1m. from York Minster & city centre.

Open all year. No smoking in dining room. Vegetarian & other diets by arrangement. Licensed. En suite, tea/coffee & T.V. in all rooms. Access, Visa. B. & B. from £21.

Pond Cottage, Brandsby Rd, Stillington, Nr York, YO6 1NY (0347) 810796

Tiny 18th C. cottage crammed with character and antiques. The garden has a terrace, croquet lawn and a natural pond.
Open Feb. to end Nov. No smoking. Vegetarian & other diets by arrangement. Children welcome. Tea/coffee in bedrooms. T.V. lounge. B. & B. from £12.

Regency House, 7 South Parade, Blossom St, York, YO2 2BA (0904) 633053

This charming Grade II listed Regency House was built in 1824 and stands in a private cobbled road just 6 minutes' walk from the railway station and less than 2 minutes' walk from Micklegate Archway and the city centre. The bedrooms have each been comfortably furnished (some have *en suite* facilities) and the dining room has an old Yorkshire Range and a low-beamed ceiling; the breakfast is excellent, and some recent guests commented that it was the best they had had on their travels! You are within easy reach of a number of interesting places at Regency House including Whitby, Harrogate, Scarborough and the Yorkshire Moors and Dales.
Open mid-Jan. to mid-Dec. Smoking banned throughout. Vegetarian and diabetic standard. Children: over 8s only. Tea/coffee-making in all bedrooms. T.V. in all bedrooms. B. & B. from £14.50.

Wellgarth House, Wetherby Rd, Rufforth, York, YO2 3QB (0904) 738592

Detached house in the delightful village of Rufforth, 4 miles from York. Glider flying, microlight flying, museum of mechanical music, car boot sales & clay pigeon shooting, all locally!
Open all year ex. Xmas. No smoking in the house. Vegetarian & other diets by arrangement. Children welcome. Pets by arrangement. En suite, TV & tea/coffee-making in bedrooms. Credit cards. B. & B. from £14.

South Yorkshire

ROTHERHAM

The Rotherham Moat House, 102/104 Moorgate Rd, Rotherham, S60 2BG (0709) 364902

Modern hotel with leisure club, member of the Queens Moat House group, serving fine cuisine prepared using only the freshest produce from local suppliers. Convenient for M1 and M18.

Open all year. Vegetarian standard. Most other special diets by arrangement. Licensed. Disabled access. Children welcome. Pets by arrangement. En suite, TV & tea/coffee-making in all bedrooms. Access, Visa, Amex, Diners. B. & B. from £22.75.

SHEFFIELD

The George Hotel Main Rd, Hathersage, Nr Sheffield, S30 1BB (0433) 50436

16th C. stone built hotel with friendly service and good food and wine.

Open all year. No smoking in dining room. Licensed. Children welcome. En suite, TV & tea/coffee-making facilities in all rooms. B. & B. from £38.

Parkfield House, 97 Norfolk Rd, Sheffield (0742) 720404

Elegant, modernised Victorian house, close Sheffield city centre.

Open all year. No smoking in the house. Vegetarian standard. Other diets by arrangement. Tea/coffee-making & TV in rooms. B. & B. £15.

West Yorkshire

HALIFAX

Collyers Hotel, Burnley Rd, Luddendenfoot, Halifax, HX2 6AH (0422) 882624

Collyers Hotel is a sympathetically converted Victorian building nestling deep in the spectacular valley of Calderdale, overlooking the River Calder and with magnificent views of the surrounding vale; the recently re-opened Rochdale Canal, with its traditional horse-drawn barges, can be also seen from the hotel. The hotel's elegant restaurant is open to non-residents and guests may choose from a wide selection of both imaginative and traditional dishes (including vegetarian) which have each been prepared from the finest, seasonal produce. The bar, which is also open to non-residents, serves coffee, traditional afternoon teas and various light lunches as well as a good selection of alcoholic beverages. You are within easy reach of a number of places including the business centres of Leeds & Manchester.

Open all year. No smoking some bedrooms. Vegetarian & other diets standard. Licensed. Disabled access. Children welcome. Pets by arrangement. En suite in most rooms. Tea/coffee-making & T.V. in all rooms. Access, Visa, Diners, Amex. B. & B. from £21.

Holdsworth House Hotel, Holdsworth, Halifax, HX2 9TG (0422) 240024

Beautifully preserved 17th C. house with panelling, open fireplaces.

Open all year. No smoking in part of restaurant. Vegetarian & other diets by arrangement. Licensed. Disabled access. En suite & T.V. in rooms.

HAWORTH

Ponden Hall, Stanbury, Nr Haworth (0535) 44154

Ponden Hall is a listed Elizabethan farmhouse with a Georgian extension which is gloriously situated on the Pennine Way amidst rugged moors and farmland; it was reputed to be the Thrushcross Grange of Emily Bronte's *Wuthering Heights* (a little booklet about the literary link is published by the proprietors), but these days is a family home which, for the best part of this century, has offered comfortable hospitality to numerous travellers and walkers on the moors. The atmosphere is 'friendly and informal' and guests dine around a huge table (which seats 18) in the large oak-beamed dining room with its mullioned windows; the food is plentiful, fresh and home-cooked, and vegetarians and vegans can be catered for with advance notice. The guest rooms are beautiful:

one is 16th C. and the other two were modernised at the time of the extension.
Open all year. Vegetarian & other diets by arrangement. Facilities for disabled. Children welcome. Pets by arrangement. B. & B. from £14.50. D. £8.

HEBDEN BRIDGE
Hebden Lodge Hotel & Restaurant, New Rd, Hebden Bridge, HX7 8AD (0422) 845272

The proprietors of the Hebden Lodge Hotel have sent me an excerpt from their visitors' book which sums up the standard of their establishment and is worth quoting in full: "A modest exterior hides a wealth of truly professional hotel management. The comfort, care and well-being of their guests is paramount. The food and its presentation is of the highest quality. Hebden Bridge should be proud of the standards set by this small hotel." High praise indeed. And Healthy Holiday Guide visitors will not be disappointed by the nutritional quality of the cuisine: everything on the extensive and daily-changing menu is prepared from fresh, seasonal produce and, as the propietors remark, the only problemis likely to be that you will be spoilt for choice!
Vegetarian standard. Other diets by arrangement. Open all year ex. Xmas. Licensed. Disabled access and ground floor rooms. Children welcome. Pets by arrangement. En suite, T.V., phones & tea/coffee in all rooms. B. & B. from £35. Special breaks.

HOLMFIRTH
Holme Castle Country Hotel, Holme Village, Holmfirth, HD7 1QG (0484) 686764

Large Victorian house standing in a mature, walled garden with magnificent views of the surrounding hills & moorland; beautifully furnished & with many original features; fabulous cuisine.

Open all year. No smoking. Vegetarian & other diets by arrangement. Licensed. Children welcome. En suite in 5 rooms. T.V., radio alarm & hairdryer in all rooms. Access, Visa. B. & B. from £25 (with reduced rates on Fri., Sat. & Sun.) D. £19.

SOWERBY BRIDGE
Wood End, Lighthazels Rd, Nr Mill Bank, Ripponden (0422) 824397

Grade II listed building set in its own grounds, surrounded by woodland.
Open all year. No smoking. Vegetarian & other diets by arrangement. Children welcome. 1 en suite. Tea/coffee both bedrooms. T.V. B. & B. from £15.

WAKEFIELD
Cedar Court Hotel, Denby Dale Rd, Calder Grove, WF4 3QZ (0924) 276310

Elegant luxury hotel with superb facilities near the M1 midway between London and Scotland.
Open all year. No smoking in part of dining room and some bedrooms. Vegetarian and other special diets by arrangement. Licensed. Disabled access. Children welcome. Tea/coffee-making, en suite & TV in all bedrooms. B. & B. from £48.50. D. from £21.50

WETHERBY
Glendales, Muddy Lane, Linton, Nr Wetherby, LS22 4HW (0937) 585915

Glendales is a lovely, large detached house which stands overlooking the village green in the attractive village of Linton near Wetherby. In spite of its country setting, you are just 10 minutes from the A1 and at the half way point between London and Edinburgh (making Glendales an ideal stop-over point for those travelling to Scotland from the South). Good English cooking is a hallmark of a stay at Glendales and, with its proximity to York, Harrogate and Leeds (each 20 minutes away), you are ideally placed for enjoying a touring holiday in the Yorkshire Dales.
Open all year. No smoking. Vegetarian and most other special diets by arrangement. Children: over 12s only. Pets welcome. En suite in 1 room. Tea/coffee-making facilities. T.V. B. & B. from £15.

Wood Hall, Linton, (0937) 67271

Lovely Georgian house set in its own parkland, sumptuously furnished and with views.
Open all year. No smoking in dining room & bedrooms. Vegetarian standard. Other diets by arrangement. Licensed. Disabled access. Children welcome. En suite & TV in rooms. B. & B. from £55.

The North East
Co Durham

BISHOP AUCKLAND
Grove House, Hamsterley Forest, Bishop Auckland, DL13 1NL (0388) 88203
Once an aristocrat's shooting box, in the middle of Hamsterley Forest with its 5,000 acres of mixed woodland, moors and becks. All food is freshly prepared from fine local ingredients; game from the forest features regularly.
Open Jan. to Nov. No smoking. Vegetarian & other diets by arrangement. Children: over 8s. Tea/coffee in all rooms. T.V. lounge. B. &. B. from £20.

BOWBURN
Bowburn Hall Hotel, Bowburn, DH6 5NH (091) 3770311
Beautifully appointed traditional-style hotel standing in 5 acres of gardens and woodlands;.
Vegetarian & low-fat standard. Other diets by arrangement. Open all year. Licensed. Children welcome. En suite & T.V. in rooms. B. &. B. from £35.

CHESTER-LE-STREET
'Crakemarsh' Guest House, Mill Lane, Plawsworth Gate, Chester-le-Street, DH2 3LG (091) 371 2464
This award-winning guest house (just voted '1990 Guest House of the Year' as we went to press) is a lovely country house with panoramic views just 5 minutes from Durham city centre, and 10 minutes from Beamish Museum and the Metro Centre. Several other amenities are close to hand including Durham County Cricket Ground, Lumley Castle and an 18-hole golf course (bookings may be made by arrangement with your hosts). Crakemarsh has been quite beautifully furnished throughout - all rooms have been tastefully designed by the owner - and, although breakfast is the only meal available at Crakemarsh, the local pub, which is a short walk away, does excellent evening meals. It is worth mentioning that Crakemarsh's award, which was sponsored by Makro in conjunction with the National Garden Festival, was based on nominations received by guests!
Open all year. No smoking. Vegetarian & other diets by arrangement. Children welcome, family room available. Tea/coffee making & T.V. in all rooms. B. &. B. from £18 (£22 single, children 3 - 12 half price). ETB listed & Commended.

CONSETT
Bee Cottage Farm, Castleside, Consett, DH8 9HW (0207) 508224

Bee Cottage Farm is a working farm set in peaceful and picturesque surroundings close to the Northumberland/Durham border. It is a very friendly place: visitors are welcome to see the animals - mainly young stock - and children especially are encouraged to participate in the easier (and nicer!) bits of farming life (bottle-feeding baby lambs, perhaps even milking the goat!). The farmhouse itself has been very comfortably decorated; guests may stay as self-caterers or take breakfast if they wish, but most visitors will be tempted by the Tea Room which is open from Easter to September and serves quite delicious cream teas!
Vegetarian & other diets by arrangement. Wholefood on request. Open all year. No smoking. Disabled access. En suite & tea/coffee. B. & B. from £16.

DARLINGTON
Blackwell Grange Moathouse, Blackwell Grange, DL3 8QH (0325) 380888
Elegant Georgian country house.
Open all year. No smoking in some bedrooms & public areas. Vegetarian by arrangement. Licensed. Disabled access. Children welcome. Pets by arrangement. En suite, tea/coffee & T.V. in all rooms.

DURHAM
Bees Cottage Guest House, Bridge St, Durham, DH1 4RT (091) 384 5775
Durham's oldest cottage in a central location close to cathedral & castle. Museums, university, river walks and shops all nearby. Private parking.
Open all year. No smoking in dining room & bedrooms. Vegetarian & other diets by arrangement. Children welcome. En suite, TV & tea/coffee-making in all bedrooms. B. & B. from £19, Single £25.

Colebrick, 21 Crossgate (091) 384 9585
Lovely whitewashed house, full of character half a mile from the city centre; magnificent views of the Cathedral. Healthy options at breakfast.
Open all year. No smoking. Vegetarian and other diets by arrangement. Disabled access: 'good'. Children: over 4s only. Tea/coffee making & T.V. in all rooms. B. &. B. from £19.

Ramside Hall Hotel, Carrville, Durham, DH1 1TD (091) 386 5282

Ramside Hall is a splendid castellated building set in large grounds just off the A1(M)/A690 motor interchange. Formerly the home of the Pemberton family, it was opened as a hotel in 1964 by two businessmen whose families still own it. It has been very luxuriously appointed - there is a pleasing blend of the traditional and the contemporary in the furnishings - and bedrooms are not only individually decorated and styled but are equipped with every modern convenience you could wish for (free in-house movies, fresh fruit, trouser-presses, the lot); two presidential suites offer the ultimate in luxury. Dining is in one of 3 elegant restaurants - each serving a choice of excellent home-made dishes - and a typical evening meal would feature Tuna and Pasta Salad in Raspberrry Vinaigrette, followed by Poached Salmon with Spinach and Hollandaise Sauce, and a selection of sweets and cheeses; first-rate conference and business facilities are first-rate.
Open all year. No smoking at b'fast, in part of carvery & in some bedrooms. Vegetarian and other diets on request. Licensed. Disabled access. Children welcome. En suite, tea/coffee making & TV in all rooms. Credit cards. B. & B. from £75.

Royal County Hotel, Old Elvet, Durham, DH1 3JN (091) 386 6821
The Royal County Hotel is a first-class 150-bedroomed hotel, which has been stylishly appointed and beautifully furnished. It is in the luxury business-class category and therefore has a superb range of leisure amenities including an indoor swimming pool, a spa pool, sauna, steam room, solarium and mini-gym. The bedrooms are very comfortable and have excellent facilities,

and some smoke-free rooms are available. A wide choice of menu is served in the hotel's restaurants and these, too, have good smoke-free areas.
Vegetarian menu standard. Vegan, diabetic and other diets on request. Open all year. Licensed. Disabled access. Children welcome. En suite, tea/coffee making & TV in all rooms. Access, Visa, Amex, Diners, Airplus. B. & B. from £85. Special W/E & summer breaks avail.

TANTOBIE
The Oak Tree Inn (0207) 235445
Carefully restored manor house furnished with antiques; excellent food freshly cooked.
Vegetarian & other diets by arrangement. Open all year. No smoking in part of dining room and some bedrooms. Licensed. Some disabled access. Children welcome. Pets by arrangement. En suite, tea/coffee making & TV in all rooms. B. &. B. from £16.

WEARDALE
Pennine Lodge, St John's Chapel, (0388) 537247
Commended country house by the River Wear.
Open Apr. - Sept. No smoking in dining room. Vegetarian, diabetic & low-fat diets by arrangement. Licensed. En suite. B. & B. from £16.50.

Friarside Farm, Wolsingham (0388) 527361
17th C. farmhouse with views; home-cooking - including bread; also self-catering.
No smoking in dining room. Vegetarian & diabetic by arrangement. Low-fat standard. Children: over 5s only. B. & B. from £14. D. £8.

Northumberland

ALNMOUTH

The Grange, Northumberland St, Alnmouth, NE66 2RJ (0665) 830401

The Grange is a 200 year-old stone-built house and was formerly used as a granary when Alnmouth was a busy grain shipping port; these days it has been totally refurbished (but with care in order to retain the many period features of the house) and, standing in large landscaped gardens overlooking the River Aln just 2 minutes from the beautiful sandy beach, is a perfect place in a perfect location! All bedrooms are very comfortably furnished - some even have canopied four-posters - and the elegant lounge, with its calming river views, is the ideal place in which to relax after a day's sightseeing. Breakfast is excellent; and there is a good variety of more unusual options including fruit compôte and kippers. It is worth pointing out that the proprietors have the very civilised habit of locking the house at 11.30 p.m. to ensure that everyone gets a good night's rest.

Open Mar. to Nov. No smoking. Vegetarian by arrangement. Children: over 5s only. En suite in some rooms. Tea/coffee-making & T.V. in all bedrooms. B. & B. from £18. ETB 2 Crown Highly Commended, and holders of Heartbeat Award.

ALNWICK

Beamish Country House Hotel, Powburn, Alnwick, NE66 4LL (0665)78266/78544

Elegant Georgian-style building, originally a 17th C. farmhouse, set in 5 acres of gardens and woodlands; sumptuous furnishings and log fires; excellent Cordon Bleu cuisine.

Open Feb. to Dec. No smoking in dining room. Vegetarian by arrangement. Licensed. Some disabled access. Children: over 12s only, younger by arrangement. En suite, tea/coffee making & TV in all bedrooms. D., B. & B. from £45.

Townfoot Farm, Townfoot, Lesbury, Alnwick, NE66 3AZ (0665) 830755

Beautiful farmhouse with garden overlooking the River Aln; comfortable accommodation & open fire; excellent wholefood menu prepared from home-grown produce.

Open March to Oct. No smoking in dining room & upstairs. Vegetarian & other diets by arrangement. Children welcome. Pets by arrangement. Tea/coffee-making in all rooms. T.V. in lounge. B. & B. from £16. D.£9.

BAMBURGH

Waren House Hotel, Waren Mill, Nr Bamburgh, NE70 7EE (06684) 581

Splendid 18th C. country house set in 6 acres of wooded grounds; beautifully furnished and appointed. *ETB 4 Crowns Highly Commended.*

Open all year. No smoking ex. in library. Vegetarian by arrangement. Licensed. Some disabled access. En suite, TV & tea/coffee-making in all bedrooms. Credit cards. B. & B. from £52.

BARDON MILL

Eldochan Hall, Willimoteswyke, Bardon Mill, NE47 7DB (0434) 344465

Large 18th C. family house in rural position close to Reiver Castle; oak beams and inglenook fireplace; good home-cooking.

Open all year ex. Xmas. No smoking. Vegetarian & other special diets by arrangement. Children welcome. En suite & tea/coffee-making in all bedrooms. T.V. B. & B. £15.

Vallum Lodge Hotel, Military Rd, Twice Brewed, Nr Bardon Mill, NE47 7AN (0434) 344248

Delightful small hotel, warm and comfortable, set in open countryside by Hadrian's Wall. Good choice of fresh foods at all meals. Home-baking. All ground floor rooms.

Open Feb. to Nov. inc. No smoking in dining room. Vegetarian & other diets by arrangement. Ground floor rooms but bathrooms not accessible to wheelchair. Licensed. Children and pets welcome. En suite some rooms. TV in lounge. Tea/coffee-making in all bedrooms. B. & B. from £20, D. £14.50.

BELLINGHAM

Eals Lodge, Tarset, Bellingham, NE48 1LF (0434) 240269

200-year-old former coaching inn on the shores of Kielder Water, Europe's largest man-made

lake; very comfortably furnished; beamed lounge has its log fires. Meals are prepared from fresh, local produce & high-fibre and low-fat alternatives are available; lots of pasta and wholegrain rice dishes are also available as healthy options.
Open all year. No smoking in dining room & bedrooms. Vegetarian and diabetic standard, other special diets by arrangement. Licensed. En suite, tea/coffee-making & TV in all rooms. B. & B. from £21. ETB 3 Crown 'Commended.'

Ivy Cottage, Lanehead, Bellingham, Nr Hexham, NE48 1NT (0434) 240337
Beautiful stone-built cottage, modernised yet retaining character (beamed ceilings, etc); spacious bedrooms with views; excellent food prepared from fresh, local produce.
Open all year. No smoking in dining room & bedrooms. Vegetarian & vegan standard. Other diets on request. Bring your own wine. Children welcome. Pets by arrangement. En suite in some rooms. Tea/coffee & T.V. in all bedrooms. B. & B. from £15.

Lyndale Guest House, Bellingham, Northumberland, NE48 2AW (0434) 220361
Attractive stone-built house in delightful village; meals are home-prepared from fresh produce wherever possible (including some home-grown fruit and vegetables in season).
Vegetarian and other special diets by arrangement. Wholefood on request. Open all year. No smoking in bedrooms and all public areas ex. dining room. Children welcome. Tea/coffee-making in all bedrooms. T.V. on request. B. & B. from £16. D. £8.

Westfield House, Bellingham, Nr Hexham, NE48 2DP (0434) 220340
Lovely large 19th C. house approached by tree-lined drive (with glorious views); evening meals by arrangement prepared from fresh, local and (sometimes) home-grown produce.
Open all year. No smoking. Vegetarian & other diets by arrangement. Children welcome. Pets by arrangement. En suite in some rooms. Tea/coffee-making in all bedrooms. T.V. in lounge. B. & B. from £17. D. £12

BERWICK-UPON-TWEED

The Estate House, Ford, Berwick-upon-Tweed, TD15 2QG (089 082) 297
The Estate House is a beautiful Edwardian country house which stands amidst large, well-maintained lawned gardens in the picturesque model village of Ford. Accommodation is in comfortably furnished bedrooms, and there are welcoming open fires in each of the public

rooms. The food is wholesome and tasty - everything having been home-cooked from fresh, local ingredients wherever possible. Above all, guests will discover a welcoming, congenial and relaxing atmosphere at the Estate House and will find it a perfect base from which to explore the many impressive castles and abbeys to be found on the beautiful English and Scottish borders; walking, cycling, fishing and riding may all be enjoyed locally.
Open from April to Oct. & 'other times on request'. No smoking in dining room. Vegetarian, gluten-free and most other diets by arrangement. Children: over 5s only. Tea/coffee-making in all bedrooms. T.V. in lounge. B. & B. from £14.

'Tree Tops', The Village Green, East Ord, Berwick-upon-Tweed, TD15 2NS (0289) 330679
Tree Tops is a spacious single storey house of unusual design, which was built in 1920 and has

since been tastefully modernised and beautifully furnished. It is in a delightful setting - facing out onto the green in the peaceful village of East Ord - and a gravel path leads round the house to a truly superb garden of nearly an acre (the house has been dubbed after its many beautiful trees) with a sweeping croquet lawn, small orchard and stream. The house itself is centred around an octagonal hall with wide panelled doors of stripped oak, and dinner is served in the elegant dining room (with its dark oak and blue-ware), the delicious 3-course meal having been prepared from fresh, often garden-grown, produce; a typical evening menu might be home-made Cream of Leek Soup followed by

Asparagus Quiche (with Austrian red cabbage) and a Grand Marnier Fool garnished with Kiwi fruit.
Open Mar. to Oct. No smoking. Vegetarian standard. Disabled access: 'yes, with helper: single storey accommodation with wide doors'. En suite in all rooms. Tea/coffee making. T.V. in lounge. B. & B. from £18. D. £10.50.

CHOLLERFORD

The George Hotel, Chollerford, Nr Hexham, NE46 4EW (0434) 681611
Business-class hotel with a wide range of leisure amenities.
Open all year. No smoking in bar lounge & some bedrooms. Vegetarian standard. Other diets by arrangement. Licensed. Some disabled access. Children welcome. Pets by arrangement. En suite, TV & tea/coffee in rooms. Credit cards. B. & B. from £65.

CORBRIDGE

Chandlers Restaurant, Angel Inn, Main St, Corbridge, NE45 5LA (0434) 712119
Open all year. No smoking in part of dining room. Vegetarian, vegan & diabetic standard. Other diets standard. Licensed. Disabled access. Children welcome. En suite in all rooms. Tea/coffee-making & T.V. in all rooms. Credit cards. B. & B. from £48.

CORNHILL-ON-TWEED

The Coach House at Crookham, Crookham, Cornhill-on-Tweed, TD12 4TD (089 082) 293
Reputedly the oldest cottage in north Northumberland; home-baked cakes and tea served on arrival; most food prepared from organically produced ingredients (including the wines and the meat).
Open Mar. to Nov. No smoking in dining room & lounge. Vegetarian standard. Diabetic & other diets by arrangment. Licensed. Excellent disabled access. Dogs by arrangement. En suite in most rooms. Tea/coffee & TV in all rooms. B. & B. from £21.

Tillmouth Park Hotel, Cornhill-on-Tweed, TD12 4UU (0890) 2255
Tillmouth Park is a 19th C. country house built in the grandest style from stones from a local castle, to the design of Charles Barry (son of the designer of the houses of Parliament). Set amidst a splendid 1,000 acre estate (complete with private salmon fishing on the River Tweed), Tillmouth Park recalls for its guests the leisurely priorities of a bygone era: furnishings are sumptuous in all of the bedrooms - each of which has a private bathroom. The reception

hall is a genuine Victorian extravaganza of stained glass and dark wood screens; there is a galleried lounge leading through the library dining room to French windows which overlook the southfacing gardens. The food is exceptionally good: fresh, local produce is used in the preparation of an imaginative menu and there is an excellent complementary wine list. Small business conferences and special anniversaries can be catered for.
Open all year. Vegetarian & other diets by arrangement. Licensed. Children welcome. Pets welcome, with no charge. En suite, tea/coffee-making & T.V. in all rooms. Visa, Mastercard, Diners, Amex. B. & B. from £43. Discounts for longer stays throughout the year.

FENWICK

The Manor House (0289) 81381
Beamed house with lots of character situated just 200 yards off the A1 near to Holy Island, Bamburgh Castle and the Cheviot Hills.
Open all year. No smoking in dining room, lounge & bedrooms. Vegetarian standard. Licensed. Children welcome. TV & Tea/coffee-making in all bedrooms. B. & B. from £14.50. D. £12.

GREENHEAD-IN-NORTHUMBERLAND

Holmhead Farm Licensed Guest House & Holiday Apartments, Hadrian's Wall, Greenhead-in-Northumberland, via Carlisle CA6 7HY (06977 47402)

Holmhead Farm is a charming old house, which stands amidst pretty gardens (complete with stream) surrounded by the unspoilt and rugged beauty of the Northumberland countryside. Accommodation is in 4 cosy and comfortable en suite bedrooms - each of which have lovely rural views - and there is a separate self-catering cottage for non-smokers in which the range of excellent amenities includes first-class facilities for disabled guests. Perhaps the best thing about

a stay at Holmhead is the food: the proprietors boast correctly that their breakfast menu is the longest in the world: I have no reason to doubt them and wish I could do justice to the range of dishes on offer; suffice to say that if you are in Northumberland and wish to dine at 8 a.m. on a choice of English or Scottish porridge followed by devilled kidneys, waffles and raspberry tea - Holmhead Farm would be your best bet. The evening meal lacks choice - most guests doubtless welcome a break from menu-reading - but does not lack quality: fresh, local ingredients are used in the preparation of an imaginative and tasty 3-course meal, and guests dine together by candlelight at a large, oak table in the cosy beamed dining room.
Open Jan 6th to Dec. 20th. No smoking throughout. Vegetarian & other special diets by arrangement. Licensed. Disabled access to holiday flat & B. & B. Noov. - Mar. Children welcome. En suite in all rooms. Tea/coffee-making & TV in lounge. Access, Visa. B. & B. from £19.50. D. £15.50. Heartbeat Award.

HALTWHISTLE

Ashcroft Guest House, Haltwhistle, NE49 0DA (0434) 320213
Victorian vicarage in private grounds in the quiet market town of Haltwhistle. Comfortably furnished bedrooms, one with a 4-poster. Healthy breakfast with lighter meal options.
Open all year. No smoking throughout. Vegetarian by arrangement. Children welcome. T.V. in lounge. B. & B. from £14. Winners of Heartbeat Award.

White Craig Farm, Shield Hill, Haltwhistle, NE49 9NW (0434) 320565
White Craig Farm accommodation is in a 17th C. croft-style farmhouse on a working farm where sheep - including some prizewinning rare breeds - and English Longhorn cattle are raised. The house has been sympathetically modernised and the sitting room, with its lovely open fireplace, has retained the timber ceiling beams; in addition to bed and breakfast accommodation, four comfortable, well-equipped stone-built self-catering cottages are also available. Your hostess offers a warm and friendly welcome, and prepares a wholesome and delicious breakfast which features several healthy options. With its wonderful views of the South Tyne Valley and the fells beyond, White Craig Farm is also perfectly placed for visiting the central (and best) sites of Hadrian's wall; its excellent facilities led to its selection as 1989 AA Inspectors Choice.
Open all year, ex. Xmas/New Year. Smoking banned throughout. Vegetarian and other special diets by arrangement. Disabled access. Children: over 10s only. En suite, TV & tea/coffee making in all rooms. Heartbeat Award. B. & B. from £18.50.

HAYDON BRIDGE

Geeswood House, Whittis Rd, Haydon Bridge, NE47 6AQ (0434) 684220
Charming 19th C. stone-built house and garden through which flows the Langley Burn; good home-cooking with home-baked bread.
Open all year. No smoking. Vegetarian, low-fat, gluten-free, diabetic & other diets by arrangement. Children: over 10s only. Pets by arrangement. T.V. B. & B. from £15. D. £9

HEXHAM

Beggar Bog Farm, Housesteads, Haydon Bridge, NE47 6NN (0434) 344320
Acclaimed accomm. 13 m. W. of Hexham.
Open all year. No smoking in dining room, lounge & bedrooms. Vegetarian and other special diets by arrangement. Disabled access. Children welcome. En suite in some rooms. B. & B. from £15.

Croft House, Slaley, Hexham, Northumberland (0434) 673322

Croft House is a particularly beautiful country house which stands amidst three quarters of an acre of lovely garden - with private parking - near the lovely town of Hexham. The proprietor, Mrs Taylor, has received a 2 Crown Commended status from the English Tourist Board for the high standards of accommodation, service and food: indeed she recommends her home to guests who want to be cossetted and pampered! Hers is a completely smoke-free stablishment too, so the atmosphere is always clean and fresh; food is of especial importance - vegetarian and other diets can be accommodated by arrangement - and everything is freshly prepared using low-fat cooking methods wherever possible. There is much to see and do in the area - if you can bear to leave the house! You are in perfect country for walking and cycling, and Durham, Hadrian's Wall and the Beamish Museum are all easily reached.
Open all year. No smoking in the house. Vegetarian & other diets standard. En suite & tea/coffee-making in bedrooms. TV in lounge. B. & B. £35 double.

Crowberry Hall, Allendale, Hexham, NE47 9SR (0434) 683392

Crowberry Hall is run by John and Isabel Wentzel who especially welcome walkers (they have devised eight first-rate walks for guests). Wholefood and organic ingredients are used as much as possible in the preparation of the tasty meat-free dishes.

Open all year. No smoking. Vegetarian standard. Other diets by arrangement. Children: over 5s only. Some en suite. T.V. B. & B. from £12. D. £5.50.

Dukeslea, 33 Dukes Rd (0434) 602947

Tastefully refurbished family home offering well-appointed, comfortable en suite double/family room. Quiet situation with open country views.

Open all year. No smoking throughout. Vegetarian and most other special diets by arrangement. Children welcome. En suite shower. Tea/coffee-making & TV in all rooms. B. & B. from £14. ETB Listed.

Manor House Farm, Ninebanks, Hexham, NE47 8DA (0434) 345236

Small Edwardian farmhouse situated in an area of Outstanding Natural Beauty on the Cumbrian/Durham border. Working farm breeding cattle & sheep.

Open all year. No smoking in dining room & bedrooms. Vegetarian & other diets by arrangement. Children & pets welcome. Tea/coffee-making in bedrooms. TV in lounge. B. & B. from £13-16.

Middlemarch, Hencotes, Hexham, NE46 2EB (0434) 605003

Listed Georgian house overlooking the Sele and Abbey in the centre of Hexham.

Open all year. No smoking in dining room & bedrooms. Vegetarian & other diets by arrangement. Children: over 10s only. Pets by arrangement. Some en suite. Tea/coffee & TV in rooms. B. & B. £16-£22.

West Close House, Hextol Terrace, Hexham, NE46 2AD (0434) 603307

Tucked away down a quiet leafy cul-de-sac with private parking, yet just half a mile from the pretty town centre of Hexham (first left off the Allendale Road - B6305), West Close House is a charming, detached 1920's residence set amidst pretty, prize-winning gardens which add to the pleasant secluded atmosphere. The house has been beautifully decorated and furnished with taste and care: each of the four well-appointed bedrooms have views of the lovingly-tended gardens and one double room has en suite facilities while the others have wash basins; there is a T.V. for guests' use downstairs - but there is also a separate elegantly appointed drawing room for those who prefer peace and quiet! The culinary emphasis is on wholefood

cuisine, but all tastes are catered for and only the finest products are used in cooking. The generous breakfast features a Wholefood Continental or Traditional English choice (all freshly cooked to individual requirements), and light snacks with home-made cakes, or packed lunches, can be provided on request. You are perfectly placed for enjoying some of the finest walking (and cycling!) to be had in the country with Hadrian's Wall and numerous other historic sites and buildings just a short drive away; however you may just choose to relax in situ and enjoy the many amenities and attractions of Hexham.

Open all year. No smoking in bedrooms & discouraged elsewhere. Vegetarian, vegan, gluten-free & other diets by arrangement. Children: over 2s only. One en suite. Tea/coffee making & radio alarms in all rooms. T.V. in lounge. B. & B. from £16.

KIRKWHELPINGTON

The Old Vicarage, Kirkwhelpington, NE19 2RT (0830) 40319

Beautiful Grade II listed Georgian vicarage in prize-winning village; free-range eggs and organically home-grown and wholefood fare.

Open Apr. to Oct. No smoking in dining room & lounge. Vegetarian & other diets by arrangement. Children welcome. Pets by arrangement. En suite in some rooms. Tea/coffee-making in all rooms. T.V. in lounge. B. & B. from £12.50-£16.

MORPETH

The Bakers Chest, Hartburn 0670) 72214

Beautiful stone-built house in delightful countryside in the charming village of Hartburn; comfortable accommodation and excellent food; many beautiful walks through tranquil woods.

Open Easter - Oct. No smoking in house. Vegetarian and other diets by arrangement. Children welcome. Tea/coffee-making. T.V. in lounge. B. & B. from £14.

ROTHBURY
Thropton Demesne Farmhouse, Thropton, NE65 7LT (0669) 20196
Victorian stone-built farmhouse with walled garden in an unspoilt dale; home-cooked food prepared from fresh, local ingredients.
Open all year. No smoking. Vegetarian & other diets by arrangement. Children welcome. En suite, TV & tea/coffee making in rooms. B. & B. £16.50.

SLALEY
Rye Hill Farm (0434) 673259
300-year-old stone farmhouse in 30 acres of working farm; self-catering & B. & B. (with D. by arrangement); log fires, home-cooking.
Open all year. No smoking in dining room & all bedrooms. Vegetarian & other diets by arrangement. Licensed. Children welcome. Pets by arrangement. En suite, tea/coffee-making & TV in all bedrooms. B. & B. from £16.50. D. £9.

STOCKSFIELD
The Dene, 11 Cade Hill Rd, Stocksfield, NE43 7PB (0661) 842025
Edwardian house quietly situated and surrounded by beautiful gardens and woodland; spacious rooms furnished with antiques; good home-cooking (Northumbrian and oriental menus) prepared from garden produce.
Open all year. No smoking in dining room & most of house. Vegetarian and other special diets by arrangement. Children welcome. En suite, tea/coffee making & TV in all bedrooms. B. & B. from £15.

Tyne & Wear

NEWCASTLE-ON-TYNE
'Bywell', 54 Holly Avenue, Jesmond, Newcastle-on-Tyne, NE2 2QA (091) 281 7615
Large, Victorian town house in a quiet residential cul-de-sac in the popular area of Jesmond, with its restaurants, bistros & wine bars.
Open all year. No smoking. Vegetarian standard. Other special diets by arrangement. Children welcome. B.& B. from £16.50.

Imperial Hotel, Jesmond Rd, NE2 1PR (091) 281 5511
Busy modern hotel in the centre of Jesmond; 2 mins drive from all major routes through the city.
Vegetarian standard. Vegan, low-cholesterol and other special diets by arrangement. Open all year. Licensed. Disabled access. Children welcome. Pets by arrangement. En suite, TV & tea/coffee-making in all rooms. Credit cards. B. & B. from £79.

Swallow Gosforth Park Hotel, High Gosforth Park (091) 236 4111
Large, modern hotel set in 12 acres of parkland; superbly appointed and with excellent food.
Vegetarian & other diets by arrangement. Licensed. Open all year. No smoking in some bedrooms. Disabled access. Children welcome. Pets by arrangement. En suite, TV & tea/coffee-making in all rooms. Credit cards. B. & B. from £88.

Swallow Hotel, Newgate St, NE1 5SX (091) 232 5025
Large, modern business-class hotel in city centre; well-appointed and with conference facilities.
Vegetarian & other diets by arrangement. Open all year. No smoking in some bedrooms. Licensed. Children welcome. En suite, TV & tea/coffee-making in all rooms. B. & B. from £45.

OTTERBURN
Percy Arms Hotel, Otterburn, NE19 1NR (0830) 20261
Fine country inn with open fires, beamed ceilings and lots of character; everything on excellent menu has been home-cooked from fresh ingredients.
Vegetarian, vegan, diabetic and other special diets standard. Wholefood when avail. Open all year. Licensed. Disabled access. Children welcome. Pets by arrangement. En suite, TV & tea/coffee-making in all rooms. Access, Visa, Amex, Diners. B. & B. from £42.50.

WASHINGTON
Washington Moat House, Stone Cellar Rd, High Usworth, District 12, Washington, NE37 1PH (091) 417 2626
Very well-appointed business class hotel with good conference facilities; excellent leisure facilities include gym, squash courts, sauna and championship length golf course.
Open all year. No smoking in part of dining room and some bedrooms. Vegetarian standard. Other special diets by arrangement. Licensed. Disabled access. Children welcome. Pets by arrangement. En suite, TV & tea/coffee-making in all rooms. Access, Visa, Amex, Diners. B. & B. from £87.50.

Channel Islands

GUERNSEY

The Bedford Hotel, Queen's Rd, St Peter Port, Guernsey (0481) 728430

Elegant Regency building which has been charmingly refurbished and offers comfortable accommodation and excellent cuisine prepared from fresh, local produce; four-poster avail.
Open March to Nov. No smoking in dining room and lounge. Vegetarian & other diets by arrangement. Licensed. Children welcome. En suite, TV & tea/coffee in all rooms. Credit cards. B. & B. from £31.

La Favorita Hotel, Fermain Bay, Guernsey (0481) 35666

La Favorita is an attractive white-painted building set amidst pleasant gardens in the beautiful wooded valley which leads down to Fermain Bay. It used to be a privately owned country house and, although these days it has been considerably extended and modernised, it retains the character (and of course magnificent sea views!) of its former life; from the elegant drawing room with its open fire to the intimate dining room with its lovely garden views, everywhere there is an atmosphere of peaceful tranquility and guests are encouraged to relax, unwind and enjoy. The food is excellent: the menu, which changes daily, is based around traditional English cooking (with some imaginative Continental culinary excursions) and a typical evening meal would feature Baked Blue Brie with Mushroom Sauce, followed by Cream of Chicken Soup, Baked Sea Bream with Tomato, and a delicious dessert, such as Coupe Mandarine; there is a good vegetarian option on each evening menu. A recent highly successful addition to La Favorita is its pleasant Coffee Shop, overlooking the garden, in which light meals are served throughout the day, and an indoor heated pool, spa and sauna.
Open Mar. to Nov. No smoking in dining room. Vegetarian standard. Some other special diets on request. Licensed. 1 bedroom equipped for disabled guests. Children welcome: nappy-changing room. En suite, TV & tea/coffee-making in all rooms. Visa, Amex, Mastercard. B. & B. from £36.

Midhurst House, Candie Rd, St Peter Port, Guernsey (0481) 724391

Elegant Regency town house which has been exceptionally well-restored; some bedrooms overlook the lovely south facing garden; superb food prepared from fresh ingredients.
Open Easter to Oct. No smoking in dining room. Vegetarian, diabetic, coeliac, allergy-free diets by arrangement. Licensed. Over 8s only. En suite, tea/coffee-making & TV in all rooms. D., B. & B. £32.

Old Government House Hotel, Ann's Place, St Peter Port, (0481) 724429

Elegant building, sumptuously furnished and offering good food; sea views; swimming pool.
Vegetarian and vegan standard. Diabetic and other special diets by arrangement. Open all year. Licensed. Children welcome. En suite & TV in all rooms. Credit cards. B. & B. from £58.

Windmill Hotel, Freepost, Rue Poudreuse, St Martins, Guernsey Tel: (0481) 35383 Fax: 954 728340

The Windmill Hotel is set well back from the road in an enviable location conveniently situated on a major bus route to the town and coast, with ample car parking. There is a comfortable lounge and a television cum reading room, and the charmingly intimate dining room and inviting bar area both overlook the swimming pool and sun trap garden. Good English cooking is a hallmark of a stay at the Windmill Hotel; a typical evening menu might feature Grilled Fresh Sardines with Paprika and Lemon, followed by Honey Roast Turkey with Herb Stuffing and Cranberry Sauce (or a Vegetarian Mixed Bean Casserole with Basmati Rice), and a choice of freshly-made desserts. The excellent service causes guests to return season after season and inclusive holidays can be arranged (with free car hire in Spring and Autumn).
Open Easter to Oct. No smoking in dining room and T.V. lounge. Most special diets by arrangement. Licensed. Some disabled access. Children: over 3s only. En suite, tea/coffee-making, T.V., phone & hairdrier in all rooms. Access, Visa, Amex, Diners. D., B. & B. from £31.

JERSEY

Hinchcliffe Guest House, Victoria Ave, First Tower, St Helier, Jersey (0534) 21574

Small, family-run guest house with panoramic views of St Aubins Bay; health-watcher b'kfast.
Open Mar. to Oct. No smoking Special diets by arrangement. Tea/coffee-making in all rooms. T.V. in lounge. B. & B. from £16.50.

SARK

Beauvoir Guest House and Tea Shop, Sark Tel: (0481) 832352 Fax: (0481) 832551

Situated at the centre of the island close to the Seigneurie, Beauvoir is a charming granite-built house, built at the turn of the century. It has recently undergone extensive renovations and now offers exceptionally comfortable accommodation and very good food; there is a charming tea garden (and indoor tea shop for those not inclined to al fresco dining) which specialises in home-baking and dishes prepared from organically home-grown fruit and vegetables. Resident guests at Beauvoir are really in for a treat: all meals have been home-cooked from fresh ingredients and the imaginative 5-course evening menu features such delights as home-made Smoked Mackerel Pate, followed by Orange Sorbet, home-made Brie and Herb Quiche and an irresistible dessert, such as home-made Chocolate Gateau; guests may also enjoy the benefits of a quiet lounge and a separate residents' bar. Sark is the smallest and, thankfully, the least developed of the Channel Islands: there are no street lights (bring a torch) and the beautiful sandy beaches are all reached by many steps or steep paths; this, combined with the fact that there is a short walk from the ferry to the guest house (although your luggage is taken by carrier) means that a holiday on Sark is best suited to those who find it easy to get about.
Open all year. No smoking. Vegetarian, diabetic, low-cal., gluten-free & other diets by arrangement. Licensed. Disabled access; ground-floor rooms with ramped access. Children: over 10s only. En suite, tea/coffee-making, central heating & T.V. in all bedrooms. Credit cards. B. & B. from £20, D. B. & B. from £30.

Hotel Petit Champ, Sark (0481) 832046

Charming hotel in unrivalled position on the west coast of the unique island of Sark. Restaurant renowned for good cuisine. Solar-heated swimming pool.
Open Apr. to Oct. No smoking in dining room & 1 lounge/library. Vegetarian and other diets by arrangement. Licensed. Children: over 7s only. All rooms en suite. Credit cards. Half Board £35-46.

Northern Ireland

ANTRIM

Ahimsa, 243 Whitepark Rd, Bushmills (026 57) 31383

Beautiful 200-year-old cottage peacefully set near Giant's Causeway; reflexology, relaxation & yoga therapies; wholefood cooking.
Open all year. No smoking. Vegetarian excluisvely. Children welcome. Pets welcome. Tea/coffee making. B. & B. from £9.

CO FERMANAGH

Lough Melvin Holiday Centre, Garrison (036565) 8142/8145

50 bedroom hotel offering, group activity holidays (canoeing, fishing, cycling, caving, etc.) plus individual holidays.
Open all year ex. Xmas Day. No smoking in dining room. Vegetarian and most other special diets by arrangement. Disabled access. Children welcome.

Wilmer Lodge, Carrybridge Road, Lisbellaw, Co Fermanagh (0365) 87045

New chalet bungalow on a small farm just a short walk from the lake shore; cruiser available for short trips. 5 mins from Enniskillen. Farm Nature Trail. Highly Commended Irish B'fast Award.
Open all year. No smoking in the house. Vegetarian standard. Disabled access. Tea/coffee making in bedrooms. T.V. in lounge. B. & B. from £10.

Scotland

Borders

DENHOLM

Barnhills Farmhouse, Nr Denholm, Roxburghshire, TD9 8SH (045 087) 577

Beautiful ex-farmhouse set in a wild garden with orchard and vegetables; 3m from the nearest village; excellent vegan cuisine.

Open all year. No smoking. Vegan wholefood only. Children welcome. Tea/coffee. B. & B. from £12.

HAWICK

Kirkton Farmhouse, Kirkton, Hawick, Roxburghshire, TD9 8QS (0450) 72421

Spacious farmhouse surrounded by beautiful countryside and offering a friendly welcome and good home-cooking; log fires in cooler weather; private sitting room with colour TV.

Open Mar. to Nov. Vegetarian and most other special diets by arrangement. Children welcome. Tea/coffee making in bedrooms. B. & B. £13.

Whitchester Christian Guest House & Retreat Centre, Borthaugh, Hawick, Roxburghshire, TD9 7LN (0450) 77477

Mid 19th C. manor standing in 3 acres of lawned grounds and offering 'a place of rest, rehabilitation and peace' within a Christian context; beautifully furnished throughout and with lovely views; excellent cuisine prepared from fresh, often home-grown, produce.

Open Feb. to Dec. No smoking ex. in T.V. lounge. Vegetarian standard. Most other special diets by arrangement. Disabled access. Children welcome. Pets by arrangement. En suite in 5 out of 10 rooms. Tea/coffee making in bedrooms. T.V. in lounge. B. & B. from £13.20.

JEDBURGH

Froylehurst, Friars, Jedburgh, Roxburghshire TD8 6BN (0835) 62477

Detached late Victorian house with lovely garden offering comfortable accommodation in tastefully decorated rooms; full Scottish breakfast. Further details from Mrs Irvine.

Open Apr. to Oct. No smoking in dining room & bathrooms. Vegetarian breakfasts. Children: over 5s only. Tea/coffee making & T.V. in all bedrooms. B. & B. from £13.

Harrietsfield House, Ancrum, by Jedburgh, Roxburghshire, TD8 6TZ (08353) 327

Harrietsfield House is a spacious and comfortable ex-farmhouse with a lovely garden set in beautiful countryside just 5 miles from Jedburgh. Breakfast is the only meal which is usually available at Harrietsfield (a vegetarian evening meal may be booked by prior arrangement), but all food is prepared from fresh wholefoods and, when possible, with organically home-grown produce. Accommodation is in warm, comfortable, well-equipped rooms and there is an inviting lounge where tea and home-baking are served in the evening by the log fire. You are centrally situated in this part of the world for visiting all the Border towns and are just 44 miles from Edinburgh; golf, riding and fishing may all be enjoyed locally.

Vegetarian standard. Most other special diets by arrangement. Wholefoods always. Open Easter/Apr. to Oct. No smoking in the house. One downstairs bedroom. Children welcome (at full tariff). Pets by arrangement. En suite in most rooms. Tea served in lounge at 9.30 pm. T.V. in lounge. B. & B. from £13.

KELSO

Duncan House, Chalkheugh Terrace, Kelso, TD5 7DX (0573) 25682

Lovely listed Georgian house in a beautiful elevated position overlooking the River Tweed.

Open Mar. to Oct. No smoking ex. in some bedrooms. Vegetarian and most other special diets by arrangement. Disabled access. Children welcome. Pets by arrangement. En suite in 2 out of 6 rooms. Tea/coffee making & T.V. in bedrooms. B. & B. from £11.50.

MELROSE

Collingwood, Waverley Road, Melrose, Roxburghshire TD6 9AA (0896 82) 2670

Detached Victorian house with large garden quietly situated 1m from Melrose and minutes from the River Tweed; splendid views of Eildon Hills; family home of Jack and Angela Sugden.
Open most of the year. No smoking. Vegetarian & other diets by arrangement. En suite & tea/coffee making in bedrooms. T.V. in lounge. B. & B. from £17.

Priory View, 15 Priors Walk, Melrose (0896 82) 2087

Beautiful detached house with pretty gardens in a quiet area 5 mins walk from town centre and the Abbey; all food prepared from fresh ingredients; home-cooking & home-baking
Open all year. No smoking. Vegetarian and diabetic diets by arrangement. Children welcome. Tea/coffee making in bedrooms. T.V. B. & B. from £12.

PEEBLES

Drummore, Venlaw High Road, Peebles, EH45 8RL (0721) 20336

Beautiful modern farmhouse standing in peaceful, wooded surroundings with panoramic views; all meals prepared from fresh ingredients.
Open Easter to Oct. No smoking. Vegetarian & low-fat diets by arrangement. Children by arrangement. Tea/coffee in rooms. T.V. B. & B. from £12.

Kingsmuir Hotel, Springhill Rd, Peebles, EH45 9EP Tel: (0721) 720151 Fax: (0721) 721795

Kingsmuir is a charming century old country house which stands amidst leafy grounds on the quiet, South side of Peebles looking across parkland to the River Tweed; indeed it is just 5 minutes' walk through the park to the High Street. It is a family-run hotel and as such offers friendly, efficient service: the bedrooms are exceptionally comfortable and there is a stylish new lounge for guests' use; the modern refurbishments and additions have been sympathetically undertaken, but the original character of the building is still clearly in evidence in the other comfortable lounge and in the dining room. The food is excellent: everything is prepared from fresh, local produce, and in addition to an imaginative evening à la carte menu, there are some good choices for children and vegetarians on separate menus; the Kingsmuir Hotel is "Taste of Scotland Recommended", incidentally. Peebles is a Royal and Ancient Borough just 40 mnutes' drive South of Edinburgh; there are many fine shops in the city and in addition you are close to many stately homes and castles of great historic interest.
Open all year ex. Xmas day. No smoking in dining room & lounge. Vegetarian standard. Licensed. Children & dogs welcome. En suite, TV & tea/coffee in bedrooms. Credit cards. B. & B. £27-31, single £31-37.

Tweed Valley Hotel & Restaurant, Walkerburn, by Peebles, EH43 6AA (089687) 636

Lovely Edwardian country mansion standing in its own grounds; beautifully furnished; fresh food & home-grown herbs used in cooking; activity courses & holidays throughout the year.
Open all year. No smoking in dining room. Vegetarian & other diets by arrangement. Licensed. Children welcome. Pets by arrangement. En suite, TV & tea/coffee in rooms. Credit cards. B. & B. from £45.50.

Mrs Julia Wilding, 10 Gallow Hill, Peebles, EH45 9BG (0721) 20372

Modern house in quiet residential area on the outskirts of Peebles; downstairs facilities.
Open all year. No smoking. Vegetarian & other diets by arrangement. Children welcome. Pets by arrangement. Tea/coffee making in bedrooms. T.V. in lounge. B. & B. from £17.50.

SELKIRK

Hillholm, 36 Hillside Terrace (0450) 21293

Open Mar. to Oct. No smoking. Vegetarian & other diets by arrangement. Children: over 12s only. Tea/coffee making. TV in lounge. B. & B. from £14.

Tibbie Shiels Inn, St Mary's Loch, Selkirk TD7 5NE (0750) 42231

Situated on the tranquil shore of St Mary's Loch and named after its first owner of 1823, the Tibbie Shiels inn has been offering hospitality to (some, very famous) guests for nearly 200 years; lots of character and excellent food.
Open all year. No smoking in one of three dining rooms. Extensive vegetarian menu. Licensed. Disabled access. Children welcome. Tea/coffee making in bedrooms. T.V. in lounge. B. & B. from £15.

Dumfries and Galloway

CASTLE DOUGLAS

Blairinnie Farm, Blairinnie, Parton, Kirkcudbright, DG7 3BJ (0556) 67268
Spacious stone-built farmhouse; traditional home-cooking from fresh, local produce.
Open May. to Sept. No smoking in the house. Vegetarian & other diets by arrangement. Children welcome. Tea/coffee making. T.V. lounge. B & B £10.

The Imperial Hotel, 35 King Street, Castle Douglas, DG7 1AA (0556) 2086/3009
Former coaching inn & listed building, this family-run 2 Star hotel has been tastefully decorated with antique and modern furnishings. Good quality home-cooking using fresh, local produce. Ideal as base to tour countryside; golf courses nearby. Special 3-day breaks.
Open all year. No smoking in bedrooms & 25% dining room. Vegetarian standard. Licensed. Disabled access. Children & pets welcome. En suite, tea/coffee making & TV in bedrooms. B & B £25.

The Rossan, Auchencairn, DG7 1QR (055 664) 269
The Rossan is an early Victorian ex-manse

standing well back from the A711 in over an acre of beautiful gardens between the Screel Hills and the sea; the house itself overlooks Auchencairn Bay and there are two lovely sandy beaches close by. Mrs Bardsley has been welcoming guests - especially ornitholigists and vegetarians - to her house for many years now; she is keen to point out, however, that it is, first and foremost, her (very welcoming) home; consequently, guests must make do with shared use of two bathrooms, there is a cosy atmosphere and guests are treated to very good meals prepared from fresh, organic (often home-grown) ingredients. She is a dab hand at catering for special diets, too. STB listed & approved.
Vegetarian & gluten-free standard; vegan & medical diets by arrangement. Wholefood always. Open all year ex. 2 weeks in Jan. No smoking in dining room & allowed in bedrooms after 9 pm. Well-behaved dogs free. Tea/coffee making in bedrooms. T.V. B & B £12.

Windywalls, Upper Drumwall, Gatehouse of Fleet, Castle Douglas, DG7 2DE (0557) 814249
Beautiful house-on-a-hill 1 mile from Gatehouse of Fleet; superb views of mountain & sea; excellent cuisine prepared from home-grown produce.
Open all year. No smoking Vegetarian and most other special diets. Children welcome. Pets by arrangement. Tea/coffee making in bedrooms. T.V. in lounge. B & B from £12.

DALBEATTIE

Torbay Farmhouse, Rockcliffe, by Dalbeattie, Kirkcudbrightshire, DG5 4QE (055663) 403
This former farmhouse is built in typical Galloway style and stands amidst lovely gardens (complete with sun-house and sitting-out area) just 400 yards from the sea. The farmhouse is totally surrounded by fields and, with its magnificent views over the Lake District and the Irish Sea, is a perfectly tranquil retreat. A very high standard of accommodation and service are offered, and accordingly Torbay has been awarded a 2 Crown Commended status by the Scottish Tourist Board.
Open Easter to Oct. No smoking. Vegetarian and most other special diets by arrangement. Disabled access. Children welcome. Pets by arrangement. En suite & tea/coffee making in bedrooms. T.V. in lounge. B. & B. from £14.

KIRKCUDBRIGHT

Millburn House, Millburn Street, Kirkcudbright, DG6 4ED (0557) 30926
Charming 19th C. white-painted, stone-built house of traditional design with lovely conservatory breakfast room; breakfast only.
Open all year. No smoking. Vegetarian & other diets by arrangement. Children welcome at full tariff. En suite & tea/coffee making in bedrooms. T.V. in lounge. B & B from £18.

LOCKERBIE

Ravenshill House Hotel, 12 Dumfries Road, Lockerbie, DG11 2EF (05762) 2882
Small family-run hotel in 2 acres of gardens.
Vegetarian & other diets by arrangement. Wholefood when avail. Open all year. Children welcome. Pets by arrangement. En suite, TV & tea/coffee making in bedrooms. Credit cards.

MOFFAT

Well View Hotel, Ballplay Road, Moffat, DG10 9JU (0683) 20184
Beautiful Victorian house standing in an acre of grounds in a quiet, rural situation at the foot of the hills overlooking Moffat.
Open all year. No smoking in dining room, one lounge and one bedroom. Vegetarian & other diets by arrangement. Licensed. Children welcome. Pets by arrangement. En suite most rooms. Tea/coffee & T.V. in all bedrooms. Access, Visa. D., B & B from £28.

MONIAIVE

Woodlea Hotel, Moniaive, DG3 4EN (084 82) 209
Excellent family-orientated hotel offering comfortable accommodation and very good food; beautiful indoor heated pool.
Vegetarian & other diets by arrangement. Open Feb. to Oct. No smoking in 'swimming-pool complex/patio area'. Licensed. Children welcome. Pets welcome. En suite in most rooms. Tea/coffee making & TV in all bedrooms. B & B from £22.

SANQUHAR

Nithsdale Guest House, Glasgow Road, Sanquhar (0659) 50288
Charming stone-built house set in lovely gardens overlooking the picnic area, the loch and the golf course.
Open all year. Smoking banned in dining room and bedrooms. Vegetarian and most other special diets by arrangement. Children welcome. Tea/coffee making in bedrooms. T.V. in lounge. B & B from £15.50.

STRANRAER

Broomknowe Guest House, School Brae, Portpatrick, Stranraer, DG9 8LG (077 6) 81365
Small family-run guest house standing in its own pretty gardens with stunning views over the village to the Irish Sea; home-cooking with garden produce a speciality.
Open Easter to Sept. inc. No smoking. Pets welcome. Tea/coffee & T.V. in all bedrooms. B & B from £14.

Fernlea Guest House, Lewis Street, Stranraer, Wigtownshire, DG9 7AQ (0776) 3037
Large detached Victorian guest house in a private garden close to the town centre. Traditional home-cooked food.
Open all year. No smoking. Vegetarian and most other special diets by arrangement. Children by arrangement. En suite, TV & tea/coffee making in bedrooms. B & B from £12.50.

Edinburgh

Adam Guest House, 2 Hartington Gardens, Edinburgh, EH10 4LD (031 229) 8664

Adam House is a family-run guest house which is situated in a quiet cul-de-sac (free from parking restrictions), just fifteen minutes' walk from the city centre and close to bus routes, shops, theatres and restaurants; Bruntsfield Links and The Meadows public parks are just a short walk away. The house has recently been completely refurbished by the present owners and all the rooms are now bright, comfortable and well-equipped with a T.V., hot drink facilities and wash hand basin; some of the rooms now have en suite facilities. The proprietors and staff offer warm hospitality and a very friendly service, and families and children are particularly welcome with reduced rates being available throughout the year.
Open all year. No smoking. Vegetarian and most special diets by arrangement. Children welcome. Pets by arrangement. Some rooms en suite. Tea/coffee making & T.V. in all bedrooms. B. & B. from £15 p.p.

Camore Guest House, 7 Links Gardens, Edinburgh, EH6 7JH (031 554) 7897
Original Georgian listed house with panoramic views over Leith Links. 10-15 mins from city centre on main bus route. 5 mins walk from local restaurants and Leith's new Waterworld.
Open all year. No smoking in dining room. Vegetarian by arrangement. Licensed. Children welcome. Pets by arrangement. T.V. with Satellite channels & tea/coffee making in all bedrooms. B. & B. from £14.

Camus Guest House, 4 Seaview Terrace, Edinburgh, EH15 2HD (031 657) 2003
Small, family-run guest house; very warm and friendly; breakfast only.
Vegetarian & other diets by arrangement. Open all year. Children by arrangement. Pets by arrangement. Tea/coffee & T.V. in all bedrooms. B. & B. from £13.

Ecosse, 15 McDonald Road, Edinburgh, EH7 4LX (031 556) 4967
Commended guest house near the city centre.
Open all year. No smoking in dining room & bedrooms. Vegetarian & other diets by arrangement. Disabled access "good". Children welcome. Pets by arrangement. En suite, tea/coffee making & TV in bedrooms. B. & B. from £15.

Highfield Guest House, 83 Mayfield Road, Edinburgh, EH9 3AE (031 667) 8717
Highfield is a small, friendly, guest house only ten minutes' drive from the centre of Edinburgh. The rooms are clean and comfortable, all with wash basins and centrally heated. Tuck into the full cooked breakfast and help yourself to cereals, oatcakes, yoghurt, toast, etc. Home-made porridge is also available. A cot, high chair and toys are provided for visiting children. Room notes and menu are available in braille for the use of blind guests. Personal attention is assured at all times. The house is well situated for the university and King's Buildings and within walking distance of Arthur's Seat and Blackford Hill. STB Commended.
Open all year. No smoking. Vegetarian & other diets by arrangement. Disabled access: Ground-floor bedroom & shower/room/WC. Children welcome. Guide dogs by arrangement. Tea/coffee making in bedrooms. T.V. in lounge. B. & B. from £13.

Hopetoun Guest House, 15 Mayfield Road, Edinburgh, EH9 2NG (031 667) 7691
Small, friendly family-run guest house close to university on main bus route to the city centre.
Open all year. No smoking. Vegetarian and most other special diets by arrangement. Children welcome. Tea/coffee & T.V. in bedrooms. B. & B. from £14.

Scandic Crown Hotel, 80 High Street, The Royal Mile, Edinburgh, EH1 1TH (031 557) 9797
Luxuriously appointed hotel in the centre of the city; excellent leisure and conference facilities.
Open all year. No smoking in bedrooms & 50% dining room. Vegetarian & other diets by arrangement. Licensed. Disabled access. Children welcome. En suite, tea/coffee & T.V. in rooms. B. & B. from £96.50.

Mr and Mrs Sandeman, 33 Colinton Road, Edinburgh, EH10 5DR (031 447) 8080
33 Colinton Road is a friendly family home which is conveniently situated within easy walking distance of the city centre. Your hosts take just 6 guests at any one time so are really made to feel as though you are at home. The healthy breakfast menu features oat-cakes and home-made preserves (organic in the case of raspberry & strawberry) and a good choice of teas; organically home-grown fruits are also available in season.
Vegetarian & other diets by arrangement. Organic when avail. Wholefood on request. Open Mar. to Oct. and other times by arrangement. No smoking in dining room. Children welcome. Pets by arrangement. En suite, TV & tea/coffee in rooms. B. & B. from £18.

San Marco Guest House, 24 Mayfield Gardens, Edinburgh, EH9 2BZ Tel: (031) 667 8982 Fax: (031) 662 1945

San Marco is a friendly, family-run guest house situated near Edinburgh centre on the main A7 road South of the city. Each of the 8 bedrooms has been tastefully decorated and furnished (3 have en suite facilities), and the colour TVs have Sky channels. A full Scottish breakfast is included in the price and vegetarians can be accommodated by arrangement. Private parking is available but guests choosing to leave their cars at home will find there is a good public transport system to all parts of the city. **STB 2 Crown Commended.**
Open all year. Smoking banned in part of dining room. Vegetarian standard. Some other special diets by arrangement. Children welcome. Pets by arrangement. En suite in 2 bedrooms. Tea/coffee making & T.V. in all bedrooms. B. & B. from £13.

Studio Bed & Breakfast, 173 Bruntsfield Place, Edinburgh, EH10 4DG (031 229) 2746
Friendly, informal B. & B. in spacious apartment near to lots of lovely walks and within easy

strolling distance of the city centre; varied, tasty food prepared from fresh ingredients.
Open all year. No smoking. Vegetarian standard. Other diets by arrangement. Children welcome. Tea/coffee making avail. B. & B. from £12.

Teviotdale House, 53 Grange Loan, Edinburgh, EH9 2ER (031 667) 4376

This elegant, stone-built Victorian town house stands in a beautiful tree-lined residential street in a quiet conservation part of Edinburgh; it has been beautifully refurbished - all the decor and furnishings complement the spacious proportions of the building - and the original features, such as the magnificent cedar doors and panelling, and the ornate cornices, have all been restored to their original splendour. Everywhere quality prevails: from the hand-sewn bed linen and down duvets and pillows on the finest quality beds, to the daily provision of freshly laundered towels. Breakfast at Teviotdale is, unsurprisingly, a real treat: your hosts, Jane and John Coville, always use fresh produce in cooking (including vegetables and herbs from their organic kitchen garden) and the home-made scones, bread, jams, marmalade and Scottish honey turn a simple morning meal into a banquet: there is an extensive range of other options including Teviotdale Special (a mouthwatering mix of soaked apricots, pineapple, raisins, sultanas and prunes), Loch Fyne Kippers and Old Fashioned Scotts Porridge made from Pin Head Oatmeal and Wholegrain Wheat; you may also elect to dine on a dish dubbed The Duke of Edinburgh's Favourite Breakfast ('delicately muddled eggs with Scottish smoked salmon and parsley garnish.' A truly regal repast).
Open all year. No smoking. Vegetarian & other diets by arrangement. Children welcome. En suite, tea/coffee making & T.V. in all bedrooms. Credit cards (surcharge). B & B. around £25.

The Town House Guest House, 65 Gilmore Place, Edinburgh, EH3 9NU (031 229) 1985

The Town House is, as its name suggests, a charming 3-storey Victorian town house which was built in 1876 as the manse for the neighbouring church. Today it has been beautifully renovated and sympathetically decorated in order to provide every possible modern convenience while still retaining the style, and indeed the atmosphere, of a 19th C. building. Breakfast is the only meal to be served at the Town House, but it is an exceeding generous meal with lots of healthy options; there are, of course, numerous first-rate eating places in Edinburgh. You are just a mile from the city centre at the Town House but you are also on a very good and direct bus route. Your hosts are

very friendly and welcoming and will gladly give you information to help you plan your stay.
Open all year. No smoking in the house. Vegetarian & other diets by arrangement. Children welcome. Some en suite. Tea/coffee making & TV in bedrooms. B. & B. from £14.50.

Thrums Private Hotel, 14 Minto Street, Edinburgh, EH9 1RQ (031 667) 5545

Vegetarian and most other special diets by arrangement. Open all year, ex. Xmas and New Year. Licensed. Children welcome. Pets by arrangement. En suite, tea/coffee & in all bedrooms. B. & B. from £22.

10A Dean Terrace, Edinburgh, EH4 1ND (031 332) 0403

Garden flat of Georgian building adjoining owner's flat and overlooking the Water of Leith; can be either B. & B. or self-catering.
Open all year. No smoking. Vegetarian breakfast by arrangement. Children welcome. En suite some rooms. Tea/coffee. T.V. avail. B. & B. from £14.50.

Turret Guest House, 8 Kilmaurs Terrace, Edinburgh, EH16 5DR (031 667) 6704

The Turret is a small, family-run guest house which is quietly situated in a residential area of the city near to the Royal Commonwealth Swimming Pool. The house has retained many of its original Victorian features, including a large open wooden staircase, and each of the bedrooms has been very comfortably furnished and tastefully decorated. Your hosts, Ian and Jackie Cameron, will do everything they can to make your stay as enjoyable as possible, and are always on hand to give helpful information to help you plan your stay.
Open all year ex. Xmas. No smoking in dining room. Vegetarian standard. Other diets by arrangement. Children: over 2s preferred. En suite in family room. Tea/coffee & T.V. in all bedrooms. B. & B. from £14.

Fife

ABERDOUR
Hawkcraig House, Hawkcraig Point, Aberdour, Fife, KY3 0TZ (0383) 860335
Beautiful old white-painted ferryman's house overlooking the sea. All food is prepared from fresh local produce ('Taste of Scotland').
Open Feb. to Nov. No smoking. Vegetarian and diabetic diets by arrangement. Bring your own wine. Children: over 8s only. En suite in both rooms. Tea/coffee on request. T.V. in both rooms. B. & B. from £16. STB 2 Crown Highly Commended.

CULROSS
Woodhead Farm (0383) 880270
Lovely old farmhouse standing in pretty garden in beautiful countryside. Home-grown, farm or local produce used in cooking.
Open all year. No smoking. Vegetarian & other diets by arrangement. Children welcome. Tea/coffee making & T.V. in all bedrooms. B. & B. from £15.

CUPAR
Greigston Farmhouse, Peat Inn, Cupar, Fife, KY15 5LF (033 484) 284
16th/17th C. Laird's house; home-grown vegetables, soft fruits, milk & cream.
Open Mar. to Nov. No smoking. Vegetarian by arrangement. Disabled access. Children welcome. Pets by arrangement. En suite & tea/coffee making in bedrooms. T.V. in lounge. B. & B. from £13.

FREUCHIE
Lomond Hills Hotel, Lomond Road, Freuchie, KY7 7EY (0337) 57329
White-painted hotel in the picturesque village of Freuchie. Candle-lit dinners reflect both Scottish and French influences. Small leisure centre.
Open all year. No smoking in restaurant & some bedrooms. Vegetarian standard. Other diets by arrangement. Licensed. Disabled access to restaurant; 1 bedroom ground floor. Children welcome. En suite, tea/coffee making & TV in bedrooms. Credit cards. B. & B. from £36.

GLENROTHES
Rescobie Hotel, Valley Drive, Leslie, Glenrothes, KY6 3BQ (0592) 742143 Fax (0592) 620231
Rescobie is a charming small country house standing in 2 acres of lovely gardens in (as its brochure reminds us) the *Royal and Ancient Kingdom of Fife*! Regal you will certainly feel as

a guest in this beautiful hotel: elegant furnishings complement the well-proportioned rooms and invite guests to relax, unwind and feel at home. The main dining room, with its lovely garden views, is a perfect setting for the first-rate cuisine of which the proprietors are justifiably proud: the menu features both international and traditionally Scottish dishes and these are always prepared from fresh, local produce. A typical evening selection from the table d'hote menu (which changes daily) would be Hot Brown Bread Basket filled with Seafood and Saffron and Sweet Pepper Sauce, followed by Fillet of Wild Salmon (dressed with prawn tails and Orange Butter Sauce) and a choice of sweets, such as Raspberry Cranachan (oatmeal, honey, whisky and raspberries in a special Gaelic combination!); excellent vegetarian options.
Open all year ex. Xmas. Vegetarian standard. Other diets by arrangement. Licensed. Children welcome. En suite, tea/coffee making & T.V. in all bedrooms. Access, Visa, Amex, Diners. B. & B. from £30.

PITTENWEEM
Victoria Cottage, 11 Viewforth Place, KY10 2PZ (0333) 311998
Charming Victorian house in a small but active fishing village within the East Neuk of Fife.
Open Apr. to Sept. No smoking. Vegetarian & other diets by arrangement. Children welcome. Tea/coffee making & TV in bedrooms. B. & B. from £11.

ST ANDREW'S
Edenside House, Edenside, by St Andrews, KY16 9SQ (0334) 838108
Edenside House is a beautiful, white-washed listed 19th C. farmhouse which is set back from the A91 St Andrews road on the Eden Estuary nature reserve and bird sanctuary. It has been very carefully renovated and beautifully

refurbished throughout and each new twin and double room has luxury en suite facilities and

views of the estuary; there are some ground floor rooms for those who find stairs difficult and each room has been designated its own parking space. A generous breakfast is served to guests and, as the proprietors are demi-vegetarians, interesting meat-free options are available (diabetic, low-calorie & low-cholesterol on request).

Open all year. No smoking. Vegetarian standard & other special diets by arrangement. Disabled access good: some ground floor rooms available. Children welcome. Pets by arrangement. En suite, tea & coffee making & T.V. in all bedrooms. B. & B. from £16.

Lathones Manor Hotel, by Largoward, St Andrew's, KY9 1JE (0334) 84494

Splendidly renovated inn with open fires, exposed stone work and oak beams in the picturesque East Neuk of Fife; excellent cuisine.

Open Feb. to Dec. Smoking banned in dining room. Vegetarian standard. Other diets by arrangement. Licensed. Disabled access. En suite, tea/coffee making & TV in bedrooms. B. & B. from £20.

Mrs Sally McGilchrist, 3 Dempster Terrace, St Andrew's (0334) 72504

Edwardian terraced house overlooking duck-filled burn 4 mins from town

Open Apr. to Nov. Smoking banned throughout. Vegetarian by arrangement. Tea/coffee making in bedrooms. B. & B. from £12-13.

Rufflets Country House, Strathkinness Low Rd, St Andrews, Fife, KY16 9TX Tel: (0334) 72594 Fax: (0334) 78703

Designed by Dundee architect Donald Mills and built in 1924, this outstanding country house stands in 10 acres of award-winning gardens and has been privately owned and personally managed by the same family since 1952. Over the years the house has been extended and refurbished, but all additions have been in keeping with the original building, and an overall atmosphere of gracious calm prevails: each of the spacious public rooms overlooks the magnificent gardens, and the 21 en suite bedrooms have been furnished to a very high standard and are equipped with a range of useful amenities including a direct dial phone; a cottage in the grounds has equally splendid accommodation for 3 further sets of guests. The food is excellent: everything is prepared from fresh, seasonal and local produce; indeed many of the vegetables, fruits and herbs come from the hotel's kitchen garden. This idyllic retreat offers the best of both worlds: a sense of rural tranquillity, yet the proximity to the world famous "Home of Golf", St Andrews.

Open Feb. to Dec. No smoking in part of dining room, bar and some bedrooms. Vegetarian standard. Diabetic on request. Licensed. Children welcome. En suite, TV & tea/coffee-making in bedrooms. Credit cards.

St Andrews Golf Hotel, 40 The Scores, St Andrews (0334) 72611

Situated on the cliffs overlooking St Andrews Bay and links, and 200 metres from the 'old course', St Andrews Hotel is a tastefully modernised, listed Victorian building with comfortable bedrooms and elegant public rooms (including a charming oak-panelled restaurant).

The food is excellent: everything is prepared from fresh, local sea-food, game and meats, and is complemented by a first-rate choice of wines; meals are served by candlelight in the aforementioned dining room or, if you prefer a more informal atmosphere, you could dine in Ma Bells basement bar and restaurant with its vast array of foreign and local beers. The hotel is owned and run by the Hughes family and specialises in providing golfing holidays for individuals and small groups.

Open all year. No smoking in restaurant. Vegetarian & other diets by arrangement. Licensed. Children welcome. Pets by arrangement. En suite, TV & tea/coffee making in bedrooms. Credit cards.

Glasgow & Central

DOLLAR

Strathdevon House, Harviestoun Road, Dollar, FK14 7PT (0259) 42320
Pre-Victorian listed building; log fires; good home-cooking; goats and poultry kept.
Open all year. No smoking in the house. Vegetarian & other diets by arrangement. Children welcome. En suite in all rooms. Tea/coffee making on request. T.V. lounge. Credit cards. B & B from £12.

FALKIRK

"Chez-Nous", Sunnyside Road, Brightons, Falkirk (0342) 715953
Pleasant B. & B. operating in conjunction with a local restaurant to cater for special diets - especially 'additive-free' and 'allergic'.
Open Feb. to Nov. No smoking. Vegetarian & other diets by arrangement. Disabled access. Children welcome. En suite Tea/coffee. T.V. lounge.

GLASGOW

The Busby Hotel, Field Road, Clarkston, Glasgow, G76 8RX (041) 644 4417
Hotel in tree-lined avenue beside the River Cart; food prepared from fresh ingredients.
Open all year. No smoking in some bedrooms. Vegetarian & other diets by arrangement. Licensed. Children welcome. Pets by arrangement. En suite, TV & tea/coffee making in bedrooms. Credit cards.

The Copthorne Glasgow, George Square, Glasgow, G2 1DS (041) 332 6711
Luxury-class hotel in the centre of Glasgow; beautifully furnished and appointed.
Open all year. No smoking in some bedrooms & 50% of restaurant. Vegetarian & other diets by arrangement. Licensed. En suite, TV & tea/coffee in rooms. Credit cards. B. & B. from £43.

Alison Couston, 13 Carment Drive, Shawlands, Glasgow (041) 632 0193
Victorian house; friendly atmosphere.
Open Apr. to Sept. or by arrangement. No smoking. Vegetarian & other diets by arrangement. Tea/coffee making in bedrooms. T.V. in lounge. B. & B. from £12.

Mrs J Freebairn-Smith, 14 Prospect Avenue, Cambuslang, Glasgow, G72 8BW (041) 641 5055
Large Victorian villa in lovely gardens.
Open all year. No smoking in public rooms & some bedrooms. Vegetarian by arrangement. Children welcome. Pets by arrangement. Tea/coffee making & T.V. in all bedrooms. B & B from £11.

Regent Guest House, 44 Regent Park Square, Strathbungo, Glasgow, G41 2AG (041) 422 1199
The Regent Guest House is a charming 'B' listed Victorian terraced house at the quiet end of a busy street just 2 miles south of Glasgow city centre (and, even more conveniently, just one mile north of the splendid Burrell Collection

which is one of Glasgow's principal attractions). The Regent has been exceptionally well-appointed: the welcome-trays in the bedrooms, for instance, do not just contain the usual tea and coffee, but also have Perrier, hot chocolate, Horlicks and shortbread. Likewise the breakfast menu features not just the usual platter of cooked fare but also offers some healthy options such as fresh fruit and yoghurt. Breakfast and evening meals are available, and there is also a good selection of restaurants at the other end of the street offering a wide range of culinary choices including Greek, Italian and Indian.
Vegetarian & vegan standard. Diabetic and some other special diets by arrangement. Organic and Wholefood when avail. Open all year. No smoking in the house except in 3 bedrooms. Children welcome. Pets by arrangement. Tea/coffee making & TV in bedrooms. Credit cards. B. & B. from £20.

STIRLING

Mrs Thelma Harper, 67 Burnhead Road, Larbert, Stirling (0324) 553168
Pleasant house in rural setting in close proximity to both Glasgow and Edinburgh.
Open all year. No smoking. Vegetarian & other diets by arrangement. Tea/coffee in rooms. T.V. on request.

Mr and Mrs D McLaren, "Allandale", 98 Causewayhead Rd, Stirling (0786) 65643
Warm and friendly B. & B.
Open all year. No smoking. Vegetarian & other diets by arrangement. Children welcome. Tea/coffee

Grampian

The Green Inn, 9 Victoria Road, Ballater, AB3 5QQ (03397) 55701

The Green Inn is a granite-built former temperance hotel which overlooks Ballater village green. All the food has been prepared on the premises and maximum use is made of local, fresh produce. Traditional Scottish specialities are a regular feature of the menu and a set vegetarian menu is also available; a typical dinner menu might feature Bisque of West Coast Langoustines served with Lochnagar Whisky followed by Scotch Lamb with a light curry, Mango and Banana Sauce garnished with Grilled Scallops, or perhaps a Fricassée of locally caught Seafood and Shellfish served with a Lime and Avocado Salad. For dessert there is Sticky Toffee Pudding served with Citrus Fruits and a Whisky Butterscotch Sauce, or 'Crowdie Cake' - a blend of Crowdie Cheese, lemon and buttermilk served with Blairgowrie Fruit and Berries in a raspberry and red wine sauce. There is a wine list with items representing every region from Alsace to Australia & from Champagne to Chile.
Open all year. No smoking in dining room. Vegetarian standard. Other diets by arrangement. Licensed. Disabled access. Children welcome. En suite, TV & tea/coffee in rooms. Access, Visa. B. & B. from £18.50.

Monaltrie Hotel, 5 Bridge Square, Ballater (03397) 55417
Splendid 19th C. hotel on the Dee; cuisine prepared from fresh produce; Thai restaurant.
Open all year. No smoking in restaurant. Vegetarian & other diets by arrangement. Licensed. Disabled access. Children welcome. Pets by arrangement. En suite, TV & tea/coffee making in bedrooms.

Netherley Guest House, 2 Netherley Place, Ballater (03397) 55792
Charming 19th C. white-painted house, with pretty blue paintwork; home-cooking.
Open Mar. to Oct. No smoking in dining room. Vegetarian & other diets by arrangement. Children welcome. En suite, TV & tea/coffee in 4 bedrooms.

BANFF
Bankhead Croft, Gamrie, by Banff, AB45 3HN (02615) 584
Vegetarian, vegan, diabetic and most other special diets catered for. Wholefood always. Open all year. Disabled access. Children welcome. Pets by arrangement. Tea/coffee making & T.V. in all bedrooms. Credit cards accepted. B. & B. from £11.

GLENLIVET
Minmore House Hotel, Glenlivet, Ballandalloch, AB3 9DB (08073) 378
Splendid house, individually furnished rooms; fresh flowers, log fires; good home-cooking from fresh, organic vegetables.
Open May to Nov. No smoking ex. bar. Vegetarian, & other diets by arrangement. Licensed. Children welcome. Pets by arrangement. En suite & tea/coffee making in bedrooms. B. & B. from £28.

HUNTLY
Faich-Hill Farmhouse Holidays, Gartly, Huntly, Aberdeenshir (046688) 240
19th C. farmhouse; excellent home-cooking; prepared from fresh and farm produce. Twice winner of *Scottish Farmhouse of the Year.*
Open all year. No smoking ex. sun lounge. Vegetarian & other diets by arrangement. Children: over 4s only. En suite. Tea/coffee, radios & electric blankets in bedrooms. T.V. in lounge. B. & B. from £12.

The Old Manse of Marnoch, Huntly, Aberdeenshire, AB54 5RS (0466) 780873
Fine 19th C. country house in 3 acres of splendid gardens. All food home-prepared (including the after dinner mints) & only fresh produce (some organically home-grown) is used in cooking
Vegetarian, vegan, diabetic and almost any other exclusion diet by arrangement. Open all year. No smoking in dining room. Licensed. Children: over 12s only. Dogs welcome. En suite in all bedrooms. Tea/coffee making in bedrooms. T.V. in lounge.

KEITH
The Haughs Farm Guest House, Keith (05422) 2238
Beautiful and comfortable farmhouse with an interesting history; very well-appointed; home-cooking from fresh produce.
Open 1 Apr. to 15 Oct. Smoking banned throughout the house. Vegetarian and diabetic diets by arrangement. Disabled access. Children welcome. En suite in 3 out of 4 rooms. Tea/coffee making & TV in bedrooms. B. & B. from £12.

Highlands

ACHARACLE

Glencripesdale House, Acharacle, Argyll, PH36 4JH (096 785) 263

Glencripesdale House is a beautifully renovated 18th C. farmhouse overlooking Loch Sunart and the peak of Ben Laga in Ardnamurchan; it is very remotely situated in Morvern, a peninsula on the south shore of the Loch which is frequently by-passed by visitors and is consequently an isolated and unspoilt wilderness, rich in flora and fauna. The proprietors are well aware that most guests come to appreciate the peace, tranquillity and richness of natural beauty that the surrounding region has to offer; consequently they have made their home into a haven of rest and a place to escape from the cares and worries of the 20th C. Rooms are beautifully decorated and furnished and meals are stupendous - almost everything having been prepared from fresh ingredients (the proprietors freeze some of their own produce - but nothing has ever been commercially frozen); a typical evening menu would feature Vegetable Soup, Lochy Trout in White Wine and Fennel, and Bramble and Apple Crumble with Bramble Cordial.
Open Mar. to Oct. & Xmas & New Year. No smoking in dining room. Vegetarian & other diets by arrangement. Licensed. Children welcome. En suite in rooms. Tea/coffee in hall. Full board from £55.

AULTBEA

Cartmel Guesthouse, Birchburn Road, Aultbea, Achnasheen, Wester Ross, IV22 2HZ (0445) 731375

Highly commended guest house offering first-rate accommodation and food.
Open Mar. to Oct. No smoking in the house. Vegetarian & other diets by arrangement. 'Good' disabled access. Children welcome. Pets by arrangement. En suite in 1 bedroom. Tea/coffee making. T.V. D. B. & B. from £18.

Mellondale Guest House, 47 Mellon Charles, Aultbea (0445) 731326

Small, family-run guest house with garden overlooking Loch Ewe; home-cooked meals prepared from fresh, local ingredients.
Open Mar. to Oct. No smoking. Vegetarian & vegan by arrangement. Disabled access. Children welcome. En suite 3 rooms. Tea/coffee & TV in rooms.

Oran Na Mara, Drumchork, Aultbea, Ross-shire, IV22 2HU (0445) 731394

Spacious, comfortable hill side guest house with stunning loch views from all rooms. Also 2 STB "Highly Commended" self-catering apartments.
Open Easter to end Oct. No smoking. Vegetarian and vegan standard. All on ground floor? Children: over 8s welcome. Pets by arrangement. Wash-hand basin, tea/coffee & T.V. in all rooms. B. & B. from £13.

AVIEMORE

Aviemore Self Catering, 17 Craig-na-Gower Avenue, Aviemore, Inverness-shire, PH22 1RW (0479) 810031 (24 hrs)

Comfortable family home with open views to the hills & peat fire! Self catering also available.
Open all year. No smoking. Vegetarian & other diets by arrangement. Children welcome. En suite all rooms. Tea/coffee on request. T.V. lounge.

BOAT OF GARTEN

Avingormack Guest House, Boat of Garten, Inverness-shire, PH24 3BT (0479) 83614

Converted croft superbly situated on a hillside with magnificent views of the Cairngorms; mountain bikes for hire; ski instruction avail.
Open all year. No smoking. Vegetarian standard. Children welcome. Tea/coffee making & TV in bedrooms. B. & B. from £13.

Heathbank House, Boat of Garten, Inverness-shire, PH24 3BD (0479) 83234

Detached Victorian house decorated in turn of the century style and full of interesting bits and pieces; large garden; beautiful views over the RSPB Reserve & the forest to the Cairngorms.
Open Dec. to Oct. No smoking in dining room and in bedrooms. Vegetarian & other diets by arrangement. Licensed. Children accepted. En suite & tea/coffee making in bedrooms. T.V. D., B. & B. from £28.

BRORA

Ard Beag, Badnellan, Brora, Sutherland, KW9 6NQ (0408) 621398
Small, comfortable former croft house with a homely atmosphere in a pleasant south-facing garden. Good, wholesome, home-cooked food prepared from fresh garden produce where possible; the delicious bread is home-baked.
Open May to Sept. No smoking in dining room & bedrooms. Vegetarian by arrangement. Children welcome. Tea/coffee in bedrooms. B. & B. from £11.

Carrol Guest House, Golf Road, Brora, Sutherland, KW9 6QS (0408) 21065
Guest house in quiet residential area close to both the golf course & the beach. Exceptionally well-appointed; excellent cuisine.
Open May to Sept. No smoking. Vegetarian & other diets by arrangement. Children welcome. En suite 2 rooms. Tea/coffee & TV in bedrooms.

Sumundar Villa, Harbour Road, Brora, Sutherland, KW9 6QF (0408) 21717
Peaceful family home superbly situated at the mouth of the River Brora on the shores of the North Sea; home-baking; vegetarian household but traditional meals also served.
Open Feb. to Nov. No smoking. Vegetarian & diabetic standard. Disabled access. Children welcome. Tea/coffee making & T.V. in rooms. B. & B. from £13.

Tigh Fada (Non-Smokers Haven), Golf Road, Brora, KW9 6QS (0408) 621332
Lovely spacious house peacefully situated in pleasant gardens with fine, uninterrupted views of the sea and hills; the garden gate leads to both the golf course and sandy beach. Cosily furnished; home-cooked wholesome food.
Open all year. No smoking. Vegetarian & other diets by arrangement. Children welcome, 'not toddlers'. Pets by arrangement. Tea/coffee making in bedrooms. B. & B. from £12.50 - 15.50.

CARRBRIDGE

Kinchyle Guest House, Carrbridge, Inverness-shire, PH23 3AA (047984) 243
Beautiful detached house with lots of character centrally situated in the village of Carrbridge.
Open all year. No smoking. Vegetarian and low-fat diets by arrangement. Children welcome. Tea/coffee making in bedrooms. T.V. in lounge. B. & B. from £14.

DORNOCH

Dornoch Castle Hotel, Dornoch, IV25 3SD (0862) 810216
Formerly the palace of the Bishops of Caithness, this imposing 15th/16th C. mansion offers exceptionally good accommodation & food.
Open all year. No smoking in the dining room. Vegetarian by arrangement. Licensed. Disabled access. Children welcome. En suite avail. Tea/coffee making in bedrooms. T.V. B. & B. from £28.

DULNAIN BRIDGE

Auchendean Lodge Hotel, Dulnain Bridge, Inverness-shire, PH26 3LU (047) 985347

Visitors to Auchendean Lodge Hotel will feel that they have stepped back into another era: beautifully appointed throughout with period antiques, furnishings and paintings which have been chosen to complement the building's many original Edwardian features, Auchendean Lodge has outstanding views across the River Spey and over the Abernethy Forest to the Cairngorm Mountains. Its owners, Eric Hart and Ian Kirk, have created an ambience of comfort, style and good service, which prevails in an atmosphere of informality and great friendliness; both owners share the cooking and specialize in an imaginative cuisine (and some traditional Scottish dishes), which have been prepared not only from local and home-grown produce but from ingredients culled from the moors and woods (such as the wild mushrooms which Eric picks daily in late summer and autumn). Staying at Auchendean Lodge is an enjoyable and unique experience, & whether your strongest memories will be of the house, the food or the magnificent surroundings will be for you to decide.
Open all year. No smoking in dining room & sitting room. Vegetarian, vegan & other diets by arrangement. Licensed. Disabled access. Children welcome. Pets by arrangement. En suite most rooms. Tea/coffee & T.V. in rooms. B. & B. from £20.

DURNESS

Port-na-Con House, Port-na-Con, Loch Eriboll, By Altnaharra, Lairg, Sutherland, IV27 4UN (0971) 511367
Port-na-Con stands on the west side of Loch Eriboll, 6 miles east of Durness, and was built

200 years ago as a Custom House and harbour store. Completely renovated in 1984, it is now a comfortable, centrally heated guest house in which all bedrooms overlook the loch: the first floor lounge and balcony have particularly impressive views and here guests can enjoy not only the scenery, but also the varied wild life, including seals, otters and birds. The food is the very best of Scottish fare: all dishes are home-cooked from fresh, local ingredients and a typical evening meal would feature Salmon and Crab Terrine with home-made bread, followed by Roast Beef with fresh vegetables, and a delicious dessert, such as Chocolate and Orange Cheesecake.
Open April - Oct. inc. No smoking in the house. Vegetarian & other diets by arrangement. Licensed. Children & well-behaved dogs welcome. Tea/coffee-making in bedrooms. Access, Visa. D., B. & B. £26, single £32.

ELGIN

Mansion House Hotel, The Haugh, Elgin, Moray, IV30 1AW (0343) 540728
Imposing Scottish mansion with picturesque riverside outlook in the ancient burgh of Elgin; excellent leisure facilities including sauna, Turkish bath, and gym.
Vegetarian, vegan dishes avail. & other special diets by arrangement. Organic and wholefood on request. Open all year. Children welcome. En suite, TV & tea/coffee making in bedrooms. B. & B. from £55.

'Carronvale', 18 South Guildry Street, Elgin, Moray, IV30 1QN (0343) 546864
Beautiful stone-built Victorian town house, quietly situated within easy walking distance of town centre; excellent b'fast; snacks available.
Open all year ex. Oct. No smoking. Vegetarian & other diets by arrangement. Children welcome. Tea/coffee in bedrooms. T.V. lounge.

Non Smokers Haven, 63 Moss Street, Elgin, Moray, IV30 1LT (0343) 541993
Traditional stone-built 19th C. town house in

quiet location; ideal for touring, birdwatching, golf and fishing.
Open all year. No smoking. Children welcome. Tea/coffee & TV in bedrooms. B. & B. from £10.

FORT WILLIAM

The Lodge On The Loch, Onich, Nr Fort William, Inverness-shire, PH33 6RY Tel: (08553) 237 Fax: (08553) 463
Beautiful hotel in spectacular setting on the shores of loch; tasteful furnishings; relaxed yet impeccable service.Outstanding Scottish cuisine; use of nearby pool & leisure club.
Open Xmas and New Year, Easter to end Oct. No smoking in dining room. Vegetarian & other diets. Licensed. Disabled access. Children welcome. Pets welcome. En suite, TV & tea/coffee in bedrooms.

Mrs B Grieve, 'Nevis View', 14 Farrow Drive, Corpach, Fort William, Inverness-shire, PH33 7JW Tel: (0397) 772447 Fax: (0397) 772800
Beautiful architect-designed house on a small, quiet estate looking out with stupendous views to lochs and mountains. The food is excellent; fresh & local ingredients are used in the preparation of home-cooked cuisine; the vegetarian options are imaginative and tasty.
Open all year. No smoking. Vegetarian standard. Vegan by arrangement. Children welcome. Pets by arrangement. Tea/coffee making & T.V. in all bedrooms. B & B from £11.50. D. £6.

Rhu Mhor Guest House, Alma Rd, Fort William, Inverness-shire, PH33 6BP (0397) 702213
Family-run, traditional & old-fashioned guest house in 1 acre of wild tree-shrouded garden on a hill behind town. Vegetarian proprietors. Tea & biscuits serve a.m. & 10 p.m. Dinner booked.
Open April - Sept. No smoking in dining room & 1 lounge. Vegetarian & other diets by arrangemet. Children & pets. B. & B. £13-14.30, D. £8 - 8.50.

Taransay, Seafield Gardens, Fort William, PH33 6RJ (0397) 703303
Comfortable, modern family home in a quiet area off the A82 close to the town centre; panoramic views over Loch Linnhe and the Artgour Hills.
Open Jan. to Oct. Smoking banned throughout Vegetarian standard. Other special diets by arrangement. Children welcome. Tea/coffee making in bedrooms. T.V. in lounge. B. & B. from £12.50.

GLENFINNAN
The Stage House, Glenfinnan, Inverness-shire, PH37 4LT (0397 83) 246
17th C. coaching inn superbly situated in picturesque glen at the head of Loch Shiel; beautifully renovated; excellent and imaginative cuisine prepared from fresh, local produce; fishing rights and boats for hire.
Open Mar. to Jan. No smoking ex. 2 bars. Vegetarian standard. Licensed. Over 5s only. Pets by arrangement. En suite, tea/coffee making & TV in bedrooms. Access, Visa. B. & B. from £25.95.

GRANTOWN-ON-SPEY
Kinross House, Woodside Avenue, Grantown-on-Spey, Morayshire, PH26 3JR (0479) 2042

Peacefully situated in the delightful country town of Grantown-on-Spey, Kinross House is an attractive Victorian villa which has been beautifully decorated and furnished throughout. David and Katherine Elder, your Scottish hosts, have established a well-deserved reputation for the warmth of their hospitality and their excellent home-prepared food. David will be wearing his MacIntosh tartan kilt when he serves your evening meal which, typically, might feature Stilton and Leek Soup followed by Baked Trout (with fresh vegetables) and an imaginative dessert such as Oranges in Cointreau with Orange Sorbet; a good mature Scottish cheddar with biscuits and oatcakes, followed by fresh coffee and mints, would complete the meal. The Kinross House brochure will tell you more about the lovely surrounding area in which you can visit Balmoral or Braemar, Loch Ness and Inverness, Cawdor Castle, Culloden Battlefield as well as numerous woollen mills and whisky distilleries.
Open Mar to Nov No smoking. Vegetarian & other diets by arrangement. Licensed. Children: over 7s only. No pets. En suite in most bedrooms. Tea/coffee making & T.V. in all bedrooms. B. & B. en suite £16-£22, B. & B. without en suite £13 - 19.

Stonefield Cottage, 28 The Square, Grantown-on-Spey, Moray, PH26 3HF (0479) 3000
Beautiful stone-built dwelling on the square in Grantown-on-Spey; friendly family atmosphere.
Open Easter to end Oct. No smoking in the house. Vegetarian & other diets by arrangement. Children welcome. Tea/coffee making in rooms. B. & B. £12.

INVERGARRY
Glendale Vegetarian Guest House, Mandally Road, Invergarry, Inverness-shire, PH35 4HP (08093) 282
Spacious attractive house situated on the outskirts of a pretty village; run by a mother-and-daughter team it has a very friendly atmosphere & offers excellent home-cooking.
Open all year ex. Xmas and New Year. No smoking in dining room & sitting room. Vegetarian exclusively. Most other meat-free special diets by arrangement. Licensed. Children welcome (under 4s free). Pets by arrangement. 1 room en suite. Tea/coffee making in bedrooms. T.V. lounge. B. & B. from £13. D. £8.50.

INVERNESS
Ardmuir House Hotel, 16 Ness Bank, Inverness, IV2 4SF (0463) 231151
Charming stone-built house of character; excellent and imaginative home-cooking prepared from fresh ingredients.
Open all year. No smoking in dining room. Vegetarian and other diets by arrangement. Licensed. Disabled access. Children welcome. En suite in all bedrooms. Tea/coffee making. T.V.

Glendruidh House, Old Edinburgh Road, Inverness, IV1 2AA Tel: (0463) 226499 Fax: (0463) 710745

Glendruidh House is a charming and unusual building standing in its own pleasant grounds overlooking Inverness, the Moray Firth and the Black Isle. Its design is extraordinary: with its interesting tower over the entrance hall, the many dormer windows and an amazing circular drawing room which has beautiful garden views; its rare peace and tranquillity bely the fact that it is just 2 miles from the centre of Inverness. The cuisine reflects a largely traditional menu and

offers home-cooked dishes which have been superbly prepared from fresh local produce. A typical table d'hote dinner selection might be Cream of Potato and Chives Soup or Chicken Liver Paté with cranberries, followed by Poached Fresh Wild Salmon with Parsley and Lemon Butter or Roast Leg of Chicken Stuffed with Raisins and Nuts (and fresh vegetable accompaniments); dessert might be Toffee Apple Sponge or Poached Victoria Plums in Port. Whilst many small hotels are totally smoke-free, Glendruidh House is unusual in that it has a small luxurious bar open to the public which is also smoke-free. The Glendruidh House brochure rightly eulogises the Highlands as a place for all seasons: spring is the time of endless days (blue skies at midnight!) and autumn is the time when heather purples the mountains; winter is not just when the skiers repair to Aviemore, but is the season when the cognoscenti come to appreciate Scotland's beautiful frozen lochs and to see waterfalls hanging like crystal from the mountains.
Open all year. No smoking. Vegetarian and most other special diets by arrangement. Licensed. Disabled access: 'with assistance; ground floor rooms & wide doors'. Children welcome. En suite, tea/coffee making & T.V. in all bedrooms. Credit cards accepted. B. & B. from £29.

Glen Mhor Hotel and Restaurant, 9-12 Ness Bank, Inverness, IV2 4SG (0463) 234308

Beautiful large old country house overlooking the River Ness; excellent cuisine.
Vegetarian standard. Vegan & other diets by arrangement. Organic when available or on request. Wholefoods on request. Open all year ex. New Year. No smoking in part of dining room. Licensed. Disabled access. Children welcome. Pets by arrangement. En suite, TV & tea/coffee making in bedrooms. Credit cards. D., B. & B. from £45.

Kingsmills Hotel, Culcabock Road, Inverness, IV2 3LP (0463) 237166

Superb hotel, with 18th C. origins, set in several acres of beautiful gardens and adjacent to Inverness golf course; beautifully furnished; excellent cuisine and good leisure facilities.
Vegetarian standard. Open all year. No smoking in 40 bedrooms. Licensed. Disabled access. Children welcome. Pets by arrangement. En suite, TV & tea/coffee in bedrooms. Credit cards.

Sky House, Upper Cullernie, Balloch, Inverness IV1 2HU (0463) 792582

Spacious, modern home in beautiful open countryside yet just 5 mins' drive from Highland capital and its airport; magnificent views across the Moray Firth; wholesome, fresh food.

Open all year. No smoking throughout. Vegetarian by arrangement. Pets by arrangement. En suite in some rooms. Tea/coffee making & T.V. in all rooms. Access, Visa. B. & B. from £18.

KINGUSSIE

The Cross, 25/27 High Street, Kingussie, PH21 1HX (0540) 661166

'A Restaurant with Rooms'; excellent and imaginative home-prepared cuisine.
Open all year except 3 weeks, May/June, 5 weeks Nov/Dec. No smoking in dining room & bedrooms. Vegetarian by arrangement. Licensed. En suite in all rooms. Access, Visa. B & B from £26.50.

Homewood Lodge, Newtonmore Road, Kingussie, Inverness-shire, PH21 1HD (0540) 661507

Charming country house offering excellent accommodation; log fires & delicious dinners with home-made bread, scones & icecreams.
Open all year ex. Xmas. No smoking. Vegetarian & other diets by arrangement. Licensed. Children welcome. Pets by arrangement. En suite & tea/coffee in bedrooms. T.V. in lounge. B. & B. from £19.

The Royal Hotel, 29 High Street, Kingussie, Inverness-shire, PH21 1HX (0540) 661898

Family-owned and run hotel in the quiet village of Kingussie; excellent cuisine prepared from fresh, local produce.
Open all year. No smoking in dining room & part of bar. Vegetarian & other diets by arrangement. Licensed. Disabled access. Children welcome. Pets by arrangement. En suite, TV & tea/coffee making in bedrooms. Credit cards B. & B. from £26. D. £12.

KYLE OF LOCHALSH

Culag, Carr Brae, Dornie, Kyle, Ross-shire, IV40 8HA (059 985) 341

Modern bungalow situated just outside Dornie village with spectacular views over Loch Duich and Loch Alsh; exclusively vegetarian B. & B.
Open all year. No smoking. Vegetarian and vegan exclusively. Disabled access: 'Ground floor only (bungalow)'. Children welcome. Tea/coffee making in bedrooms. B. & B. from £10.50.

Kirkbeag, Kincraig, Kingussie, Inverness-shire, PH21 1ND (05404) 298

Kirkbeag is a beautiful 19th C. church which has been successfully converted into a family home and workshop. Both bed and breakfast and self-catering accommodation is offered, and additionally the proprietors offer craft training courses in wood-carving or silver work. The food is excellent: everything has been home-prepared to guests' individual requirements from fresh, local ingredients and a typical evening meal would feature corn on the cob with cream sauce followed by lasagne with jacket potatoes and a home-made dessert.

Vegetarian, vegan & other diets by arrangement. Wholefoods on request. Open all year. Children welcome. Tea/coffee on request.B. & B. from £12.

The Retreat, Main Street, Kyle, Ross-shire, IV40 8BY (0599) 4308

Pleasantly furnished guest house close to station, bus terminus & ferry to Skye; excellent home-cooked cuisine.

Open all year. No smoking. Vegetarian and most other special diets by arrangement. Restricted licence. Children: over 14s only. Tea/coffee in bedrooms. T.V. lounge. Credit cards. B. & B. from £13.

Tigh Tasgaidh, Bank House, Dornie, Kyle of Lochalsh, IV40 8EH (059 985) 242

Converted village bank; home-cooked food.

Open Mar. to Nov. No smoking. Pets by arrangement. En suite & tea/coffee in bedrooms. T.V. B. & B. from £14.

KYLESKU

Kylesku Hotel, Kylesku, Sutherland (0971) 2231

Beautiful hotel overlooking sea; good home-cooking including home-baked bread.

Open Mar. to Oct. No smoking in 50% of dining room & some bedrooms. Vegetarian and other diets by arrangement. Licensed. Disabled access. Children welcome. Tea/coffee in bedrooms. B. & B. £19

Linne Mhuirich, Unapool Croft Road, Kylesku, via Lairg, Sutherland, IV27 4HW (0971) 502227

Fiona and Diarmid MacAulay welcome up to 6 non-smoking guests to their modern croft house, which is superbly situated on a hillside leading down to the rocky shore of Loch Glencoul; its quiet, peaceful, yet accessible position makes it an excellent base for exploring the north-west Highlands. Many guests return annually for the comfort and attention, peace and the delicious food (which is 'Taste of Scotland' recommended). Everything has been home-made from fresh and local ingredients, and Fiona specializes in preparing local fish and seafood dishes; quiches, pates, tasty casseroles, delicious vegetarian dishes and tempting desserts also feature on her menus (although there are also low-calorie choices for those with an eye on the waistline!). There is no T.V. reception here - so nothing can interfere with after dinner conversation or just sitting back and enjoying the spectacular views from the comfort of the lounge (or perhaps browsing through the MacAulays' extensive collection of books).

Open May to Oct. No smoking. Vegetarian, low-fat, high-fibre diets by arrangement. Not licensed - guests welcome to bring their own wine. Children welcome. Pets by arrangement. 1 room with private bathroom. Tea/coffee making in bedrooms. B. & B. from £16.50, D. £9.50. Scottish Board 2 crowns commended. "Taste of Scotland " recommended.

LAIRG

Gneiss House, Invershin, by Lairg, Sutherland, IV17 4ET (054 982) 282

New bungalow standing in pretty garden amidst the glorious unspoilt Sutherland countryside. B. & B. only but tea and home-made scones greet you on your arrival & breakfast is a splendid repast with bowls of hot porridge (or cereal if you prefer it) followed by a generous cooked platter of bacon, egg, sausage and tomato.

Open all year. No smoking. Vegetarian and most other special diets by arrangement. Pets by arrangement. En suite & tea/coffee making in bedrooms. T.V. in lounge. Credit cards.. B. & B. from £12.50.

Invercassley Cottage, Rosehall, by Lairg, Sutherland (054 984) 288

Charmingly renovated house in a beautiful rural setting complete with duck ponds and a variety of waterfowl. Excellent b'fast & everything - including the bread - is home-made. Terrain bikes are for hire and maps and packed lunches can be provided. Dinner by arrangement.

Vegetarian standard. Vegan but no other special diets by arrangement. Organic and Wholefood when avail. Open all year. No smoking in bedrooms. Disabled access. Children welcome. Pets by arrangement. T.V. in all bedrooms. B. & B. from £10.

LOCHCARRON
Ladytrek Scotland, 'Foxgloves', Leacanashie, Lochcarron, Wester Ross, IV54 8YD (05202) 238

Award-winning walking holidays based in cosy Highland cottages and offering leisurely leader-accompanied walks into mountains using ancient drove tracks; excellent and imaginative home-cooked meals.

Open Easter to Oct. No smoking. Vegetarian & other diets by arrangement. Tea/coffee making in kitchen. Inclusive holiday rates.

LOCHNESS-SIDE
The Foyers Hotel, Lochness-side, Inverness, IV1 2XT (04563) 216

Comfortable Victorian country house hotel in pleasant grounds overlooking Loch Ness. All food freshly prepared by the chef-proprietor.

Open all year. No smoking. Vegetarian standard. Vegan & other diets by arrangement. Children welcome. En suite some rooms. T.V. lounge. Credit cards. B. & B. from £27.50.

MORAY
Seaview B & B, 82 Granary Street, Burghead, Moray, IV30 2UA (0343) 830034

Commended guest house situated on the harbour front of the small fishing village of Burghead.

Open all year. No smoking. Vegetarian & other diets by arrangement. Disabled: '1 ground floor bedroom'. Children welcome. Pets by arrangement. Tea/coffee making & T.V. in all bedrooms. B. & B. from £11.

MUIR OF ORD
Ord House Hotel, Muir of Ord, Ross-shire, IV6 7UH (0463) 870492

Beautiful 17th C. country house standing in 25 acres of formal gardens and woodlands; elegantly furnished and appointed; excellent cuisine prepared from home-grown produce.

Vegetarian and diabetic diets by arrangement. Organic when avail. Wholefood on request. Open mid May. to mid Oct. No smoking in dining room annexe. Licensed. Children welcome. Pets by arrangement. En suite & tea/coffee making in bedrooms. T.V. Access, Visa, Amex, Mastercard. B. & B. from £27.

The Dower House, Muir of Ord, Ross-shire, IV6 7XN Tel & Fax: (0463) 870090

Nestling in 3 acres of mature grounds & converted to the *cottage orne* style in 1800, this Dower House offers exceptionally comfortable accommodation & award-winning food & wine.

Open all year. No smoking in dining room & some bedrooms. Vegetarian & other diets by arrangement. Licensed. Disabled access. Children welcome. Dogs by arrangement. En suite & T.V. in all bedrooms. Credit cards. B. & B. from £45.

NAIRN
Clifton Hotel, Viewfield Street, Nairn, Nairn-shire (0667) 53119

Sumptuously appointed Victorian house; elegant, spacious rooms; wonderful food prepared from fresh ingredients.

Open Mar. to Nov. No smoking in T.V. room & part of dining area. Vegetarian standard. Other diets by arrangement. Children welcome. Pets by arrangement. En suite in all bedrooms. Access, Visa. B. & B. from £43.

Dallaschyle, Cawdor, Nairn, IV12 5XS (06678) 422

Charming house offering excellent home-cooking prepared from fresh, local and some home-grown produce; home-baked cakes, biscuits, jams and marmalade. Large, peaceful garden. Evening tea & home-baking in lounge.

Vegetarian & diabetic diets by arrangement. Organic & wholefood when avail. Open Apr. - Oct. No smoking in bedrooms. Disabled: ground floor bedrooms. Children welcome. B. & B. from £12. D. from £8.

NETHYBRIDGE
Talisker, Dell Road, Nethybridge, Inverness-shire, PH25 3DG (047982) 624

Beautiful stone-built house standing in pretty gardens; tastefully furnished; excellent food home-cooked from fresh ingredients.

Open all year. No smoking. Diabetic diets by arrangement. Children: over 8s only. Tea/coffee. T.V. lounge. B. & B. from £11.50.

NEWTONMORE
Craigellachie House, Main Street, Newtonmore, Inverness-shire, PH20 1DA (0540) 673 360

Comfortable family home built in the 1800s & thought to be the oldest house in Newtonmore; excellent breakfast menu with lots of options. Evening meals by arrangement.

Open all year ex. Xmas. No smoking. Vegetarian and vegan standard. Other diets by arrangement. Children welcome. Pets by arrangement. Tea/coffee making in bedrooms. T.V. in lounge. B. & B. from £14.

Spey Valley Lodge, Station Road, Newtonmore, Inverness-shire, PH20 1AR (05403) 398
Beautiful house situated in an acre of grounds with magnificent views of the Spey Valley; good home-cooking; French, Italian & Scots spoken.
Open all year. No smoking in dining room. Vegetarian & other diets by arrangement. Children welcome. Tea/coffee & T.V. in bedrooms. B. & B. from £11.

SPEAN BRIDGE
Old Pines, Gairlochy Road, Spean Bridge, Inverness-shire, PH34 4EG (039) 781324

Old Pines is a happy family home of great character, built in Scandinavian style, which stands in 30 peaceful acres of land commanding breathtaking views of Aonach Mor and Ben Nevis. The bedrooms are comfortable and prettily decorated, and fresh flowers, interesting books and log fires all help to create a relaxing, informal atmosphere and a restful holiday! The cooking is excellent: delicious meals are imaginatively prepared from the best of fresh local ingredients, and a typical dinner menu would include cheese and fruit Salad with raspberry vinegar dressing followed by Trout stuffed with Leeks, Garlic and Orange or Pheasant with Black Grapes and Fresh Herbs and, for dessert, a Rhubarb and Banana Brulée. Old Pines is a perfect base from which to tour Scotland's beautiful West Highlands, and there is winter skiing just 6 miles away at Aonach Mor.
Open all year. No smoking indoors.Vegetarian & other diets by arrangement. Bring your own wine. Disabled access: 'Completely accessible; 3 specially adapted ground floor bedrooms.' Children welcome. Pets by arrangement. En suite in most rooms. Tea/coffee on request. T.V. in lounge. Access, Visa, Mastercard. D., B. & B. from £35. STB 3 Crowns Commended.

STRATHPEFFER
Craigdarroch Lodge Hotel, Contin-by-Strathpeffer (0997) 21265
Beautiful lodge in 12 acres of wooded grounds; fresh food; indoor swimming pool, sauna, solarium, snooker, canoes & mountain bikes.
Open 22 Mar. to 1 Feb. No smoking in dining room & leisure area. Vegetarian, diabetic standard. Other diets by arrangement. Licensed. Disabled access. Children welcome. Pets by arrangement. En suite, tea/coffee making & TV in rooms. B. & B. from £18.

Gardenside Guest House, Strathpeffer, Ross and Cromarty, IV14 9BJ (0997) 421242

Gardenside is a charming 19th C. house set in a splendid situation surrounded by woodland and fields on the southwest side of the Victorian Spa village of Strathpeffer. Accommodation is in well-appointed rooms - some with views - and there is an inviting guest lounge. Meals are served in an attractive dining room and the 3-course dinner, prepared from fresh, local produce, would typically feature Homemade Kipper Paté, Scottish Beef braised with peppercorn, garlic, red wine and cream, and a delicious dessert such as fresh fruit in a light cinnamon and lemon syrup. Strathpeffer owes its existence to the discovery in the 18th C. of a nearby spring with healing waters. Formerly one of Britain's most elegant health resorts (the village is full of opulent and spacious turn of the century villas), it is currently undergoing a modest revival. If the waters are not enough to lure you to Strathpeffer, then its proximity to so many other of the Highland's tourist attractions surely will: head out from the village in a different direction each day and come across Inverewe Gardens, Drumnadrochit, Invergordon and Bonor Bridge.
Open 1 Mar. to 4 Jan. No smoking. Vegetarian & other diets by arrangement. Licensed. Disabled access: ground floor rooms avail. Children welcome. En suite in some rooms. Tea/coffee making in bedrooms. T.V. in lounge and some bedrooms. B. & B. from £13.50.

STRUY

Chisholm Stone House, Struy, by Beauly, Inverness-shire (046) 376 222

Chisholm Stone House is named after the Chisholm Stone that sits in the front grounds close to the Cannich lane boundary. It is a very comfortable, centrally heated home (all bedrooms are en suite) which offers a true away-from-it-all break for lovers of wild, unspoilt countryside (the house is surrounded by 2,000 foot mountains); indeed its owners tell me that their enviable location is often described as being the last true wilderness in the U.K. You are surrounded by natural beauty - so it is only fair and appropriate that you ingest natural and beautiful food: no problem here - everything is cooked slowly on the woodburner, including the bread (often made with walnuts and sultanas).

Open April - Oct. inc. No smoking in the house. Vegetarian by arrangement. Children: over 10s welcome. Dogs welcome. Restricted licensed. En suite & tea/coffee-making in bedrooms. D., B. & B. £21.

TONGUE

Ben Loyal Hotel, Tongue, Sutherland, IV27 4XE (0847 55) 216

The Ben Loyal Hotel is a white-painted building standing in a quite splendid location overlooking the waters of the Kyle of Tongue and the peaks of the mountain after which it has been named. The hotel has been designed with the seemingly sole intention of enabling guests to enjoy these quite stunning panoramas in almost every room: from the comfortably furnished lounge with its picture window to the beautifully appointed bedrooms (pine furniture, pretty fabrics, fourposters). Perhaps the best views can be had from the dining room, however - although here you will find that your loyalties are torn between relishing the view and savouring the food: only fresh, local produce - some of it home-grown - is used in the preparation of a largely traditional menu and the table d'hote meal could well feature home-made Lentil Soup followed by Supreme of Salmon in a Seafood Sauce (served with fresh vegetables) and a selection of good old-fashioned puddings, such as Bread and Butter Pudding. Ben Loyal is, as I have indicated, surrounded by quite breathtaking countryside; there are lots of lovely sandy beaches to wander along and the wildlife flourishes in abundance.

Open all year. No smoking in dining room. Vegetarian & other diets by arrangement. Licensed. Disabled access: 'partial, with assistance'. Children welcome. En suite in most rooms. Tea/coffee making in bedrooms. T.V. on request. D., B. & B. from £35.50-44.50.

ULLAPOOL

Altnaharrie Inn, Ullapool, IV26 2SS (085 483) 230

Lovely old house standing on the shores of Loch Broom & reached by launch (6 trips daily); outstanding cuisine (chef rated among top few in the country - the others being in London).

Open Easter to late Oct. No smoking. Vegetarian and other diets by arrangement. Licensed. Children: over 8s only. Pets by arrangement. En suite in all rooms. D., B. & B. from £105.

Tigh-Na-Mara (House by the Sea), The Shore, Ardindrean, Nr Ullapool, Loch Broom (0854 85) 282

Unique secluded and idyllic home on the shore of Loch Broom. Gourmet Scottish and Vegetarian cuisine. Free use of boats, bikes and windsurfers. bring your own wine and wellies! (200 yd walk down steep muddy croft).

Open all year. No smoking in house. Vegetarian & vegan standard. Fish on request. Children welcome. Tea/coffee making & TV in bedrooms. D., B. & B. from £149.50. per week.

Lothian

DALKEITH
Belmont, 47 Eskbank Road, Dalkeith, Midlothian, EH22 3BH (031 663) 8676
Large, Victorian house with many original period features; conservatory and garden.
Open all year. No smoking in the house. Vegetarian and other special diets by arrangement. Children & pets welcome. En suite in 1 room. Tea/coffee available. B. & B. from £14.

EAST CALDER
Whitecroft Farm, East Calder, Near Edinburgh, EH53 0ET (0506) 881810
Large bungalow on a small farm near Almondell Country Park and golf courses.
Open all year. No smoking in the house. Vegetarian and most other special diets by arrangement. Children welcome. Tea/coffee making & T.V. in all bedrooms. B. & B. from £14.

DUNBAR
St Helen's Guest House, Queen's Road, Dunbar, EH42 1LN (0368) 63716
Charming 19th C. red sandstone house; tastefully renovated yet retaining many original features; breakfast only but vegetarian & continental options available.
Open Jan. to Oct. No smoking in the house, except T.V. lounge. Vegetarian standard. Children welcome. Pets welcome. En suite in 1 room. Tea/coffee making in bedrooms. T.V. in lounge. B. & B. from £12.

HADDINGTON
Long Newton House, Gifford, Haddington, EH41 4JW (062 081) 210
Beautiful 17th C. farmhouse with large garden at the foot of the Lammermuir Hills.
Open Apr. to Oct. No smoking in bedrooms. Vegetarian & most other special diets by arrangement. Children welcome. Pets by arrangement. En suite & tea/coffee making in bedrooms. T.V. in lounge. B. & B. from £16.

Orkneys & Shetlands

KIRKWALL
Bilmaris, Glaitness Road, Kirkwall, Orkney, KW15 1TW (0856) 4515
Vegetarian, vegan and diabetic standard. Most other special diets by arrangement. Open all year. Smoking banned in dining room. Children welcome. Pets by arrangement. En suite in most rooms. Tea/coffee making in bedrooms. T.V. Access, Visa. B. & B. from £10.

Briar Lea, 10 Dundas Crescent, Kirkwall, Orkney (0856) 2747
Bed and breakfast offering healthy breakfast options.
Vegetarian & vegan standard. Some other special diets by arrangement. Open all year. No smoking in dining room & bedrooms. Children welcome. Tea/coffee making in bedrooms. T.V. in lounge. B. & B. from £13.

2 Dundas Crescent, Kirkwall, Orkney, KW15 1JQ (0856) 2465
Central town house near St Magnus cathedral and the shopping area.
Open all year. No smoking in the house. Vegetarian and most other special diets by arrangement. Children welcome. Tea/coffee making in lounge. T.V. in lounge. B. & B. from £8.50.

LYNESS
Family Budge, Stoneyquoy, Lyness, Orkney, KW16 3NY (0856)79234
Working beef farm overlooking Longhope Bay; excellent home-baking; southfacing garden with sun porch.
Open all year. No smoking in the house ex. in part of dining room. Vegetarian and most other special diets by arrangement. Children welcome. Tea/coffee making in kitchen. T.V. in all bedrooms on request. Credit cards. B. & B. from £9.

PAPA STOUR
Mrs S Holt-Brook, North House, Papa Stour, Shetland, ZE2 9PW (059 573) 238
Stone-built house on working croft on small island of the West of Shetland. Own boat to visit caves & spectacular coast. Local crab & croft produce. Visitors welcome to participate in seasonal activities.
Vegetarian and other diets by arrangement. Organic and wholefood always. Open Apr. to Sept. No smoking in the house. Disabled access:'ground floor bedroom'. Children & pets welcome by arrangement. Tea/coffee making in bedrooms. T.V. in lounge. B. & B. from £11.

Strathclyde

AYR

Brenalder Lodge, 39 Dunure Road, Doonfoot, Ayr, KA7 4HR (0292) 43939

Brenalder Lodge is a beautiful modern bungalow superbly situated overlooking the Firth of Clyde with panoramic views of the Carrick Hills. It has been quite exceptionally well-furnished and appointed throughout: bedrooms are light, airy and spacious and the conservatory-type dining room sets the scene for the delicious meals which have all been cooked on the premises from fresh ingredients. The four-course breakfast is a generous and healthy treat, while the evening meal reflects a largely traditional menu, and would typically feature home-made soup followed by home-made Steak Pie (with fresh vegetables) and a good old-fashioned dessert, such as Apple Pie. The Lodge is an ideal base for exploring 'Burns Country' and the world famous golf courses of Turnberry and Royal Troon are nearby.

Open all year. Smoking banned throughout the house ex. T.V. lounge. Awaiting licence. Disabled access. Children: over 7s only; younger by arrangement. Pets by arrangement. En suite, tea/coffee making & T.V. in all bedrooms. B. & B. from £23. D. £16.

BIGGAR

YMCA National Training & Conference Centre, Wiston Lodge, Wiston, Biggar, Lanarkshire, ML12 6HT (08995) 228

Once a hunting lodge, this converted 19th C. mansion stands in 55 acres of countryside & offers holidays and training courses.

Open all year. No smoking. Vegetarian and most other special diets by arrangement. Disabled access. Children welcome. Tea/coffee making in bedrooms. T.V. Full board from £98 weekly.

Candybank Farm, Biggar (0899) 20422

Large, comfortable farmhouse in peaceful setting with lovely views of surrounding hills.

Open April to Oct. No smoking. Vegetarian & other diets by arrangement. Disabled access to ground floor bedrooms. Children welcome. Pets by arrangement. Tea/coffeemaking & TV in all bedrooms. B. & B. from £11.

HELENSBURGH

Thorndean, 64 Colquhoun St., Helensburgh, Dumbartonshire, G84 9JP (0436) 74922

Friendly Scottish welcome in spacious 19th C. house standing in extensive gardens; lovely sea views. Private parking. Your hosts organise barbeques, sailing in 31' cruiser & hill-walking.

Open all year. No smoking in the house. Vegetarian and other diets by arrangement. Children welcome. Most rooms en suite. Tea/coffee making in bedrooms. B. & B. from £16.

LARGS

South Whittlieburn Farm, Brisbane Glen, Largs, Ayrshire, KA30 8SN (0475) 675881

Attractive farmhouse on working sheep farm 2m NE Largs. 2 Crown Commended. Golf, horse-riding, sailing, fishing, diving & hill-walking. Ferries to Arran, Cumbrae and Bute nearby.

Open all year. No smoking in dining room & some bedrooms. Vegetarian & other diets by arrangement. Children welcome. En suite 1 room. TV & tea/coffee-making in bedrooms. B. & B. from £14.50.

LOCH GOIL

Eversley House, Carrick Castle, Loch Goil, Argyll, PA24 8AJ (03013) 535

Stone-built country manse overlooking Loch Goil near to Carrick Castle & Lochgoilhead. most bedrooms have loch views. Imaginative meals from fresh, local ingredients.

Vegetarian and other diets by arrangement. Open all year ex. 2 weeks in Feb. Licensed. Children welcome. Pets by arrangement. Tea/coffee making & TV in bedrooms. B. & B. from £19.50.

OBAN

Asknish Cottage, Arduaine, by Oban, Argyll, PA34 4XQ (085 22) 247

Small, modern house on a hillside with wonderful views over islands of Jura, Scarba, Shuna and Luing. Excellent touring base.

Open all year. No smoking in the house. Vegetarian and most other special diets by arrangement. Children welcome. Pets welcome. Tea/coffee making in bedrooms. T.V. in lounge. B. & B. from £13.

PAISLEY

Myfarrclan Guest House, 146 Corsebar Road, Paisley, Renfrewshire, PA2 9NA (041) 884 8285

Tastefully decorated house situated in a quiet residential area 1m from the town centre; some rooms have microwaves for self-caterers; safe, quiet garden has children's play area.
Open all year. No smoking in the house. Vegetarian and low-fat diets by arrangement. Children welcome. En suite in most rooms. Tea/coffee making & T.V. in all bedrooms. B. & B. from £18.

SEAMILL

Spottiswoode Guest House, Sandy Rd, Seamill, West Kilbride, Ayrshire, KA23 9NN (0294) 823131

Built in 1896, Spottiswoode is a spacious Victorian home which has been tastefully decorated and traditionally appointed by its present owners who have taken care to retain the house's original charm and character. It stands just feet away from the Firth of Clyde - the beautiful sea and island views can be appreciated from the dining room, lounge and a bedroom - and the surrounding countryside is both rich in natural wildlife and also an ideal base from which to explore Ayrshire and the nearby islands (Glasgow is just 45 minutes away by train or car). Your hosts at Spottiswoode, Christine and Jim Ondersma, are thoroughly committed to quality and guest satisfaction: each of the guest bedrooms have been decorated to a very high standard and are equipped with fluffy towels, reading materials, well-lit mirrors and other thoughtful touches. The breakfast menu is another example of the Ondersmas' attention to detail: prepared with minimum fat and salt, both Scottish and American specialities are offered, including locally-made, additive-free sausages, free-range eggs, and home-made bread and yoghurts; evening meals are creative and freshly prepared (24 hours notice, please). There is much to enjoy *in situ* - a soak in the deep Victorian bath, afternoon tea on the lawn, games and music by the fireside . . . There is no reason at all to move from base except, perhaps, to enjoy a walk in the magnificent surrounding countryside or shore, or to enjoy a game of golf arranged by your hosts.
Open all year. Non-smokers only. Vegetarian a speciality. Other diets by arrangement. Children: over 10s. En suite, TV, tea/coffee, hairdryer in rooms. Credit cards. B. & B. from £16, D. from £9.50.

ST CATHERINE'S

Arnish Cottage Lochside Guest House, Poll Bay, St Catherine's, Argyll, PA25 8BA (0499) 2405

Lovely house in conservation area midway between St Catherine's & Strachur. A truly idyllic spot on a private road 20 ft from the lochside. A wealth of wildlife & peace - walks from the doorstep.
Open all year. No smoking in the house. Vegetarian & other diets by arrangement. En suite & tea/coffee in bedrooms. TV in lounge. B. & B. from £17, D. £11.

TURNBERRY

Malin Court, Turnberry, Ayrshire, KA26 9PB Tel: (0655) 31457 Fax: (0655) 31072

Malin Court combines both residential and hotel accommodation in a modern, comfortable building set amidst tranquil gardens. Recently refurbished, each of the en suite bedrooms has

satellite and colour TV as well as a radio, direct dial phone and hairdryer; centrally heated and double-glazed, they offer a very high standard of accommodation. Meals are served in a beautiful restaurant with breath-taking views of the Isle of Arran and the Firth of Clyde; both the à la carte and table d'hôte dishes have been prepared from the finest of fresh, local produce, and there is an extensive, carefully chosen wine list. There is a also a cosy bar - with a roaring log fire in cooler weather - in which are served bar meals, afternoon teas or suppers; other amenities include a laundry and hairdressing salon. Turnberry is a wonderful centre for touring Ayrshire; the numerous local outdoor activities include tennis, sea-angling, squash, windsurfing, riding and fishing.
Open all year. Vegetarian standard. Other diets by arrangement. Licensed. Children welcome. Pets by arrangement. En suite, TV & tea/coffee-making in bedrooms. Credit cards. B. & B. £45-55.

Tayside

ABERFELDY

Dalchiorlich, Glenlyon, by Aberfeldy, Perthshire, PH15 2PX (08876) 226
Remote sheep farm amidst 3000 ft mountains in Scotland's longest glen; good home-cooking.
Open Mar. to Nov. No smoking in bedrooms. Vegetarian and low-fat diets catered for. Children welcome. Tea/coffee making in bedrooms. T.V. in lounge. B & B from £10.

Mrs Morag Tulloch, Fendoch, Fortingall, by Aberfeldy, Perthshire, PH15 2LL (08873) 322
Warm welcome in peaceful village. Ideal touring centre. Good home-cooked food. Fishing, hill-walking & pony-trekking can be arranged.
Open all year. Vegetarian, low-fat & other diets catered for. Children & pets welcome. En suite. T. V. & Tea/coffee in rooms. B & B from £12.50. D. £8.50

BLAIRGOWRIE

Dryfesands Guest House, Burnhead Road, Blairgowrie, Perthshire, PH10 6SY (0250) 3417
Spacious and attractive white-painted bungalow standing in pretty gardens on a hillside overlooking Blairgowrie; the wonderful food is freshly cooked to Cordon Bleu standards from local or home-grown ingredients.
Open all year. No smoking. Vegetarian & other diets by arrangement. Children: over 10s. En suite & tea/coffee in rooms. T.V. lounge. B & B from £20.

BRECHIN

Blibberhill Farmhouse, Brechin, Angus, DD9 6TH (030 783) 225
18th C. farmhouse set in peaceful surroundings; home-cooking including jams & marmalade.
Open all year. No smoking. Vegetarian & other diets by arrangement. En suite in most rooms. Tea/coffee making in bedrooms. B & B from £12.50.

BROUGHTY FERRY

Invermark Hotel, 23 Monifieth Road, Broughty Ferry, Dundee, DD5 2RN (0382) 739430
The Invermark is a small privately run hotel conveniently situated in the Dundee suburb of Broughty Ferry; the furnishings are modern and attractive - there are two large public rooms which can comfortably host small functions, such as weddings or birthday parties - and all bedrooms have been tastefully furnished and appointed. The food is exceptionally good: only fresh produce is used in the cooking and, while breakfast is the only meal which is usually available at Invermark, evening meals may be taken on request. Originally a fishing village, Broughty Ferry is now a bustling, residential city suburb; it still has lots of character, though: the seafront is guarded by a 15th C. castle, and the high street is full of interesting craft shops.
Open all year. Smoking banned throughout. Vegetarian and most other special diets by arrangement. Restricted licence. Children welcome. En suite in some rooms. Tea/coffee making & T.V. in all bedrooms. B & B from £17.50.

CALLANDER

Brook Linn Country House, Leny Feus, Callander, FK17 8AU (0877) 30103
19th C. house standing in 2 acres of terraced grounds in an elevated position above Callander; beautifully furnished.
Open Easter to Oct. No smoking. Vegetarian & other diets by arrangement. Restricted licence. Children welcome. Pets by arrangement. En suite, tea/coffee making & T.V. in all bedrooms. B & B from £16.

The Lubnaig Hotel, Leny Feus, Callander, FK17 8AS (0877) 30376
Beautiful 19th C. house standing in its own grounds on the outskirts of Callander; excellent home-cooking from fresh, local produce.
Open Mar. to Nov. No smoking in the house ex. in bar. Vegetarian and other diets by arrangement. Licensed. Children: over 7s only. Pets by arrangement. En suite, tea/coffee making & T.V. in bedrooms. D., B & B £33.

Orchardlea House, Main Street, Callander, FK17 8BG (0877) 30798
Lovely house in grounds on the main road; good Scottish cooking from fresh and local produce.
Open May. to Oct. No smoking. Vegetarian, low-fat, diabetic by arrangement. Disabled access: ground floor bedrooms. En suite in most rooms. Tea/coffee on request. T.V. in all bedrooms. B & B from £15.

Roslin Cottage Guest House, Lagrannoch, Callander, Perthshire, FK17 8LE (0877) 30638

Beautiful 18th C. house on the outskirts of Callander; oak beams, exposed stone walls & open fireplace; home-grown vegetables, honey from home-based hives & free-range eggs from the hens used in cooking; home-made wine.

Open all year. No smoking ex. in lounge. Vegetarian & other diets by arrangement. Children & pets welcome. Tea/coffee. T.V. lounge. B. & B. from £11.

CRIANLARICH
Portnellan Lodge Hotel, by Crianlarich, FK20 8QS (08383) 284 Fax (08383) 332

Portnellan House dates from the mid 19th C, and stands in the wooded grounds of a private estate overlooking Glen Dochart; it was originally built as a shooting lodge by the Marquis of Breadalbane, but these days it has been substantially extended and sympathetically modernised to provide spacious, warm and comfortable accommodation while retaining its original Victorian character. The en suite bedrooms have each been tastefully decorated, and the public rooms have book and music collections for guests' use; central heating supplements the cosy wood-burning stove in the lounge. The delicious home-cooked food is prepared from fresh, local ingredients and, with sufficient advance notice, special requests can be undertaken (lunch boxes can also be prepared on request); a good selection of malt whiskies and wines are available from the bar (which is, incidentally, the only room at Portnellan where smoking is permitted). Glen Dochart is rich in wild life: an abundant hunting territory for eagle, buzzard and osprey and a grazing ground for the red deer which may be seen wandering through the grounds. Private fishing and clay pigeon shooting are also available and some challenging golf courses can be reached within a short drive.

Open all year. No smoking in bedrooms, dining room & drawing room. Vegetarian & other diets by arrangement. Licensed. Children under 10 & visitors with pets accommodated in lodge suites. En suite, tea/coffee, TV, video, radio, trouser press & hairdrier in rooms. Credit cards. D., B. & B. £32

CRIEFF
Cairnleith, North Forr, Crieff, PH7 3RT (0764) 2080

Edwardian manse with walled garden and 4 acres of land with rare breeds; vegetarians welcome; mountain bikes for hire; very friendly.

Open all year. No smoking. Vegetarian by arrangement. Children welcome. Pets by arrangement. Private bathroom. Tea/coffee making in bedrooms. T.V. in lounge. B & B from £13.

St Ninian's Centre, Comrie Road, Crieff, PH7 4BG (0764) 3766

Converted and extended church offering comfortable accommodation & good food within a Christian context. Conference facilities available for business seminars, private functions or similar group activities.

Open all year. No smoking ex. in lounge. Vegetarian and most other special diets by arrangement. Children welcome. Tea/coffee making & TV B & B from £15.45.

DUNDEE
Swallow Hotel, Kingsway West, Invergowrie (0382) 641122

Stylish hotel based around a traditional Victorian manse; beautiful conservatory restaurant; conference and leisure facilites including pool.

Open all year. No smoking in 23 bedrooms and in approx. 25% of dining room. Vegetarian & other diets by arrangement. Licensed. Disabled access. Children welcome. Pets by arrangement. En suite, TV & tea/coffee making in bedrooms. Credit cards.

DUNKELD
Heatherbank, 1 Guthrie Villas, St Mary's Road, Birnam, Dunkeld, PH8 0BJ (0350) 727413

Heatherbank is an attractive 3-storey bay fronted Victorian house which used to be a hotel run by the Temperance Society at the turn of the century! It has been restored since that time and now offers very comfortable accommodation with all mod cons, but retains the interesting features of the original building (corniced ceilings, stained woodwork, etc). The cooking is imaginative and wholesome, a typical evening

menu featuring Smoked Salmon Paté followed by Ginger Beef with fresh vegetables and a delicious Highland dessert, such as Caledonian Cream; tea or freshly made coffee with chocolate mints would complete the meal. Heatherbank is situated in the heart of the peaceful village of Birnam close to the River Tay; you are just at the start of the Highlands in Birnam and can enjoy the wealth of hills, woodlands, rivers and wild flowers which make up the scenery of this beautiful part of the world.
Open April - Dec. No smoking. Vegetarian by arrangement. Children welcome. Pets by arrangement. Tea/coffee making in bedrooms. B. & B. from £12.50. D. £8.50.

Oronsay House, Oak Road, Birnam, Dunkeld, PH8 0BL (035 02) 294
Elegant Victorian villa in an attractive garden near the River Tay; 3 bedrooms have hill views; home-made preserves, oatcakes, wholemeal bread and porridge at breakfast.
Open Apr. to Oct. No smoking. Vegetarian and most other special diets by arrangement. En suite, TV & tea/coffee making in bedrooms. B & B from £16.50.

KILLIECRANKIE
Druimuan House, Killiecrankie, PH16 5LG (0796) 3214 Fax (0796) 2692
Elegant country house standing in private grounds. Excellent breakfast.
Open Apr. to Oct. No smoking. Vegetarian diets. Children welcome. En suite, tea/coffee making & TV in all bedrooms. B. & B. from £17.50.

KINLOCH RANNOCH
Cuilmore Cottage (08822) 218
18th C. stone croft nestling under wooded hills on the edge of village; log fires; home-cooking from organically home-grown vegetables & fruit; home-baked bread and free-range eggs.
Open all year. No smoking Vegetarian & other diets by arrangement. Children welcome. Pets by arrangement. Tea/coffee in bedrooms. D., B & B from £29.

Glenrannoch House (08822) 307
Former manse standing in 1 acre of fruit and vegetable-producing gardens; views of Schiehallion and Loch Rannoch; superb cuisine prepared from own and local produce.
Open all year. No smoking ex. in lounge. Vegetarian & other diets by arrangement. Children welcome. Pets by arrangement. Tea/coffee making on request. T.V. in all bedrooms. B & B from £12.

KIRRIEMUIR
Purgavie Farm, Lintrathen (05756) 213
Beautiful old stone-built farmhouse situated at the foot of Glen Isla on a mixed farm near the lovely Lintrathen Loch; many bedrooms have wonderful views. All food is home-prepared from fresh, local produce.
Open all year. No smoking in bedrooms or dining room. Vegetarian & other diets by arrangement. Children welcome. Pets by arrangement. En suite 1 room. Tea/coffee making in rooms. T.V. B & B £10.

'Lismore', Airlie (05753) 213
Detached bungalow on the A926 overlooking the valley of Strathmore; peaceful situation; good food prepared from fresh, local produce.
Vegetarian & other diets by arrangement. Open Mar. to Oct. No smoking in dining room & bedrooms. Disabled access. Children welcome. Tea/coffee making & TV in bedrooms. B & B from £9.50.

LOCHEARNHEAD
Stronvar Country House Hotel, Balquhidder, Lochearnhead, FK19 8PB (08774) 688

Stronvar Country House Hotel is an elegant 19th C. mansion standing on the shores of Loch Voil overlooking the Braes O'Balquhidder. It has had a very interesting history and indeed much of the Stronvar brochure is dedicated to describing it and the activities of its founding family, the Carnegies. These days the house has been completely renovated and restored to its former glory and offers first-class accommodation to guests: bedrooms are sympathetically furnished - many have brass beds or fourposters - and all have spectacular views over the surrounding mountains and countryside; within the house is a fascinating collection of bygones. Stronvar is an excellent touring base for the Trossachs and central Scotland; additionally fishing (brown trout and salmon) can be arranged on Loch Voil (mid-March to October) & there are 30 golf courses nearby including, of course, Gleneagles.

Open Mar. to Oct. No smoking in dining room & bedrooms. Vegetarian & diabetic by arrangement. Licensed. Children welcome.En suite, TV & tea/coffee in bedrooms. Access, Visa. B. & B. from £29.

PITLOCHRY

Burnside Apartments, 19 West Moulin Road, Pitlochry, PH16 5EA (0796) 2203

Beautifully converted Victorian building offering award-winning serviced apartments with taste of Scotland coffee shop. STB 4 & 5 Crown Highly Commended.

Open all year. No smoking in coffee shop & some apartments. Vegetarian dishes avail. and most other special diets by arrangement. Licensed. Disabled access. Children welcome. Pets by arrangement. En suite bathrooms, TV & gallery kitchen in apartments. Access, Visa. From £50 (2/3 persons) daily.

Tigh-Na-Cloich Hotel, Larchwood Road, Pitlochry, PH16 5AS (0796) 472216

Tigh-Na-Cloich (its name means 'house on the sentinel stone') is a beautiful stone-built Victorian villa, southfacing and peacefully situated in its own lovely gardens just a short walk from the centre of Pitlochry. It has been beautifuly restored and furnished in keeping with the original period features of the building with its high ceilinged-rooms, and all bedrooms have been exceptionally well-appointed (each has an electric blanket just in case what they say about the Scottish weather turns out to be true!) The food is exceptionally good: everything is home-made from fresh and local ingredients, and a typical evening menu would feature Broccoli and Stilton Soup followed by Lamb Cutlets in a Fresh Herb Crust or Fishy Parcels with Vermouth Sauce, and a delicious dessert, such as Iced Chocolate Souffle with Orange Cream. The proprietors are not only very helpful to those with special dietary needs, but will even offer to cook a favourite dish for you on request! Pitlochry is Scotland's premier inland tourist resort and as such offers something for everyone, from sailing on rivers and lochs or walking amidst the beautiful hill scenery to visiting the many woollen mills, distilleries or craft centres in the region.

Open mid-Mar. to end Oct. No smoking throughout. Vegetarian and most other special diets by arrangement. Licensed. Children welcome. En suite in most rooms. Tea/coffee making & TV in bedrooms. B & B from £25.

"Tom-na-Monachan" Vegetarian B. & B., Cuilc Brae, Pitlochry (0796) 473744

Large family house quietly situated in an acre of wooded garden just 10 minutes walk from both the railway station and shopping centre.

Open all year. No smoking in the house. Exclusively vegetarian/vegan/wholefood. D. by arrangement. Disabled access: '1 ground floor bedroom & bathroom. Ramp'. Children welcome. Tea/coffee making in bedrooms. B & B from £15.

Western Isles

ISLE OF ARRAN

Glencloy Farmhouse, Brodick, Isle of Arran, KA27 8BZ (0770) 2351
Farmhouse in peaceful glen; home-grown vegetables, free-range eggs, poultry and meat.
Open 1 Mar. to 7 Nov. No smoking ex. in bedrooms. Vegetarian, vegan and diabetic by arrangement. Children welcome. En suite in 2 rooms. Tea/coffee making in rooms. B. & B. £26.

Grange House Hotel, Whiting Bay, Isle of Arran, KA27 8QH Tel: Whiting Bay 263
Grange House Hotel was built in 1896 and stands amidst delightful gardens overlooking the sea with views to the Ayrshire coast and out towards Holy Island. Recently refurbished to a very high

standard, and in a style in keeping with the period features of the house, Grange House Hotel has every modern convenience including (for those who wish to pamper themselves a little!) a sauna and spa bath suite; on cooler evenings a log fire welcomes you in the lounge. The cooking is first rate: your hosts, Janet and Clive Hughes, base the evening's menu selection around the availability of good, fresh local produce: accordingly, while dishes are often Victorian or Scottish in flavour (Steak Kidney and Oyster Pie followed by Bread and Butter Pudding with whisky cream), everything has been expertly prepared on the premises from fresh, organic (wherever possible) produce; the proprietors also have a sound awareness of healthy nutritional principles: wholefoods are used wherever possible, and cream and animal fats are only used in moderation. Arran is popularly known as 'Scotland in miniature' - within the confines of this small island you will find no less than 7 golf courses, 4 pony-trekking centres, and numerous opportunities for mountaineering and fishing.
Open Mar. to Oct. inc. No smoking in house. Vegetarian & other diets avail. Licensed. Disabled facilities: converted downstairs bedroom. Children welcome. Tea/coffee making & T.V. in all rooms. Access, Visa. B. & B. from £25, D. £15. 3 Crowns Commended.

Kilmichael House Hotel, Glen Cloy, by Brodick, Isle of Arran, KA23 14PQ (0770) 2219
Small historic mansion set in 4 acres of lovely grounds on a property said to have been gifted to the ancestors of its builders by King Robert the Bruce; organic and wholefood ingredients are used in cooking. Trad. & Scottish menus.
Open all year. No smoking in dining room & bedrooms. Vegetarian standard. Table licence. Children welcome. T.V. lounge. B. & B. from £13.

ISLE OF BUTE

"Palmyra", 12 Ardbeg Road, Rothesay, Isle of Bute, PA20 0NJ (0700 50) 2929
Charming stone-built dwelling by the sea shore, in an acre of grounds. The food is oustandingly good: fresh fish features highly on the menu - much of it bought in by the hotel's own trawler - and lobster is a regular treat at Palmyra.
Vegetarian, vegan, diabetic, coeliac and some other special diets by arrangement. Open all year. No smoking in dining room. Licensed. Children welcome. Pets by arrangement. En suite, TV & tea/coffee making in bedrooms. B & B from £18.

ISLE OF HARRIS

Minchview House, Tarbert, Isle of Harris, PA85 3DB (0859) 2140
Guest house serving excellent home-cooking prepared from fresh produce.
Open all year. No smoking in dining room & bedrooms. Vegetarian and most other special diets by arrangement. B. & B. from £12.

Scarista House, Isle of Harris, PA85 3HX Tel: (085 985) 238 Fax: (085 985) 277

Situated on the magnificent Atlantic coast of Harris overlooking a 3-mile shell-sand beach, Scarista House, once the principal Church of Scotland manse for Harris, is one of the most remote hotels in Great Britain. Furnished with

antiques and decorated in a manner in keeping with the understated architecture of the exterior, Scarista House is a haven of tranquillity: no newspapers, television or radio interrupt the silence - just peat fires (to supplement the central heating!), books and a large collection of baroque and classical music. Each of the 3 bedrooms has beautiful views - most over the sea - and there are two lawned gardens. Your hosts pay particular and assiduous attention to the freshness and integrity of the ingredients used in cooking: all meat, for instance, is from free-range animals (including the fish and shellfish) cheeses are obtained direct from farm or dairy, and all breads cakes, preserves and confectionary are home-made. Breakfasts are prepared with similar care and feature freshly squeezed juices, local puddings, kippers, herring and venison sausages. Meals are served in a candlelit dining room with fine silverware and china chosen to complement the quality of the food served thereon.
Open Easter to mid. Oct. No smoking ex. 2 sitting rooms. Vegetarian and most other special diets by arrangement. Licensed. Disabled access: '4 bedrooms, dining rooms and library on ground floor'. Children: over 8s only. Pets by arrangement. En suite & tea/coffee making in bedrooms. B. & B. from £44.

ISLE OF IONA
Argyll Hotel, PA76 6SJ (068 17) 334

This beautiful sea-facing hotel (the front lawn runs down to the shore and jetty) is one of hotels about which I invariably receive a large number of recommendations throughout the year; guests comment on the peace and tranquility which seems to pervade the place - a sense doubtless partly attributable to the fact that the beautiful louges (with their open fires), spacious dining room and plant-filled sun lounge all look out over the Sound of Iona to the hills of Mull; external beauty recreating inner peace. I am sure that the excellence of the food is also an inexorable part of the lure of the place, too: wholefood and organically home-grown vegetables and produce are used in the preparation of excellent meals typically featuring Hummus followed by Chicken Paprika and Lemon and Blackberry Sponge; excellent vegetarian options.

Open Easter to mid Oct. No smoking in dining room & lounge. Vegetarian & other diets by arrangement. Licensed. Children welcome. Pets by arrangement. En suite in 10 of 19 rooms. Tea/coffee making in rooms. Access, Visa. B. & B. from £24.50.

ISLE OF ISLAY
Ceol-na-Mara, Bruichladdich, Isle of Islay, PA49 7UN (049 685) 419
Pleasantly situated house in small coastal distillery village overlooking Loch Indaal. Own & local produce used where possible in cooking.
Open all year. No smoking. Vegetarian, vegan & other diets by arrangement. Children welcome. Pets by arrangement. TV in lounge. B & B from £10, D. £7.

Taigh-Na-Creag, 7 Shore Street, Port Charlotte, PA48 7TR (049 685) 261
Lovely guest house with magnificent views over Loch Indaal, situated opposite the jetty; warm and comfortable accommodation;
Open all year. No smoking. Vegetarian standard. Children welcome. B. & B. from £15.

ISLE OF LEWIS
Baile-na-Cille, Timsgarry, Isle of Lewis, PA86 9JD (085 175) 241
Converted manse and stables on the shore at Timsgarry. The food is excellent: almost everything having been home-made - including the delicious bread - and from the wonderful breakfast (with its 'mighty but not compulsory Stornoway black pudding') to the exceedingly generous evening meal (lots of local produce, including trout, mackerel and salmon) you are wined and dined in truly splendid style.
Open mid-Mar. to mid-Oct. No smoking in dining room, 2 sitting rooms & bedrooms. Vegetarian & other diets by arrangement. Licensed. Children & pets welcome. Some rooms en suite Tea/coffee in rooms. T.V. in sitting room. Credit cards. B. & B. from £24.

Eshcol Guest House, Breasclete, Isle of Lewis, PA86 9ED (0851 72) 357
Lovely guest house on a small croft in a little weaving village; superb views overlooking Loch Roag.
Open Mar. to Oct. No smoking. Vegetarian by arrangement. Children welcome. Most rooms en suite Tea/coffee & TV in rooms. B. & B. from £17.

ISLE OF MULL
Bellachroy Hotel, Dervaig, Isle of Mull, PA75 6QW (06884) 225/314
Pleasant hotel standing at the head of the picturesque village of Dervaig; fresh local produce used in cooking.

Vegetarian, diabetic and some other special diets by arrangement. Open all year. Licensed. Children welcome. Pets by arrangement. Tea/coffee making & T.V. in lounges. B & B from £17.

Bruach Mhor, Fionnphort, Isle of Mull, PA66 6BL (068 17) 276

Small modernised croft house standing alone on the slopes of Tor Mor half a mile from Fionnphort; centrally heated & comfortable,. Wholesome home-cooked meals prepared from healthy, fresh ingredients; vegetarians & vegans especially welcome.

Vegetarian standard. Most other special diets by arrangement. Organic when avail. Wholefood almost always. Open all year. Children welcome. Tea/coffee making in bedrooms. T.V. lounge. B & B from £12.

Druimard Country House, Dervaig, Isle of Mull, PA75 6QW (06884) 345

Award-winning country house hotel and restaurant. Excellent food prepared from fresh, local produce. Seafood specialities. 6 comfortable, well-furnished bedrooms. STB Highly Commended. AA Red Rosette. 1992 Catering and Care Award.

Open Mar. to Oct. No smoking in restaurant. Vegetarian standard. Most other special diets by arrangement. Licensed. Children welcome. Pets by arrangement. En suite in 4 rooms. Tea/coffee making & TV in bedrooms. Access, Visa. B. & B. from £33.

Druimnacroish, Dervaig, Isle of Mull, PA75 6QW (06884) 274

Small, exclusive country house hotel in the beautiful Bellart Glen; home-grown fruit and vegetables; local produce used in cooking.

Open mid-Apr. to mid-Oct. No smoking ex. in bedrooms & smoking lounge. Vegetarian & other diets by arrangement. Licensed. Disabled access. Children: over 12s only. Pets by arrangement. En suite, TV & tea/coffee making in bedrooms. Access, Visa, Amex, Diners. B. & B. from £48.

The Glenforsa Hotel, Salen by Aros, Isle of Mull, PA72 6JW (0680) 300535

Attractive Norwegian chalet-style hotel standing in 6 acres of secluded grounds overlooking the Sound of Mull; excellent home-cooking using fresh produce and home-grown herbs.

Open all year. No smoking in dining room. Vegetarian standard. Other diets by arrangement. Licensed. Disabled access. Children welcome. Pets by arrangement. En suite & tea/coffee making in rooms. T.V. lounge. Access, Visa, Amex. B. & B. from £26.50.

Keeper's Cottage, Torloisk, Ulva Ferry, Isle of Mull, PA74 6NH (06885) 265

Traditional stone-built cottage with garden and stream situated in a remote yet sheltered position close to a waterfall near the west coast of Mull; good home-grown food and good conversation!

Open all year. No smoking. Vegetarian by arrangement. T.V. B & B from £15.

Ulva House Hotel, Tobermory, Isle of Mull, PA75 6PR (0688) 2044

Beautiful 19th C. house with lots of character; log fires, excellent food (including home-made chocolates) beautiful views.

Open Mar. to Oct. No smoking in dining room. Vegetarian, vegan & diabetic standard. Other diets by arrangement. Licensed. Children welcome. Pets by arrangement. En suite in some rooms. Tea/coffee making & TV in bedrooms. B. & B. from £19.50.

ISLE OF RAASAY

Isle of Raasay Hotel, Raasay, by Kyle of Lochalsh, IV40 8PB (047862) 222/226

Renovated mansion with views; excellent home-cooking using fresh, local produce.

Open Apr. to Oct. No smoking in dining room & T.V. lounge. Vegetarian & diabetic by arrangement. Licensed. Disabled access. Children welcome. Pets by arrangement. En suite, tea/coffee making & TV in bedrooms. B. & B. from £26.

ISLE OF SKYE

Dunringell Hotel, Kyleakin (0599) 4180

Beautiful country house in 4 acres of secluded grounds; fresh food.

Open Mar. to Oct. No smoking in dining room & one lounge. Vegetarian & other diets by arrangement. Disabled access. Children welcome. En suite in some rooms. Tea/coffee making in bedrooms. T.V. in lounge. B. & B. from £14.

Janet Kernachan, 4 Lephin, Glendale, Isle of Skye (047 081) 376

Small, modern crofthouse on 6 acre working croft; home-cooking from fresh, local produce including bread, cakes, soups and jams.

Open all year except Oct. No smoking in dining room. Vegetarian and most other special diets by arrangement. Children welcome. Pets by arrangement. B. & B. from £10.50

Skye Environmental Centre Guest House, Harapool, Broadford (04712) 487

Wildlife holidays about the wildlife of Skye based in a guest house overlooking the bay. All profits from guest house and wildlife holidays go directly into wildlife conservation work & the centre's wildlife rehabilitation hospital.

Open all year. Smoking banned in dining room. Vegetarian standard. Other diets by arrangement. Licensed. Children welcome. Pets by arrangement. Tea/coffee making & TV in lounge. B. & B. £16.

Wales

Clwyd

BODELWYDDAN
The Manor, Faenol Fawr Country Hotel, Bodelwyddan (0745) 591691
Beautiful 16th C. Grade II listed manor with Jacobean fireplace & panelled drawing room.
Open all year. No smoking in dining room, some bedrooms & part of the bar. Vegetarian standard. Licensed. Disabled access. Children welcome. Pets by arrangement. En suite, tea/coffee-making & TV in bedrooms. Credit cards. B. & B. from £28.

BRYNEGLWYS
Cae Crwn Farm, Bryneglwys, LL21 9NF (049085) 243
Detached farmhouse peacefully situated; home-cooked meals & good vegetarian option.
Open all year. No smoking. Vegetarian standard. Children welcome. Pets by arrangement. Tea/coffee-making. T.V. in lounge. B. & B. from £13.

DENBIGH
Fron Haul, Bodfari, LL16 4DY (074 575) 301
Charming house with superb country views. There is a 50 acre hill farm which supplies the freshest and best quality vegetables and meat from which the excellent cuisine is prepared.
Open Feb. to Nov. No smoking in dining room, sitting room & all bedrooms. Vegetarian by arrangement. Children welcome. Pets by arrangement. En suite in 1 room. Tea/coffee-making. T.V. in lounge. B. & B. from £15.50. 'Taste of Wales' Commended.

HANMER
Buck Farm, Hanmer, SY14 7LX (094 874) 339

This beautiful unspoilt half-timbered 16th C. farmhouse stands in eight acres of woodland and paddocks (alive with butterflies, wild flowers...) on the A525 midway between Whitchurch and Wrexham. It is appropriate that it should be situated straddling two counties for the proprietors themselves have a cosmopolitan background (Frances a Trinidadian of Chinese ancestry, and Cedric a naturalized Canadian) which makes for great diversity in the culinary styles to be sampled at Buck Farm: Spanish, African and Indian influences combine with Frances' already wide culinary experience. The main nutritional influence, however, is that of healthy food preparation: generous portions of simply cooked food prepared from fresh, local, wholefood and, where possible, organic ingredients make for very good dining indeed! Breakfast is enormous (home-baked bread, fruit compote, etc.) and an evening meal might feature Watercress or Sorrel Soup followed by Vegetable Croustade and warm Blackcurrant Cake with Egg Custard. Food apart, Buck Farm is an exceptionally nice place to stay: beautifully furnished (and with a little library and music facilities), friendly (your hosts will lend you maps, guide books, cycle shelter, and offer a maildrop service for tourers), and with excellent nearby walks (you can now follow footpaths directly from Buck Farm onto the link between Offa's Dyke and the Sandstone Way).
Open all year. No smoking. Vegetarian & other diets by arrangement. Disabled access to dining room and toilets. Children welcome. Tea/Coffee on request. T.V. in lounge. B. & B. from £13.50.

LLANGOLLEN
Hillcrest, Hill Street, Llangollen, LL20 8EU (0978) 860208
Victorian house which in an acre of pretty gardens 3 mins from Llangollen & the River Dee.
Open all year. No smoking. Vegetarian & other diets by arrangement. One downstairs double room. Children welcome. En suite & tea/coffee-making in all bedrooms. Separate T.V. lounge. B. & B. from £19. D. from £9. W.T.B 3 Crowns Commended.

Hyfrydle Guest House, Upper Garth, Trevor, Nr Llangollen, LL20 7UY (0978) 822992
Victorian red brick house (hyfrydle is Welsh for 'beautiful place') quietly situated in the village of Upper Garth high above the Vale of Llangollen
Open Feb to Dec. No smoking. Vegetarian and most other special diets by arrangement. Not licensed, but complimentary drink with dinner. Children welcome. En suite & tea/coffee-making in bedrooms. T.V. in lounge. B. & B. from £16.

Dyfed

ABERYSTWYTH
Glyn-Garth Guest House, South Road, Aberystwyth, SY23 1JS (0970) 615050

A pleasantly appointed family-run guest house situated close to the South Promenade of Aberystwyth; bedrooms have been comfortably furnished and many enjoy sea views. Mr & Mrs Evans, offer wholesome food in the pleasant dining room, and the comfortable lounge, with its colour TV has drinks available at most times; the service is excellent and Glyn-Garth has received the Highly Commended status by the Mid Wales Tourism Council together with several other high acclamations.

Open all year ex. Xmas. No smoking in dining room & some bedrooms. Vegetarian & other diets by arrangement. Children welcome. Sorry, no pets. En suite in most rooms. Tea/coffee-making & T.V. in all bedrooms. B. & B. from £15.

BONCATH
Gwelfor Country Guest House, Blaenffos, Boncath, Pembrokeshire, SA37 0HZ (0239) 831599

Guest house with panoramic views of the Preseli Hills. Wholesome traditional & vegetarian dishes; home-grown, local or organic produce used in cooking; great for country lovers, bird watchers, painters; ancient sites, golf, riding, water sports. WTB 2 Crowns.

Open all year. No smoking in the house. Vegetarian and vegan standard. Other diets by arrangement. Children welcome. Pets by arrangement. En suite in some rooms. Tea/coffee-making in bedrooms. T.V. in lounge. B. & B. from £16. D. available.

CARDIGAN
Trellacca Guest House, Tremain, Cardigan, SA43 1SJ (0239) 810730

Trellacca Guest House has been superbly converted from two slate and stone cottages; beautifully furnished with much handcrafted pine furniture and fittings; lovely rural setting.

Open all year. No smoking in bedrooms & dining room. Vegetarian and diabetic diets by arrangement. Children welcome. Some rooms en suite. Tea/Coffee-making in bedrooms. T.V. in lounge & bedroom on request. B. & B. £14. D £6.

CRYMYCH
Felin Tygwyn Farm, Crymych, SA41 3RX (023 979) 603

Traditional farmhouse built of earth(!) & slate; beamed ceilings; part of organic smallholding; home cooking from own produce.

Open all year. No smoking in the house. Vegetarian and most other special diets by arrangement. Licensed. Children welcome. Pets by arrangement. Tea/coffee. T.V. lounge. D., B. & B. from £17.

FISHGUARD
Coach House Cottage, Glendower Square, Goodwick, Fishguard, Dyfed, SA64 0DH (0348) 873660

This traditional Pembrokeshire stone cottage stands in a secluded location by a mountain stream, yet is conveniently situated in the heart of the village of Goodwick, 1 mile from the centre of Fishguard and a few minutes' walk from the harbour and seafront. Centrally heated accommodation is provided for just two people in a prettily decorated bedroom, with beautiful hill and sea views (and almost exclusive use of the bathroom), and guests are also welcome to use the rest of the cottage including the large, eclectic collection of books, the lovely garden (with its sea views) or the sitting room with T.V. The proprietors specialise in providing delicious vegetarian, vegan and wholefood fare (prepared with organic produce wherever possible), but light, 'snack' type meals can be provided in the evening for meat-eaters (there are several other good eating places within walking distance).

Pembrokeshire is a beautiful county and is said to have the highest number of working craftsmen within its boundaries (including, incidentally your host, 'Max' Maxwell-Jones, who is a well-known local artist and calligrapher).
Open all year. No smoking in the house. Vegetarian standard; other diets by arrangement. Bring your own wine. Children welcome. Pets by arrangement. Tea/coffee-making in bedrooms. T.V. in lounge. B. & B. from £12. D. £8.50.

Gellifawr Country House, Pontfaen, Nr Fishguard, SA65 9TX (0239) 820343

Beautiful country house once the centre of a 700 acre estate with many original farm buildings, including water wheel in the millhouse, still standing; excellent cuisine imaginatively prepared from fresh, local produce.
Vegetarian standard. Vegan, diabetic and other special diets by arrangement. Open all year. Licensed. Disabled access. Children welcome. Pets by arrangement. En suite in some rooms. Tea/Coffee-making on landings. T.V. in lounge. Access, Visa. B. & B. from £20.

Tregynon Country Farmhouse Hotel, Gwaun Valley, Nr Fishguard, SA65 9TU Tel: (0239) 820531 Fax: (0239) 820808

It is over a decade since Peter Heard decided to abandon the stress-filled London rat race for a more peaceful way of life in a Welsh farmhouse cum smallholding. A tremendous amount of renovation work had to be done on Tregynon but, with a lot of hard work and enthusiasm, the run-down farmhouse soon became a thriving smallholding and a guest house which has won several awards and received much national acclaim. Such is the extent of Tregynon's success that nowadays all energies are devoted to looking after guests. Much of the recognition is due not just to the wonderfully comfortable surroundings (log fires in the inglenook fireplace in the oakbeamed lounge, beautiful bedrooms) but to the superlative quality of Jane's cuisine: fresh produce - much of it local - is used wherever possible in the preparation of all meals:

free-range eggs, organic and unpasteurised cheeses, home-smoked bacon and gammon are all part of the Tregynon gastronomic experience - as are the range of speciality additive-free breads and rolls. But Tregynon's surroundings provide the enduring lure for guests who return year after year...situated on the edge of the Gwaun Valley with its ancient oak forest, this beautiful part of the world is a haven for wildlife - badgers, buzzards and herons are regularly seen whilst red kites and peregrine falcons are also spotted from time to time.
Open all year. Smoking discouraged throughout. Vegetarian & other diets standard/request. Licensed. Disabled access. Children welcome. En suite, tea/coffee making & T.V. in rooms. B. & B. from £22.50.

HAVERFORDWEST
Druidston Haven (0437) 781221

Hotel and self-catering cottages standing in 20 acres of wild garden overlooking the sea; educational courses; excellent healthy food.
Vegetarian standard. Vegan and other special diets by arrangement. Wholefoods always. Open Feb. to Oct. plus Xmas. Licensed. Children welcome. Pets by arrangement. Tea/coffee-making . B. & B. from £20.

NEWQUAY
Nanternis Farm, Nanternis, Newquay, SA45 9RP (0545) 560181

Small 8 acre farm set on a hillside with beautiful views; a stream runs by the farm along which a footpath leads to the sea just over a mile away.
Open Easter to end Sept. No smoking in bedrooms & dining room. Vegetarian & other diets by arrangement. Children welcome. Tea/coffee-making in rooms. T.V. B. & B. from £13.

Ty Hen Farm Hotel & Cottages, Llwyndafydd, Nr Newquay, SA44 6BZ (0545) 560346

This charming stone-built farmhouse (Ty Hen means simply 'Old House') offers a very high standard of accommodation to guests and stands

in spacious gardens in a peaceful location just 2 miles from the rocky cliffs and sandy beaches of the Cardiganshire coast. Health is a priority at Ty Hen where the generous breakfast features a number of very laudable items such as yoghurt, muesli and fresh fruit as well as a huge platter of bacon, eggs, mushrooms and anything else breakfasty you care to name. The 4-course evening meal is similarly generous and a full range of options are offered including some vegetarian and fish specialities. There is a leisure centre at Ty Hen which has a superb indoor heated pool (tuition available), together with a gymnasium, sauna, sunbed & bowls/skittles alley.
Open all year. No smoking in the house & in leisure centre. Vegetarian standard. Most other special diets by arrangement. Licensed. Disabled access. Children welcome. Pets by arrangement. En suite, tea/coffee-making & T.V. plus video channel in all rooms. Visa, Mastercard. B. & B. from £21.

PENCADER

Argeod Fach, Pencader, SA39 9AG (0559) 384800

Pretty single-storey cottage in lovely secluded spot just 2 miles from Pencader; vegan cuisine prepared from fresh, organically and veganically home-grown produce. *Grid Ref: SN 433382*
Open Apr. to end Sept. No smoking. All food vegan, other diets by arrangement. Disabled access. Children welcome. Pets by arrangement. T.V. in lounge. B. & B. from £11. D. £6.

RHYDLEWIS

Broniwan, Rhydlewis, Llandysul, SA44 5PF (023975) 261

Cosy Victorian farmhouse 10 mins from Penbryn Beach. Part of a working organic farm (Member of the Soil Association), much of the delicious food been prepared from home-grown produce; vegetarian meals are a speciality
Open all year. No smoking. Vegetarian & other diets by arrangement. Children welcome. Pets by arrangement. En suite in 1 room. Tea/coffee available. T.V. in lounge. B. & B. from £12. D. £7.

ROBESTON WATHEN

Robeston House Hotel & Restaurants, Robeston Wathen (On main A40), Pembrokeshire, SA67 8EU Tel & Fax: (0834) 860392 & 861195

Elegant, country house hotel in 5 acres of grounds. Log fires in winter. Acclaimed restaurant serves first-class meals prepared exclusively from fresh meat, fish and vegetables.

Open all year. No smoking in dining room. Vegetarian & other diets by arrangement. Licensed. Children in Buttery only. Pets by arrangement. En suite, tea/coffee & T.V. in all bedrooms. B. & B. from £25.

TREGARON

The Edelweiss Country Guest House, Penuwch, Tregaron, SY25 6QZ (0974) 821601

The Edelweiss is a charming oak-beamed house

set in 1½ acres of grounds in the beautiful Ceridigion countryside; the proprietors find that the stunning scenery with which their home is surrounded makes it a natural magnet for artists, walkers, ornithologists, flower arrangers, botanists and naturalists as well as holiday-makers in search of peace, tranquillity and good food. The Edelweiss is 6 miles from both the coastal road and Tregaron, the pony-trekking centre of Mid-Wales; and as such is a perfect place from which to enjoy both rural and sea-side vacational delights. A beautiful self-contained caravan for up to 6 people is also available, with all amenities provided, and meals available in the guest house if required.
Open all year . No smoking in the house. Vegetarian & other diets by arrangement. Bring your own wine. Children welcome. Tea/Coffee served 7 - 11. T.V. in all bedrooms. B. & B. from £12-£14, £73 weekly. B., B. & D. £17-£19.50, £111 weekly. Caravan £100 weekly. B. B. & D. 3-day specials £55 Sept. - June.

YSTRAD MEURIG

Hillscape Walking Hols, Blaen-y-ddol, Pontrhydygroes, Ystrad Meurig, Dyfed, SY25 6DS (097422) 640

Walking holiday supervised by experienced walkers; imaginative cuisine using fresh, often home-grown, produce.
Open Feb. to Nov. No smoking. Vegetarian & other diets by arrangement. Bring your own. wine Children: over 11s. En suite in all rooms. Tea/coffee-making in lounge. B. & B. from £20. D. £7.

Wales

Glamorgan

CARDIFF

Annedd Lon Guest House, 3 Dyfrig Street, Pontcanna, Cardiff, CF1 9LR (0222) 223349
Lovely Victorian guest house in a quiet close on Cathedral Road; interestingly furnished in keeping with the period.
Open all year. No smoking. Vegetarian & other diets by arrangement. Children welcome. En suite in some rooms. Tea/coffee-making & TV in bedrooms. B. & B. from £15.

Cardiff Marriott, Mill Lane, Cardiff, CF1 1EZ (0222) 399944
Well-appointed business-class hotel, with a wide range of leisure amenities, in the centre of Cardiff.
Open all year. No smoking in part of dining room & in some bedrooms. Vegetarian standard. Other diets by arrangement. Licensed. Disabled access. Children welcome. Pets by arrangement. En suite, TV & tea/coffee-making in bedrooms. Credit cards. B. & B. from £40.

RHOOSE

Lower House Farm Guest House and Cottage, Rhoose Road, Rhoose, South Glamorgan, CF6 9ER (0446) 710010
Lovely Georgian farmhouse with a nearby thatched cottage avail. to self-caterers. B & B.
Open all year. No smoking. Vegetarian available. Children welcome. Pets by arrangement. Tea/coffee-making. T.V. available. B. & B. from £15. Cottage from £165 per week.

SWANSEA

The Bays Guest House, 97 Mumbles Road, Mumbles, Swansea, West Glamorgan, SA3 5TW (0792) 404775
Detached guest house with large gardens on the sea-front; recent winners of Health Award.
Open all year. No smoking in the house. Vegetarian and other diets by arrangement. Children: over 10s only. 1 en suite rooms. Tea/coffee-making & TV in lounge. B. & B. from £16.

Gwent

ABERGAVENNY

Pentre House, Brecon Rd, Llanwenarth, Abergavenny, NP7 7EW (0873) 853435
Small, pretty country house in lovely award-winning gardens; comfortably furnished; generous breakfasts with a variety of options.
Open all year. No smoking in dining room, & bedrooms. Vegetarian & other diets by arrangement. Children & pets by arrangement. Tea/coffee-making in bedrooms. T.V. sitting room. B. & B. from £15.

CAERLEON

Clawdd Farm, Bulmore Road, Caerleon (0633) 423250/421788
Edwardian farmhouse, set on 19 acres of hillside in the peaceful vale of Usk; excellent food prepared from organic & wholefood ingredients.
Vegetarian, vegan and other special diets by arrangement. Organic & wholefoods when avail./on request. Open all year. Separate area of dining room for smokers & no smoking in some bedrooms. Bring your own wine. Children 'if controlled'. Pets by arrangement. Tea/coffee-making & TV in bedrooms. Credit cards. B. & B. from £14. D. £7.50.

CHEPSTOW

The George Hotel, Moor Street, Chepstow, Gwent (0291) 625363
Built originally as an inn in 1610 this beautifully renovated and appointed hotel offers excellent accommodation and first-rate food.
Open all year. No smoking in part of dining room & some bedrooms. Vegetarian & other diets by arrangement. Licensed. Children welcome. Pets by arrangement. En suite, TV & tea/coffee-making in bedrooms. Credit cards. B. & B. from £35.

St Pierre Hotel Golf and Country Club, St Pierre Park, Chepstow, Gwent, NP6 6YA (0291) 625261
Set in 400 acres of magnificent gardens, complete with 11 acre lake, two excellent golf courses and conference rooms, this beautifully renovated country house has been elegantly furnished and serves very good food.
Open all year. No smoking in 50% of dining room, country club & some bedrooms. Vegetarian and other diets by arrangement. Licensed. Disabled access. Children welcome. Pets by arrangement. En suite, TV & tea/coffee-making in bedrooms.

CWMBRAN

The Parkway Hotel and Conference Centre, Cwmbran Drive, Cwmbran, NP44 3UW (0633) 871199
Independently-owned hotel & conference centre which has been designed & built on a Mediterranean theme in 7 acres of grounds. Excellent food & well-equipped Leisure Complex with swimming pool, sauna, steam bath, gymnasium and spa as well as a sports shop and Cafe Bar. *W.T.B. 5 Crowns Commended.*
Open all year. No smoking in dining room & some bedrooms. Vegetarian & other diets by arrangement. Licensed. Disabled access. Children welcome. Pets by arrangement. En suite, TV & tea/coffee in bedrooms. Credit cards. B. & B. from £51 - 58.

NEWPORT

Anderley Lodge Hotel, 216 Stow Hill, Newport, NP9 4HA (0633) 266781
Award-winning family-run 19th C. hotel with spacious, elegant bedrooms; evening meal by arrangement prepared from fresh produce.
Open all year. Smoking allowed only in 2 bedrooms. Not licensed, but wine offered when available. Children welcome. Tea/coffee-making & T.V. in all bedrooms. B. & B. from £15.

Chapel Guest House, Church Road, St Brides, Wentloog, Nr Newport, NP1 9SN (0633) 681018
Converted chapel in a small country village adjacent to Elm Tree Restaurant; B. & B. only.
Open all year. No smoking. Vegetarian & other diets by arrangement. Children welcome. Pets by arrangement. En suite in 1 room. Tea/coffee available. T.V. in lounge. B. & B. from £12.

The West Usk Lighthouse, St Brides, Wentlodge, Nr Newport (0633) 810126

The West Usk Lighthouse was built in 1821 by James Walker, a Scottish architect, on the estuaries of the rivers Usk and Severn; as you might imagine it has quite magnificent views of the Bristol Channel and stands on its own beautiful promontory. Its design is quite extraordinary: 50 feet in diameter, the walls are 2 feet thick and the rooms are shaped like pieces of a pie: there are 6 guest bedrooms and the dining room is decorated in a nautical style; log fires blaze in the lounge. A variety of courses are held at the lighthouse on a wide selection of themes; there is also an amazing stress-release flotation tank for guests' use (10 inches of water, a ton of Epsom salts and you!). Breakfast is the only meal to be offered at the Lighthouse, but it is a healthy repast with good vegan options.
Open all year. No smoking. Vegetarian, vegan and most other special diets by arrangement. Children welcome. 3 rooms en suite. TV & Tea/coffee-making in bedrooms. Credit cards. B. & B. from £16.

PONTYPOOL

Ty'r Ywen Farm, Mamhilad (049528) 200
Charming white-washed, slate-tiled longhouse with oak beams, inglenook fireplaces & oak panelling; pretty garden; delicious meals made from fresh, often home-grown, produce.
Open all year. No smoking in dining room & bedrooms. Vegetarian & other diets by arrangement. Pets by arrangement. En suite, tea/coffee & TV in rooms. D., B. & B. from £25

TINTERN

The Old Rectory, Tintern, NP6 6SG (0291) 689519
Lovely old house, once used as a rectory for the Church of St Mary's (now in ruins on the hillside opposite the Abbey); own produce used in home-made cuisine.
Open all year. Smoking allowed only in the sitting room. Vegetarian and most other special diets by arrangement. Children welcome. Pets by arrangement. B. & B. from £12.50 D. £7.50.

Valley House, Raglan Road, NP6 6TH (0291) 689652
Charming Georgian residence opposite picturesque woods 1m from Tintern Abbey.
Open all year. No smoking in dining room, bedrooms & lounge. Vegetarian by arrangement. Children welcome. Pets by arrangement. En suite, tea/coffee & TV in bedrooms. B. & B. from £15.

USK

Glen-yr-Afon House, Pontypool Road, Usk, NP5 1SY (02913) 2302
Elegant country house 5 mins from Usk; excellent home-cooked food.
Open all year. No smoking in dining room. Vegetarian & other diets by arrangement. Licensed. Disabled access. Children welcome. En suite in all rooms. T.V. Access, Visa. B. & B. from £21.

Gwynedd

ABERDOVEY

The Harbour Hotel, Aberdovey, LL35 0EB (0654) 767250
The Harbour Hotel is a lovely, award-winning, Victorian hotel which stands on the seafront in the heart of the picturesque village of Aberdovey overlooking miles of golden sandy beaches. Owned and run by the resident proprietors, the Harbour Hotel has been beautifuly restored and its furnishing and decor are of an exceptionally high standard; bedrooms are very comfortable and family suites are available (with separate children's and parents' bedrooms). Excellent, home-cooked food may be enjoyed in the Alacarte (sic.) Restaurant, and there is a family restaurant, 'Rumbles', which has good children's options; the hotel also has a basement wine bar, called Wellies.
Open all year. No smoking in dining room, sitting room & some bedrooms. Vegetarian standard. Other diets by arrangement. Licensed. Children welcome. Pets by arrangement. En suite, TV & tea/coffee in bedrooms. Credit cards. B. & B. from £32.50.

1 Trefeddian Bank, Aberdovey, LL35 0RU (0654) 767487
Lovely house in quiet, elevated position with stunning views over the Dovey Estuary, golf course, beach and sea; good home-cooking.
Open all year. Smoking allowed only in the conservatory. Vegetarian & other diets by arrangement. Children welcome. Pets by arrangement. Tea/coffee-making in bedrooms. T.V. in lounge and conservatory. D. B. & B. from £28.

BALA

Palé Hall Hotel, Llandderfel, Bala, LL23 7PS (067) 83285
Splendid country house (once visited by Queeen Anne who found the house 'enchanting') in landscaped gardens overlooking the Dee Valley; magnificent carved oak staircase and hall; sumptuous furnishings; excellent cuisine prepared from fresh, local produce.
Open all year. No smoking in dining room & 1 guest lounge. Vegetarian & other diets by arrangement. Licensed. Disabled access. Children welcome. Pets in kennels in grounds. En suite & TV in all rooms. Room service. B. & B. from £42.50.

BARMOUTH

Lawrenny Lodge Hotel and Restaurant, Aberamffra Road, Barmouth, LL42 1SU (0341) 280466
Stone-built house commanding a superb position overlooking the Mawddach Estuary and Barmouth Harbour; pleasingly furnished and offering very good freshly prepared food.
Open Mar. to Dec. No smoking in dining room. Vegetarian standard. Other diets by arrangement. Licensed. Children welcome. Pets by arrangement. En suite in most rooms. Tea/coffee-making & T.V. in all bedrooms. Visa, Mastercard. B. & B. from £15.

Pen Parc Guest House, Park Road, Barmouth, LL42 1PH (0341) 280150
Small guest house in a quiet location overlooking the bowling and putting green, and tennis court, 4 mins walk from the sea; a choice of vegetarian or traditional cuisine is served.
Open all year. No smoking. Vegetarian standard. Other diets by arrangement. Bring your own drinks. Older children by arrangement. Tea/coffee-making facilities. T.V. in lounge. B. & B. from £14. D. £7.

BANGOR

Rainbow Court, Pentir, Nr Bangor, LL57 4UY (0248) 353099
Excellent restaurant just outside Bangor (on B4366 at Caerhun turnoff), which specialises in serving many, delicious original dishes. Vegetarian options are tasty and imaginative. Low/non alcoholic wines and beers are available or you are welcome to bring your own wine.
Open all year. No smoking. Vegetarian & other special diets by arrangement. Not licensed, but guests welcome to bring their own. Children by arrangement. En suite in most rooms. Tea/coffee-making & T.V. in all bedrooms. Credit cards. B. & B. from £12.50.

BETWS-Y-COED

Plas Hall Hotel and Restaurant, Pont-y-Pant, Dolwyddelan, Nr Betws-y-Coed, LL25 0PJ (06906) 206/306
Beautiful old house with scenic riverside views superbly converted to country house hotel; excellent food prepared from fresh, local produce.
Open all year. No smoking in dining room. Vegetarian standard. Vegan & other special diets by arrangement. Licensed. Disabled access. Children welcome. En suite, tea/coffee-making & TV in all bedrooms. Access, Visa. B. & B. from £29.50.

Ty'n-y-Celyn House, Llanrwst Rd, Betws-y-Coed, Gwynedd, LL24 0HD Tel: (0690) 710202 Fax: (0690) 710800

Ty'n-y-Celyn is a large Victorian house which nestles in a quiet elevated position overlooking the picturesque village of Betws-y-Coed. It has been very comfortably furnished: there are 8 bedrooms - 3 of which are family rooms - and each has been tastefully refurbished with new beds and fitted furniture, together with a range of helpful amenities including TV, hairdryer, radio-cassette and tea-making facilities; most bedrooms have magnificent views of the Llugwy Valley, surrounding mountains or the Conwy River. Your hosts, Maureen and Clive Muskus, will do all they can to make your stay a happy and comfortable one - including picking you up from the station if you are arriving by rail. Betws-y-Coed is a perfect touring base: it is in the heart of the Snowdonia National Park, yet is also within easy reach of the fine coastlines; in addition to walking and climbing, it is an excellent centre for other outdoor pursuits such as fishing (which can be arranged in the nearby streams, rivers and reservoirs) and horse riding (there are good facilities nearby).

Open all year. No smoking in the dining room. Vegetarian & other diets by arrangement. Licensed. Children & pets welcome. En suite, TV & tea/coffee-making in bedrooms. B. & B. £18 - 20.

CAERNARFON

'Maesteg', High Street, Llanberis, Caernarfon, LL55 4HB (0286) 871187

Private house overlooking the lake in Snowdonia; very friendly atmosphere.

Open all year. No smoking. Vegetarian & some other special diets by arrangement. Tea/coffee-making in bedrooms. T.V. in some bedrooms. B. & B. from £12.

Ty'n Rhos, Seion, Llanddeiniolen, Caernarfon, LL55 3AE (0248) 670489

From the outside Ty'n Rhos is an unashamedly modern looking building, but inside it's everything you'd expect a *proper* Welsh farmhouse to be complete with Welsh Dressers, log fires, and bedrooms with cottagey windows which look out onto cottagey scenes. Until the advent of milk quotas Ty'n Rhos was a working dairy farm: these days the proprietors, Linda and Nigel Kettle, have turned their considerable energies into running a guest house (there's still enough of the Jersey herd left to provide milk, yoghurt and cream). The food is first-rate: organic and wholefood ingredients are used wherever possible to prepare delicious meals which would typically feature home-made Fish Paté followed by Local Welsh Trout (baked in lemon butter) and a generous slice of Ty'n Rhos Cheesecake (made with Ty'n Rhos cheese). Ty'n Rhos nestles at the foot of Snowdonia and as such is nearby to first-rate climbing 'for the serious minded' (and some energetic strolling, for the not-so-intent).

Vegetarian, vegan and other special diets by arrangement. Organic when avail. Wholefoods on request. No smoking in dining room. Open all year. Licensed. Disabled access. Children: over 6s only. Pets by arrangement. En suite, TV & tea/coffee-making in all bedrooms. B. & B. from £18.

CONWY

Castle Hotel, High Street, Conwy, LL32 8DB (0492) 592324

A coaching house in the 19th C. (some parts of the building date from the 15th C.) this superbly converted hotel offers very comfortable accommodation and excellent cuisine.

Open all year. No smoking in dining room. Vegetarian standard. Other diets by arrangement. Licensed. Children welcome. Pets by arrangement. En suite, tea/coffee-making & T.V. in all bedrooms. Credit cards. B. & B. from £35.

The Lodge Hotel, Tal-y-Bont, Conwy, LL32 8YX (0492) 69766

Highly acclaimed country hotel & restaurant.

Open all year. No smoking in most of dining room & most bedrooms. Vegetarian & other diets by arrangement. Licensed. Disabled access. Children welcome. Pets by arrangement. En suite, TV & tea/coffee in bedrooms. B. & B. from £22.50.

The Old Rectory, Llansanffraid Glan Conwy, Nr Conwy, LL28 5LF Tel: (0492) 580611 Fax: (0492) 584555

There has been a rectory on this beautiful site on the Conwy Estuary with its spectacular views from Conwy Castle to Snowdonia, for the last 5 centuries. Sadly, in 1740, the Tudor House was burnt down, but the elegant Georgian replacement is a splendid house - skilfully restored by the Vaughan family and now functioning as a comfortable and charming small country house: sympathetically decorated and

furnished with antiques (the collection of Victorian watercolours is a delight) and all the individually styled bedrooms have excellent facilities (including bathrobes, ironing centres and hairdryers). The cuisine is exceptionally good: the finest local produce is used to prepared dishes of imagination and flair, a typical evening menu featuring Mediterranean Vegetable and Herb in Strudel Pastry with Tomato Sauce followed by Spinach and Salmon Terrine, Lamb with Leek Garnish and a delicious dessert, such as Chocolate and Raspberry Roulade; a selection of Welsh Cheeses would complete the meal.
Open Feb. to Dec. No smoking. Vegetarian & other diets by arrangement. Licensed. Children: over 10s only. En suite & TV in all rooms. Room service. Access, Visa. Dinner, B. & B. from £56.

Tir-y-Coed Country House Hotel, Rowen, Conwy, LL32 8TP (0492) 650219
Beautiful country house set in an acre of mature landscaped gardens on the outskirts of the picturesque village of Rowen; most bedrooms have superb garden/mountain views.
Open Feb. to Nov. No smoking in dining room. Vegetarian, vegan and other special diets by arrangement. Licensed. Children welcome. Pets by arrangement. En suite, TV & tea/coffee-making in all bedrooms.B. & B. from £19.50.

The Whins, Whinacres, Conwy, LL32 8ET (0492) 593373
Designed by the well-known local artist, Hubert Coop, at the turn of the century, The Whins has lots of character (panelled lounge with log fire, cosy dining room); good, home-cooking.
Open Mar. to Oct. No smoking. Vegetarian & other diets by arrangement. Well-behaved children welcome. En suite in 2 rooms. Tea/coffee-making in bedrooms. T.V. in lounge. B. & B. from £16. D. £9.50.

CRICIETH
Muriau, Cricieth, LL52 0RS (0766) 522337
Lovely granite-built house, part 17th and part 19th C., in small coastal town of Cricieth.

Open all year. No smoking. Vegetarian & other diets by arrangement. Children welcome. Tea/coffee in bedrooms. T.V. in lounge. B. & B. from £10.

DOLGELLAU
Bontddu Hall Hotel, Bontddu, Nr Dolgellau, LL40 2SU (0341 49) 661
Built in 1873 as a country mansion for the sister of Joseph Chamberlain; 14 acres of landscaped gardens and rhododendron forest; best local and home-grown produce is used in cooking.
Open Easter to Oct. No smoking in lounge, 50% of dining room & some bedrooms. Vegetarian & other diets by arrangement. Licensed. Children welcome. Pets by arrangement. En suite, tea/coffee-making & TV in rooms. B. & B. from £35.

Penmaenuchaf Hall, Penmaenpool, Dolgellau, Gwynedd, LL40 1YB Tel & Fax: (0341) 422129
It would be difficult to imagine a more beautiful and idyllic situation than the one enjoyed by this lovely country manor hotel which nestles in the foothills of Cader Idris overlooking the famous Mawddach Estuary. Upon entering the hall you are instantly transported back to an age of gracious living: the oak panelling, exquisite furnishings, fresh flowers and blazing log fires encourage a feeling of relaxation and well-being. Lulled thus into a condition of happy anaesthesia with respect to 20th C. concerns, the most stressful decision you are likely to have to make is whether your choice of afternoon tea will spoil your appetite for the superb evening meal: the food is fabulous and not to be missed, an evening menu choice perhaps featuring Tomato Consommé with Corriander, Madeira and Herb Dumplings followed by Pan-fried Pork with Apple and Rosemary and some outstandingly irresistible desserts (Apricot Soufflé on an Orange Caramel Sauce, Mille Feuille of Chocolate on a Compote of Cherries). Vegetarian choices are always included on the menu and other diets can be accommodated by arrangement.
Open all year. No smoking in the dining room, 2 lounges & 1 bedroom. Vegetarian & other diets by arrangement. Licensed. Children welcome. En suite, TV & tea/coffee-making in bedrooms. Credit cards. B. & B. from £47.50.

HARLECH
Aris Guest House, Pen-y-Bryn, Harlech, LL46 2SL (0766) 780409
Modern detached house set above the village of Pen-y-Bryn with magnificent views of Harlech Castle and Cardigan Bay; garden and local produce.

Gwynedd

Open all year. No smoking Vegetarian, vegan and most other special diets by arrangement. Children welcome. Pets by arrangement. Tea/coffee-making in bedrooms. T.V. in all bedrooms. B. & B. from £12.50.

Hotel Maes-y-Neuadd, Talsarnau, Nr Harlech, LL47 6YA (0766) 780200

This ancient Welsh manor house standing on a

wooded mountainside in 8 acres of landscaped grounds, is a gracious blend of 14th, 16th, 18th and 20th C. additions and has played host to travelling bards for centuries (many lines in Welsh literature bear witness to its hospitality). Now less bard-like travellers may also linger and enjoy this beautiful old house with its exposed stone-work, elegant dining room with stupendous views and woodburning stoves; bedrooms are individually styled - many with a pleasing medley of antique and contemporary craftmanship - and look out over mountain or sea views. The food is tremendous: home-grown vegetables and herbs are culled daily from the kitchen garden to be used in the making of stupendous meals such as Cream of Fennel Soup, followed by Grapefruit Sorbet, Roast Goose with Chestnut, a selection of desserts and some Welsh Farmhouse Cheeses.

Open all year ex. 2 weeks mid-Dec. No smoking in dining room. Vegetarian & other diets by arrangement. Licensed. Disabled access. Children by arrangement. Pets by arrangement. En suite in all rooms. T.V. Credit cards. B. & B. from £48.

Tremeifion Vegetarian Country Hotel, Talsarnau, Near Harlech, LL47 6UH (0766) 770491

Charming house, with beautiful views of Portmeirion, the estuary and the wonderful mountains of Snowdonia; individually styled bedrooms; everything is home-baked and much of the organic produce comes fresh from the garden. Tremeifion is a wonderful base from which to explore the many scenic attractions of North Wales from the beautiful mountains and hills to the safe sandy beaches of the estuary.

Open all year. No smoking. Exclusively vegetarian and vegan; other meat-free special diets by arrangement. Licensed. Children welcome. Pets by arrangement. En suite in some rooms. Tea/coffee-making in bedrooms. T.V. in lounge. Access, Visa. D., B. & B. from £27.

LLANDUDNO

Brin-y-Bia Lodge Hotel, Craigside, Llandudno, LL30 3AS (0492) 549644

This charming hotel, built in the 19th C., stands in its own walled grounds on the Little Orme overlooking the town and the sea. It has been beautifully decorated and furnished throughout - a gracious and yet relaxed atmosphere prevails - and bedrooms are appointed to a very high standard with everything you could possibly need, including direct dial phones. The spacious yet intimate dining room sets the scene for the wonderful meals which have been carefully prepared from the finest of fresh, local produce, a typical evening meal featuring Asparagus Crêpes followed by Chicken en Croute (with fresh vegetables) and a delicious dessert, such as Hot Peaches in Marsala Sauce with Toasted Almonds. Llandudno has a unique charm, and its proximity to the Snowdonia National Park makes it an ideal location for a holiday in North Wales.

Open all year ex. Xmas & New Year. No smoking in dining room. Vegetarian and most other special diets by arrangement. Licensed. Children welcome. Pets by arrangement. En suite, TV & tea/coffee-making in bedrooms. Access, Visa, Amex. B. & B. from £25.

The Chandos Hotel, 6 Church Walks, Llandudno, LL30 2HD (0492) 878848

Charming small hotel situated close to the beach, pier and Great Orme; first-rate food prepared from fresh, local ingredients.

Open all year ex. Xmas. No smoking in all public areas. Vegetarian & other diets by arrangement. Licensed. Children welcome. Pets by arrangement. En suite, tea/coffee-making & TV in bedrooms. Access, Visa, Amex. B. & B. from £15.

The Cliffbury Hotel, 34 St David's Rd, Llandudno, Gwynedd, LL30 2UH (0492) 877224

The Cliffbury is a small, non-smoking, licensed, family-run hotel just 5 minutes' walk from all the main attractions of Llandudno. It is run by Janet and Michael Cook who aim to offer a real home-from-home welcome to guests: Michael will collect you from the station if you arrive by coach or rail and Janet does all her own

home-cooking - and delicious home-cooking it is, too, a typical evening menu featuring melon followed by Fresh Salmon with Hollandaise Sauce and a choice of home-made desserts, cheese, biscuits, tea and coffee. Llandudno is a large, thriving holiday centre with a huge assortment of leisure pursuits including a ski/toboggan slope, bowls, horse-riding and golf; the secret of its success lies in its safe, sandy beach - and, of course its proximity to so many other places of interest such as Snowdonia and Conwy.
Open all year. No smoking in the house. Vegetarian & other diets by arrangement. Licensed. Children & pets welcome. En suite, TV & tea/coffee-making in bedrooms. B. & B. from £12.50.

Cranberry House, 12 Abbey Rd, Llandudno, Gwynedd, LL30 2EA   (0492) 879760

Cranberry House is a small, elegant Victorian house which stands just a few minutes' walk from the pier, promenade and shops of Llandudno. Your hosts, Mr and Mrs Aldridge, offer a very high standard of comfort and service, and have taken tremendous trouble to furnish and decorate their lovely home in a manner which complements its period origins: each of the bedrooms is beautifully equipped and there is a comfortable lounge for guests' use. The dining room is particularly attractive - a perfect setting in which to enjoy the delicious home-cooked meals which have been prepared from fresh ingredients: the Aldridges will meet guests' special dietary needs wherever possible, and a typical evening meal would feature home-made Cream of Leek Soup followed by Fresh Chicken Breasts with Herb Stuffing (with fresh vegetables) and a choice of tempting desserts; cheese, biscuits and coffee would complete the meal. **WTB Commended. AA QQQ**
Open mid Mar. - mid Oct. No smoking in the house. Vegetarian & other diets by arrangement. En suite, TV & tea/coffee-making in bedrooms. Credit cards. B. & B. from £16.

Gogarth Abbey Hotel, West Shore, Llandudno, LL30 2QG   (0492) 76211/2
Fine old hotel offering first-rate cuisine prepared from fresh and local produce.
Open all year. No smoking in dining room, leisure facilities & in some bedrooms. Vegetarian standard. Other diets by arrangement. Licensed. Disabled access. Children welcome. Pets by arrangement. En suite, tea/coffee & TV in bedrooms.

The Grafton Hotel, Promenade, Craig-y-Don, Llandudno, LL30 1BG (0492) 876814
Pleasantly appointed small hotel situated on quieter part of promenade; excellent vegetarian meal options.
Open Feb. to Nov. No smoking in dining room & some bedrooms. Vegetarian by arrangement. Licensed. Disabled access. Children welcome. Pets by arrangement. En suite, tea/coffee & TV in bedrooms. Credit cards. B. & B. from £15.50.

Plas Madoc Private Hotel, 60 Church Walks, LL30 2HL   (0492) 76514
Family-run hotel at the foot of the Great Orme with magnificent views over Llandudno and the wonderful mountains of Snowdonia; fresh local ingredients used in cooking; vegetarian and other special diets by arrangement.
Open all year. No smoking in dining room & bedrooms. Vegetarian & other diets by arrangement. Licensed. Children welcome. En suite, tea/coffee-making & TV in rooms. B. & B. from £15.

Tan Lan, Great Ormes Rd, West Shore, (0492) 860221
18-bed-roomed hotel. Good, home-cooking.
Open Mar. to Oct. inc. No smoking in dining room & lounge. Vegetarian & other special diets by arrangement. Licensed. Easy disabled access. Children welcome. Pets by arrangement. Tea/coffee making & TV in bedrooms. B. & B. from £21.

LLANFAIRFECHAN

Rhiwiau Riding Centre, Llanfairfechan, Gwynedd, LL33 0EH   (0248) 680094
Family owned and run riding centre with friendly and relaxed atmosphere; excellent home-cooking.
Open all year. Smoking banned throughout the house. Vegetarian & other diets by arrangement. Licensed. Children welcome. Tea/coffee-making. T.V. in 2 lounges. W/E FB & riding from £75.

LLWYNGWRIL
Pentre Bach, Llwyngwril, LL37 2JU
(0341) 250294

A former manor house, Pentre Bach is splendidly situated in a secluded (but not isolated!) position and has wonderful views of the sea and the mountains. There is a great emphasis on the use of healthy produce and guests can also buy free-range eggs, organic fruit and vegetables and preserves, all produced on the premises. Llwyngwril is a pretty coastal village with a British Rail station and regular bus service. There is no need to leave the house during the day - guests can just sit and enjoy the glorious scenery with its wealth of wildlife (including cormorants, buzzards and herons), all with the sea as a backdrop. The more energetic can stagger the 20 yards to play table tennis, 330 yards to the local pub or around the same to go pony-trekking; those who wish to travel further afield by car, public transport or Pentre Bach mountain bikes, will find themselves within easy reach of castles, craft centres, steam railways and the Centre for Alternative Technology. Packed lunches and evening meals may also be ordered by arrangement.

Open all year ex. Xmas. No smoking in the house. Vegetarian standard. Other diets by arrangement. Children welcome. En suite, TV & tea/coffee making in rooms. Private parking. B. & B. from £18.

MAENTWROG
The Old Rectory Hotel, Maentwrog, (076 685) 305

The Old Rectory stands in its own grounds in the delightful Vale of Ffestiniog in the village of Maentwrog bounded on one side by the River Dwyryd which meets the sea at Tremadog Bay. It is a lovely old building - over 200 years old, and with a wealth of interesting features including some quite extraordinary chimneys! The house has been comfortably decorated with taste and style and there is a very good restaurant, open to non-residents, in which delicious freshly-prepared meals are served, such as

home-made Lentil and Coriander Soup followed by a special dish of sweet potatoes, sweetcorn, peas, coriander, coconut and cumin (there is a strong African and Eastern influence in the Old Rectory kitchen!) and a delicious dessert such as home-made Bramley Apple Pie; many dishes are suitable for vegetarians and vegans. The area boasts many attractive features including the beach at Black Rock which is not only one of the safest for children, but also has the added advantage of being a 'drive-on' beach.

Vegetarian, vegan, diabetic standard. Other diets by arrangement. Organic & wholefoods when avail. Open all year. Licensed. Children welcome. Pets by arrangement only. En suite, tea/coffee-making in all bedrooms. T.V. Credit cards. B. & B. from £16.

PORTHMADOG
Bwlch-y-Fedwen Country House Hotel, Penmorfa, Porthmadog, LL49 9RY
(0766) 512975

Bwlch-y-Fedwen was built in 1664 and used to be a coaching inn. Now beautifully renovated yet retaining the oak beams, stone walls and huge open fireplaces of the original building, this charming small hotel invites visitors to relax and unwind in an atmosphere of gracious living: guests dine by candlelight in the beautiful dining room where delicious meals featuring both traditional English and Welsh dishes are served; a typical evening menu might feature Asparagus Spears followed by Fresh Scotch Salmon with Parsley Sauce (and fresh vegetables) and a tempting home-made dessert, such as Hazelnut Meringue. All rooms are very comfortably

appointed - there is a sun room with a view of the mountains and a large, comfortable drawing room with an open fire.
Open Apr. to Oct; closed Aug. No smoking. Vegetarian by arrangement. Licensed. En suite & tea/coffee in rooms. T.V. lounge. D., B. & B. from £32.

PORTMEIRION
The Hotel Portmeirion, Portmeirion, LL48 6ET (0766) 770228
Beautiful hotel based around a Victorian villa in the Italianate village of Portmeirion; open air pool; fresh produce used in French-based menu.
Open all year. No smoking in dining room, 'Mirror room' and 'Ivy Room'. Vegetarian & other diets by arrangement. Licensed. Children welcome. En suite & TV in all rooms. Room service. Credit cards. B. & B. from £37.50.

TALYLLYN
Minffordd Hotel, Talyllyn, Tywyn, LL36 9AJ (0654) 761665
17th C. Drover's Inn; real fires, beautifully furnished and appointed bedrooms and excellent food prepared on the kitchen Aga: all meals are prepared from fresh, local produce
Open Mar. to Dec. No smoking in dining room, sitting room & bedrooms. Vegetarian by arrangement.

Licensed. Children between ages of 3 and 12 accepted. En suite & tea/coffee-making in bedrooms. Access, Visa, Diners. D., B. & B. from £40.

TRAWSFYNYDD
Old Mill Farmhouse, Fron Oleu Farm, Trawsfynydd, Snowdonia National Park, LL41 4UN (0766) 87397
Traditional built 18th C. Welsh farmhouse with inglenooks; fresh home-cooked food a speciality; own produce, including goat's milk, free-range eggs, used in cooking.
Open all year. No smoking in all public areas. Vegetarian & other diets by arrangement. Bring your own wine. Disabled access. Children welcome. Pets by arrangement. En suite, TV & tea/coffee-making in rooms. B. & B. from £14.50.

TRIFRIW
Crafnant Guest House, Main street, Trefriw, LL27 0JH (0492) 640809
Detached Victorian residence; candlelit dinners (traditional or vegetarian) have been prepared from fresh ingredients including some home-grown salad vegetables.
Open all year. No smoking. Vegetarian food a speciality. Other diets by arrangement. Children welcome. Pets by arrangement. En suite in some rooms. Tea/coffee-making & T.V. in all bedrooms.

Pembrokeshire

CAREW
Old Stable Cottage, Carew, Pembs., SA70 8SL (0646) 651889

A Grade II listed stone cottage, Old Stable Cottage was originally a stable and carthouse for Carew Castle, one of Pembrokeshire's finest castles which is reflected idyllically in the tidal waters of River Carew which it overlooks. The entrance porch to the cottage was a trapshed and leads into the old stable and from thence to the large lounge with its low beams and inglenook (there is a log fire and bread oven therein). A wrought iron spiral staircase leads to three double en suite bedrooms which have been well-equipped with colour TV, a tea and coffee-making tray and bathrobes. There is an attractive conservatory adjoining the country kitchen where delicious meals, prepared from fresh produce and cooked on the Aga by Joyce, are temptingly and creatively presented (Lionel specializes in the bread making). Breakfast is a healthy feast of muesli, oats, almonds, yoghurts, seeds and fresh fruit followed by the traditional English platter. Your hosts, Joyce and Lionel Fielder, are keen sailors who now, having sailed across the Atlantic, keep their yacht in the British Virgin Islands where they sail during the winter months.
Open 10 Mar. - 30 Nov. No smoking in the house. Vegetarian & other diets by arrangement. Children: over 5s welcome. En suite, TV & tea/coffee-making in bedrooms. B. & B. £22.50, D. £17.50, single £30.

Pembrokeshire

CRYMYCH

**Felin Tygwyn Farm, Crymych, SA41 3RX
(023 979) 603**

Felin Tygwyn is a traditional earth and slate farmhouse which nestles at the foot of the Preseli Mountains, some 9 miles from Cardigan and Newport beach. It is very welcoming and has lots of character including beamed ceilings from which are hung bunches of home grown dried flowers, and an inviting open fire in the lounge. The farmhouse forms part of an organic smallholding in which your hosts, Tom and Beryl Hazelden, do everything they can to preserve the habitat for all forms of wildlife: they even allow dandelions to grow in the spring to provide a feast for gold finches and linnets! The house has a very friendly and relaxed atmosphere, and the freshly cooked meals are prepared from home-grown vegetables and herbs or local produce. You will find much at Felin Tygwyn to help you relax and unwind - the surrounding countryside is rich in different varieties of flora and fauna - and there are many places to visit nearby, including nature reserves, castles, standing stones and craft workshops.

Open all year. No smoking in the house. Vegetarian & other diets by arrangement. Licensed. Children welcome. Pets by arrangement. Tea/coffee available. T.V. in lounge. D., B. & B. from £20.80.

FISHGUARD

Coach House Cottage, Glendower Square, Goodwick, Fishguard, Pembrokeshire, SA64 0DH (0348) 873660

This traditional Pembrokeshire stone cottage stands in a secluded location by a mountain stream, yet is conveniently situated in the heart of the village of Goodwick, 1 mile from the centre of Fishguard and a few minutes'walk from the harbour and seafront. Centrally heated accommodation is provided for just two people in a prettily decorated bedroom, with beautiful

hill and sea views (and almost exclusive use of the bathroom), and guests are also welcome to use the rest of the cottage including the large, eclectic collection of books, the lovely garden (with its sea views) or the sitting room with T.V. The proprietors specialise in providing delicious vegetarian, vegan and wholefood fare (prepared with organic produce wherever possible), but light, 'snack' type meals can be provided in the evening for meat-eaters (there are several other good eating places within walking distance). Pembrokeshire is a beautiful county and is said to have the highest number of working craftsmen within its boundaries (including, incidentally your host, 'Max' Maxwell-Jones, who is a well-known local artist and calligrapher).

Open all year. Smoking banned throughout the house. Vegetarian standard. Most other special diets by arrangement. Not licensed but guests welcome to bring a bottle. Children welcome. Pets by arrangement. Tea/Coffee-making in bedrooms. T.V. in lounge. B. & B. from £11. D. £7.50.

Powys

BRECON

Beacons Guest House, 16 Bridge St, Brecon, Powys, LD3 8AH (0874) 623339

The Beacons Guest House is a beautiful Georgian family-run house close to the River Usk. Its owners, Mr and Mrs Cox, have taken great care to ensure that the period atmosphere of their lovely home has been retained: bedrooms have been furnished in a sympathetic style and the Master Bedroom has a four-poster bed which complements the moulded ceiling and the marble fireplace. The food is delicious - and very much prepared to suit guests' needs: there is a choice of a traditional or lighter continental breakfast, and light snacks, packed lunches and mid-day meals are served in the Beacon Coffee Shop. The Beacons is "Taste of Wales Recommended" and as such offers wholesome home-cooked meals, prepared from fresh local produce (some home-grown); before enjoying your meal you may linger over a drink in the old meat store, now a cosy bar although it still retains the old ceiling hooks as testament to its original purpose.

Open all year. No smoking in dining room. Vegetarian & other diets by arrangement. Children & pets welcome. Licensed. En suite, tea/coffee & TV in bedrooms. Credit cards. B. & B. £16-19.

Forge Farm House, Hay Road, Brecon, LD3 7SS (0874) 611793

Beautiful 17th C. house with adjacent historical fulling mill in a quiet, secluded position in the valley of the River Honddu; good home-cooking including bread and jams.
Vegetarian, vegan & other diets by arrangement. Wholefoods when avail. Open all year ex. Xmas. No smoking. Children welcome. Tea/Coffee-making & TV in sitting room. B. & B. from £12.50. D.£8.

BUILTH WELLS

The Court Farm, Aberedw, Nr Builth Wells, LD2 3UP (0982) 560277

Spacious stone-built house with working farm set in beauiful unspoilt valley; traditional home-cooking with home-produced meat, poultry, eggs, honey and organically home-grown vegetables and fruit. Farm, riverside and hill walking.
Vegetarian by arrangement. Open Easter to Nov. No smoking. Children: over 12s only. En suite 1 room. Tea/coffee on request. T.V. lounge. B. & B. from £13.50. D.£8.

Nant-y-Derw Farm, Builth Wells, LD2 3RU (0982) 553675

Working sheep farm 4 miles north of Builth Wells on a south-facing slope in the centre of 45 acres of farmland; home-produce used in cooking. Only four guests at any one time.
Vegetarian, vegan and other special diets by arrangement. Organic when avail. Wholefoods always. Open May to Dec. ex. Xmas. No smoking. Disabled access. Children: over 7s only. Pets by arrangement. Private bathroom. Tea/Coffee in bedrooms. T.V. in lounge. B. & B. from £14. D. from £5.

CRICKHOWELL

The Dragon Hotel, High Street, Crickhowell, NP8 1BE (0873) 811868

Early 18th C. building within original boundaries of Alisby Castle and supposedly built from its ruins; a listed building full of charm, open fires and oak beams; excellent food prepared from fresh, local produce.
Vegetarian standard. Vegan and other special diets by arrangement. Wholefoods when avail. Open all year. No smoking in lounge, part of dining room & some bedrooms. Licensed. Children welcome. En suite & TV in most bedrooms. Tea/coffee-making in bedrooms. Access, Visa. B. & B. from £16.

LLANBRYMAIR

Barlings Barn, Llanbrynmair (0650) 521479

When Terry and Felicity Margolis arrived at Barlings Barn some years ago they were prepared to have to undertake a tremendous amount of renovative work on their lovely 18th century stone farm buildings. Their efforts were well rewarded, however, and now, in addition to the main building, a cottage and self-catering wing now provide absolutely first-class accommodation to guests; not only is there a microwave, automatic washer and tumble dryer, but your hosts will provide you with home-cooked frozen meals on request, and will send you a grocery shopping list when you book to ensure that your first few days' worth of provisions is there to greet you when you arrive. A stay at Barlings Barn is healthy indeed; in addition to the excellent cuisine which is prepared wherever possible from fresh and wholefood ingredients, there is a first-class range of leisure and sports amenities including an outdoor heated pool, squash court, sauna and solarium.
Vegetarian standard. Vegan and other special diets by arrangement. Organic and wholefood almost always. Open all year. No smoking in main leisure areas and discouraged throughout. Children welcome. Pets by arrangement. En suite in all rooms. Prices: various.

LLANDRINDOD WELLS

Corven Hall, Howey, Llandrindod Wells, LD1 5RE (0597) 823368

Corven Hall is a large Victorian house with spacious rooms and large windows which overlook the four acres of peaceful gardens, bounded by trees and open country, near the small village of Howey. Most of the comfortable bedrooms have en suite facilities and there is a ground floor room for disabled guests. Traditional English and Welsh cooking is a house speciality, and a variety of home-made dishes are freshly prepared from local produce. The area is particularly rich in bird life - indeed

it is the only part of Britain where the Red Kite can still be seen - and additionally you will find yourself excellently placed for enjoying pony trekking, riding tuition, fishing and golf (the 18 hole course at Llandrindod Wells commands spectacular views of the town and surrounding countryside).
Open Feb. to Nov. No smoking in dining room & lounge. Vegetarian & other diets by arrangement. Licensed. Disabled access. Children welcome. Pets by arrangement. En suite in most rooms. Tea/coffee-making in bedrooms. T.V. in lounge and some bedrooms. B. & B. from £14. D. £8.

The Metropole Hotel, Temple Street, Llandrindod Wells (0597) 823700
Vegetarian, vegan and diabetic standard. Low-cal., low-fat or wheat-free by arrangement. Organic on request. Wholefoods when avail. Smoking discouraged and banned in some bedrooms. Open all year. Licensed. Children welcome. Pets by arrangement. En suite, TV & tea/coffee-making in all bedrooms. Credit cards. B. & B. from £34.

LLANGAMMARCH WELLS
The Lake Country House Hotel, Llangammarch Wells, Powys, LD4 4BS (05912) 202
Exceptional award-winning hotel. First-class cuisine prepared from the finest, fresh local produce.
Vegetarian, vegan and other special diets by arrangement. Open mid Jan. to end Dec. No smoking in dining room & some bedrooms. Licensed. Disabled access. Children welcome. Pets by arrangement. En suite & T.V. in all bedrooms. Access, Visa, Amex. B. & B. from £42.50.

MACHYNLLETH
Gwalia, Cemmaes, Machynlleth, SY20 9PU (0650) 511377
Exclusively vegetarian, family-run 10 acre smallholding; lovely house with beautiful views just outside Snowdonia National Park; virtually all food home-grown or home-produced spring water. Therapeutic massage available.
Vegetarian and vegan diets standard. Open all year. No smoking. Children welcome. Pets by arrangement. Tea/coffee on request. B. & B. from £13. D. £7

MONTGOMERY
The Dragon Hotel, Montgomery, SY15 6AA (0686) 668359
Parts of the black & white timbered Dragon Hotel date back to the 17th C. when it was used as a coaching inn. Panoramic views. Meals prepared from fresh, local produce. The hotel has an indoor heated swimming pool.
Vegetarian standard. Vegan & other special diets by arrangement. No smoking in some bedrooms & part of dining room. Open all year. Licensed. Reasonable disabled access. Children welcome. Pets by arrangement. En suite, tea/coffee-making & TV in all bedrooms. Credit cards. B. & B. from £28.50.

RHAYADER
Tre Garreg, St Harmon, Nr Rhayader, LD6 5LU (0597) 88604
Converted stone barn offering comfortable accommodation with log fires & wholesome food.
Vegetarian & other special diets, but not vegan, by arrangement. Organic when avail. Open Easter to Oct. No smoking. En suite in all rooms. Tea/coffee & T.V. in lounge. B. & B. from £15. D. £10.

READER'S OBSERVATIONS

I would be very glad to hear your comments about the establishments you have visited as a result of *The Healthy Holiday Guide*. If you think I have ommitted anyone who ought to be included - do please let me know. Write to me at Saddlers Cottage, York Rd, Elvington, York, YO4 5AR (no phone calls please!).

Hotel/ Guest House

....
....
....
....

Comments

....
....
....
....
....
....
....
....
....
....
....
....
....
....
....
....
....
....
....
....
....
....
....
....
....
....
....
....
....
....
....
....